Financial Services Authority Regulation and Risk–based Compliance

Second Edition

D1438180

Financial Services Authority Regulation and Risk–based Compliance

Second Edition

by

Stuart Bazley LL.B (Hons), LL.M (Lond)

and

Dr Andrew Haynes B.A. (Hons) Law, PhD, Cert Ed, FRSA, FSALS

Tottel
p u b l i s h i n g

Tottel Publishing Ltd, Maxwelton House, 41–43 Boltro Road, Haywards Heath, West Sussex, RH16 1BJ

© Tottel Publishing Ltd 2007

Second edition published 2007.
Reprinted 2009.

A CIP Catalogue record for this book is available from the British Library.

ISBN   978 1 84592 249 8

Typeset by Kerrypress Ltd, Luton, Beds

Printed and bound in Great Britain by Digital Book Print Ltd, Milton Keynes, MK1 1DR

Authors' biographies

STUART BAZLEY LL.B (Hons), LL.M (Lond)

Stuart has worked in the financial services industry since 1980 and read law at the University of London. In 1996 he undertook postgraduate studies in the Law of Banking and International Finance at Queen Mary College and is now undertaking research at the Institute of Advanced Legal Studies. He has lectured and written extensively on legal matters concerning financial services compliance. His previous publications include Risk-Based Compliance 1st edition, published by Butterworths in 2001 and Money Laundering: Business Compliance 1st edition published by Lexis Nexis in 2004. Between 1991 and 1996 Stuart was the head of the legal function for the UK life assurance operation of Irish Life Assurance and between 1999 and 2004 was the Director of Compliance and General Counsel for the UK operation of Edward Jones. Stuart joined Momenta in 2004 where he is head of its regulatory consulting business. Momenta is a specialist outsourcing, consulting and training business serving the financial services industry. Stuart specialises in the regulation relating to banking and financial markets.

DR ANDREW HAYNES B.A. (Hons) Law, PhD, Cert Ed, FRSA, FSALS

After originally training as a solicitor Andrew worked at the British Bankers Association and as an adviser at Deloitte's in London. He later went on to become an academic and in this role he has written, edited and contributed to a wide range of books, encyclopaedias and articles on financial services law, financial crime and international banking law. He has also spoken at a wide range of academic conferences; recently including those at the University of Cambridge, the University of Macau (People's Republic of China) and the Institute of Advanced Legal Studies at the University of London. He has delivered specialist sessions for banks, solicitors' practices, financial regulators and financial services firms throughout the world.

At the University of Wolverhampton he has developed a specialist LLM in International Financial and Corporate law which operates in Wolverhampton and Hong Kong. The Law School also supervises a number of doctoral students in this area.

Preface

This culture of risk based compliance is one that is being widely adopted through the financial world, largely as a result of the conclusions of the Basel Committee and a range of other bodies and has emerged as the primary methodology in financial services regulation. The British Financial Services Authority has as a consequence adopted a regulatory approach that is based on the premise that a financial services business poses risks to the regulator's objectives as well as the stability of the firms themselves. The regulations that the FSA passes are thus a means to making sure that these risks are being managed in an appropriate way. So, as seen in the 1st edition, the days of 'compliance', where maintaining a satisfactory set of systems was determined by whether a set of rules were being complied with, are gone. What it has been replaced with is a system of risk based compliance which involves satisfying a series of principles and rules in the course of managing the necessary risks.

Whilst such a move presents both the FSA and authorised firms with great flexibility in their approach to compliance, it will undoubtedly place pressure on firm's senior management and their advisers to fully understand FSA expectations and properly apply approaches to compliance that suit the nature and complexity of their firm's own business model. Thus, the text analysis risk based compliance in this context.

When publishing the 1st edition of this book our aim was to assess the FSA's then emerging approach to risk based regulation and introduce the reader, perhaps for the first time, to concepts of risk assessment and a risk based application of compliance through a discussion of key elements of the FSA's rule book and the Financial Services and Markets Act 2000. We received a very positive response from practitioners, lawyers, academics and students in compliance, and we learned that the book's appeal extended beyond the UK to international students and compliance practitioners as far a field as South Africa. In producing the 2nd edition we have expanded the book's coverage to include an analysis of key areas of the FSA's operation, including its accountability as well European and International influences. Importantly, however, we have extended the exploration of the FSA approach to risk based regulation. The book provides a combination of academic discussion and practical insight into what has been learned during the past five years concerning the framework of financial services regulation in UK and the financial service industries approach to risk based compliance.

The book focuses on the FSA's supervision of firms conducting investment business in UK and makes reference to key FSA texts, materials and speeches that give an insight into the topics we have addressed. The law and regulation is stated as at 1 November 2006.

We have to thank those friends and colleagues that have supported us with our endeavour: Andy Hill of Tottel Publishing for always believing that the book would be published, Nick Smith of Momenta for his views and help in understanding the FSA's Training and Competence rules, Professor Barry Rider for his ongoing support for our work and our families for their constant support. We dedicate this book to Kenneth Bazley and Ronald Haynes.

Stuart Bazley and Andrew Haynes
London
November 2006

Contents

Contents

Table of Cases

xiii

Table of statutes

Table of Statutory Instruments

Chapter 1

Relevant provisions in the Financial Services and Markets Act 2000

'Originally a stockbroker was just a broker of stocks and shares, an insurance broker a broker of insurance policies, a commodity broker a broker of commodities, a banker a provider of banking services and a unit trust manager a manager of unit trusts. And by and large, each stuck to his last. Today all these rules, and others, may, and often will be undertaken by the same firm or group. And groups offering a full range of financial services are tending to become multinational with ultimate control of the British operations not necessarily being British.'

Prof LCB Gower

Introduction

1.1   The main purpose of the regulatory structure which the Financial Services and Markets Act 2000 ('the Act') brought about was to create a single system of regulation in which the Financial Services Authority regulates almost the entire financial services industry. An industry which, as the above quote highlights, has become one where many firms operate as financial supermarkets offering a range of products, sometimes in more than one country. This process had already started with the passing of the Bank of England Act 1998 which transferred the regulation of banks from the Bank of England to the FSA. The regime now consists of the FSA being responsible for the regulation of: investment business, banks, building societies, friendly societies, credit unions, insurance companies and a supervisory relationship with Lloyd's insurance underwriting market[1].

---

1 See FSMA 2000, Pt XIX, ss 314–324 and also the FSA Lloyd's Sourcebook.

1.2   The other crucial parts of the Act in this context are:

(1)   that it is not possible carry on investment business without FSA authorisation unless you are either an authorised or an exempt person[1].

(2)   that if this requirement is breached a criminal offence is committed. On summary conviction up to six months in prison can be imposed and/or a fine. On indictment up to two years in prison can result and/or a fine[2].

(3)   If a financial services activity is carried on without FSA authorisation then any contracts entered into by the party acting illegally can only be enforced on their behalf at a judge's discretion. However, any such contracts can be enforced against them[3].

(4)   That a new right of action is available to private clients to sue where loss is caused to them by an FSA regulated party as a result of the FSA rules being breached[4]. This can be useful where for technical reasons there are barriers to more usual causes of action such as negligence or breach of contract. This right does not extend to a breach of Lloyd's of London rules[5].

(5)   This is extended[6] to a right of action also being available to a private person who suffers loss as a result of a breach of an FSA prohibition order. These are issued where the FSA believe that an individual is not a fit and proper person to carry out regulated activities[7] and can relate to a specific activity or be general.

(6)   The same right of action exists where a private person suffers loss as a result of an authorised person not taking reasonable care to make sure that someone does not carry out a controlled function without FSA permission[8].

---

1 FSMA 2000, s 19.
2 FSMA 2000, s 23.
3 FSMA 2000, ss 26–29.
4 FSMA 2000, s 150.
5 LLD 25.1.1.
6 FSMA 2000, s 71.
7 FSMA 2000, s 56(1)–(3).
8 FSMA 2000, s 59(1), (2).

The Financial Services Authority

1.3   The Act provides the FSA with the power to regulate all categories of financial business and also makes it the competent authority for Official Listing of securities which will entail, *inter alia*, specifying the requirements to be complied with for listing. The FSA is responsible for maintaining the official list and applications for listing have to be made to them. A detailed analysis of the listing rules is however beyond the scope of this book.

1.4   The purpose of the listing rules is to provide a regulatory framework for the issuing of new (primary) securities and the selling of existing (secondary) ones. The aim of the regulations is to keep a balance between the interests of those in industry who wish to raise capital and those of the public at large who may wish to subscribe. Securities will only be admitted to listing if the applicant is suitable and it is appropriate for the securities concerned to be publicly held and traded. They must be brought to the market in a way that is appropriate to their nature and number and which will facilitate an open and efficient market for trading in those securities. Issuers must make full and timely disclosures about themselves and the listed securities both at the time of issue and afterwards. The continuing obligations imposed on issuers are designed to promote investor confidence in standards of disclosure, in the conduct of listed companies' affairs and in the market as a whole. Holders of equity securities must be given adequate opportunity to consider in advance and vote upon major changes in the company's management and constitution.

1.5   The other ingredients of the FSA's powers are:

(1)   controlling insurance business and banking transfers;

(2)   combating market abuse (see Chapter 4);

(3)   recognising and supervising investment exchange and clearing houses;

(4)   overseeing the compensation scheme; and

(5)   overseeing the ombudsman scheme.

1.6   The Act also sets out the FSA's objectives. These are:

(i)   The maintenance of confidence in the UK financial system[1].

(ii)   The promotion of public understanding of the financial system. This objective involves the promotion of public awareness of the risks and benefits of investment and financial dealing and also making available the necessary information and advice for the public to be able to do this[2].

(iii) To secure an appropriate degree of protection for consumers. In considering what to provide in this context the FSA must consider both the degree of risk and experience that consumers may possess, and their need for accurate information[3].

(iv)   The reduction of the extent to which it is possible for financial services business to be used to facilitate financial crime. The FSA is required to make sure that regulated businesses are aware of the risk of their business being used in connection with the commission of financial crime and to make sure that the necessary steps are taken to monitor, detect and prevent financial crime. The main target in this area is money laundering[4] (see Chapter 5).

Although this appears to leave the FSA with an enormous degree of power they are scrutinised by Parliamentary Committee and the Treasury. In the final analysis Parliament has the overriding power.

1 FSMA 2000, s 3.
2 FSMA 2000, s 4.
3 FSMA 2000, s 5.
4 FSMA 2000, s 6.

Approved persons

1.7 In addition to financial services businesses requiring authorisation all significant individuals involved in a business that requires authorisation by the FSA must be 'approved'. This means that the FSA must be convinced that the person concerned is fit and proper and has suitable abilities, relevant qualifications and/or experience and an appropriate level of honesty and integrity. The people concerned fall into two main groups: those who carry on controlled functions themselves, such as advising clients or arranging contracts and those who manage such people. The other group are those who are in such senior positions that the FSA need to be satisfied that they are suitable. Examples are: the chief executive, directors, partners (if relevant), senior managers, compliance officers, money laundering reporting officers and finance officers. However, it does not include the head of the legal department!

1.8 Despite this the regulated firm remains primarily responsible for compliance with the regulations. There is however a Code of Practice affecting approved persons that sets out the conduct to be expected of them. Its main purpose is to make sure that those people realise the legal obligations being imposed on them in the area of risk based compliance.

The FSA have determined that controlled functions fall into seven categories of job function.

Significant influence functions

Governing body functions

1.9 These consist of being:

● a director of either a company or a holding company;

● a non-executive director of a company;

● a chief executive officer. This is widely interpreted and covers joint chief executives operating under the immediate control of the board where there is more than one. In the case of a UK branch of a non-EEA insurer the role includes the principal UK executive.

4

- Partners and limited partners (where appropriate) are all regarded as carrying on controlled functions where the firm is primarily carrying on regulated investment business. Limited partners are excluded where their role is only that of an investor. If a partnership's primary business does not relate to specified investments but a separate part of the business does, then provided a distinct partner or set of partners deal with that aspect of the business only they need be approved.

- Directors of unincorporated associations.

- Those directing or regulating the specified activities of a small friendly society.

- Sole traders.

Required controlled functions

1.10   There are four of these:

- the director or other senior member responsible for apportionment and oversight;

- the director or senior manager responsible for investment business compliance;

- the money laundering reporting officer; and

- in the case of insurance companies, the appointed actuary.

Management functions

1.11   These consist of the members of senior management reporting to the governing body in relation to the following activities:

- the financial affairs of the firm;

- setting and controlling risk exposure; and

- internal audit.

Significant management functions in relation to business and control

1.12   The functions set out below are added to cover those situations where the firm concerned has senior managers whose function is equivalent to that of a member of the firm's governing body. They do not apply if the activity is a specified activity as this would automatically then be an approved persons' role. They fall into five categories of senior management:

- those operating in relation to investment services, such as the head of equities. This will often be a controlled function in any event;

- those operating in relation to other areas of the firm's business than specified investment activity, eg, head of personal lending or corporate lending, head of credit card issues etc;

- those responsible for carrying out insurance underwriting other than in relation to contractually-based investments, eg, head of aviation under-writing;

- those responsible for making decisions concerning the firm's own finances, eg, chief corporate treasurer; and

- those responsible for back office functions.

Temporary and emergency functions

1.13   Should the function of undertaking such a role continue for more than eight weeks in a twelve-month period then the person primarily responsible will need to be an approved person.

Dealing with customer functions

1.14   There are seven main functions within this category:

- life and pensions adviser;

- life and pensions advisers when acting under supervision;

- pension transfer advisers, such people can also give ancillary advice in relation to packaged products;

- investment advisers, including those advising in relation to packaged products, but not life and pensions advice;

- investment advisers acting under supervision;

- corporate finance advisers; and

- advisers to underwriting members of Lloyd's in relation to becoming a syndicate member.

Dealing with customers' property

1.15   This covers two main types of activity:

6

- those individuals who deal or arrange deals on behalf of customers. It does not extend to execution only business and feeding orders into automatic execution systems; and

- discretionary fund management.

Appointed representatives

1.16   An 'appointed representative' is defined[1] as being someone who is:

'(a) a party to a contract with an unauthorised person (his principal) which-

(i)   permits or requires him to carry on business of a prescribed description, and

(ii)   complies with such requirements as may be prescribed, and

(b) is someone for whose activities in carrying on the whole or part of that business his principal has accepted responsibility in writing.'

1 FSMA 2000, s 39(1)(a), (b).

1.17   Anyone satisfying this description is exempt from the general prohibition in relation to any regulated activity when they are acting within the remit of the area of business for which their principal has accepted responsibility. Thus the principal will be responsible for the appointed representative's acts and the principal will therefore need to be an authorised person. There is some protection for the principal though:

'nothing ...is to cause the knowledge or intentions of an appointed representative to be attributed to his principal for the purpose of determining whether the principal has committed an offence, unless in all the circumstances it is reasonable for them to be attributed to him'[1]

Applications to carry on regulated activities can be made by individuals as well as corporate entities, partnerships and unincorporated associations[2].

1 FSMA 2000, s 39(6).
2 FSMA 2000, s 40.

FSA rules

1.18   The FSA has the power to issue rules, both generally[1] and has statutory authority to issue them in certain specific areas[2] such as price stabilisation, financial promotion, money laundering and the control of information. The full FSA handbook includes a glossary, high level standards and prudential standards to determine the financial resources or capital adequacy requirement as the case may be. The business standards cover the general conduct of business rules, market conduct requirements, training and competence, and money laundering. The regulatory manuals cover authorisation, supervision, enforcement and decision making. In addition there are manuals on redress, specialist areas, listing, prospectus requirements and disclosure, handbook guides for specialist areas and in particular the energy and insurance markets and regulatory guides.

---

1 FSMA 2000, s 138.
2 FSMA 2000, ss 144–147.

1.19   The rules themselves are preceded by general principles (see below) which the FSA require authorised persons to obey and are followed by guidance notes, which are not technically part of the rules but which assist in explaining how the rules are expected to operate. The FSA have made clear that should the guidance notes be followed a firm or approved person will be safe from disciplinary proceedings should the guidance transpire to be inaccurate.

1.20   The FSA regulated firms find their clients divided into three categories. Private customers, intermediates and market counterparties[1]. Private customers are precisely that and a client is automatically in this category if the firm is providing advice on stakeholder products. The definition in the FSA rules largely defines a private customer as anyone who is not an intermediate or a market counterparty. Significant parts of the conduct of business rules only apply to private customers as they have a consumer protection element. Intermediate customers are: local or public authorities, body corporates, special purpose vehicles, partnerships with net assets of at least £5 million, trusts with assets of at least £10 million other than occupational pension and stakeholder pension schemes. These are included where they have at least 50 members and assets under management of at least £10 million. Market counterparties are lifted out of the regime and left to look after themselves as they are not believed to need protection. However, they are governed by the Code of Inter-Professional Conduct (see below).

---

1 FSA Conduct of Business Rules at 4.

1.21   Market counterparties are defined as: governments, monetary authorities, supranational authorities whose members are countries or monetary authorities, state investment bodies and overseas financial institutions or their associates. It excludes regulated collective investment schemes.

1.22   The firm is required[1] to classify clients appropriately. There is no reason why a client in a higher category cannot opt for a lower level of classification and thus acquire greater protection. However, if the contrary is to be done the FSA must be informed. This can be appropriate in some cases, such as expert private investors wishing to opt up to intermediate status.

---

1 FSA Conduct of Business Rules at 4.1.3.

FSA Principles for Business

1.23   These are the initial part of the rules and in some respects the most important. The Principles overarch the various detailed regulations and a breach of either can potentially lead to disciplinary steps being taken by the FSA, though a breach of the Principles will not in themselves give rise to potential civil action by clients. This is in contrast to the FSA rules which can give rise to civil liability where the action is at the suit of a private person. The Principles are widely worded and thus can represent an opportunity for the FSA to take disciplinary steps where the regulations do not deal with the issue that has arisen. In practice however the vast majority of disciplinary actions involve clear breaches of the other rules and in some cases the law.

The Eleven FSA Principles

1.24   **(1) Integrity**

A firm must conduct its business with integrity.

(2) Skill, care and diligence

A firm must conduct its business with due skill care and diligence.

(3) Management and control

A firm must take reasonable care to organise and control its affairs responsibly and effectively, with adequate risk management systems.

(4) Financial prudence

A firm must maintain adequate financial resources.

(5) Market conduct

A firm must observe proper standards of market conduct.

(6) *Customers' interests*

A firm must pay due regard to interests of its customers, and treat them fairly.

(7) *Communications with customers*

A firm must pay due regard to the information needs of its customers, and communicate information to them in a way which is clear, fair and not misleading.

(8) *Conflicts of interest*

A firm must manage conflicts of interest fairly, both between itself and its customers and between one customer and another.

(9) *Customers' relationships of trust*

A firm must take reasonable care to ensure the suitability of its advice and discretionary decisions for any customer who is entitled to rely upon its judgment.

(10) *Customers' assets*

A firm must arrange adequate protection for customers' assets when it is responsible for them.

(11) *Relations with regulators*

A firm must deal with its regulator in an open and cooperative way, and must tell the FSA promptly anything relating to the firm of which the FSA would reasonably expect notice.

There are additional Principles specifically applied to approved persons. The first four apply to all of them but the last three only to those with a 'significant influence function', ie, directors and in larger firms the senior managers.

Statements of Principle for Approved Persons

1.25

(1)   An Approved Person must act with integrity in carrying out his controlled function.

(2)   An Approved Person must act with due skill, care and diligence in carrying out his controlled function.

(3)   An Approved Person must observe proper standards of market conduct in carrying out his controlled function.

(4)   An Approved Person must deal with the FSA and with other regulators in an open and cooperative way and must disclose appropriately any information of which the FSA would reasonably expect notice.

(5)   An Approved Person performing a significant influence function must take reasonable steps to ensure that the business of the firm for which he is responsible in his controlled function is organised so that it can be controlled effectively.

(6)   An Approved Person performing a significant influence function must exercise due skill, care and diligence in managing the business of the firm for which he is responsible in his controlled function.

(7)   An Approved Person performing a significant influence function must take reasonable steps to ensure that the business of the firm for which he is responsible in his controlled function complies with the regulatory requirements imposed on that business.

Wholesale market activities

The Inter-Professionals Code

1.26   Market counterparties are not seen as requiring supervision in their market activities. The parties are perfectly capable of taking legal action to protect their interests should it be necessary. In addition if a party refused to abide by the rules they would quickly be squeezed out of the market. There is however the Inter-Professionals Code[1] which applies to inter-professional business. This consists of dealing in investments as principal or agent, acting as an arranger and providing transaction specific advice provided it is in respect of an inter-professional investment entered into with a market counterparty. It does not extend to financial promotions, between those operating in the same collective investment scheme, corporate finance business, safeguarding and administering assets, distance contracts with retail customers and activities related to life policies.

---

1 FSA Conduct of Business Handbook at MAR 3.

1.27   The FSA Principles do apply here but they are to be interpreted in a different way. The starting point is an assumption that market counterparties do not need the level of protection of intermediaries, never mind private customers[1].

It is not necessary for example to ascertain whether the counterparty understands the risks involved in entering into a particular contract. There is however a requirement to communicate with them in a way which is not misleading. Principle 7 requires this if information is provided as to the various types of action that may follow from a misrepresentation. However, unless a requirement to update information has been given there is no need to do so. Should a conflict of interest arise it should be appropriately managed and the nature of it disclosed to the counterparty.

The FSA have indicated that isolated departures from the IPC will not normally cause FSA action, though that would of course be determined by what exactly the departure consisted of.

---

1 FSA Conduct of Business Handbook at MAR 3.4.2.

Investment business in the UK

Specified Investments

1.28   The Financial Services and Markets Act 2000 (Regulated Activities) Order 2001 as amended[1] provides full definitions of specified investments and activities.

---

1 SI 2002/1518, SI 2003/1475, SI 2003/1476, SI 2004/1610, SI 2004/2737 and SI 2005/1518.

1.29   As far as the Order is concerned, the investments that are specified are as follows.

(1)   **Deposits.** The investment itself is effectively left undefined but there is a definition of 'accepting deposits' at **1.38** below.

(2)   **Issuing electronic money**[1].

(3)   **Contracts of insurance.** These are defined in Schedule 1 to the Instrument. The definition covers the following categories of insurance policy: accident, sickness, land vehicles, railway rolling stock, aircraft, ships, goods in transit, fire and natural forces, damage to property, motor vehicle liability, aircraft liability, liability of ships, general liability, credit, suretyship, miscellaneous financial loss, legal expenses, travel assistance, life and annuity, marriage and birth, linked long-term, permanent health, tontines, capital redemption contracts, pension fund management, collective insurance contracts and social insurance.

(4)   **Shares.** This is widely defined as 'shares or stock in the share capital of:

(a)   any body corporate (wherever incorporated), and

(b) any unincorporated body constituted under the law of a country or territory outside the United Kingdom.'

---

1 Inserted by SI 2002/682, art 4.

1.30 It also includes deferred shares within the meaning of s 119 of the Building Societies Act 1986 and any transferable shares in a body incorporated under the UK law relating to industrial and provident societies or credit unions, or under equivalent laws in other EEA states.

Shares were defined by Farwell J as being 'the interest of a shareholder in the company measured by a sum of money, for the purpose of liability in the first place, and of interest in the second, but also consisting of a series of mutual covenants entered into by all the shareholders *inter se*.' The definition appears to extend to stock.

The Instrument's definition excludes shares in open ended investment companies, building societies, industrial and provident societies, credit unions or an equivalent entity in another EEA jurisdiction.

1.31

(5) **Instruments creating or acknowledging indebtedness.** The definition of debentures is a wide one and in addition to normal debentures, loan stock and bonds it includes certificates of deposit and any other instrument creating or acknowledging indebtedness.

It is generally accepted that 'debenture' has never been properly defined. The most widely accepted definition is that of Chitty J, who described a debenture as being 'a document which either creates a debt or acknowledges it'. This is the wording adopted by the Statutory Instrument, and as a result of it being so wide certain other financial instruments are excluded, namely:

- an instrument acknowledging indebtedness for money borrowed to provide the cost of goods or services;

- cheques, bills of exchange, bank drafts and letters of credit, but not a bill of exchange accepted by a banker;

- bank notes and bank statements, a lease or other disposition of property or a heritable security; and

- contracts of insurance.

1.32

(6) **Government and public securities.** This covers loan stock, bonds and other instruments issued by central, regional and local government in the

EEA. Excluded are those instruments excluded under 'debentures' above and instruments issued by the National Savings Bank and under the National Loans Act 1968 and s 11(3) of the National Debt Act 1972.

(7)   **Warrants.** The definition applies regardless of whether the instrument relates to something that is or is not already in existence. They have been defined as 'transferable option certificates issued by companies and trusts which entitle the holder to buy a specific number of shares in that company at a specific price ... at a specific time in the future.' As is made clear in the definition this state of affairs applies regardless of whether the shares are already in existence.

(8)   **Certificates Representing Securities.** Certificates providing contractual rights in respect of shares, instruments creating or acknowledging indebtedness, government and public securities and warrants where the interest is held by someone other than the person on whom the rights are conferred and where the transfer can be carried out without the consent of that person. This paragraph effectively debars the creation of investments which amount to an indirect interest so as to facilitate carrying on business in such investments outside the jurisdiction of the FSA regime.

Excluded are instruments conferring rights in respect of two or more investments issued by different persons, or in respect of two or more types of government or public security issued by the same person. The first of these exclusions covers legal and equitable mortgages because such an arrangement involves a transfer of property interest from the party granting the mortgage to that receiving it.

1.33

(9)   **Units in collective investment schemes.** Such schemes are defined in s 235 of the Act as:

'(1)   *any arrangements with respect to property of any description, including money, the purpose or effect of which is to enable persons taking part ....(whether by becoming owners of the property or any part of it or otherwise) to participate in or receive profits or income arising from the acquisition, holding, management or disposal of the property or sums paid out of such profits or income.*

(2)   *The arrangements must be such that the persons who are to participate ... do not have day-to-day control over the management of the property, whether they have the right to be consulted or give directions.*

(3)   *The arrangements must also have either or both of the following characteristics-*

(a)   the contributions of the participants and the profits or income
      out of which payments are to be made to them are pooled;

(b)   the property is managed as a whole by or on behalf of the
      operator of the scheme.'

If the property is held on trust for the participants the fund will be
known as a unit trust. An open ended investment company on the other
hand is a collective investment scheme where the property concerned
belongs beneficially to and is managed by or on behalf of a body
corporate. The aim of such a scheme must be to spread investment risk
and give the members the benefit. The investment must however appear
to a reasonable investor to be one from which he can realise the
investment within a reasonable period and be satisfied that the value of
that investment would be calculated by reference to the value of
property into which the scheme has invested.

1.34

(10) **Rights under stakeholder pension schemes**. These are defined by s 1 of
the Welfare Reform and Pensions Act 1999 which in essence states that
such a scheme is one which is registered with OPRA and meets a series of
conditions which are set out in s 1(2)–(9) and any others that may be
added by statutory instrument.

(11) **Options**. The definition covers options to buy or sell:

●   a security or contractually-based investment;

●   UK or foreign currency; or

●   palladium, platinum, gold or silver.

There are two main categories: put options, which involve the party
paying a deposit acquiring the right to sell one of the above commodities whilst the counterparty takes on the obligation to buy, and call
options which operate in reverse. The party paying a deposit acquires a
right to buy whilst the counterparty must sell. In each instance the party
who has the right to perform can also decide to walk away from the
contract and the only cost to them will be the loss of the deposit. Their
counterparty has no such right.

(12) **Futures.** This covers rights under a contract to sell a commodity or
property where the price is agreed now but delivery is in the future where
such an agreement is made for an investment rather than a commercial
purpose. A contract will be regarded as being for investment purposes if it
is traded on a recognised investment exchange or where it is not but is
expressed to be traded as such. A contract will be regarded as being for
commercial purposes if delivery is to be made within seven days or where

one of the parties is a producer of the commodity or property or uses it in their business, or where delivery is intended.

The contract must be for sale, hire, loan or bailment. In practice it is usually a contract for sale. The definition has been widened, for example to cover a weakness in the previous definition that did not clearly cover futures contracts in indexes.

1.35

(13) **Contracts for differences**. This covers agreements the aim of which is to secure a profit or avoid a loss by either or both of the parties by reference to fluctuations in the value of property or an index or other factor. There are two types of contract which would potentially appear to be caught by this wording: swaps and forward rate agreements.

Swap contracts exist in a number of forms, but essentially they all consist of a contractual arrangement whereby two counterparties will agree to notionally swap similar or dissimilar assets or debts. The original type – currency swaps – evolved as a method of circumventing exchange control restrictions prior to their suspension in 1979. Rather than use traditional methods, such as parallel and back-to-back loans, the parties would enter into a spot exchange transaction to sell one currency and use a forward exchange contract to reverse the original contract. As loans were not being made as such it did not constitute borrowing and the transaction could be left off the balance sheet. Any necessary payments between the parties were then made on a net basis, commonly every six months. The net major development was the emergence of the interest rate swap, where one party who had a greater quantity of fixed rate debt that they wished to retain arranged with a counterparty who had a surplus of floating rate debt, to 'swap' the respective debts. The arrangement did not consist of a transference of the legal title to the debts but the periodic payment of net amounts needed to place the parties in the financial position they would have been had the legal transfer of the debt taken place. Recent years have seen the emergence of a wide range of swap contracts of which the most important are credit swaps where one party exchanges an income stream against another's asset holdings. This can facilitate a transfer of risk that better suits the respective parties financial needs.

Excluded by the Instrument are contracts under which delivery is going to take place to one of the parties, and contracts in relation to money deposits where interest or another return will be paid by reference to fluctuations in an index or other factor. Also excluded are contracts in relation to deposits at the National Savings Bank or money raised under the National Loans Act 1968 or under s 11(3) of the National Debt Act 1972.

(14) **Lloyd's syndicate capacity and syndicate membership.** Lloyd's is an insurance underwriting market. Those who underwrite risks are the underwriters who work in syndicates to spread the risk between them. They do not carry all this risk themselves but spread it to 'names' in return for passing them a share of the premium. These names fall into two categories. The traditional names who are wealthy individuals who risk all their assets in return for a premium income and the corporate names who, subject to limited liability receive a premium income on behalf of their shareholders. Syndicate capacity and membership are specified investments.

Largely as a consequence of the problems that beset Lloyd's in the 1990s, The Council of Lloyd's that traditionally ran the market is now subject to oversight by the FSA. Section 314 requires the FSA to keep itself informed about the Council's running of Lloyd's and the manner in which regulated activities are being carried out with a view to exercising their own powers if necessary.

1.36

(15) **Funeral plan contracts.** This issue is discussed below at **1.44(13)**

(16) **Regulated mortgage contracts.** This is arguably the most important addition to the range of investments covered by the financial services regulatory regime. It is for most people the largest or second largest financial investment they make. Although the banks and other main lending institutions had adopted a code of practice with regard to mortgage lending, the involvement of the FSA now means that tighter control can be taken of advice given to those taking out one of the various types of mortgage contract now available. Lifetime mortgages are also regulated but, as yet, other types of equity release products are not (see below at **1.45**).

(17) **Other financial arrangements involving land.** This covers an arrangement for the provision of finance where the person providing the finance either acquires a major interest in land from the person to whom the finance is provided or disposes of a major interest in land to that person as part of the arrangement. A 'major interest' in land covers a fee simple or a term of years absolute whether at law or in equity. (In Scotland it covers owners and a tenant's rights over or interest in property subject to a lease. In Northern Ireland it covers freehold estates and leaseholds at law and in equity).

(18) **Rights or interests in investments.** Essentially this covers any right or interest in the above. Excluded are interests under trusts of an occupational pension scheme and certain interests in contracts of insurance or under certain trusts. This is effectively a safety net provision to catch instruments that would otherwise have been covered by one of the above but are technically outside it, for example because the beneficiary of the

investment has a legal or equitable charge or mortgage over the property or a beneficial interest in a trust rather than a direct involvement with the investment.

---

1 Inserted by the Regulation of Financial Services (Land Transactions) Act 2005, s 1.

Specified activities

1.37   The Financial Services and Markets Act 2000 (Regulated Activities) Order 2001 as amended also defines the activities that are regulated in the new regime where they relate to specified investments. These activities are:

1.38

(1)   **Accepting deposits**. This covers the receipt of deposits (other than those immediately exchanged for electronic money[1]) that will be repaid, either with or without interest, and either on demand or at another time agreed by the parties. It does not cover payments referable to the provision of property other than currency, or services or giving security. There are a range of exclusions, namely sums paid by:

- central banks in Europe;
- an authorised person who has permission to accept deposits;
- EEA authorised firms;
- The National Savings Bank;
- A municipal bank;
- Keesler Federal Credit Union;
- A certified school bank;
- Local authorities;
- A body which is enacted to issue a precept to local authorities in England and Wales or by requisition in Scotland;
- The European Community, the European Atomic Energy Community or the European Coal and Steel Community;
- The European Investment Bank;
- The International Bank for Reconstruction and Development;
- The International Finance Corporation;
- The International Monetary Fund;

- The African Development Bank;

- The Asian Development Bank;

- The Caribbean Development Bank;

- The inter-American Development Bank;

- The European Bank for Reconstruction and Development;

- The Council of Europe Resettlement Fund.

Also sums paid by any other party in the course of wholly or significantly carrying on the business of moneylending; sums paid by one company to another where they are both members of the same group or when the same individual is a majority shareholder in both of them; or the making of a payment by a person who is a close relative of the person receiving it or who is a close relative of a director or manager of that person or a partner in it. Likewise, a sum received by a solicitor, or anyone dealing in investments, acting as agent in relation to investments, arranging deals in investments, managing investments, or establishing, operating or winding up a collective investment scheme or stakeholder pension scheme. Also excluded are sums received in consideration of the issue of debt securities.

---

1 Inserted by SI 2002/682, art 3(2).

1.39

(2) **Insurance.** This covers both effecting and carrying out a contract of insurance. Excluded from this are where such contracts are effected or carried out by an EEA firm falling within Sch 3, para 5(d) of the 2000 Act and motor vehicle breakdown insurance. Contracts of insurance are defined in Sch 1 to the Instrument in two main categories – general and long-term insurance. These are explained at **1.29(3)** above. This activity has been extended to cover insurance mediation as a consequence of the Insurance Mediation Directive. It covers dealing, arranging, making arrangements with a view to transactions, assisting on, advising and agreeing to carry on insurance business.

(3) **Dealing in investments as principal.** This covers buying, selling, subscribing for or underwriting securities or contractually-based investments (other than funeral plan contracts and rights to, or interests in, investments). Excluded are situations where the person concerned holds themselves out as willing to deal at prices determined by him generally and continuously or holds themselves out as engaging in the business of buying or underwriting investments of the type concerned. Also excluded are those who hold over 20% of the shares in a company and who seek to

buy the shares of other shareholders or sell those shares to them, or someone acting on behalf of such a person. Finally, there is a general exception for those whose head office is outside the UK and whose ordinary business consists of dealing as principal or agent, arranging, managing, safeguarding and administering investments and advising on investments. Likewise those who are establishing, running or winding up a collective investment scheme or stakeholder pension scheme, and, where relevant, those agreeing to carry on any of these.

This category does not extend to those who:

- enter into contractually-based transactions with or through an authorised or exempt person;

- accept instruments creating or acknowledging indebtedness;

- are companies issuing shares or share warrants;

- are contracting as principal in relation to options and contracts for differences where the counterparties are not individuals and the principal is contracting with a view to limiting an identifiable business risk other than one arising as a result of regulated activities (or matters that would be regulated activities but for the exclusions in Part III of the Instrument).

- trustees;

- contracts for the sale of goods and supply of services;

- groups and joint enterprises;

- sale of a body corporate; and

- overseas persons.

1.40

(4) **Dealing in investments as agent.** This covers buying, selling, subscribing for or underwriting securities or contractually-based investments (other than funeral plan contracts and rights or interests in specified investments) as agent.

The exclusions are:

- dealing through authorised persons where the transaction is entered into or the advice given to the client by an authorised person or where it is clear that the client is not seeking and has not sought advice from the agent regarding the transaction. This exclusion does not apply if the agent receives payment from anyone other than the client, for which he does not account to the client.

- Transactions relating to options, contracts for differences or rights or interests in either of those, between parties who are not individuals where the sole or main purpose is that of limiting the extent to which the business may be affecting by an identifiable risk other than one arising as a result of carrying on a regulated activity.

- Activities carried on in the course of a profession or non-investment business.
- Activities carried on in connection with the sale of goods or supply of services.
- Groups and joint enterprises.
- Activities carried on in connection with the sale of a body corporate.
- Activities carried on in connection with employee share schemes.
- Overseas person.

1.41

(5) **Arranging deals in investments.** This covers the making of arrangements for another person to buy, sell, subscribe for or underwrite investments which are either a security, a contractually-based investment, an interest in investments or syndicate capacity or membership of Lloyd's. It also extends to making such arrangements with a view to someone participating. It does not extend to merely introducing someone to another party unless it is done for a fee or on a recurrent basis. The wording is clearer here than in the previous legislation in that it makes overt that the act of arranging must be a causative element in the transaction following.

The exclusions are:

- arrangements which would not bring about the transaction;
- merely providing the means of communication;
- where the person entering into the contract does so as principal or as agent for another;
- arranging deals through authorised persons where the client is acting on the advice of an authorised person, or where it is clear that the client is not seeking advice from the person acting (or if he has and it has been refused and the client advised to seek advice from an appropriate person);
- arranging transactions in connection with lending on the security of insurance policies;
- arranging the acceptance of debentures in connection with loans;

- providing finance to enable a person to buy, sell, subscribe for or underwrite investments;

- introducing persons to either an authorised person, an exempt person acting in the course of a regulated activity for which he is exempt, or someone who is lawfully dealing, dealing as agent, arranging, managing, safeguarding and administering investments, sending dematerialised securities, establishing, operating or winding up a collective investment scheme or stakeholder pensions scheme or advising. The introduction must be made with a view to the provision of independent advice;

- arrangements for the issue of shares, share warrants, debentures or debenture warrants by the company issuing them;

- international securities self-regulating organisations who have been approved as such by the Treasury;

- Trustees;

- activities carried on in the course of a profession or non-investment business;

- activities carried on in connection with the sale of goods or supply of services;

- groups and joint enterprises;

- sale of a body corporate;

- employee share schemes;

- overseas persons.

1.42

(6) **Managing investments.** This is a specified activity if the assets concerned consist of or include an investment which is a security or a contractually-based investment. It is limited to discretionary management. If there is no discretion it would normally then be covered by 'arranging deals in investment' at (5) above.

The exclusions are:

- where the assets are being managed under a power of attorney and all day-to-day decisions are taken by an authorised person acting within the scope of their authorisation;

- trustees;

- activities carried on in connection with the sale of goods or supply of services; and

- groups and joint enterprises.

(7) **Safeguarding and administering assets.** This category applies regardless of whether the securities are held in a certified form.

The exclusions are:

- where responsibility has been accepted by a qualified third party;
- making introductions to a qualified custodian;
- providing information as to the units or value of assets held, converting currency or receiving documents relating to an investment solely for the purpose of onward transmission to, from, or at the direction of the person to whom it belongs;
- trustees;
- activities carried on in connection with professional or non-investment business;
- activities carried on in connection with the sale of goods or supply of services;
- groups and joint enterprises; and
- employee share schemes.

(8) **Sending dematerialised instructions.**

The exclusions here are:

- acting on behalf of a participating issuer;
- acting on behalf of settlement banks;
- instructions in connection with takeover offers;
- instructions in the course of providing a network;
- trustees; and
- groups and joint enterprises.

1.43

(9) **Establishing, operating or winding up a collective investment scheme.** The definition of 'collective investments schemes' is considered at (8) above.

(10) **Establishing, operating or winding up a stakeholder pension scheme.** The definition of 'stakeholder pension schemes' is considered at (9) above.

(11) **Advising on investments.** This covers giving advice to an investor or prospective investor on the merits of buying, selling, subscribing for or underwriting an investment which is a security or a contractually-based investment or exercising any right conferred by such an investment. It

applies whether the advice is given to someone in their own capacity or as agent or another. However, generic advice is not covered, so for example it is possible to advise on the relative merits of direct and indirect investments or of investments of a particular nature.

The exclusions are:

- advice given in newspapers, journals or broadcast transmissions where that media is neither essentially giving advice or leading or enabling people to buy, sell, subscribe for or underwrite securities or contractually-based investments;

- trustees;

- activities carried on in connection with professional or on-investment business;

- activities carried on in connection with the sale of goods or supply of services;

- sale of a body corporate; and

- overseas persons.

1.44

(12) **Lloyd's.** This covers advising a person to become or to cease to be a member of a Lloyd's syndicate; managing the underwriting capacity of a Lloyd's syndicate as a managing agent or arranging deals in contracts of insurance written at Lloyd's. The background to this is discussed at (14) above. The Society of Lloyd's itself is an authorised person and has permission to carry on the following regulated activities

- arranging deals in insurance written at Lloyd's (basic market activity);

- arranging deals in participation in Lloyd's syndicates (secondary market activity); and

- activities carried on in connection with basic and primary market activities.

However, the FSA retains the legal capacity to involve itself by applying core provisions of the Act to a member of Lloyd's or the Society of Lloyd's generally if it thinks so fit bearing in mind the interests of policyholders and potential policyholders. The FSA can do this either by giving a direction to the Council of Lloyd's or to the Society acting through the Council.

Former underwriting members can carry out each contract of insurance that they have underwritten at Lloyd's whether or not they are authorised. However, the FSA can impose on them such requirements as the

FSA thinks fit to protect policyholders against the risk that the underwriter may not be able to meet their liabilities.

(13) **Funeral plan contracts.** This covers contracts under which one person makes payments to another in return for the provision of a funeral on the first person's death provided it is not expected to occur within the first month.

The exclusion is that of plans covered by insurance or trust arrangements.

(14) **Regulated mortgage contracts.** This covers entering into or administering a regulated mortgage contract. Such an arrangement arises where a lender provides the credit to an individual or trustee in return for an obligation to repay which is secured by a first legal mortgage on land in the UK, at least 40% of which is to be used as a dwelling by the borrower or (if it is the beneficiary of a trust the beneficiary), or a related person. In this context administering means notifying the borrower of changes in interest rates on payments due and taking any necessary steps to collect or recover payments from the borrower. Merely exercising the right to take action does not amount to administering.

Exclusions cover arranging administration by an authorised person or pursuant to an agreement with one.

(15) **Agreeing to carry on activities.** Agreeing to carry on any other specified activity other than accepting deposits, effecting and carrying out contracts of insurance, or establishing, operating or winding up a collective investment scheme or stakeholder pension scheme.

Future developments

1.45 The FSA have announced that further developments are to be made to the categories of investment business. These are Self Invested Personal Pensions (SIPPS), Home Reversion Plans (HRs) and Home Purchase Plans (HPPs).

1.46 A SIPPS is a pension fund where the person saving has a greater degree of control over how the money is invested. They have existed for some time, but recent changes have made them much more attractive and their use is expected to expand rapidly. HRs are equity release arrangements involving a sale and leaseback to provide finance for an existing home owner by accessing equity. HPPs are sale and leaseback arrangements as well, but for different reasons. A sale and leaseback is permissible under Islamic Law as a method of providing a *de facto* mortgage. HRs are seen as higher risk than conventional mortgages but not HPPs, which will impact on the manner in which the FSA treat them[1]. HPPs will be treated along the same lines as existing mortgages or lifetime mortgages, as appropriate. At the time of writing the new rules on SIPPS are expected in late 2006 and those on HRs and HPPs early in 2007.

---

1 See FSA Consultation Paper 06/8.

Gaming

1.47 Gaming contracts are unenforceable as being for an illegal consideration and any monies loaned to another person with the intention that the borrower shall use those monies for gambling is also an unenforceable debt. This gives rise to problems with the increased use of derivative contracts (ie, futures, options and contracts for differences) which could, in some instances be viewed as having similar characteristics to gaming contracts. Indeed this misconception is reflected in part in Lord Wilberforce's judgment in *Hazell v Hammersmith and Fulham London Borough Council* where he stated:

> '*A swap contract based on a notional principal sum of £1 million under which the local authority promises to pay the bank £10,000 if LIBOR rises by 1% and the bank promises to pay the local authority £10,000 if LIBOR falls by 1% is more akin to gambling than insurance*'

1.48 Hopefully, the greater understanding of derivative instruments and their usage that now exists will stop this judicial approach in the future. In any event to stop contracts of such financial importance being rendered unenforceable the Act states that:

> '*(1) No contract to which this section applies is void or unenforceable because of-*
>
>   (*a*) *section 18 of the Gaming Act 1845, section 1 of the Gaming Act 1892 or Article 170 of the Betting, Gaming, Lotteries and Amusements (Northern Ireland) Order 1985; or*
>
>   (*b*) *any rule of the law of Scotland under which a contract by way of gaming or wagering is not legally enforceable.*
>
> (*2*) *This section applies to a contract if-*
>
>   (*a*) *it is entered into by either or each party by way of business;*
>
>   (*b*) *the entering into or performance of it by either party constitutes an activity of a specified kind or one which falls within a specified class of activity; and*

(c) it relates to an investment of a specified kind or one which falls within a specified class of investment.[1]'

---

1 FSMA 2000, s 412.

1.49 *Morgan Grenfell & Co Ltd v Welwyn Hatfield District Council*[1] *was a case on the virtually identical wording of the equivalent section in the preceding statute.* The judge made clear that in this context 'business' would be very widely interpreted and cover any situation where one of the parties was entering into the arrangement for other than recreational purposes.

---

1 [1995] 1 All ER 1.

1.50 The definition of 'contracts for differences' is extremely wide and should thus continue the tradition already seen in *City Index Ltd v Leslie*[1] where it was held that a contract in relation to stock market index movements was not a gaming contract and could be enforced as it fell within the definition of 'contracts for differences' and the party seeking to enforce it was properly authorised to carry on the relevant category of investment business. Indeed the definition of 'contracts for differences' in Article 85 of the Instrument appears wide enough to cover most spread betting.

---

1 [1992] QB 98.

1.51 Perhaps the other issue is that of speculative forex trading which had been suggested as being at risk from the gaming laws. This risk appears to remain as exemption under s. 412 only exists where the activity involves a specified investment. This could give rise to problems as forex contracts do not fall within any of the above categories.

Compensation scheme

1.52 The Act requires the FSA to set up a compensation scheme. The purpose of this is to provide a fallback position for those who have a claim against an authorised firm which cannot be satisfied financially by a claim against the firm or their insurers. The compensation scheme applies even if the firm is acting outside or in breach of its authorisation, but not if it is unauthorised. The claim may be for money that has been paid over to an authorised person, money due to be paid to them by an authorised person or an amount owing as a result of a legal claim or an ombudsman's ruling.

1.53 As the function of the compensation scheme is to provide cover for those who need it, claims may only be made by a restricted group of people, which excludes larger businesses. As is normally the way with compensation schemes there is a limit on the size of payouts for any individual claim. The funds that finance the scheme cover three areas of the financial services markets: investment services, deposit protection and insurance. The authorised firms are required to pay a levy according to which of these areas the business concerned operates in.

1.54 The scheme manager can require the authorised person against whom a claim is being made to provide information and documents within a given period where this is believed by the manager to be necessary to fairly determine the claim. The manager can also inspect documents held by an administrative receiver, administrator or liquidator, or trustee in bankruptcy of an insolvent person or in Scotland a permanent trustee of an insolvent person where this is necessary for the manager to discharge his function. This will normally occur where the authorised person against whom a claim has been made is in insolvency. If either type of request is not met it is possible to request a court order to that effect.

Chapter 2

The Financial Services Authority, its duties, objectives, governance and accountability

Introduction

2.1

> "... I agree with what the Select Committee said about self-regulation: let us end it ... Self-regulation is a misnomer. The present system is rooted in statute. The problem with self-regulation is the public's perception that trade interest dominates, which is extremely damaging ..."

Alistair Darling, 14 December 1995[1].

---

1 House of Commons debate 14 December 1995 cc 1184–85.

2.2   In this chapter we will consider the legal basis of the Financial Services Authority's role in regulating the UK financial services markets. In particular we will review the FSA's functions and powers and the mechanisms the UK government has put in place to ensure that the FSA is accountable for the actions and functions it performs.

The regulatory challenge

2.3   The Financial Services Authority is the single regulator for the Financial Services industry in the United Kingdom. Within days of its election success in 1997 the new Labour government announced plans to reform the way the UK financial Services industry was to be regulated. Until that date the Financial Services industry had been subject to a multi-channelled and hybrid regulatory regime. The banking sector was regulated under the Banking Act 1987 and subject to the supervision of the Bank of England. Friendly Societies, Building Societies and Insurance Companies were subject to prudential regulation created by specific legislation, and the Investment Industry was regulated under a regime created by the Financial Services Act 1986. The 1986 Act had established a system of two-tiered statute backed self-regulation. In essence the system created a requirement for persons conducting investment business in the United Kingdom to be authorised. Authorisation was granted in a number of ways, although mainly granted by either the government's designated agency, the Securities and Investment Board or by Self regulating organisations which in turn were recognised by SIB. Authorised firms were then required to comply with rules created by the SIB or their relevant SRO.

2.4 The Regulatory system created by the Banking Act 1987 and Financial Services Act 1986 became subject to much criticism and a series of financial failures in the 1990s, including the pensions transfer scandal, the collapse of Barings Bank, and criticism in the Bank of England's supervision of BCCI led to a momentum for change. Fundamental weaknesses existed in the Financial Services Act, in particular the role and often the functions of the SIB were hindered by certain restrictions in the 1986 Act. Moreover, the Bank of England's supervisory functions were subject to a review by Anderson Consulting following the collapse of BCCI. The review reported that the Bank's supervisory function was under-resourced, under-trained and inexperienced.

2.5 During the late 1990s, comment on the perceived shortcomings in the regulatory regime created by the 1986 Act became more common and although wide ranging concerns were expressed by Government, practioners and consumer groups three particular significant shortcomings featured with some regularity[1]:

(a) **SIB's dual role**. SIB's role was originally intended to be focused towards the authorisation and ongoing recognition of the Self Regulating Organisations. The 1986 Act, however, did make provision allowing persons to be authorised and regulated directly by SIB. This structure allowed firms the choice of being directly regulated or becoming members of an SRO. This would have perhaps not been a major failure had it not been for the limitation on SIB's powers. In relation to SROs it only possessed the ultimate sanction of derecognition and in relation to authorised businesses lacked the power to levy fines. It is difficult to determine why SIB lacked a range of powers that would have enabled it to take effective action against authorised firms. It may have been something that was overlooked when the legislation was being drafted or have been due to some constitutional objection to an organisation exercising an executive function being able to involve itself in matters viewed as quasi-judicial[2].

(b) **The absence of clear objectives**. The regulatory regime created by the Financial Services Act lacked any clear objectives. and stated that the remit was 'To protect investors'. Because of the lack of clarity there was often too little effort to identify risk so as to allocate resource and regulation toward issues that were more likely to give rise to problems. Regulators often applied a full audit approach when supervising firms and were often criticised for encouraging a tick box approach to regulation and compliance[3].

(c) **Self-regulation in the life and pensions industry.** Professor Gower's recommendation for a statute backed system of self-regulation arguably assumed some pre-existing experience of self-regulation which the Life Assurance Industry had little of. At the same time that the Financial Services Bill was being debated in Parliament, the government was also making plans to introduce legislation to allow Personal Pensions and provide savers with the freedom to choose whether or not to join their employer's Occupational Scheme. In retrospect the government lacked a proper appreciation of the inexperience within the regulatory regime it was creating and the life insurance industries naivety towards conduct of business regulation. At that time sales forces began focusing on the opportunities presented by the freeing up of pension planning and as now appears to be the case had little appreciation for their client advisory responsibilities, focusing merely on the arrangements necessary to confirm a sale. What followed was the mis-selling of hundreds of thousands of personal pension policies, a retrospective industry-wide review that lasted over five years and a compensation bill running into £100s of millions. The so-called pensions scandal came to be one of the major failings of the self-regulating regime and perhaps a key driver for a change to the UK's regulation of its financial markets[4].

---

1 For further detail on the criticism of the regulatory regime created by the Financial Services Act 1986 see House of Commons research paper 99/68: Financial Services and Markets Bill. Christopher Blair 24 June 1999.

2 In particular see Guide to Financial Services Regulation 3rd Edition, Barry Rider, Charles Abrams, Michael Ashe, CCH Editions Ltd, 31 July 1997.

3 See Financial Services and Markets Act 2000, Butterwortsh New Law Guides. Edited by D Sabalot and R Everett, July 2000.

4 See The Regulatory Leviathan: Will Super SIB work?, Dr Michael Taylor, 1997. CTA Financial Publishing.

2.6   There was also a growing to move to a single entity model of financial regulation. In addition the UK financial marketplace was beginning to evolve and fundamental changes to the structure of the market were removing the traditional compartmentalising of business. Multi-function banking was emerging and banks such as HSBC, Barclays and Lloyds TSB were offering clients multi range services under one roof. Under the then current regime each of such services might be regulated by a different Self Regulating Organisation as well as the Bank of England. The formation of multi-function banking made an appreciation of group wide matters an imperative for any holistic and effective regulatory supervision. This inevitably created increased regulatory cost for organisations and in the event of problems with the services provided, confusion for consumers wishing to pursue their complaints through the variety of organisations that would then have been involved in regulating the different services provided. By 1997 single regulator systems had already begun to emerge in countries such as Austria, Denmark, Malta, Norway and Sweden[1], although single regulatory systems were not without their own criticism and with a belief that a single regulator responsible for the oversight of a country's entire financial market would be an unwieldy and inefficient machine[2].

---

1 See Directory of Financial Regulatory Agencies 1996 London: Central Bank Publications.
2 Refer to Dr Michael Taylor The Regulatory Leviathan, Will super SIB work? CTA Financial Publishing 1997.

2.7 On 20 May 1997 Gordon Brown MP Chancellor of the Exchequer in a statement to the House of Commons on the Bank of England stated *inter alias:*

'... there is a strong case in principle for bringing the regulation of banking, securities and insurance together under one roof. Firms organise and manage their businesses on a group-wide basis. Regulators need to look at them in a consistent way. This would bring the regulatory structure closer into line with today's increasingly integrated financial markets. It would deliver more effective and more efficient supervision, giving both firms and customers better value for money. This would improve the competitiveness of the sector and create a regulatory regime to meet the challenges of the twenty-first century.'

2.8 The intention indicated by the government was to establish a single financial regulator combining the regulatory functions of nine existing bodies. These were:

(1) The Building Societies Commission,

(2) Friendly Societies Commission,

(3) Insurance Directorate of the Department of Trade and Industry,

(4) Investment Management Regulatory Organisation,

(5) Personal Investment Authority,

(6) Registry of Friendly Societies,

(7) Securities and Futures Authority,

(8) Securities and Investments Board,

(9) Supervision and Surveillance Division of the Bank of England.

2.9 The government also took the decision to make two fundamental changes to the role of the Bank of England. The first was to withdraw the government's involvement in establishing monetary policy. This had the effect of granting to the Bank of England monetary policy independence. The second was to use a Bank of England Bill to transfer to SIB (later known as the FSA) the banking supervisory powers of the Bank of England. This decision immediately extended the functions of SIB from that of overseeing financial services consumer protection into the realms of protecting the financial and banking system itself.

2.10   The Chancellor of the Exchequer instructed the then SIB Chairman Sir Andrew Large to lead a working party that included representatives of the nine regulatory bodies whose functions were to be brought together, to report on the detailed preparation requirements for the new regulator. The report was prepared in seven weeks and presented on 29 July 1997. Although the report only deals in outline in the planning for the new regulatory regime and is now almost nine years old, it does provide an insight into the source of some of the structural and accountability mechanisms that exist to support the operation of the FSA. In relation to the accountability of the New Single Regulator, the report highlighted the need for the regulator to be accountable to the government and Parliament and that it would have obligations to all whose interests it protects so as to deal with them in an open and accessible way. The report stated, '*[the regulator]... will take into account the continuing need – especially given its size and scope – to ensure that it is responsive to the concerns of those affected by its activities. This implies continued emphasis on high levels of accountability ...*'[1]

---

1 Report to the Chancellor of the Exchequer on the Reform of the Financial Regulatory System, July 1997.

2.11   The Financial Services Authority (FSA) was created on 28 October 1997 as a result of a relaunch of the Securities and Investments Board. On the June 1998 the supervisory powers of the Bank of England were transferred to the FSA soon followed in January 1999 the transfer of responsibility for insurance business supervision and the transfer of regulatory activities on behalf of the existing SROs. By January 1999 the Treasury had created from a practical point of view and without the FSMA 2000 being in force, a single regulator for the major parts of the UK's financial markets. The (SIB) FSA's early new role was encapsulated in a letter from Sir Andrew Large, the then Head of the SIB, responding to Gordon Brown MP Chancellor of the Exchequer's Statement to the House of Commons. He stated, '... you asked me to bring forward a plan ...involving the transfer to the SIB of responsibility for banking supervision and the functions of the SROs. You invited us to consider the logistical and organisational issues, the eventual architecture when the legislation is in place ...'

2.12   Following publication of a draft consultation Bill in July 1998, The Financial Services and Markets Bill was introduced into the House of Commons on June 1999. Its passage through Parliament caused a great deal of discussion and comment, particularly in relation to the overriding concept of the creation of a single regulator with statutory powers to enable the proposed regulatory authority to create rules, set standards of behaviour, supervise firms and take enforcement action against firms and individuals that it deemed were acting in breach of its rules. It should be remembered that in November 1998 the Labour Government adopted into the UK law the European Convention on Human Rights by way of the Human Rights Act 1998. Section 16 of that Act requires a Government Minister to certify, as compatible with convention rights, all new legislation and as a consequence specific attention was given by Parliament as to whether the regime to be created by the Financial Services and Markets Bill would comply with the European Convention. Particular concern was expressed about the FSA's multiple role in rule making, monitoring and enforcement.

2.13 In a clear response to the criticism aimed at the FSA's role in the new regulatory system Howard Davies Chairman and Chief Executive of the FSA stated:

> 'The second crucial advantage of the new regime is that it incorporates clear lines of accountability. There is clearly no doubt about who is responsible in the event of a regulatory failure. I may live to regret that clarity of responsibility, but at least as a theoretical proposition it is attractive. There is a clear separation of duties between the Treasury and the FSA, with Ministers responsible for the statutory framework while the Authority is responsible for acting effectively within that framework.[1]'

---

1 Howard Davies 1999 Travers Lecture 'Building the Financial Services Authority: Whats new' London Guildhall University, 11 March 1999.

2.14 Between October 1997 and 30 November 2001 (being the date that the substantial parts of the Financial Services and Markets Act 2000 was brought into effect) the FSA's role was twofold, it first operated as the provider of regulatory services to the SROs and the Bank of England. Staff at the SROs, building societies commission, friendly societies commission and the insurance directorate of the DTI as well as Banking Supervision staff at the Bank of England found that their employment was transferred to the FSA and regulated firms were introduced to the FSA in the form of correspondence and supervision visits, albeit acting on behalf of the existing regulators. Secondly the FSA took an active role in supporting HM Treasury in the design and crafting of the new legislation and consequent regulation. As a consequence of its involvement a curious situation occurred as although the new law was required to create a single regulator, the FSA had already been created in October 1997 and as a practical consequence the legislation would merely confirm the FSA's role as the single regulator.

2.15 During the period from 20 May 1997 and 30 November 2001, the FSA's was required to undertake a monumental task in the drafting, consultation and introduction (pending the bringing into force of the new law) of a new regulation that would provide both the cornerstones as well as detail of the regulation of the UK's financial marketplace. It was responsible for the publication of 113 Consultation papers plus a series of general communication documents and discussion papers. In addition, in response to the principles of good regulation set out in the FSMA 2000, s 2(3), the FSA determined to change the approach to the supervision of regulated firms. In its publication, a New Regulator for a New Millennium in January 2000, it set out a revised approach, moving away from the approach utilised by many of the legacy regulators and towards to a risk-based approach to supervision and compliance. One key principle of the new regulatory system was an approach for the FSA to identify and prioritise risks within the financial system to enable it to place greater resource toward those risks that presented the greatest potential of failure in the financial system[1]. In essence, the new risk-based approach to regulation accepted that some failures neither can nor should be avoided.

---

1 The subject of risk-based supervision is discussed in more detail in Chapters 4 and 5.

2.16   The transfer of the Bank of England's supervisory functions was initially dealt with under the Bank of England Act 1998. This Act had the effect of transferring to the FSA from the Bank of England the then current UK Banking markets supervision. It in effect provided a temporary solution to the FSA's role in Banking supervision while HM Treasury negotiated the Financial Services and Markets Bill's passage through Parliament.

2.17   As part of its role as a single financial regulator the FSA was also given the role as the UK Listing Authority, a role previously carried on by the London Stock Exchange. The government's view was that the growing commercial pressures on the London Stock Exchange and its plans for demutualisation made it essential to split the LSE's regulatory functions to admit firms to listing from its role of facilitating trading. The FSMA 2000 established the FSA under s 72(1) as the competent authority. FSMA 2000, Sch 7 sets out a number of modifications of the FSA's general duties in s 2 as Regulator of Investment Business to facilitate the FSA as the UK listing authority. Although an analysis of the FSA role as UK listing authority is outside the scope of this book further detail about the FSA's powers and role as competent authority are set out in Chapter 1 Relevant provisions of the Act.

2.18   The Financial Services and Markets Act 2000 (which we shall now refer to as the Act) received Royal Assent in June 2000 and the new regulatory system was brought into effect at midnight on 30 November 2001.

As a result, a series of safeguards were established in the legislation, each designed to create accountability of the FSA and act as a check and balance over the FSA's powers. These include within the Act:

- Under s 7 and Sch 1, the FSA is subject to strict corporate governance requirements.

- Section 2(2) sets out that the FSA's operation must meet four specified Statutory Objectives.

- Under s 2(3) the FSA must operate within a framework of principles of good regulation, including a requirement to ensure that all new regulation is subject to a cost benefit analysis.

- Under para 10 to Sch 1 the FSA is obliged to make an annual report to the Treasury a copy of which must be presented to Parliament by the Treasury and within three months of its publication be presented in public meeting.

- The FSA has a duty to consult in relation to its rule making and guidance function. Under s 8 it must consult with the Consumer and Practioner Panels and under s 65 (in relation to a new approved persons code), s 155 (in relation to new rules) and s 121 (in relation to a new code of market conduct) it must consult with the public.

- Section 10 creates a Consumer Panel with the role of being consulted about new rules and making representations to the FSA.

- Section 9 Creates a Practitioner Panel with the role of being consulted about new rules and making representations to the FSA.

- Under para 7, Sch 1 the Establishment of an independent Complaints Commissioner whose role is to adjudicate on any complaints about the discharge of the FSA's powers and make, where necessary, recommendations for change to the FSA.

- To directly deal with the concern of the FSA becoming Legislator, Judge and police force, the FSA established an internal Regulatory Decisions Committee which would act as a protective barrier between the FSA's supervisory and enforcement functions. The committee would be chaired by a person independent of the FSA and have the role of determining whether enforcement action should or should not be taken against authorised firms or approved persons.

- Under s 132 and Sch 13 The Financial Services and Markets Tribunal acts as an adjudicator of those decisions of the FSA specified under the Act which are referred to it by the aggrieved person.

- The FSA has established a number of other panels with whom it consults in connection with the discharge of its functions. This includes a Small Business Practitioner Panel, a Training Advisory Panel and Collective Investment Scheme Forum.

The Financial Services Authority's general duties, objectives and principles of good regulation

FSA general functions

2.19   Section 2 of the Act sets out the FSA's general functions and specifies that the FSA must when discharging these (in so far as is reasonably possible) act in a way which is compatible with its regulatory objectives and which is considered by the FSA to be most appropriate for the purpose of meeting those objectives.

2.20   The FSA's general functions are[1]:

(1)   that of making rules under the Act. This would include those rules set out in the FSA's handbook whether of general application considered by the FSA necessary to protect the interest of customers[2] or relating to matters specifically required by the Act. For example rules relating to Financial Promotions under s 145;

(2)   preparing and issuing codes under the Act. This would include the Code of Market Conduct issued under s 119 to the Act and the Approved Persons Code issued pursuant to s 64 to the Act;

(3)   the giving of general guidance under s 157 of the Act;

(4)   determining the general policy and principles by reference to which it performs particular functions.

---

1 Financial Services and Markets Act 2000, s 2(4)
2 Financial Services and Markets Act 2000, s 138(1).

Monitoring

2.21   The FSA is required under para 6(1), Sch 1 of the Act to have appropriate monitoring arrangements to enable it to determine whether persons subject to obligations in the Act are complying with them. Although the FSA retains responsibility for monitoring functions it may delegate them to any person that is competent to perform them. Further information about the FSA monitoring activities appear in Chapter 4 'Risk-based approach to regulation' and Chapter 5 'FSA supervision of firms'.

Enforcement

2.22   The FSA is also required under para 6(3), Sch 1 to establish and maintain arrangements for the enforcement of the Act. Unlike its arrangements for monitoring, its enforcement activities may not be delegated. Further information about the FSA's enforcement arrangements appear in Chapter 5 Supervision of firms.

Statutory objectives

2.23 FSMA 2000, s 2(1) requires that in discharging its general functions the FSA must (in so far as is reasonably possible) act in a way that is compatible with the four Statutory objectives set out in s 2(2) and particularised in ss 3–6. A criticism of the SIB's role in the regulatory regime under the Financial Services Act 1986 was that SIB lacked any clear and meaningful objective.

2.24 During the preparation for the new regulatory regime the Chancellor of the Exchequer said:

'The objectives we set will give the new regulator a clear sense of its priorities. And will provide a benchmark against which the performance of the regulator can be measured. They will form the basis of the regulator's annual report to me[1]'.

---

1 Speech of Rt hon Gordon Brown MP Chancellor of the Exchequer, 28 October 1997.

2.25 These four Statutory Oobjectives are applied directly to the FSA's operations including its rule-making and policy-making functions, however they do not in themselves impose specific statutory duties on the FSA but require the FSA to carry out its general functions in a way which is compatible with the objectives. The Statutory Objectives are:

2.26

(1) **Market Confidence**: Maintaining Confidence in the financial system[1].

The Financial System is described as including (a) financial markets and exchanges, (b) regulated activities, and (c) other activities connected with financial markets and exchanges[2].

---

1 Financial Services and Markets Act 2000, s 3(1)
2 Financial Services and Markets Act 2000, s 3(2).

2.27

(2) **Public Awareness**: Promoting public understanding of the financial system[1.]

In relation to this objective the financial system has the same definition as that in s 3 and the objective is further defined by specifying that it includes promoting awareness of the benefits and risks associated with different kinds of investments or other financial dealing; and the provision of appropriate information and advice[2].

1 Financial Services and Markets Act 2000, s 4(1).
2 Financial Services and Markets Act 2000, s 4(2).

2.28

(3) **Protection of consumers:** Securing the appropriate degree of protection for consumers[1].

1 Financial Services and Markets Act 2000, s 5.

2.29 Consumers are specifically defined and it is important to note that the definition is not limited to private or retail customers. In general terms the definition of consumer applies to a person using, having used or contemplating using services provided by authorised persons or appointed representatives carrying on regulated activities or those that have rights or interests derived from or attributable to the use of such services by other persons or those that may be adversely affected by the use of such services by persons acting on their behalf[1].

1 Financial Services and Markets Act 2000, ss 5(3), 138(7).

2.30 Section 5 specifies that in considering what degree of protection may be appropriate, the FSA must have regard to the following matters:

(a) the differing degrees or risk involved in different kinds of investment or other transactions,

(b) the differing degrees of experience and expertise that different consumers may have in relation to different kinds of regulated activity,

(c) the need consumers may have for advice and accurate information, and

(d) the general principle that consumers should take responsibility for their decisions.

2.31

(4) **Reduction of financial crime.** Reducing the extent to which it is possible for business carried on by a regulated person or in contravention of the general prohibition to be used for a purpose connected with financial crime.

2.32 *The Financial Services Authority, its duties, objectives etc*

It should be noted that the objective relates to both regulated business and activities carried on by non-authorised persons conducting business in contravention of the general prohibition.

2.32 Financial crime is defined as including fraud and dishonesty, money laundering, insider dealing and financial market misconduct and it is made clear that in the context of the objective relates to criminal activities of employees as well as activities commissioned by a regulated person's criminal customers[1].

---

1 Financial Services and Markets Act 2000, s 6(2)(b).

2.33 Section 6(2) states that the FSA must have regard to the desirability of:

(a) regulated persons being aware of the risk of their businesses being used in connection with financial crime,

(b) regulated persons taking appropriate measures to prevent financial crime, facilitate its detection and monitor its incidence,

(c) regulated persons devoting adequate resources to financial crime prevention, detection and monitoring.

Principles of good regulation

2.34 In carrying out its general functions the Act at s 2(3) requires the FSA to have regard to seven 'principles of good regulation' the FSA describe the application of the principles as:

'In all our work we believe in the principles of a risk-based approach; the desirability of regulation working with the grain of the market rather than against it; the restriction of regulation to those circumstances where the market does not provide adequate answers and where regulation has the prospect of doing so at reasonable cost; and an acceptance that a regulatory system neither can nor should aim at avoiding all failures.[1]'

---

1 See FSA web site www.fsa.gov.uk/pages/about/what/index.shtml

---

2.35 The seven principles of good regulation are:

(1) the need to use the FSA's resources in the most efficient and economic way;

(2) recognising the responsibilities of regulated firms' own management;

(3) the principle that the burdens and restrictions imposed by regulation should be proportionate to the benefits;

(4)   the international character of financial services and the desirability of maintaining the UK's competitive position;

(5)   the desirability of facilitating innovation;

(6)   the desirability of facilitating competition;

(7)   the need to minimise the adverse effects of regulation on competition.

FSA's strategic aims

2.36   To help achieve its Statutory Objectives the FSA structures its work around three strategic aims:

(1)   to promote efficient, orderly and fair markets, both retail and wholesale;

(2)   to help retail consumers to achieve a fair deal; and

(3)   to improve business capability and effectiveness.

Financial Services Authority funding, independence, corporate governance, and accountability

2.37   The Financial Services Authority (FSA) was given statutory powers by the Financial Services and Markets Act 2000. Schedule 1 to the Act sets out a series of corporate governance requirements for the FSA, each designed to contribute to both the FSA's independence from Government and the industry it regulates but at the same time to ensure that the FSA is appropriately managed and is accountable for the functions it performs. The FSA is a company limited by guarantee[1] and financed wholly by the financial services industry[2]. Paragraph 17(1), Sch 1 allows the FSA to make rules to provide it payment in connection with the discharge of any of its functions under or as a result of the Act to enable it[3]:

(a)   to meet its expenses of carrying out its functions or incidental matters;

(b)   to maintain adequate reserves.

---

1 FSMA 2000.
2 FSMA 2000, Sch 1, para 17.
3 Paragraph 17(1) also enable fees to be raised to fund the transfer of the Bank of England's supervision functions to the FSA.

2.38   The FSA when fixing the level of fees must not take into account any sums which it receives or expects to receive by way of penalties imposed under the Act[1], however the FSA is obliged[2] to operate a scheme that ensures that penalties imposed under the Act are applied for the benefit of authorised persons. Paragraph 17(4) specifies that any fee owed to the FSA may be recovered as a debt and thus may be enforced in the Courts if left unpaid.

---

1 FSMA 2000, Sch 1, para 17(2).
2 FSMA 2000, Sch 1, para 16.

2.39   In its business plan for the financial year 2006 to 2007 the FSA's cost for its ongoing regulatory activity for the year is budgeted to be £276.1m. This includes cost such as £202.8m for employment and related costs, £15.2m on IT costs and £31.1m on professional fees. These costs are split between FSA business units, the retail markets business unit accounts for the largest share of expenditure at £99.2m, compared to £70.1m on the wholesale and institutional markets business unit, £37.1m on enforcement costs and £1.6m for the cost of running panels. The FSA budget to raise by way of levy from fee payers £276.1m to cover its operating costs for 2006/07. In addition fines and penalties levied against authorised businesses subject to civil enforcement also contribute to the FSA's funding. The notion of such monies contributing to the running costs of the FSA reconcile with the notion that non-performing authorised businesses should contribute more to the running costs of the regulator then those firms or individuals that operate a compliant regime[1]. This annual fee requirement raised by way of subscription is reduced by the amount the FSA collects in financial penalties, as at January 2006 the FSA had recovered £17m which it predicted would result in a 6.2% reduction in fee levies for firms.

---

1 The impact of this for 2006/07 is referred to at **2.46** below.

2.40   In the FSA's business plan for 2005 to 2006 John Tiner FSA Chief Executive stated:

> '... against the background of a buoyant employment market in financial services, significant challenges in the external environment and increasing pressures on us to do more, we have managed to keep increases in our budget to within modest levels. Our budget for 2006/07 will be £276m compared to £267m in the previous year. This funds the £2m of annual costs from the new enforcement process ...and an overall increase in staff remuneration of 4.5%... to meet this budget we will need to improve productivity by £7m ...'[1]

---

1 John Tiner, Chief Executives overview FSA Business Plan 2006/07, 1 February 2006.

2.41   The FSA's rules setting out the precise requirements for the calculation and payment of fees is set out in the FSA handbook FEES. In outline the FSA collects fees to meet its: annual funding requirement through fees charged in respect of:

- application fees, payable by those applying for authorisation,

- waiver fees,

- transaction reporting fees.

2.42   Moreover the FSA's annual funding requirement to cover its operating budget is collected by:

- Periodic fees, payable by authorised firms and certain other bodies.

2.43   The substantial part of the FSA's budget is recovered by periodic fees referred to as the annual levy. The calculation of the levy is apportioned amongst firms by reference to the type of business they conduct. In the setting of fee blocks, where possible the FSA attributes costs and a share of its overheads based on the firm specific activities it undertakes in each fee block together with regulatory activities in relation to the type of business of a fee block.

2.44   Each business type is referred to as a fee block. Authorised firm fee blocks are grouped together in a series of fee blocks coded as A. Authorised firms must identify the fee blocks their business falls within and calclulate the levy they are responsible for by reference to the fee formula known as the tariff-base applying to their fee block. Depending on the fee block, the fee is calculated by reference to the amount of business conducted by the firm or the number of approved persons, or both where a firm falls into multiple fee blocks.

2.45   Each year, however, the FSA consults on its proposals for the collection of its operating budget. The calculation of the levy from fee payers for 2006/07 is set out in FSA Consultation paper 'CP06/02, Regulatory fees and levies 2006/07.' By way of example for the year 2006/07 the FSA propose that the following fee blocks have fee responsibilities as follows:

A1   (deposit acceptors) proportion of annual funding requirement (after reserves adjustment) £54m

A4   (Insurers: Life) proportion of annual funding requirement (after reserves adjustment) £40.5m

A10   (Firms dealing as principal) proportion of annual funding requirement (after reserves adjustment) £13.4m.

2.46   The impact of enforcement penalties can give rise to an adjustement to the fees ultimately incurred by individual fee blocks. FSMA 2000, Sch 1, para 16, requires that the FSA apply any penalties recovered to the benefit of authorised persons. This is particularly pronounced in 2006/07 where a £13.9m penalty recovered from Citigroup Global Markets Lld on 28 June 2005 in relation to proprietary trading activities when applied to fee block A10 exceeded the annual funding requirement for that block by £641,000. This has the effect of causing a 100% reduction in the fees payable within the A10 block and providing a credit for the block for 2007/08.

FSA governance

2.47   Constitutional and governance requirements are established for the FSA and specified in FSMA 2000, Pt 1, Sch 1, which specifies requirements relating to the establishment, structure and functions of the FSA Governing body (its board), its chairman, directors (specifically its non-executive directors and chief executive officer. Although the FSA is an independent non-governmental body, HM Treasury is responsible for making these appointments.

Governing body

2.48   Paragraph 2 to Sch 1 to the Act requires that the FSA must maintain a governing body of members who are appointed to and removed from office by the Treasury. The FSA Board sets the overall policy, including the operation of the FSA's legislative functions which cannot be delegated. The FSA's legislative functions are listed in para 1(2), Sch 1 to the Act and may only be performed by the FSA governing body. The functions are:

(a)   making rules,

(b)   issuing approved persons and market conduct codes,

(c)   issuing statements of

　　　(i)   principle for approved persons,

　　　(ii)   policy relating to approved person financial penalties,

　　　(iii)   policy relating to market abuse financial penalties,

　　　(iv)   policy relating to disciplinary action financial penalties.

(d)   Directions relating to investment business carried on by members of Lloyd's Underwriting Market and members of the professions,

(e)   General Guidance[1]

The FSA role in rule making and issuing codes of practice are considered in more detail in Chapter 5.

---

1 FSMA 2000, s 157.

2.49   The FSA is also required to appoint a Chairman. Although since 2003 FSA has appointed separate Chairman and Chief Executive, between May 1997 and September 2003 the Treasury decision to combine the roles of FSA Chairman and Chief Executive was the focus of criticism (with Howard Davies occupying roles of both Chairman and Chief Executive). The government at the time believed this combined role would create efficiencies as well as improve FSA accountability, despite it not conforming to principles of corporate governance set out in the Combined code[1]. Although the Combined code is a voluntary code it supports the concept of the separations of the role of Chairman and Chief Executive on the basis that there should be a clear division of responsibilities at the head of the company between the running of the board and the executive responsibility for the running of the company's business. No one individual should have unfettered powers of decision[2]. In the government's response to the Joint Committee First Report in 1999 justifying its decision to combine the roles of FSA Chairman and Chief Executive, it said:

'... it is however mindful of the fact that parallels with other models of corporate governance are not exact. There is also a good case for a strong line of direct accountability to Treasury ministers from the senior executive of the regulator. These views are shared by the non-executive board members ...'

---

1 At the relevant time the applicable code was that issued by the Hempel Committee on corporate governance in June 1998.

2 Paragraph A2 of the Combined Code on corporate governance. Financial Reporting Standards Council issued in July 2003 now provides that 'There should be a clear division of responsibilities at the head of the company between the running of the board and the executive responsibility for the running of the company's business. No one individual should have unfettered powers of decision.'

2.50   Undoubtedly in the early period of the FSA's existence a great deal of legislation and policy development was required together with the logistical, political and management demands of drawing together nine different regulatory organisations. The timescale of the change together with the competing demands of all affected by the change where better served by a singly focused management structure derived from a combined chairman and chief executive.

2.51   The majority of the FSA governing body are, under para 3 to the Act, required to be non-executive directors. We will now consider the specified responsibilities of the non-executive members. Paragraph 3(1), Sch 1 to the Act requires that a governing body committee comprising solely of non-executive directors is established for the purpose of discharging specified functions. The non-executive committee members are appointed by the FSA and the committee's chairman, who is selected from the committee's members must be appointed by the HM Treasury. The committee's specified functions are as follows:

(a)   to keep under review whether the FSA uses its resources in the most efficient and economic way when discharging its functions with the governing bodies' decisions,

(b)   keep under review whether the FSA's internal financial controls secure the proper conduct of its financial affairs,

(c)   determine the remuneration of the FSA's Chairman and executive members of the governing body.

2.52   In addition the non-executive committee may appoint a subcommittee to discharge its functions save those in (a) above. Any subcommittee must have as its chairman the chairman of the non-executive committee but may include additional persons to the non-executive members of the main committee[1].

---

1 FSMA 2000, Sch 1, para 4(4), (5).

2.53   The non-executive committee is required to prepare an annual report on the discharge of its functions. This report is included in the FSA's annual report to the HM Treasury. Further details of the FSA annual report are set out in 2.62 to this Chapter.

2.54   Paragraph 5(1) to the Act permits the FSA to discharge any of its functions, (save its legislative functions) by way of arrangements through any committee, subcommittee, officer or member of its staff. By way of example, within its general organisation, the FSA has established sectoral teams specialising in topics or particular importance spanning many of the FSA's regulating activities.

The current FSA Board structure is as follows:

● Chairman, Sir Cullum McCarthy

● Deputy Chairman, Dame Deirdre Hutton

● Chief Executive, John Tiner

● The Board comprises nine non-executive directors, and

● Three executive directors; David Kenmir, Clive Briault and Hector Sants.

2.55   Day-to-day decisions and management of the staff are the responsibility of the Executive and on 3 November 2003, following the appointment of John Tiner as Chief Executive Officer, a restructure of the executive management of the FSA was announced. This review resulted in the restructuring of the management executive of the FSA and the creation of three managing director posts responsible for regulatory services, wholesale markets and retail markets respectively. This restructuring had the effect of splitting the FSA operations into two supervisory divisions reflecting the differing needs and demands of the wholesale and retail markets that the FSA regulates[1].

---

1 Management structure of FSA. FSA/PN/116/2003.

Regulatory decisions committee

2.56   To deal with concern and criticism of the draft Bill that the FSA would be in the unique role of enforcing the rules that it makes, the Act requires that the investigation and enforcement recommendation functions of the Authority are carried out separately from the FSA's functions of taking of decisions and issuing of statutory notices.

2.57   Section 395(1) to the Act provides that the FSA must determine the procedure that it proposes to follow in relation to the giving of a) supervisory notices; and b) warning notices and decision notices.

2.58   Section 395(2) to the Act provides that procedures must be designed to secure, among other things, that the decision which gives rise to the obligation to give any such notice is taken by a person not directly involved in establishing the evidence on which that decision is based.

2.59   To meet this requirement the FSA Board has established the Regulatory Decisions Committee to take those enforcement, authorisation and supervisory decisions that are of material significance for the firms and individuals concerned. The committee has 29 members and operates under the chair of Timothy Herrington and four deputy chairman each responsible for separate decision groups. The committee is a subcommittee of the FSA Board but is operationally independent. The principle of separation is made more effective by the committees members, drawn from industry and consumer groups who introduce independence and objectivity to the committee's deliberations.

2.60   The FSA have stated that notwithstanding the statutory requirement to separate its investigation and recommendation functions from its decisions functions, it is also vital that the FSA's decisions and disciplinary process is perceived as being fair to ensure confidence in the system.

2.61   The role of the regulatory decisions committtee and recent changes to its operational structure will be considered in more detail in Chapter 'FSA Supervison of Regulated Firms'.

A package of business planning and public reporting

2.62   Schedule 1 to the Act sets out a requirement and structure for reporting to the HM Treasury, and Parliament on how the FSA has met its regulatory objectives during the previous year and then offering the public and regulated persons in general meeting the opportunity to provide feedback to the FSA on its functions. Each year a timetable for each of these steps is followed.

2.63 The FSA's framework of planning and publications is as follows:

- Business plan: January
- Risk outlook: January
- International risk outlook January
- Annual report published: June
- Annual report presented to Parliament: June
- Annual meeting: July

Responsibility and reporting to the HM Treasury

2.64 The FSA works closely with the HM Tresury in the performance of its general duties. A tripartite agreement between HM Treasury, the FSA and the Bank of England has been entered into establishing a framework for co-operation in the field of financial stability, setting out the role of each institution, and explaining how they are to work together towards the common objective of financial stability. The division of responsibilities is based on four guiding principles[1]:

- **Clear accountability**. Each authority must be accountable for its actions, so each must have unambiguous and well-defined responsibilities;
- **Transparency**. Parliament, the markets and the public must know who is responsible for what;
- **No duplication**. Each authority must have a clearly defined role, to avoid second-guessing, inefficiency and the duplication of effort. This will help ensure proper accountability;
- **Regular information exchange**. This will help each institution to discharge its responsibilities as efficiently and effectively as possible.

---

1 Memorandum of Understanding between HM Treasury, the Bank of England and the Financial Services Authority, March 2006.

2.65 On 13 December 2001[1] by way of letter to Howard Davies the then FSA Chairman and Chief Executive, the Chancellor of the Exchequer set out how the FSA would be accountable to the government, Parliament and the public, but additionally set out the extent to which the government would use its powers as part of the new regulatory regime. The letter set out in particular that it would use its powers in:

- directing the FSA to cover particular issues in its public Annual Report, so that, over time, the reports will establish an important public information base, through which Parliament and others will hold the FSA and its Board to account. The Chancellor stated that *'I will encourage Parliament and the Treasury Select Committee to consider the Report carefully. The Treasury Committee may also want to take evidence on it'*;

- the annual report would be required to cover the FSA's performance against its Statutory Objectives. They would also have to set out how the FSA dealt with major regulatory cases, or regulatory issues;

- under s 12 of the Act the government would undertake periodic reviews to establish whether the FSA provides value for money;

- periodically reviewing the Act's secondary legislation;

- under s 14 of the Act, the Government has power to undertake a statutory inquiry into possible serious regulatory failure.

---

1 Rt Hon Gordon Brown Chancellor of Exchequer Letter to Howard Davies 13 December 2001.

2.66   In relation to the government's power to undertake a statutory inquiry the Chancellor stated, '… such circumstances may arise where … it appears that serious regulatory failures or gaps in the regulatory regime allowed events to occur which posed, or could have posed, significant damage to the market confidence or consumer protection objectives. In such cases, where it is in the public interest to do so, I may want to use my power to launch a statutory inquiry; we have agreed that you will formally write to Ministers as soon as circumstances or issues arise which you and your Board judge are serious enough to be likely to prompt me to consider launching a statutory inquiry at some point in the future.'

2.67   FSMA 2000, Sch 1, para 10 sets out the FSA's obligation to report at least once each year to HM Treasury. In turn the Treasury is obliged under Sch 1, para 10(3) to the Act to present a copy of the FSA's annual report to Parliament.

2.68   The content of the FSA's annual report is described in para 10(1) to the Act which provides that the FSA must report on:

(a)   the discharge of its functions,

(b)   the extent to which, in the FSA's opinion, the regulatory objectives have been met,

(c)   The FSA's consideration of the principles of good regulation set out in FSMA 2000, s 2(3). These will include the need to use its resources in the most efficient way, that the burden or restriction imposed on any person or

49

activity under the Act must be proportionate to the benefits which are expected to result from the imposition, the desirability of facilitating innovation in connection with regulated activities, the responsibility of those that manage the affairs of authorised persons, and

(d)   such other matters that the Treasury may direct.

2.69   The FSA's annual report must be accompanied by a report from the FSA's non-executive committee on the discharge of its functions, and such other reports that the Treasury may direct.

2.70   In addition to its formal annual report, the FSA also publishes annually in January a series of reports that serve to provide a framework and justification for its planned work in the year ahead in the context of what it has identified as risks to its Statutory Objectives. This series of publications contributes to the framework of accountability mechanisms in the Act by setting out in clear and transparent terms both the FSA's budgeted operating costs for the forthcoming year as well as how the FSA proposes to conduct regulatory activities to deal with the risks it has identified. As well as providing firms with advance notice of the work that the FSA is planning on conducting the annual plan and budget allows all interested parties to assess later the FSA's success against the work it has targeted to undertake. In its business plan for 2006/07 Cullum McCarthy stated:

'The outline and purpose of this, the FSA's plan for our activities in 2006/07, should be familiar to those who take an interest in our work. It sets out, as specifically as is now possible, with dates for the most important outcomes, what we plan to do in the next year, under the three headings which give coherence to the many and various activities of the FSA: promoting efficient, orderly and fair markets (wholesale and retail); helping retail consumers achieve a fair deal; improving our business capability and effectiveness, thus making the FSA more efficient and easier to deal with. It is an essential part of our accountability. We seek to set out as clearly as we can our priorities for the year ahead, so that at the end of the year we can report – and be judged – on how we have measured up against our intentions …[1]'

---

1. FSA Business plan 2006/07 Chairman's foreword, January 2006.

Reporting to Parliament

2.71   Once the FSA's annual report has been presented to HM Treasury, the Treasury must in turn, pursuant to FSMA 2000, Sch 1, para 10(3) lay a copy of the report before Parliament. Parliament has also established a House of Commons select committee to examine the expenditure, administration and policy of HM Treasury and a number of public bodies including, the Bank of England and the Financial Services Authority. Its terms of reference are to examine the expenditure, administration and policy of the bodies it overseas including the FSA. Within its terms of reference, the Committee chooses its own subjects of inquiry which can last for several months and lead to a report to the House of Commons or take up just a days oral evidence. The committee has the powers to insist upon the attendance of witnesses and the production of papers and other material. The committee routinely examines representatives from the FSA. By way of example on 8 November 2005 evidence was taken from Sir Cullum McCarthy and John Tiner concerning various aspects of the Financial Services Authority including questions about the cost to the financial services industry of implementing the EU Markets in Financial Instruments Directive.

Annual public meeting

2.72   Within three months of the publication of its annual report, Sch 1, para 11(1) to the Act requires that the FSA must hold a public meeting to facilitate general discussion of the content of its report and to allow questions relating the FSA's discharge of its functions to be put forward. One month following the annual meeting the FSA is obliged to publish a report of the annual meeting. Copies of the transcript of the FSA annual meetings are published on the FSA's website.

The role of the consumer panel

2.73   The Consumer Panel represents the interest of consumers and its panel members are appointed by the FSA and although it is given statutory effect by FSMA 2000, s 9 it has been operating since November 1998 consulting with the FSA about its new rule planning in the lead up to the implementation of the new regulatory regime on 30 November 2001.

2.74   The FSA is required to appoint such consumers to the panel or persons representing the interest of consumers, as it considers appropriate. Despite the wide scope of opportunity to appoint persons plus the wide definition of Consumer[1] the FSA is obliged to appoint persons to the panel to ensure that it gives a fair representation to those persons using, or those that are or may contemplate using, the services of authorised persons or appointed representatives. One of the Consumer Panel members must be appointed as chairman by the FSA although such appointment and any subsequent removal must be approved by the Treasury. The Panel funding is provided by the FSA together with the provision of a small secretariat in the FSA's offices in Canary Wharf. In its annual report for 2005 Consumer Panel reported its operating budget for the 12 months ending 31 March 2005 as £440,000. The FSA's influence over Panel member selection, its funding of its operation and provision of support staff might evidence a lack of Panel independence and the potential of an element of 'capture' by the FSA. If this were the case it would seriously hinder the accountability mechanism sought by the establishment and consultation with the Panel. Notwithstanding this the panel manage to maintain a high degree of operational independence and, as can be seen from many of its representations, it is not constrained in its criticism of the FSA's efforts to protect the interest of consumers. By way of example, in its annual report for 2004/05 it reported:

> '... Disappointingly, the FSA has still not introduced Key Facts for investment products. This has been put on hold pending the outcome of its review of prescribing projection rates which will not be complete until 2006. This delay is unacceptable ...'[2]

---

1 See **2.29** above.
2 Paragraph 1.18, Financial Consumer Panels annual report 2005/05, June 2005.

2.75 The current Panel consists of 13 members with John Howard as Chairman. The Panel members have wide ranging experiences including working with vulnerable consumers, consumer education and advice, trade unions, consumer and public policy, law, market research, media issues and broadcasting, as well as the financial services industry itself. They also have close links with the main consumer organisations in the UK and Europe.

2.76 Under s 8 to the Act, the FSA is required to have arrangements in place to consult with the Consumer Panel on the question of whether its general policies and practices are consistent with its general duties[1] Furthermore to ensure that the Consumer Panel's views are taken into account ss 8 (4) and 11(2) of the FSMA 2000 require that the FSA must have regard to and consider any representations made to it by the Panel. Moreover where the FSA disagrees with any view of the Panel or proposal made by it, the Panel must receive a statement in writing setting out the reasons for the disagreement.

---

1 The FSA's General Duties are described in s 2 of the FSMA 2000.

2.77 Members of the Panel meet about once a month, both in working groups and as a full Panel. The Panel operates in accordance with a 10 point terms of reference which requires inter alia:

(a) The main purpose of the Panel is to provide advice to the FSA. As such it does not carry out responsibilities on behalf of the FSA. For example, the Panel does not undertake consumer education, nor does the Panel take up individual consumer complaints. (Terms of reference Paragraph 3)

(b) The emphasis of the Panel's work is on activities that are regulated by the FSA, although it may also look at the impact on consumers of activities outside but related to the FSA's remit. (Terms of reference Paragraph 4)

(c) The Panel:

  (i) represents the interests of consumers by advising, commenting and making recommendations on existing and developing FSA policy and practices as appropriate,

  (ii) speaks on behalf of consumers by reviewing, monitoring and reporting to the FSA on the effectiveness of the FSA's policies and practices in pursuing its duties,

  (iii) keeps under review and influence actual and potential developments in financial services to enable it to fulfil (a) and (b) effectively. (Terms of reference paragraph 6)

(d) The Panel publishes an Annual Report on its work and expenditure. (Terms of reference paragraph 9)

(e) The Panel can speak out publicly when it wishes to draw attention to matters in the public interest and when it disagrees with the FSA. (Terms of reference paragraph 10)

2.78 The FSA Board meets with Panel members at various times each year and a formal meeting takes place each year with the Chair of the Panel to discuss the Panel's annual report. A written response to the Panel's annual report is printed in the FSA annual report.

Information about the work of the Panel can be found on its website at www.fs-cp.org.uk.

2.79 The Panel describes itself in the following terms:

'The Panel is an independent voice for consumers of financial services. We provide advice to the FSA on the interests and concerns of consumers and we assess the FSA's effectiveness in meeting its objectives to protect consumers' interests and promote public understanding of the financial system. As well as being consulted by the FSA on its policy proposals, the Panel also raises its own concerns and initiates its own research.'

2.80 A significant element of the Panel's work is devoted toward formulating responses to FSA, UK government and European Commission consultation papers and other consultations where the intended policy might affect consumers' interaction with financial services. In 2005 the Panel published 28 formal responses. Copies of all the Panel's response documents are archived on their website. In addition the Panel also spends time formulating comments and responses together with presenting evidence to Parliamentary committees and communications with the European Commission. The Panel is also active in engaging in public debate on matters that affect consumers in financial services. To assist in the formulation of its views and opinions on matters the Panel also commission research into areas including consumer opinion. For example in October 2005 the Panel published a research paper entitled 'Consumer Confidence in the Financial Services Industry'.

2.81 In June of each year the Panel publishes its annual report detailing its activities in the previous year. The FSA in turn includes in its annual report its response to the Consumer Panel's report. In its report for the year 2004/05 the Panel specifically raises priority matters for its forthcoming year where the panel wishes to press for change. Although each of these relate to consumer driven matters 1 specifically relates to the operational effectiveness of the FSA for which the Panel outlines a desire for adopting an holistic rather than a piecemeal approach to assessing the FSA's effectiveness and to meet this desire the Panel would commission an overall audit and assessment of the effectiveness of the FSA as a regulator from the consumer perspective.

The role of the practitioner panel

2.82 The Practitioner Panel comprises persons representing the interests of practitioners in the financial services industry. Appointments to this Panel are made by the Financial Services Authority which is required to appoint persons to the Panel as it considers appropriate who are:

(a) Individuals who are authorised persons,

(b) Persons representing authorised persons,

(c) Persons representing recognised investment exchanges,

(d) Persons representing recognised clearing houses.

2.83 The FSA is required to appoint from amongst the Panel members a Chairman although, that appointment and any subsequent dismissal required at the approval of HM Treasury.

2.84 The Practitioner Panel is established under FSMA 2000, s 9 for the purpose of enabling the FSA to consult under s 8 with practitioners about the extent to which its general policies and practices are consistent with its s 2 General Duties. The FSA is obliged to consider any formal representations under s 11 of the FSMA 2000 from the Practitioner Panel and where it disagrees with the views or proposals of the Panel it must set out in writing to the Panel, its reasons.

2.85 The Practioner Panel's relationship with the FSA is in some respects the same as the Consumer Panel, although currently the Practitioner Panel does not request an annual budget from the FSA, (despite it having the facility to do so) although it has a small support budget funded by the FSA which was around £300,000 in 2003. It does, however, request approval from the FSA for funding for certain projects such as research. These costs are incorpated within the FSA's overall budget and covered by the levies rasied from authorised firms. Notwithstanding the foregoing, the Practioner Panel provided an important and strong voice for Financial Services Pratitioners.

2.86 The Practitioner Panel currently comprises 13 members chosen to represent the various sectors in which financial services businesses operate and effect a balanced mix of retail and wholesale firms. The Panel's current chairperson, appointed on 1 November 2005, is Roy Leighton Chairman of Nymex Europe. In addition the Panel meet regularly with the FSA. The Panel Chairman meets regularly with the Chairman of the FSA, providing an opportunity to communicate important and developing issues. There are frequent meetings between the Panel members and FSA senior executives to allow the Panel's views to be expressed before matters are sent on for formal consultation. Moreover, the FSA Managing Directors regularly attend Panel meetings to provide an update on issues within their responsibility.

The Panel's Annual Report is the subject of a formal presentation to the FSA Board.

2.87 The Panel members operate in accordance with a terms of reference which includes the following two key provisions:

Scope

Paragraph 5: The main remit of the Panel is to provide input to the FSA from the industry in order to help it meet its Statutory Objectives, comply with the seven principles of good regulation and to represent the interests of practitioners. It does not carry out responsibilities on behalf of the FSA, and does not seek to duplicate the work of trade associations.

Purpose

Paragraph 6: The Panel:

(a) Reviews the impact of the FSA's policies at the pre-consultation, formal consultation and publication stages, insofar as they affect regulated firms, individuals and markets.

(b) Reviews and reports to the FSA on the effectiveness of the FSA in meeting its objectives and ensure that the FSA, in setting out its priorities, takes into account the various considerations set out in the legislation.

(c)   Is available to be consulted by the FSA on specific high-level issues.

(d)   Is active in bringing to the attention of the FSA issues which practitioners feel are likely to be of major significance or controversy.

(e)   Commissions such research as it wishes in order to help it in fulfilling these terms of reference.

(f)   Has access to all information which it reasonably requires to conduct its work, except for confidential information about specific regulated firms, individuals or markets.

(g)   Has access to the FSA Chairman and Board and will meet them formally at least once a year.

2.88   The Panel operates in the context of two core principles of:

(1)   Practitioners' interests are best served by ensuring clients' prosperity and financial awareness.

(2)   A clear distinction must be drawn between wholesale and retail markets

and measures its own performance in meeting its statutory function against six objectives established by the original Panel members.

2.89   These objectives are:

(1)   **Monitor Overall Effect of FSA Activities on the Industry** To gauge the cumulative burden of incremental regulatory initiatives and regulation as a whole.

(2)   **Assess FSA Effectiveness, as seen by Practitioners, Against Its Objectives** To evaluate FSA compliance with all objectives and principles of good regulation, including the desirability of facilitating innovation and of maintaining the UK's competitive position.

(3)   **Actively Communicate Industry Concerns to FSA** To voice to FSA issues of general concern to the regulated community over developments that could impact the UK financial services industry.

(4)   **Actively Promote Broad Industry Views and Interests** To play an active role in formulating and communicating to FSA a broad practitioner view on the requirements for fair, efficient, and innovative markets.

(5)   **Provide Practitioner View to FSA on Specific Regulation** To respond when requested to by FSA with a practitioner view on early drafts of regulatory initiatives and discussion papers.

(6)   **Promote International Competitiveness of the UK Markets** To safeguard the competitive standing of the UK financial markets in the context of developments in the European Union and internationally, and to encourage innovation.

2.90   One key tool of the Practitioner Panel is its biannual survey of Regulated Firms. This is aimed at determining practitioners' views of the FSA's efficiency and the outcome of its activities.

Each year around April, the Panel publishes an annual report setting out its activities during the year. In turn the FSA's annual report includes the FSA's responses to the Practitioner Panel activities.

2.91   The true worth of the work of both the Consumer and Practitioner Panels is best understood through a comparison of its views and responses on the same FSA Consultation papers. Whilst there are occasions when the views of both panels are in alignment, there are occasions when the Panles responses take opposing viewpoints. Although, as noted above, the FSA is not required to take into account the views of either Panel, any opposing stand-points will undoubtedly have the effect of pulling the FSA's policy development and rules development in two directions and creating a necessary balance between consumer and practitioner interests.

The role of the small business practitioner panel

2.92   The FSA has a duty under FSMA 2000, s 8 to consult with other practitioners and consumers. Although not being formally required under the Act, the Small Businesses Practitioner Panel was established by the FSA in 1999 to represent the interests of small regulated firms in providing views and input to the FSA on the impact on small firms of regulatory policy and practice. It also monitors the FSA's performance more generally in the context of its treatment of small firms.

2.93   The panel currently has 14 members and is chaired by Ruthven Gemmell. Appointments to the Panel are generally based on nominations made by relevant trade associations. The Panel meets every month and regularly receives representations from FSA staff on the development of regulatory policy and the FSA's operation. Of particular value is the work the Panel does in responding to FSA consultations. The FSA uses these responses to help frame its approach to regulatory development.

2.94   Each year the small business Practitioner Panel publishes an annual report setting out its activities in the year.

Given that around 80% of the business regulated by the FSA would probably be classified as small firms, the work of the Small Business Practitioners Panel is invaluable in helping the FSA to understand and appreciate the impact of its activities on the operation and financial viability of small businesses.

The independent complaints commissioner

2.95 Schedule 1, para 7(1) to the Act requires the FSA to establish a complaints scheme to allow for the investigation of complaints arising in connection with the exercise of or failure to exercise any of its functions, other than its legislative functions. As part of its obligation to establish a complaint scheme, the FSA is required to appoint a person to be responsible for the conduct of investigations under the scheme under para 7(3) to the Act. HM Treasury's approval of the appointed investigator is required. The rules of the scheme are contained in the FSA handbook at its sourcebook COAF.

2.96 Schedule 1, para 7(4) requires that the terms and conditions on which the investigator is appointed are such that in the opinion of the FSA that will reasonably secure that:

(a)   the investigation is free at all times to act independently of the FSA, and

(b)   complaints will be investigated under the scheme without favouring the FSA.

2.97 Although in relation to the original scheme rules drafting and any amendments to the scheme the FSA was and is obliged to consult and have regard to any representations made to it, there is no requirement for the rules to be approved by the Treasury. The FSA's duties are satisfied provided it complies with paras 7 and 8 of Sch 1 and is only required to provide the Treasury with a copy of the scheme details.

2.98 Schedule 1, para 8 sets out further requirements for the complaints scheme in particular that:

(a)   the investigator must have the means to conduct a full investigation of the complaint,

(b)   to report on the result of the investigation to the FSA and the complainant,

(c)   be able to publish the report if he considers that it ought to be brought to the attention of the public.

2.99 To assist in investigations, the investigator may appoint other persons to conduct investigations on his behalf albeit under his direction, this presumably means acting within a terms of reference and in accordance with the scheme rules. The investigator, is however, prohibited under para 8(9) to Sch 1 of the Act from appointing an officer or employee of the FSA. This is seemingly to ensure that the investigation is conducted independently and without bias towards the FSA.

2.100 The scheme is required to deal with any complaints arising in connection with the exercise of or failure to exercise any of the FSA functions (other than its legislative functions). There is no limitation on who may bring a complaint and thus a complaint may be brought by authorised or regulated persons, approved persons, persons applying for authorisation or approved person status, actual consumers or persons contemplating investing and third parties affected by the FSA's activities. There is, however, overlap between the scheme and those matters dealt with by the Financial Services and Market Tribunal. Paragraph 8(1) does state that the FSA is not obliged to investigate a complaint in accordance with the scheme where it reasonably considers that the matter would be more appropriately dealt with in another way such as by the Tribunal.

2.101 Following an investigation, where the investigator considers it appropriate he may recommend that the FSA makes a compensatory payment to the complainant and remedy the matter complained of[1]. Where the investigator has criticised the FSA or where it reports that the complaint is well founded the FSA is required to inform the investigator and complainant of the steps it proposes to take. There is, however, no obligation placed on the FSA to adhere to the recommendations of the investigator and although theoretical, in the event that the investigator makes a recommendation of an award in favour of the complainant, the complainant has no remedy enabling him to enforce the recommendation. Between 1 April 2005 and 31 March 2006 the complaint scheme received 126 new allegations and complaints, with over half of these from consumers[2].

---

1 FSMA 2000, Sch 1, para 8(5).
2 Office of the Complaints Commissioner Annual report 2005/06.

The function of the Financial Services and Markets Tribunal

2.102 The Financial Services and Markets Tribunal was created by the Act as part of the FSA's accountability framework. The Tribunal's jurisdiction relates to both FSA enforcement work and certain aspects of the FSA's decision making. The Tribunal's establishment is in accordance with Schedule 17 of the Act and operates in accordance with rules of procedure. The Tribunal's independence is also safeguarded by it being a part of the Department for Constitutional affairs and for administrative purposes is part of the UK Finance and Tax Tribunals.

2.103 The impact of the Tribunal's decisions can be significant, for example following its decisions in the matter of *Legal and General Assurance Society Ltd v the FSA*[1] in which it criticised the FSA's enforcement process the FSA undertook a root and branch review and made changes to its internal enforcement process and the functions of the Regulatory Decisions Committee. Nonetheless the Tribunal operates within a statutory structure where it can only determine matters that have been specifically referred to it by a person subject to an FSA enforcement or administrative decision. Although such a system facilitates an early and economic settlement of FSA decisions it has resulted in relatively few FSA decisions being subjected to the external scrutiny of the Tribunal.

Further analysis of the Tribunal is contained in Chapter 13.

---

1 *Legal and General Assurance Society Ltd v Financial Services Authority* Case number 11, 18 January 2005.

FSA performance evaluation

2.104 Demonstrating that it operates in an efficient, cost effective and proportionate manner is a critical element for the FSA's discharge of its responsibilities. In its document, 'A new regulator for a new millennium' published in January 2000, the FSA set out its initial thinking into how it could evaluate its performance. In January 2002 the FSA introduced its methodology for performance measurement and implemented a package of measures against which the performance of its general duties could be judged. These measures comprised two key elements:

(1)   performance indicators for the strategic outcomes, which are mostly be high-level outcome-based indicators, but which also include some more traditional process-based measures; and

(2)   stories' about how the FSA have 'fixed important problems'.

2.105 The FSA formally publishes the results of its performance evaluation each year in its annual report. In relation to its performance evaluation measurements, David Kenmir FSA Managing Director stated in 2005, *'We will continue to introduce further service standards where necessary and are constantly striving to improve our performance to ensure that we meet the needs of our stakeholders.'*[1]

---

1 FS/PN/114/2005.

The FSA's role in other legislation

2.106 The FSA has certain other powers and functions under other legislation. Although a detailed analysis of such functions is outside the scope of this book. It is however, worth noting some areas of its more significant functions:

Enterprise Act 2002

2.107   The FSA is designated as a consumer enforcer under the Enterprise Act. The FSA has the power to apply to the courts to stop traders infringing a wide range of consumer protection legislation where those infringements harm the collective interests of consumers.

Unfair Terms in Consumer Contracts Regulations 1999

2.108   The FSA may seek an injunction to prevent the use of a contract term drawn up for general use in a financial services contract that appears to the FSA to be unfair.

Distance Marketing Regulations 2004

2.109   The FSA is designated as the body responsible for considering and, if necessary, taking action against persons responsible for breaching specified contracts.

Electronic Money Directive

2.110   The FSA is responsible for regulating the issuing of e-money (money stored on an electronic device such as a chip card or computer memory). Electronic Commerce Directive: The FSA has a number of powers under the directive including the power to direct that an incoming provider may no longer carry on a specified incoming electronic commerce activity, or may only carry it on subject to specified requirements.

Chapter 3

International and European Influences

'..Everything's got a moral, if only you can find it'

Lewis Carroll, Alice in Wonderland

Relevant international bodies

Introduction

3.1 Recent years have seen the increasing internationalisation of banking, insurance and other financial services businesses. Coupled with this has been a breaking down of the barriers that traditionally existed between the various parts of the financial services industry. This is against a background of an ever increasing proportion of the world's wealth being reflected in capital flows, some related to international trade but the majority by way of investment. As a consequence the regulation of financial services has become a task requiring a far wider range of activities than used to be the case. This is a primary reason for the creation of the Financial Services Authority in the UK. In addition, it is necessary in an increasingly interlinked world for there to be an agreed set of international standards by which financial institutions should be regulated. This does not require total commonality, but a large degree of equivalence is certainly highly desirable to facilitate economic stability and sustained economic growth. A failure to create high quality economic regulation can also both facilitate a financial crisis and aggravate it when it arises. In addition, the extent to which world capital markets have become integrated has limited the ability of national regulators to monitor firms effectively without a considerable degree of international co-operation.

3.2 The proposals considered below which help develop a set of international financial regulations articulate five key features. It represents a reform of the nexus of international financial regulation; a bringing together of a group of limited codes and standards; international collaboration between a disparate set of linked codes and standards; international collaboration between a disparate set of states, markets, financial regulators and financial institutions. It engages both international and domestic compliance assessments and there is a clear acceptance that there is a direct relationship between adopting such regulation and codes, and maintaining financial stability.

3.3   The motivation is also clear. In the words of a G7 Communiqué:

'Close international co-operation in the regulation and supervision of financial institutions and markets is essential to the continued safe-guarding of the financial system and to prevent erosion of necessary prudential standards.'

Organisations

3.4   A number of bodies stand out as being key players in this process. In alphabetical order they are:

The Basel Committee on Banking Supervision

3.5   This provides a meeting place for the central banks of the G10 countries and facilitates co-operation on the regulation of banking. Over recent years it has developed into a standard setting body on all aspects of banking supervision. Member countries are represented by their central bank and also by the authority with formal responsibility for the prudential supervision of banking if this is a separate body. Its secretariat is provided by the Bank for International Settlements in Basel.

Committee on Payment and Settlement Systems

3.6   Also created by the G10 central banks this, as its name suggests, provides a meeting place for those central banks on matters arising in relation to payment and settlement systems. Their concern is not limited to domestic considerations but extends to cross-border operations and netting. Much of their work concerns supervisory standards and recommendations of best practice. It sates its aim as 'strengthening the financial market infrastructure through promoting sound and efficient payment and settlement systems'.

Financial Action Task Force

3.7   Created by the G7, its role is to ascertain the threat to financial institutions from money laundering and to recommend steps that can be taken to counter this. There are now a large number of member states and a key function of the Task Force is to monitor the extent to which these countries are taking appropriate steps to deal with the problem.

Financial Stability Forum

3.8 Following a meeting of the Finance Ministers and Central Bank Governors of the G7 countries, Hans Tietmeyer, the then President of the Bundesbank, was commissioned to draft a report considering what new structures might be appropriate to improve co-operation between the existing national and international regulatory bodies. The aim was to facilitate increased stability in the regulation of world finance and financial services. As a consequence of the report he produced the Forum was created.

International Accounting Standards Board

3.9 The aim of this institution is to bring about the convergence of accounting standards. This is of importance, partly in increasing the financial safety by having high common standards, and also in reducing the risk of financial failure or loss to investors due to accounts not representing a true and fair view in the generally understood meaning of the words. Its progress in this area is well advanced.

International Association of Insurance Supervisors

3.10 Its purpose is to develop a set of generally accepted standards in this area to increase the effectiveness of insurance regulation. Over 100 states have become members.

International Federation of Accountants

3.11 This is made up of the national accountancy bodies that represent those accountants who are involved in the public sector, large organisations and commerce and industry. Its primary aim is to increase the quality of the accounting regulations and increase their international equivalence.

International Monetary Fund

3.12 This is the body that sets international standards in relation to overseeing the world's monetary system. It has created a range of standards in relation to monetary and fiscal policy and has assisted in creating methods of assessment for the standards used for the supervision of banking and insurance.

International Organization of Securities Commissions

3.13   As its name implies, this is an organisation made up of the securities and derivatives regulators of the member countries. Its main purpose is to create high standards to govern the regulation of the securities markets to exchange information, provide effective surveillance of international securities markets and to protect the integrity of markets.

Organisation for Economic Cooperation and Development

3.14   The aim of this body is to promote world economic growth and to this end it promotes the development of financial markets regulation to a high common standard. Much of its significance arises from the statistics that it provides. It plays a prominent role in fostering good governance in both public service and corporate activity. It also assists governments in ensuring the responsiveness of key economic areas with sectoral monitoring.

The World Bank

3.15   The World Bank is a key source of financial and technical assistance for developing countries. It is a combination of two institutions, the International Bank for Reconstruction and Development and the International Development Association. It aims to reduce poverty in the world by facilitating private investment in the regions concerned through low-interest loans, interest-free credit and grants.

Key standards

3.16   In its role as a facilitator of increased international co-operation the Financial Stability Forum has issued a set of 12 standards which it believes are a prerequisite to creating a system of stable, well-regulated financial systems. These are as follows:

Code of Good Practices on Transparency in Monetary and Financial Policies

3.17   The essence of this is that it highlights the approaches that creates the appropriate level of transparency to enable the public to assess what is happening and thus facilitate accountability. The Code specifically highlights four key areas:

- roles, responsibility and objectives should be clearly stated;

- policy decisions should have clearly defined processes determining how they are reached and reported;

- policies and information pertinent to them should be publicly available; and

- accountable systems should exist to guarantee integrity.

Code of Good Practices on Fiscal Transparency

3.18 The role of transparency is critical in that it makes the regulatory authorities more accountable. To facilitate this the code provides four principles:

- that the roles and responsibilities of those involved should be clear;

- there should be access to the information by the public;

- that key financial steps such as budgets, accounts and financial reports should be publicly available; and

- integrity should be underpinned by independent means.

Data Dissemination

3.19 There are two key agreements in this area. The first is the Special Data Dissemination Standard issued by the IMF. This was produced to resolve the problem of instability induced, if only in part, by insufficient information being available in the marketplace. Those countries who subscribe (and the significant economies already do) agree to satisfy this function in four key regards and to do so in standard form:

- that data, particularly regarding reserves and foreign currency holdings should be made publicly available, promptly and at appropriate periods;

- that the public should be informed of the dates on which such data will be available;

- clear laws determining both the above and proposed changes in the same, coupled with government access to data and comment being released by the relevant government officials; and

- the making available to the public of information to articulate how the data should be formulated and of any other material against which it can be assessed.

3.20   The second is the General Data Dissemination System, also issued by the IMF. This is more severe in its demands than the Special Data Dissemination Standard and the developed economies are expected to apply it. It requires that detailed, high-quality information relating to financial, economic and social issues be made publicly available on a timely basis. It adopts the same four-stage structure as the Special Data Dissemination Standard.

Principles and Guidelines for effective Insolvency and Creditor Rights Systems

3.21   The existence of a clear, fair set of rights for creditors is a key ingredient for a stable economy. It also assists commercial lenders in determining the degree of risk they are taking on. This has been primarily driven by the World Bank, the United Nations Commission of International Trade Law, the IMF and INSOL.

Principles of Corporate Governance

3.22   This is a system of corporate regulation which applies to a company when it determines its objectives, when it seeks to achieve them and in assessing its performance. It is crucial to have such regulation to create a high quality corporate environment to attract international capital. Key issues to be found within corporate governance regulations are:

- shareholder rights;
- stakeholder rights (this is a contentious area in terms of its future development);
- disclosure of information; and
- Board responsibility.

International Accounting Standards

3.23   A succession of international accounting standards have been issued to determine the extent of the detail, range, relevance and reliability of the information to be included in the accounts. To represent a true and fair view accounts must be regulated by clear and detailed regulation. There are specific types of accounts, those relating to banks, securities houses and insurance companies for example, which give rise to specific issues when determining what should be included.

International Standards on Auditing

3.24   If there are to be accepted standards of accountancy then it follows that there must also be internationally accepted standards of auditing to maintain it. The standards on auditing that have been issued cover:

- audit responsibilities;
- audit planning;
- internal controls;
- evidence;
- practice statements relating to international auditing;
- external auditing; and
- audit characteristics and considerations.

Core Principles for Systemically Important Payment Systems

3.25   To function in a stable way financial markets require stable, effective settlement systems. The aim of the Core Principles is to facilitate this by requiring a degree of safety and efficiency in these systems. The Principles themselves require that domestic and international payment systems satisfy criteria relating to design and operation. Guidance is also provided on interpreting the Principles.

The Forty Recommendations of the Financial Action Task Force on Money Laundering

3.26   These were intended to provide a set of recommendations which, if followed, would optimise the response of banking and financial bodies that were being used to launder illegal money. They cover areas such as:

- criminal justice systems;
- law enforcement;
- the banking and financial systems;
- banking and financial regulation; and
- international co-operation.

3.27   All members states are subject to periodic mutual analysis to determine whether they are satisfying the recommendations. They must also carry out an annual self-assessment exercise to the same end.

Core Principles for Effective Banking Supervision

3.28   To assist in stabilising the world's banking system the Basel Commit-tee on Banking Supervision have published a set of 25 core principles and additional criteria for banking supervision. These cover issues such as:

- the preconditions for effective banking supervision;
- licensing requirements;
- ongoing banking supervision;
- powers of supervisors; and
- cross-border banking.

Objectives and Principles of Securities Regulation

3.29   IOSCO have published a set of objectives and principles to help bring about a system of sound regulation of the securities markets. The key objectives are:

- protecting investors;
- making sure the markets function in a manner that is fair, efficient and transparent; and
- reducing the risk of systemic failure.

There are also 30 principles relating to securities regulation.

Insurance Core Principles

3.30   As their name implies these were produced to facilitate that the regulatory supervision of the insurance industry is taking place at a suitably proficient and effective manner. The Principles themselves cover key areas such as:

- the role of supervisors;
- licensing insurance companies;
- corporate governance of insurance companies;
- prudential controls;
- market conduct;
- monitoring by the regulator; and

● sanctions for failure to satisfy the regulations.

Monitoring regulatory observance

3.31 Clearly it is insufficient to create a series of desirable standards without some system for ascertaining whether they are being subscribed to in practice. States themselves will sometimes carry out research into the state of affairs within their own jurisdiction. In addition the IMF and the World Bank both produce reports on the extent to which the standards and codes discussed above are being met. The IMF has produced them in relation to the distribution of data and fiscal transparency. The World Bank has done so in relation to accounting, auditing, corporate governance, insolvency and creditors' rights. How well standards in the financial sector are carried out and what the priorities need to be to rectify any shortcomings are dealt with under the auspices of the joint IMF and World Bank 'Financial Sector Assessment Programme'.

Facilitating regulatory observance

3.32 The Financial Stability Forum has suggested that member states could take a number of key steps to facilitate awareness and observance of regulatory standards:

● an ongoing campaign should be run to raise the level of awareness in their financial centres as to the requirements of the standards;

● that the bodies creating the standards in the first place should themselves facilitate and encourage this process of education;

● that the bodies creating the standards and the national regulators should help explain how satisfying the requirements of the standards will help avoid certain types of risk. In this context explaining how past market problems have led to the standards will assist;

● external assessments of the application of standards should be undertaken by the bodies setting the standards;

● peer discussions should be encouraged to facilitate the implementation of standards; and

● technical advice and training should be provided by the more developed states to the others.

3.33 There are a number of reasons why this is thought necessary. The importance of the standards is primarily in that they facilitate a sound financial system. To this end it is important that not only the authorities but also relevant private bodies should put them into effect.

Key issues other than regulatory observance

3.34   Turning to the regulated financial institutions themselves, there are factors other than the quality of regulation that will determine whether institutions will proceed with a financial arrangement. A suitable legal system and framework are vital. Key elements are efficiency, transparency and a predictable outcome in the sense that it should be determined by clearly stated laws rather than other factors. In some states it can prove difficult to successfully pursue certain parties through their courts due to corruption. Political risk and economic fundamentals also need to be within acceptable levels. If not there will be no point pursuing a financial arrangement further. Parties do not always fully understand how the regulations relate to the risks they were created to try and manage.

3.35   Some firms are by their very nature less concerned with regulatory issues. The international investment portfolios managed by those such as hedge funds, pension funds and insurance companies are more concerned with market analysis that relates to capitalisation.

Rating agencies are a key source of information and their role in providing assessments will involve an analysis of supervisory and regulatory issues as well as financial and market issues.

Consequences of regulatory failure

3.36   There are instances of countries having lax regulatory controls and surviving for some time with no serious problems. However, the absence of a system of decent controls both increases the risk of a crisis arising and of it becoming systemic, leading to a larger scale problem when it does. The Asian financial crisis of 1998 has been generally regarded as having been partly caused by lax regulation. In addition the crisis was able to develop to a greater extent before it became apparent that it was occurring than should have been the case because of poor corporate governance and a lack of transparency. This was exacerbated by the high proportion of businesses in the area that were owned and managed by the same people, which coupled with traditional business practices resulted in weak corporate governance. Then as the crisis accelerated those outside the countries concerned were unable to draw a distinction between those institutions in the states concerned that were a real risk and those that were not. This resulted in a flight of matured short-term debt and a refusal by those outside the jurisdictions to hold debt and equity securities denominated in those states' currencies due to fear of devaluation.

3.37   The key steps that were deemed necessary to reduce the risk of such a crisis in the future were:

71

- increasing transparency;
- enhancing the free flow of capital;
- strengthening states' financial systems;
- leaving the responsibility and risk associated with lending with the private institutions responsible; and
- increasing the involvement of international financial institutions.

It has been suggested that the larger credit rating agencies have an important role to play in this context.

Co-operation between regulators

Introduction

3.38 At a national level co-operation is much less of a problem. Home state regulators have long since had agreements in place to deal with the issues of co-operation. In the United Kingdom the wideness and extent of the FSA's powers reduce the scale of the problem. It can carry out most of the regulatory steps itself. In instances where it cannot do so there are provisions in place to facilitate them. The real issues arise in the context of international and pan European regulation.

Memoranda of Understanding

3.39 The main way in which international co-operation has been put in place is through memoranda of understanding. Originally these tended to be bilateral, but more recently a multilateral approach seems to have gained ground. A considerable amount of work has gone into key issues such as the exchange of information between regulators to arrive at the best design for such memoranda. These agreements do not impose legally binding obligations on the signatories. Nor can they override domestic laws and regulations. What they can do however is give rise to a much freer flow of information between regulators than would otherwise be the case. This facilitates the national regulators building a more accurate picture of the financial scene of which they are regulating one part. It is important to bear in mind that an MoU is not always a prerequisite to co-operation being provided. For example, the US Exchange Act specifically allows the SEC to utilise its powers to assist foreign regulators if there is not an MoU in place. They are also mandated to try and develop reciprocal arrangements with states that are not in a position to sign them. Nonetheless they represent the most effective and comprehensive way of proceeding.

3.40 The Principles that the IOSCO Report of 1990 suggested as giving rise to an optimal Memorandum of Understanding are:

That Memoranda should provide for assistance to an investigation from an overseas state requesting information even if the behaviour under investigation would not be a breach of the laws or regulations of the country from which it is requested. If that is not possible because of the laws of a state signing a memorandum then they should request a change in their domestic law to permit it. This Principle overrides what has been a long-standing principle of extradition type laws, namely that someone can only be extradited if the offence concerned is one in both the requesting state and the requested. This has to be overridden in the context of financial regulation as otherwise it would be impossible to police international financial organisations effectively. A decision could be made in a part of a financial organisation in one country to do something that was a breach of financial regulation in another. If the regulator in the state where the offence occurred were to find out there would be little they could do to proceed against the parties responsible without a Memorandum drafted on the basis of this principle. They could otherwise only take steps against the branch or subsidiary in their own jurisdiction which may be insufficient.

3.41 This has been a particular issue for the United States. US law does not require that when a non-US regulator seeks assistance the events concerned must also be an offence in the US. This is important as US securities laws generally tend to be wider than the securities laws of other countries. However, reciprocity arises in another way in that the Exchange Act requires the SEC to consider whether the overseas regulator would reciprocate were the SEC to request assistance from them. If not then assistance should be refused.

3.42 That a memorandum should provide that information received by a regulator should be treated 'with the highest possible level of confidentiality'. This is stated to mean that the information should be treated with the same degree of confidentiality as domestically acquired information. The memorandum should also give the authority that is asked for information the opportunity to say what degree of confidentiality should be attached to the information provided.

3.43 The memorandum should also set out the procedures to be followed in requesting information and in responding to such requests. This is a fundamental issue to be agreed, and in most cases one that should not be too difficult for the parties to agree on.

3.44 The memorandum should state that when an investigation is going on in one state as a result of a request from a regulator in a second state it should not impact on the rights that a person has in the first state. This is necessary because otherwise the memorandum will find itself inoperable in the first state. In many nations the rights concerned will be constitutional ones, and so the matter is not negotiable.

3.45   The memoranda should contain an agreement that the signatories will consult with each other during the period of operation of the memorandum. The need for this could become apparent when there is a difference of view as to whether assistance should be provided in a particular case. It is also hoped that the facility for consultation will give rise to a relaxed relationship between the regulators concerned. Highlighted by IOSCO are three situations where consultation is likely to be particularly important; namely where unforeseen circumstances arise, where there is an overlap of jurisdiction and where one country's laws or regulations change.

3.46   As a matter of political and legal reality it is accepted that there must be a public policy exclusion. This permits a regulator to refuse to provide assistance to a request where to do so would violate the public policy of its state. The IOSCO Report defines public policy in this context as being 'issues affecting sovereignty, national security or other essential interests.' This may prove a narrower definition than that which some states' judges may give it.

3.47   The memoranda should provide that the signatories should take all reasonable steps to fully utilise their powers when faced with a request for information. This should include obtaining documents, where appropriate testimony from witnesses, giving access to any relevant non-public files they may have and carrying out inspections of the regulated entity concerned in the investigation. This is a particularly important principle given that there have been instances of regulators refusing to provide information that it can obtain from the regulated firm on a voluntary basis because of an unwillingness to enforce requests for information against the firm. In some cases this has occurred for legal reasons.

3.48   There should be an agreement allowing an authority requesting assistance to take part directly in its execution. This can be useful in cases where the investigating authority is the one with most of the background information on the issue concerned. In addition it may be the case when the investigation proceeds further that the requesting authority starts to find information that it would not have been able to request in the first place because it could not have known of its existence.

3.49   Finally, the memorandum should allow the regulator being requested to provide assistance to share the costs with the regulator requesting it. This would be important in cases where an investigation were likely to prove expensive, especially where the regulator being requested to provide assistance has limited resources. It could also prove relevant if, over a period of time, one regulator finds itself requesting more information from another than is requested in return. It is useful to have a mechanism for dealing with this.

European considerations

Introduction

3.50   The recent and ongoing developments in the European Union relevant to the area covered by this book are grouped under the umbrella of the Financial Services Action Plan, the aim of which is to develop a single market in financial services in the European Union. It was created following the European Council in Cardiff in 1998 when the European Commission was invited to set out a framework to develop such a market. Forty two measures are being, or have been adopted so far. The aim is to:

- reduce the cost of accessing capital and improve the allocation of capital across the EU;

- give firms increased opportunities to access markets in other Member States and to carry out business effectively on a cross-border basis; and

- give retail customers access to a wide range of more competitively priced financial services products[1].

---

1 H M Treasury 'The EU Financial Services Action Plan in the UK', May 2004.

3.51   The Financial Services Action Plan has a number of key objectives. These cover developing a single wholesale market to facilitate the raising of corporate finance across Europe on an optimised cost efficient basis. It also involves allowing investors to invest across Europe from one point of access and creating a state of affairs where the trading of investments and settling of transactions are carried out as safely as possible. To facilitate access there needs to be suitable availability of information, and available electronic communication services. Clearly there also need to be equal standards of prudential regulatory standards to maintain satisfactory financial stability.

3.52   For these reasons the Directives and Regulations passed are disparate in nature and in some cases extensive in content. The former must be incorporated by national law within a stated period. The latter apply directly although the UK makes a habit of bringing legislation or delegated legislation to put it into effect and in many cases this is necessary to achieve full impact. Under the Lamfalussy process which has been utilised in the Action Plan there are four levels of bringing laws into effect.

Level 1 This is used for framework issues and matters of broad principle. Once agreed at an EU level the Commission will engage in consultation and then make a proposal for legislation to the Council of Ministers and European Parliament. Legislation, normally in the form of a regulation, will then be passed.

Level 2 This is utilised to bring in the more detailed rules under the principles already discussed. Under the comitology procedure The Council of Ministers delegates power to the Commission and representatives of the Member States[1]. These representatives sit on committees to help the Commission. Such committees were set up in banking, securities and insurance. The focal point of drafting and issuing European legislation falls to the European Securities Committee chaired by the Commission, who are in turn advised by the Committee of European Securities Regulators.

Level 3 This consists of contact and co-operation between national regulators. This is necessary because many of the Directives and Regulations passed could potentially have a significantly different effect if interpreted in a disparate way between Member States.

Level 4 This is the level of enforcement of the Directives and Regulations which is carried out by the European Commission. They in turn are assisted by the Member States and the national financial, banking and insurance regulators.

---

1 Parlour 'European Law Considerations' in the Financial Services Law Guide, Ed Haynes. Tottel, 2006 p 489.

Markets in Financial Instruments Directive

3.53 In the context of this book some of the Directives and Regulations are more relevant than others. Of particular importance is the Markets in Financial Instruments Directive, commonly referred to as 'MiFID' which will result in an extensive series of changes being needed to the FSA rules. It is planned that the Directive will be fully in force by 1 November 2007. In essence it extends the coverage of the existing Investment Services Directive (which it will replace) adopting the same key approaches of establishing high level provisions for conduct of business and internal organisation. It also seeks to harmonise the operation of regulated markets. To achieve this it widens the range of core investment services and activities that are available to be provided on a passported basis across the EEA. The home state continues to be responsible for conduct of business and organisational issues though the host state's rules on such matters as advertising would apply where appropriate. If however a matter is not carried out on a cross-border basis but through a branch then the host state's conduct of business rules will apply. The services and activities that MiFID applies to are:

3.54 Services

(1) Reception and transmission of orders in relation to one or more financial instruments;

(2) Execution of orders on behalf of clients;

(3)   Dealing on own account;

(4)   Portfolio Management;

(5)   Investment advice;

(6)   Underwriting of financial instruments and/or placing of financial instruments on a firm commitment basis;

(7)   Placing of financial instruments without a firm commitment basis;

(8)   Operation of Multilateral Trading Facilities.

3.55   Ancillary services

(1)   Safekeeping and administration of financial instruments for the account of clients, including custodianship and related services such as cash/ collateral management;

(2)   Granting credits or loans to an investor to allow him to carry out a transaction in one or more financial instruments, where the firm granting the credit or loan is involved in the transaction;

(3)   Advice to undertakings on capital structure, industrial strategy and related matters and advice and services relating to mergers and the purchase of undertakings;

(4)   Foreign exchange services where these are connected to the provision of investment services;

(5)   Investment research and financial analysis or other forms of general recommendation relating to transactions in financial instruments;

(6)   Services related to underwriting;

(7)   Investment services and activities as well as ancillary services of the type included under **3.54** or **3.55** related to the underlying of the derivatives included under **3.56** points 5, 6, 7 and 10, where these are connected to the provision of investment or ancillary services.

3.56   Financial Instruments

(1)   Transferable securities;

(2)   Money market instruments;

(3)   Units in collective investment undertakings;

(4)   Options, futures, swaps, forward rate agreements and any other derivative contracts relating to securities, currencies, interest rates or yields, or other derivatives instruments, financial indices or financial measures which may be settled physically or in cash;

(5) Options, futures, swaps, forward rate agreements and any other derivative contracts relating to commodities that must be settled in cash at the option of one of the parties (otherwise than by reason of a default or other termination event);

(6) Options, futures, swaps, and any other derivative contracts relating to commodities that can be physically settled provided that they are traded on a regulated market and/or an MTF;

(7) Options, futures, swaps, forwards and any other derivative contracts relating to commodities that can be physically settled not otherwise mentioned in (6) immediately above and not being for commercial purposes, which have the characteristics of other derivative financial instruments, having regard to whether, inter alia, they are cleared and settled through recognised clearing houses or are subject to regular margin calls;

(8) Derivative instruments for the transfer of credit risk;

(9) Financial contracts for differences;

(10) Options, futures, swaps, forward rate agreements and any other derivative contracts relating to climatic variables, freight rates, emission allowances or inflation rates or other official economic statistics that must be settled in cash or may be settled in cash at the option of one of the parties (otherwise than by reason of a default or other termination event), as well as any other derivative contracts relating to assets, rights, obligations, indices and measures not otherwise mentioned in this list of financial instruments, which have the characteristics of other derivative financial instruments, having regard to whether, inter alia, they are traded on a regulated market or a multilateral trading facility, are cleared and settled through recognised clearing houses or are subject to regular margin calls

3.57 Key issues here in comparison with the Investment Services Directive are that MiFID has upgraded the advice that engages in making personal recommendations to a core investment service that can be passported on a stand-alone basis. Operating a multilateral trading facility has been added as a new core investment service covered by the passport and there is an extension of the passport to cover commodity derivatives, credit derivatives and financial contracts for differences. However, not all firms trading commodity derivatives are covered by the Directive. There is an exemption in the Directive and firms that are unsure whether they fit within it should check the FSA's guidance note[1].

---

1 FSA Draft Guidance Note 06/9 'Organisational Systems and Controls: Common Platform for Firms'.

3.58 There are more detailed requirements covering organisation, conduct of business and the operation of regulated markets and multilateral trading facilities. Pre and post-trade transparency requirements for equity markets are introduced across three main types of facility:

- regulated markets such as the London Stock Exchange;
- multilateral trading facilities or, as they are sometimes known, alternative trading systems; and
- over the counter trading.

3.59   In all these instances MiFID will require greater pre-trade transparency, especially where future transactions are below the size threshold or traders are trading outside their order book. The introduction of new rules for systemic internalisers regarding liquid equities' retail order flow will also result in changes. 'Systemic internalisers' are investment firms that deal on their own account executing client orders on a regulated market or multilateral trading facility on an organised, frequent and systematic basis. The change will involve firms in providing definite bid and offer quotes in liquid shares for transactions that are below 'standard market size'. There is however the facility to execute orders from professional clients at other prices than those quoted in certain situations of which the commonest is likely to be where large orders are concerned.

3.60   Transaction reporting requirements, ie, those relating to post-trade reporting have also been amended. This covers post-trade reporting to the regulator of the home or host state of the firm as is appropriate. These will now receive the reports rather than the authority governing the market on which the instrument is traded. The range of investments is also being extended from equity and debt related products to any instrument, including commodity instruments traded on a regulated market. However, MiFID does not go as far as the current FSA rules and the higher FSA standard is likely to continue. These cover transactions on AIM and Ofex and transactions in OTC instruments where these are referenced to instruments on prescribed markets. Investments traded on exchanges outside the EU are not likely to need to be reported except as required by the exchanges concerned or the rules applying there.

3.61   MiFID also goes into greater detail than the FSA Conduct of Business Rules and this will result in changes to the latter, in particular in the areas of compliance arrangements, internal systems and controls, outsourcing, record keeping, managing conflicts of interest, best execution and safeguarding clients' money and financial instruments and the new client categorisation regime. The main effect of the last of these on the UK will be the need to change the client classification to a new one of market counterparty, professional clients and retail clients. These do not exactly fit the three-category classification that the FSA currently applies, in particular not all intermediate customers under the current regime will be reclassified as professional clients. Nor does the capacity to move between categories remain the same. Overall the FSA will end up having to impose a greater range of obligations on all three client categories under the new regime.

3.62 Perhaps one of the biggest advantages of the MiFID approach is that it will improve the working of the passport approach, ie, that firms constituted in one EEA state and acting in line with the passport provisions can carry on business through a branch in another such state, subject to local conduct of business and advertising rules. The main advantage of the new regime is that this system can be used for a wider range of investment activities. The relationship between home and host states is clarified and the jurisdictional position is made clearer. Marketing communications themselves are going to see change as a result of the Directive and this will result in changes to the financial promotions regime. The FSA anticipate that there will be changes in the direction of more high level rules placing greater responsibility on senior management.

3.63 The information disclosure rules governing the provision of information to clients will see changes to the FSA rules concerning what is stated, when it must be provided, its form and when updates are required. There will also be restrictions on the offering of execution-only business. Under MiFID these can only be offered where:

● the transaction concerned involves an instrument that satisfies the definition of 'non complex'. This includes shares admitted to trading on a regulated market or an equivalent third country market, money market instruments, bonds (other than bonds embedding a derivative), securitised debt, UCITS and it is possible that others will be added as part of the Level 2 measures adopted;

● the transaction consists only of executing orders and or their transmission/reception;

● it is provided on the client's initiative; and

● the client has been given a warning that no suitability assessment has been carried out.

3.64 Where other investments are concerned there is a new requirement that firms obtain from their clients sufficient information to assess whether a service is appropriate for that client. Such information includes knowledge and experience. If it is then concluded that the service is not suitable for the client concerned the firm must warn them that this is the case, or if insufficient information had been forthcoming, that the assessment cannot be carried out. This is distinct from the suitability test which applies to investment advice and portfolio management. The latter requires the client's financial situation, investment objectives, knowledge and experience to be considered. Appropriateness focuses only on the last two of these.

The best execution rule will also see change. This will require the firm to take all reasonable steps to make sure the best possible result is obtained for the client bearing in mind: price, cost, speed and the likelihood of execution and settlement taking place in an appropriate way. An order execution policy needs to be created along these lines, including disclosing to clients how it operates and getting their consent.

3.65 Firms are required under MiFID to execute client orders promptly and fairly along the lines of the existing FSA rules. Clients must also be promptly provided with the key details of transactions entered into on their behalf and they must receive a regular statement with the relevant information concerning their investment portfolio. The rules that will be brought in are likely to preclude the more flexible approach sometimes adopted to provide particular clients with information in a tailored form or at times to suit the client as can be done under the current FSA rules.

3.66 The majority of firms covered by MiFID will also have to satisfy the Capital Requirements Directive which determines the amount of capital that a firm must maintain. An analysis of the contents of this Directive is beyond the scope of the text. However, it does develop further the requirements imposed on firms to maintain sufficient financial resources to increase the likelihood of long-term financial stability. The calculation of the necessary resources for any particular firm is a matter for financial specialists. For most of those engaged in compliance the day-to-day issue will be to make sure that the transactions and activities engaged in do not breach the specific limits that will exist within the firm.

Regulations, Directives, Decisions and Recommendations making up the Financial Services Action Plan

3.67

809/2004	Regulation implementing Listing Amendment Directive
2273/2003	Regulation implementing Market Abuse Directive exemptions
2001/2560	Cross Border Euro Payment Regulation
1999/1228/EC	Insurance Statistics Data Series Regulation
1999/1227/EC	Insurance Statistics Format Regulation
1999/1226/EC	Insurance Statistics Derogation Regulation
1999/1225/EC	Insurance Statistics Regulation
EC/3605/93	Protocol on the Excessive Deficit Procedure Regulation

EC/3604/93	Prohibition of Privileged Access to Financial Institutions Regulation
EC/3603/93	Prohibition of Privileged Access to Financial Institutions Regulation
EEC/2155/91	EEA and Switzerland Non-Life Insurance Regulation
EEC/1534/91	Insurance Agreements Regulation
EEC/1969/88	Medium Term Financial Assistance Regulation
Proposed	MiFID Deadlines Amendment Directive
Proposed	Financial Services Distance Marketing Directive
2005/14/EC	Motor Vehicle Insurance Directive
2005/1/EC	Financial Services Committees Amending Directive
2004/109/EC	Transparency Directive
2004/72/EC	Market Abuse Amending Directive
2004/69/EC	Second Banking Amending Directive
2004/39/EC	Markets in Financial Instruments Directive
2003/125/EC	Market Abuse Implementing Directive
2003/124/EC	Market Abuse Implementing Directive
2003/71/EC	Listing Amendment Directive
2003/51/EC	Annual and Consolidated Accounts Directive
2003/20/EC	Motor Insurance Decision
2003/6/EC	Market Abuse Directive
2002/92/EC	Insurance Mediation Directive
2002/87/EC	Supplementary Supervision Directive
2002/83/EC	Supervision Directive
2002/12/EC	Life Insurance Solvency Directive
2001/108/EC	UCITS Further Amending Directive
2001/107/EC	UCITS Amending Directive
2001/34/EC	Listing Directive
2001/24/EC	Winding Up of Credit Institutions Directive
2001/17/EC	Winding Up of Insurance Companies Directive
2000/64/EC	Third Country Information Exchange Directive
2000/46/EC	Electronic Money Institutions Directive
2000/35/EC	Late Payments Directive
2000/28/EC	Banking Amending Directive
2000/26/EC	Fourth Motor Insurance Directive

2000/12/EC	Consolidated Banking Directive (amended the Self Employed Activities of Banks Directive 73/183/EEC; First Banking Directive 77/780/EEC; Own Funds Directive 89/299/EEC; Second Banking Directive 89/646/EEC; Solvency Ratio Directive 89/647/EEC; Second Banking Consolidated Supervision Directive 92/30/EEC; Large Exposures Directive 92/121/EEC)
98/78/EC	Supplementary Insurance Supervision Directive
98/33/EC	Banking, Solvency Ratio and Capital Adequacy Amending Directive
98/32/EC	Third Solvency Ratio Directive
98/31/EC	Second Capital Adequacy Directive
98/26/EC	Settlement Finality Directive
97/9/EC	Investor Compensation Scheme Directive
97/5/EC	EU Credit Transfers Directive
96/13/EC	Second Banking Exclusion Amendment Directive
96/10/EC	Netting Directive
95/67/EC	Third Solvency Ratio Amendment Directive
95/26/EC	Prudential Supervision of Financial Institutions 'BCCI' Directive
95/15/EC	Second Solvency Ratio Amendment Directive
94/19/EC	Deposit Guarantee Directive
94/18/EC	Admissions Directive
94/7/EC	Solvency Ratio Amendment Directive
93/43/EEC	Motor Vehicle Insurance Decision
93/22/EEC	Investment Services Directive
93/6/EEC	Capital Adequacy Directive
92/121/EEC	Large Exposures Directive
92/96/EEC	Third Life Assurance Directive
92/49/EEC	Third Non-Life Insurance Directive
92/30/EEC	Second Banking Consolidated Supervision Directive
92/16/EEC	Third Own Funds Directive
91/675/EEC	Insurance Committee Directive
91/674/EEC	Insurance Company Accounts Directive
91/633/EEC	Second Own Funds Directive
91/308/EEC	Money Laundering Directive
91/31/EEC	Second Solvency Ratio Directive
90/619/EEC	Second Life Assurance Directive
90/618/EEC	Second Non-Life Insurance Directive

90/605/EEC	Consolidated Accounts Directive
90/232/EEC	Motor Liability Insurance Directive
90/211/EEC	Listing Mutual Recognition Directive
89/647/EEC	Solvency Ratio Directive
89/646/EEC	Second Banking Directive
89/592/EEC	Insider Dealing Directive
89/299/EEC	Own Funds Directive
89/298/EEC	Listing Particulars Directive
89/117/EEC	Publication of Branch Annual Accounting Documents Directive
88/627/EEC	Listing Particulars Directive
88/361/EEC	Free Movement of Capital Directive
88/357/EEC	Direct Insurance Services Directive
88/220/EEC	UCITS Amending Directive
87/345/EEC	Admissions Directive
87/344/EEC	Legal Expenses Insurance Directive
87/343/EEC	Credit Surety Insurance Directive
86/635/EEC	Bank Accounts Directive
86/566/EEC	Free Movement of Capital Directive
86/524/EEC	First Banking Exclusion Amendment Directive
85/611/EEC	UCITS Directive
85/583/EEC	Free Movement of Capital Directive
85/345/EEC	First Banking Amendment Directive
84/641/EEC	First Non-Life Insurance Second Amendment Directive
84/253/EEC	Eighth Accounts Directive
84/5/EEC	Second Motor Vehicle Insurance Directive
83/350/EEC	Consolidated Supervision Directive
83/349/EEC	Seventh Consolidated Accounts Directive
82/148/EEC	Admissions Amending Directive
82/121/EEC	Admissions Information Directive
80/390/EEC	Listing Particulars Directive
79/279/EEC	Admissions Directive
79/267/EEC	First Life Assurance Directive
78/660/EEC	Fourth Company Accounts Directive
78/473/EEC	Coinsurance Directive
77/780/EEC	First Banking Directive
77/92/EEC	Insurance Agents Directive

77/91/EEC	Public Limited Company Directive
76/580/EEC	First Non-Life Insurance Amendment Directive
73/240/EEC	Non-Life Insurance Establishment Directive
73/239/EEC	First Non-Life Insurance Directive
73/183/EEC	Self-employed Activities of Banks Directive
72/430/EEC	Motor Vehicle Insurance Amendment Directive
72/166/EEC	Motor Vehicle Insurance Directive
64/225/EEC	Reinsurance Directive

2004/332/EC	Motor Insurance Decision
2004/10/EC	Decision establishing European Banking Committee
2004/9/EC	Decision establishing European Insurance and Occupational Pensions Committee
2004/8/EC	Decision amending Committee of European Securities Regulators Decision
2004/7/EC	Decision amending European Securities Committee Decision
2004/6/EC	Decision establishing Committee of European Insurance and Occupational Pensions Supervisors
2004/5/EC	Decision establishing Committee of European Banking Supervisors
2001/528/EC	Decision establishing European Securities Committee
2001/527/EC	Decision establishing Committee of European Securities Regulators
1999/103/EC	Motor Vehicle Insurance Decision
1999/61/EC	WTO Negotiations of Financial Services Decision
97/828/EC	Motor Vehicle Insurance Decision
91/371/EEC	EEA and Switzerland Non-Life Insurance Directive
91/370/EEC	EEA and Switzerland Non-Life Insurance Decision
91/323/EEC	Motor Liability Insurance Decision
88/369/EEC	Ninth Motor Insurance Decision
88/368/EEC	Eighth Motor Insurance Decision
88/367/EEC	Seventh Motor Insurance Decision
87/373/EEC	Commission Implementation Powers Decision

2004/384/EC	Recommendation on simplified prospectus for UCITS
2004/383/EC	Recommendation on use of derivatives for UCITS
2000/408/EC	Recommendation on Financial Instrument Disclosure

95/198/EC	Late Payments Recommendation
92/48/EEC	Insurance Intermediaries Recommendation
90/109/EEC	Cross-border Financial Transactions Recommendation
88/590/EEC	Payment Systems Recommendation
87/598/EEC	Electronic Payments Code of Conduct Recommendation
87/63/EEC	Deposit Guarantee Recommendation
87/62/EEC	Large Exposures Recommendation
85/612/EEC	UCITS Directive Recommendation
81/76/EEC	Motor Vehicle Insurance Recommendation
77/534/EEC	European Securities Code of Conduct Recommendation
74/165/EEC	Motor Vehicle Insurance Recommendation

3.68   As will be noted the majority of these are already in force. The consequences of such changes manifest themselves as new laws and regulations in the UK and where appropriate are dealt with as such elsewhere in the text.

Chapter 4

A risk-based approach to regulation and internal compliance

4.1   The concept of risk-based regulation was highlighted in the Report to the Chancellor of the Exchequer on the Reform of the Financial Regulatory System in July 1997 which stated at paragraph 2, Style and process of regulation: Risk-based approach, *'[FSA] will adopt a flexible and differentiated risk-based approach to setting standards and to supervision, reflecting the nature of the business activities concerned, the extent of risk within particular firms and markets, the quality of firms' management controls and relative sophistication of the consumers involved ...'*.

4.2   This chapter will consider the design and methodology behind the FSA's risk assessment operating framework as it relates to both the marketplace and the FSA's approach to its risk mitigation programme for regulated businesses. It will go on to consider risk assessment obligations placed on firms by the FSA rules together with standard approaches and tools that can help firms build risk-based approaches to compliance.

Moving to a risk-based approach to regulation

4.3   In its publication 'A New Regulator for a New Millennium' the FSA set out its then proposed approach to the supervision of firms conducting Investment Business in the United Kingdom. The approach was referred to as a risk-based approach to regulation and had been developed around the notion that maintaining market confidence does not aim to prevent all collapses or lapses in conduct in the financial system. Given the nature of financial markets, which are inherently volatile, achieving a no-failure regime is impossible and undesirable. In fact a zero-risk regime would most likely damage the economy as a whole as it would be both uneconomic from a cost benefit point of view as well as stifling market innovations and competition. Moreover risk is an inherent feature of any financial market. Certain risks should not be eliminated at all. Taking consumer investment as an example, investment performance risk is a necessary feature of a financial market and provided an investment firm has made the investor aware of the nature of all the risk involved and not made excessive claims about the investment the FSA should have no role protecting the consumer from an economic fall in the value of their investment. In fact a zero-failure regime would engender a view by consumers that firms might never be permitted to fail and thus act as a disincentive for customers to assess the risk associated with their investment decisions. The FSA's approach to risk, however, was described as one way of minimising the impact of failure in the financial market.

4.4 Issues surrounding the desirability for risk-based regulation and the balance between regulatory intervention and a regime that allowed some risk to materialise was addressed by Kari Hale in a speech entitled Risk-based compliance for financial services in which the concept or risk-based compliance in the markets. He stated,

'After all, most markets have some element of market failure. Often those who favour intervention argue that any market failure justifies intervention. But, the real test goes beyond that: there must be both market failure and the prospect that intervention will provide a net benefit. This involves recognising that regulatory intervention has a cost; and that regulatory intervention, like reliance on market operations, has a non-zero probability of failure ...'[1] Kari Hale Director Finance FSA

---

1 25 November 2004.

4.5 This approach further developed the requirements of the Principles of Good Regulation in the Financial Services and Markets Act 2000, s 2(3) which states in particular:

'(3) In discharging its general functions the Authority must have regard to-

(a) the need to use its resources in the most efficient and economic way

(b) ...

(c) the principle that a burden or restriction which is imposed on a person, or on the carrying on of an activity, should be proportionate to the benefits, considered in general terms, which are expected to result from the imposition of that burden or restriction ...'

4.6 The FSA's approach to risk-based regulation has continued to be developed in the five years since 30 November 2001 and continues to be an approach the FSA strives to develop and improve. It is at the very core of the FSA's activities, how it supervises firms and the market as well as being a concept that is closely aligned to the FSA's approach to the structure and design of its rules which are now undergoing a simplification process.

What is risk and what is risk-based regulation?

4.7   At the root of the FSA's operating risk framework is the issue of cost for the utilisation of its resources, the fact that it has finite resources and how it can best demonstrate that it has met its statutory objectives. A risk-based approach allows the FSA to focus its resources on the areas of greatest risk to its objectives as well as allowing it to develop a bias towards proactively identifying and then reducing those risks before any can cause major damage or failure in the markets.

4.8   There is, however, no definition of risk provided in the FSMA or the FSA Handbook. The FSA look at the potential for risk in the context of each of its four Statutory Objectives where risk relevant to one objective may not be relevant to another. Historically, however, there have been key risks that are of regulatory concern. Although this is not an exhaustive list, key risks would include:

● Systemic risk,
● Financial risk,
● Market risk,
● Credit risk,
● Currency risk,
● Legal risk,
● Regulatory risk,
● Counterparty risk,
● Operational risk,
● Bad faith risk.

FSA's risk-based operating framework

4.9   As highlighted earlier the FSA's risk-based approach to its regulatory activities emanates from the Principles of good regulation and an acceptance that because of its limited resources it must establish a process allowing it to focus its attention towards those matters that are more likely to impact upon its Statutory Objectives. The FSA focuses its risk assessment towards consumers and the marketplace and secondly in relation to the firms it regulates. We will analyse its approach in relation to both of these below.

4.10   As we will see later in this chapter, as part of its risk identification programme, the FSA seeks to identify those risk that are both probable and have the greatest impact in meeting its Statutory Objectives. Having done this, it then establishes an operating risk framework for mitigating against such risks. Equally, each of these types of risk will be important for firms to identify to ensure the effective and sound management of their businesses. Regulated businesses now have regulatory responsibilities to identify those risk that will impact what they do and take steps to mitigate them.

The FSA's risk map: markets and consumers

4.11   The FSA has developed a risk mapping framework as an operational approach to identifying risk. The framework acts as a bridge between the FSA's regulatory functions and its Statutory Objectives. The process of risk identification, mitigation and performance evaluation is a central part of how the FSA determines its activities. The process is both thoroughly mapped out and comprehensibly managed. In its second progress report the FSA described its risk mapping system in the following terms:

'... designed to enable [the FSA] to assess risks, whether at the firm specific level or at the consumer, product, market or industry level ...'[1]

---

1 FSA Building the New Regulator. Progress report 2, February 2002.

The main elements of the FSA's risk mapping process include the following stages:

Environmental assessment and risk identification

4.12   The FSA conducts a forward looking exercise to identify risks to its Statutory Objectives from the external environment such as economic and legal matters both domestic and international as well as demographical issues. It draws on information from external sources asking whether external issues might affect firms, consumers, products, markets or industries in a manner that will impact on the statutory objectives. In addition other risks are identified throughout the year as part of the FSA's general regulatory activities. These may be risk caused by firms' activities or product developments. Once again as any such risks are identified they are related back to the FSA's Statutory Objectives. The FSA publishes the outcome of its environmental and general risk assessment each year its annual the Financial Risk Outlook. The impact of this document described in more detail below.

Strategic aims

4.13   Having identified risks the FSA is then able to put these in the context of its strategic aims. The FSA sets for a three-year period strategic aims which represent the areas on which the FSA will focus in its regulatory plan. These are designed to help the FSA achieve their statutory objectives by dealing with the most significant risk, together with any new demands placed upon it and its regulatory responsibilities. Each year the FSA sets out its strategic aims for the forthcoming year in its annual plan and budget.

Risk prioritisation and resource allocation

4.14   In terms of its risk operating framework, the FSA has to determine whether or not to respond to a particular risk given its significance to its ability to meet its Statutory Objectives. To help determine the timing of the FSA's response to identified risk and the resources to be allocated to dealing with them, at the Risk assessment and prioritisation stage the FSA assesses and prioritises the identified risks against probability and impact factors. A probability factor considers the likelihood of the risk manifesting itself as an event, and the impact factor indicates the significance of the event if it were to take place. The FSA then use a combination of the probability factor and impact factor to measure the overall risk posed to its Statutory Objectives and prioritise the risks enabling it to provide an appropriate regulatory response.

4.15   The resources necessary to satisfy the regulatory responses to identified risks are allocated by the FSA Board. The Board also review previous years' work, including what was achieved against targets and goals previously set, what they were able to perform successfully and those things which can be discontinued because there were ineffective.

Decision on regulatory response and use of regulatory tools

4.16   Having assessed and prioritised risks the FSA then go on to determine an appropriate response to the risk both in terms of the resources it has available, the most appropriate regulatory tools to deal with the matter and having regard to the principles of good regulation. Further analysis of the FSA supervision of regulated businesses and its use of its regulatory tools is dealt with in more detail in Chapter 5.

4.17   The FSA has a wide ranging armoury of tools available to enable it to deal with specific identified risks as well as enabling it to operate an effective response to risks across the sectors it regulates. The FSA refers to this as its Operating Framework Response. The response will be split between the work it conducts with consumers and the financial industry at large and the work it undertakes with individual firms as well as approved persons. The FSA uses in particular the following regulatory tools:

Tools directed towards the industry at large

4.18

(a)   Raising standards through the requirement for the industry to comply with training and competence regime requirements,

(b)   Making rules to set regulatory standards,

(c)   Sector-wide projects to address risks arising across particular sectors, discharged through thematic reviews,

(d)   Monitoring market activities, such as transaction date or complaints statistics,

(e)   Communications and letters. These may highlight specific issues of concern and require responses.

Tools directed towards consumers in general

4.19

(a)   Consumer education and public awareness,

(b)   Public statements about threats or scams,

(c)   Disclosure requirements, allowing the FSA to prescribe that firms provide clearer information on product sales to ensure consumers are in a better position to understand the nature of risks associated with their investment decisions,

Tools directed towards individual firms and approved persons

4.20

(a)   Supervision of firms to monitor, identify and deal with firm-specific risk. This can be achieved through desk-based reviews, on-site visits or a combination of these. The FSA also rely significantly on thematic reviews to deal with risk across categories of firms.

(b) Although not published, the FSA maintain a 'watch list' system that identifies those firms that historically have given rise to regulatory problems as well as firms where risks have manifested themselves requiring some type of remedial work.

(c) Investigations enabling the FSA to develop a more in-depth appreciation of the risks identified within particular firms, but where further information about the extent of the risk may be required.

(d) Intervention, allowing the FSA to deal with a firm that will not voluntarily undertake appropriate remedial action.

(e) Discipline and enforcement which provides a signal to the regulated industry about the seriousness which the FSA attaches to a particular problem.. It also enables the FSA to respond to a particular risk in a targeted manner, by censuring and imposing a financial penalty on a firm. In very serious cases the FSA can use disciplinary action to enable it to act as a gatekeeper of the quality of those entering and participating in the financial market by withdrawing or suspending a firm's authorisation. Any such withdrawal of authorisation has the galvanising effect of removing certain types of firm risk.

4.21 The use of regulatory themes has increasingly become a major regulatory tool, allowing the FSA to allocate its resource towards assessing the probability and impact of identified risk amongst a sample of regulated businesses. Each year the FSA publishes in its Plan and Budget the themes for the forthcoming year. In terms of a firm's own responsibility towards identified risk, the FSA state that themes should be sufficiently important to justify the attention of senior management within firms, and provide output which firms can assess to enable them to take steps in order to deal with the identified risks themselves.

Performance evaluation

4.22 The FSA set performance indicators and evaluate their performance to assess whether their activities in dealing with identified risk have satisfied the principles of good regulation and have been effective in meeting their statutory objectives and whether their activities. Further information about the way the FSA evaluates its performance is set out in Chapter 2.

The FSA risk map: individual firms and risk mitigation programmes

4.23 A substantial element of the FSA Risk Operating framework relates to the time and resources it devotes to the assessment of risk posed by individual firms and the impact that firm-specific risk may have on its success in meeting the Statutory Objectives. The firm-specific risk assessment framework starts from the point that the FSA assesses new applications for authorisation and continues through their ongoing supervision of firms' activities[1]. The FSA's relationship with firms is risk-based and as part of this approach the FSA aims to give firms a greater incentive to conduct business in a way that reduces their regulatory attention. This can result in well managed firms experiencing a lighter touch of supervision than poorly managed firms. The FSA's publication Building the new regulator progress report 2 stated the following:

'Our relationship with firms will be risk based. This means that there will be a base level of supervisory activity or intensity with each firm ...the base level of supervisory intensity will depend on impact (i e the effect on the statutory objectives if risk crystallising). These will help determine the nature of the relationship that we expect to have with that firm, with a higher proportion of our resources devoted to supervising those firms that pose a higher risk to our objectives.'

1 The FSA firm risk assessment programme is set out in Financial Services Authority: The firm risk assessment framework, February 2003.

4.24 In developing its approach to risk assessment at firm level the FSA focus on three critical areas[1]:

(a) Improving industry performance by creating incentives for firms to maintain their own standards,

(b) Flexible and proactive regulation by focusing their resources on the areas of greatest risk to their statutory objectives, as well as having a preference towards identifying and reducing risk before they cause significant damage. To identify the most important risk the FSA will draw upon research and analysis (see **4.26** below)

(c) Maximising effectiveness by focusing their work on targeted and specific issues as opposed to open-ended information collection and routine on-site inspections.

1 Financial Services Authority. A new regulator for the new millennium, page 12, January 2000.

4.25 To assess the risk that each authorised firm poses to its Statutory Objectives the FSA has developed a risk assessment programme commonly referred to as Arrow. (This stands for Advanced Risk Response Operating Framework). One of the outcomes of the firm specific programme is to place firms into one of four relationship categories: A High, B medium high, C medium low, and D low. A firm's individual categorisation is determined during risk assessment work by way of the impact (the potential effect the risk will have on the Statutory Objectives) and probability factors (the likelihood of a particular risk event crystallising). (these have been explained in further detail in section **4.14** above). The allocation of a firm to a particular category may change over time if the risk assessment of the firm alters. Over 80% of the firms supervised by the FSA are allocated to the low level relationship category. One key aspect of the FSA's approach to risk mitigation has been the bringing together of prudential and conduct of business supervision for all firms. An additional improved approach relates to groups with multiple authorised entities and those that are part of an overseas group. In the former although different divisions of the group are likely to have different supervisors, the FSA allocates a lead supervisor to act as a single point of contact communicating and understanding group-wide risk issues and to co-ordinate the individual risk mitigation programmes. Furthermore firms that are either subsidiaries of overseas entities or UK authorised firms with overseas operations will experience FSA working with the relevant overseas regulator to better understand the nature and implications of group risks and where issues arise will see the FSA working in close liaison with the overseas regulator agency. This helps the FSA to identify risk to objectives arising from overseas operations as well being able to carry out work with firms where the overseas regulator is deemed to be less effective. We have discussed the main FSA regulatory tools for firms in [ ] above. Certain of these tools might be used depending on the risk identified in the firm. For example where high-level risks are identified this might lead to remedial or preventative FSA action, whereas medium low risk issues may lead to monitoring actions and if further information is needed the FSA may carry out further diagnostic tests.

Base line monitoring and site visits

4.26   The FSA's first step in its firm risk assessment is to understand the impact of an individual firm. It does this by conducting baseline monitoring of firms in all relationship categories by way of reviews of regulatory returns such as audited accounts, financial returns, complaint returns and notifications. Returns are monitored to identify potential breaches of regulatory requirements. Further preparation is conducted into a firm's legal, business and management structure as a way of deciding what areas within a firm need to be assessed. In most cases where the FSA find that firms' business structures are simple enough for its risk assessment the framework can be applied to the entire firm. A number of firms, however, are more complex. They may be within a large group where there is a layered legal, management and business structure. Where this type of complexity arises the FSA will most likely identify and risk assess the firm's material business units together with its group-wide control and support functions (such as internal audit and IT).

4.27   Once the FSA has completed its impact assessment it will conduct a probability assessment of a firm to assess the likelihood of a risk crystallising and its potential effect on the statutory objectives. The probability assessment is also used to provide the early stages of a risk mitigation programme for an individual firm. The probability assessment comprises desk-based assessment of existing and new information supplied by firms and where the risk category of the firm is A,B or C, the FSA supervisor will conduct a visit to a firm to carry out on-site assessment. An element of the probability assessment is to review the potential for environment risks external to a firm that might directly or indirectly affect a firm's business or control of risk. These will include risks across categories such as political/legal, socio-demographic, technological, economic, competition and market structure.

4.28   An early indication that the FSA is conducting a risk assessment of an individual firm will be a request for specific information. This might include a request for information concerning:

(a)   up-to-date business unit, legal and management structure charts;

(b)   samples of board minutes;

(c)   recent strategy documents;

(d)   management accounts;

(e)   risk reports;

(f)   compliance reports;

(g)   money laundering reports to senior management;

(h)   internal audit plan and methodology;

(i)   external audit management letter.

4.29   On-site visits are conducted in response to risks identified from the FSA's base-line monitoring work although sample visits to monitor compliance in a sector and visits as part of sector-wide reviews are regularly carried out. The visits to individual firms conducted as part of the risk assessment framework are often referred to as ARROW visits and are used to gather further information to enable the FSA to complete its risk mapping for a firm. Such visits will often be used to fill in gaps in the information held as part of the FSA base-line morning and follow up on issues that have previously been identified as part of the FSA previous work relating to the firm. Occasionally the FSA will also undertake a limited review of the controls within a firm to enable it to verify any views or concerns it has about a firm. During a visit the FSA will often want to interview key individuals at the firm. The types and number of individuals that the FSA will want to interview will depend on the size and complexity of the firm in question although the FSA will almost certainly want to interview the Chief executive officer and other board members together with the head of compliance.

4.30 The period between formal risk-assessments and thus the length of a firm's risk mitigation programme is typically between one and three years depending on the identified risk of the firm. If the period of risk assessment is longer than 12 months then FSA will undertake a periodic review. During this period a firm may experience other supervisory activity such as thematic work (refer to Chapter 5). This additional work may contribute to the identification of further risks that affect the FSA's impact and probability assessment of the firm and cause further risk mitigation work or the utilisation of other regulatory tools.

4.31 Potential firm specific risks are broken down between risk elements categorised as either business risk and control risk. All identified risks are then assessed by the FSA against the Statutory Objectives they may affect. The FSA then apply to any identified firm specific risk, seven Risk to Objectives (RTOs). These RTOs are:

(1)   financial failure of the firm,

(2)   misconduct or mismanagement

(3)   lack of consumer understanding,

(4)   market abuse

(5)   market quality,

(6)   incidence of fraud or dishonesty within the firm, and

(7)   incidence of money laundering conducted through the firm.

4.32 As a result of its assessment the FSA arrive at what it refers to as a multi-dimensional picture of where the risks might arise in a firm's business and control structures and how they may affect the Statutory Objectives.

4.33 Once the FSA supervisory team has completed the risk assessment for an individual firm and completed a proposed risk mitigation programme, its work is subjected to internal validation as a way of challenging the supervisory team about the identified risk issues, help the FSA make sector comparisons, check that the Risk Mitigation Programme is proportionate and provide an overall quality control of the teams risk assessment work. The validation process for higher risk firms is conducted by a committee chaired by the relevant FSA director or head of department. The validation process for lower risk firms may be conducted by a manager who does not have day-to-day responsibility for the individual firm.

Communicating individual Risk Mitigation Programmes

4.34 FSA will usually conclude a firm's risk assessment once it has completed its onsite visit at the firm. Once that visit its completed the firm's managememt may receive preliminary feedback as a way of enabling the FSA to share any significant findings from the risk assessment with senior management at the firm. It is often the case that this preliminary feedback takes place before the FSA internal validation takes place (described in **4.33** above).

4.35   All firms (save those classified as low risk) are told the results of their risk assessment and will receive a Risk Mitigation Programme (RMP) together with an explanatory letter. To stress the importance the FSA place on senior managements' responsibility for compliance arrangements within a firm a letter from the FSA setting out its RMP for the firm is sent to the individual firm's governing body. A copy of the letter is also sent to any individuals within a firm that act as key points of contact with the FSA, usually being the individual with responsibility for compliance oversight and the firm's Chief Executive Officer. In addition were a firm is a branch or subsidiary of an overseas firm a copy of the letter and the RMP will also be sent to the firm's UK general manager and any individual responsible for the UK branch. Moreover, if the firm is a branch or subsidiary of an EEA authorised firm a copy of the letter will be sent to the home country supervisor. Firms are asked to formally respond to the letter confirming that the RMP will be followed. Under the FSA's current system there is limited scope to disagree with the findings in an RMP (although see **4.37** and **4.38** below). Any disagreements the firm may have about the requirements of the RMP or the matters relied on to determine those requirements should usually be raised with the firm's individual supervisor, the supervisor manager of the head of department. The decision about raising concerns about the RMP should be carefully considered. It must be remembered that the RMP is not a report of findings following a thorough audit and as such the mitigation programme itself is often very general relying on outcomes driven by the firm itself. Where, however, the outcomes are more intrusive, and the firm considers the determining factors are misconceived, these might be appropriate matters to be raised with the firm's supervisor. If a firm declines to carry out the actions in the RMP the FSA will consider utilising other regulatory tools as a way of ensuring the identified risks are appropriately mitigated.

4.36   Each firm's RMP will include both an impact score for the firm and a probability score against each of the Statutory Objectives. The scoring levels are High, Medium High, Medium Low or Low. The report will show against each identified risk, the outcome sought by the FSA together with the date by which it is to be achieved as well as any action to be taken by the FSA or the firm to allow the FSA to achieve the results it desires. There tends to be an emphasis in the RMP for work to be conducted by the firm rather than the FSA, however, if serious concerns have been identified the FSA will not hesitate to use more intrusive regulatory tools to help achieve their desired outcome. As part of the regulatory incentives provided by the FSA a firm that takes prompt and effective remedial action to any risk highlighted in an RMP might experience a reduction in the intensity of its supervisory relationship. The FSA also view the role of senior management within a firm as an important element in the progress of each Risk Mitigation Programme both in terms of risk identification and the determination of any necessary regulatory actions. The commitment shown by senior management to any risk identified by the FSA can and do have an impact on the regulatory tools the FSA may choose to use to deal with the matter as well as determining a shift between preventative work and less intrusive monitoring work.

The future for the FSA's risk assessment framework

4.37 There have been a number of evolutions of the FSA Risk Mitigation Programme, the latest of which began in the summer of 2005 following an announcement by John Tiner in the FSA's Business plan for 2005/06[1]. The FSA has stated that its planned Risk Mitigation Programme changes are aimed at providing greater proportionality and consistency in response to risks together with a more flexible resourcing model. It is planned that the changes will allow for the timely transfer of FSA resources to the greatest risks and will facilitate a lighter touch regime for the least risky firms. In addition the FSA intendes to enhance the use of thematic work and improve its ability to undertake sector intelligence and analysis work. Overall the changes should lead to firms being better informed of emerging risks and other industry trends that are likely to impact the operation of their business.

---

1 FSA Business Plan 2005/06 26 January 2005, Chief Executive's foreword.

4.38 The notable changes to the FSA Risk Mitigation Programme are beginning to feature in 2006 are:

(a) Risk Assessment letters being revised, to add more value to the process including:

- More focus on the main issues and what the FSA expect firms to do about them,

- More helpful explanation of the FSA's views of the risks, and

- An indication of how the FSA views individual firms in the context of their peer group

(b) More communication of the FSA's findings in 'close-out' discussions following the assessment visits.

(c) RMP letters will be provided in draft form to enable firms to comment on factual inaccuracies and misunderstandings and to reduce any 'surprises' in the final letter.

(d) Better communication to relevant sectors of good and bad practice found on focused thematic visits.

(e) There will be abridged one day visits for medium-low risk firms.

How the FSA communicates identified risk

Financial Risk Outlook

4.39 Each January as part of its environmental assessment and risk identification, the FSA publish a paper entitled 'Financial Risk Outlook'. The financial risk outlook is essential reading for all senior management and every compliance officer as the paper puts the FSA's regulatory work into the context of identified risk and as priority risks. Research leading to the preparation of the paper looks at a range of external factors which might affect the FSA's ability to meet its Statutory Objectives. All identified risks are highlighted in the report with key risks presented as Priority Risk. These are the risks that the FSA believe pose the most significant risk to its Statutory Objectives and strategic aims. Through publication of the report the FSA aim to increase awareness of the risks identified and the actions it aims to take in relation to each of them. The factors set out in the report typicaaly include:

(a) Economic conditions;

(b) Performance of financial markets;

(c) Social change;

(d) Political development.

4.40 By way of example, in its 2006 Financial Risk outlook the FSA identified weaknesses in the development of firms' stress testing. It stated '… In a period of low market volatility, it is important for firms to evaluate how they would respond to extreme risk scenarios … stress testing can help senior management evaluate how their firm may respond to extreme, but plausible, risks and so test the risk appetite of their business … fully embedding stress testing into their risk management processes remains a key challenge for many firms …'.

FSA's Business plan and budget

4.41 Each year the FSA publish a business plan setting out it's priorities for the coming year, the timing of major projects and the resources the FSA needs to enable it to meet its commitments for the year. The work planned in the report is shaped by a number of factors including the FSA's annual Financial Risk Outlook. Once more the business plan is used to communicate any identified risks posed to the FSA by either firms, sectors of the industry or external factors.

By way of example in the FSA's 2004/05 plan and budget, John Tiner high-lighted the unprecedented volume of international regulatory change as an area of risk for firms. In the main body of the report the FSA stated that '... all these measures taken together involve very substantial preparations by UK firms ... against this background we have kept to a minimum the number of fresh initiatives which we plan to pursue in the coming year ...'.

FSA communications: CEO Letters and themed reports

4.42   The FSA use letters to the industry as an effective way of raising the profile of particular risk issues that require urgent attention. Often the FSA will require that specific work is undertaken in response to the letters and alert firms to increased supervisory attention in the relevant area. Firms that overlook such letters even if such letters are not directly addressed to them are running the risk of not keeping pace with matters that are of concern to the FSA. Often such letters can be a precursor to major regulatory issues that have given rise to risks to a firm's ability to operate compliantly without further action by the firm. By way of example in September 2005 The FSA wrote to all Chief Executive Officers of investment banks raising concerns about the management of con-flicts of interest within their organisations. The letter asked that each bank satisfy itself that it had effective arrangements in place.

4.43   In particular the letter stated:

'In the light of a number of high-profile cases in Europe and the US and recent regulatory reviews by the FSA, I am writing to remind you of your responsibility to implement appropriate processes and procedures for the effective risk management of conflicts of interest and risks arising from financing transactions ... our supervisors will wish to be assured that firms in our regulatory sphere are operating to professional standards when arranging and executing all financing transactions. Among the most important issues to be addressed by these standards are:

- the need for senior management to take full responsibility for transactions within the businesses for which they are responsible;

- the need for mechanisms designed to draw out information and analysis to permit decision-makers to reach appropriate decisions on risks;

- the need for a clear audit trail relating to the business intent of the transactions;

- the need for adequate disclosure and documentation;

101

- the need for risk disclosures to recognise the possibility of the product being sold on to retail customers.

Our concerns and interest in the important areas of conflicts management and financing transactions will be reflected in the risk mitigation programmes implemented for individual firms as well as cross-firm work that I am initiating ...[1]'

---

1 FSA Letter to Chief executive officers of investment banks, September 2004.

Regulated business and internal risk-based compliance

4.44 Firms need to appreciate the major risks faced by their business. Failure to do so will leave an individual firm exposed to the likelihood of it not being able to deal fully or in a co-ordinated way with such risks if they manifest themselves. Successful risk management allows a firm to identify and then mitigate significant risk that might otherwise prevent a firm from achieving its business objectives. A firm which co-ordinates its activities without first having conducted any form of risk assessment will be operating blindly, unaware of matters which may get in the way of the success of its business and even cause the business to fail.

4.45 A risk-based approach to firms' regulatory obligations does, however, go further than managing and eliminating risk. A thorough risk assessment can be used to focus compliance resources towards those areas of the firm's business which are more likely than other areas to face regulatory risk and leave the lower risk facing business to a lower level of compliance scrutiny. Moreover, businesses do have finite financial and precious resources and senior management and a compliance department will be viewed as providing enhanced value if they are able to apply the firm's resources in a responsible manner. A well thought out risk assessment programme might contribute to a positive view of how compliance is managed throughout the firm.

4.46 The concept of risk-based compliance is one that is also encouraged in firm's own compliance arrangements. Since 2001 many regulated firms have altered their approach to internal compliance supervision to allow them to focus more resources towards the risk to their business and consequently less resources toward those parts of their business that are viewed as presenting less of a risk. Firms' compliance arrangements have become more sophisticated as a result and many firms now incorporate within their organisation arrangements for regular risk identification. Moreover many larger firms have changed the face of compliance establishing regulatory risk departments in place of their previous compliance departments. Firms' internal compliance arrangements are driven to a large extent by FSA rules and in relation to risk identification FSA rule SYSC 3.2.6 R provides as follows:

'A firm must take reasonable care to establish and maintain effective systems and controls for compliance with applicable requirements and standards under the regulatory system and for countering the risk that the firm might be used to further financial crime.'

4.47   Further guidance to this rule in relation to risk assessment is provided at SYSC 3.2.10 G which encourages firms of a certain size and complexity to have a dedicated risk assessment function. It defines a risk assessment function as one that is appropriately resourced by competent staff who can undertake their duties independently and are responsible for assessing risks faced by the firm. The guidance states:

'Depending on the nature, scale and complexity of its business, it may be appropriate for a firm to have a separate risk assessment function responsible for assessing the risks that the firm faces and advising the governing body and senior managers on them. The organisation and responsibilities of a risk assessment function should be documented. The function should be adequately resourced and staffed by an appropriate number of competent staff who are suffi-ciently independent to perform their duties objectively.'

4.48   What is made clear in the guidance, however, is that it is senior management that are responsible for dealing with any identified risks rather than being a matter which is delegated to the compliance team and left with them to resolve.

4.49   Further guidance is provided at 3.2.11G which provides:

'(1) A firm's arrangements should be such as to furnish its governing body with the information it needs to play its part in identifying, measuring, managing and controlling risks of regulatory concern. Three factors will be the relevance, reliability and timeliness of that information.

(2) Risks of regulatory concern are those risks which relate to the fair treatment of the firm's customers, to the protection of consumers to confidence in the financial system and to the use of that system in connection with financial crime.'

4.50   Further development to risk-based compliance was introduced by the FSA on 27 January 2006 as part of its programme of rule book simplification[1]. With effect from 1 March 2006 the FSA's money laundering sourcebook is replaced with specific anti-money laundering risk assessment requirements[2].

These will oblige firms to conduct an assessment of the risk of money laundering to enable them to develop and maintain effective systems and controls to identify, assess, monitor and manage money laundering risk. The FSA require that the systems and controls developed are proportionate to the nature, scale and complexity of the firm's activities. At SYSC 3.2.6C R the FSA have introduced an additional requirement for firms to carry out regular assessments of the adequacy of their money laundering systems and controls.

---

1 SYSC 3.2.6A does not apply to all firms. See the exclusions in SYSC 1.1.3A R.
2 FSA rules SYSC 3.2.6A R.

4.51   This departure from prescriptive anti-money laundering rules allows firms more scope to design systems that suit the nature and complexity of their businesses. However, it does introduce an obligation to design systems that are appropriate in the context of both an initial and ongoing risk assessment of the firms business, clients and product development. It will undoubtedly be the case that to demonstrate compliance with this new rule the FSA will expect firms to show the risk assessment programmes they have carried out to arrive at the systems they have implemented and maintained are logical, well planned, objective thought out and robust.

4.52   This risk-based approach to anti-money laundering should not be viewed by firms as a reduction in the FSA's attention to financial crime. Moreover, firms must remember that many areas of money laundering compliance are required by statute and there is little scope for them to move away from the statutory requirements. For example firms have an obligation to verify the identify of their customers. They must do so even if they consider the client presents limited risk of laundering the proceeds of crime. In introducing the new SYSC requirements Philip Robinson, FSA Financial Crime sector leader said *'... the changes ...do not mean we are going soft on money laundering, they are part of delivering a more proportionate and effective regime to counter money laundering ...*[1]*'.*

---

1 FSA press release, FSA to streamline money laundering rules for firms, 27 January 2006.

4.53   A risk-based approach to compliance will serve to balance the cost of otherwise burdensome internal procedures and provide a realistic assessment of higher impact regulatory breaches occurring.

4.54   A risk-based approach, however, inherently carries with it its own risk as it will divert resources from lower risk matters toward issues of high risk and thus on occasions compliance breaches and failures may very well occur in those lower risk areas. Management must be prepared to accept this. Overall senior management and the FSA may conclude that the potential for minor breaches is outweighed by the benefits of more focused resource. A common misconception of less experienced management, however, is that risk-based compliance only gives benefit to matters which are lower risk. The converse is also important and thus higher risk matters will require greater emphasis and resources than any standard compliance arrangements might previously have necessitate.

4.55 Compliance risk analysis and surveying has developed significantly in recent years with a number of tools becoming commonplace. Methodologies for identifying risks and their mitigating controls are now used by compliance managers. Frameworks for managing compliance risk and the use of action plans to improve the framework elements are increasingly employed. However, the specialised needs of compliance managers must continue to be taken into account and the issues raised embraced by line management.

4.56 Managing and mitigating the compliance risk of an organisation is probably the most difficult challenge facing compliance managers. Compliance risk is a very wide category of risk bounded only by the imagination of employees and, sometimes, external events completely beyond management's control.

4.57 Over recent years compliance risks have become more and more prominent partly as a result of changes in many sectors of the financial services industry, for example:

- The boundaries of existing business processes have been stretched by a continuing need to innovate through new product launches, the use of more complex investment instruments and the use of increasingly complex structures. The compliance responses to these have ranged from increasing compliance awareness through training to simple changes to existing processes, that in some cases can be manually intensive and lack the appropriate systems support. The increased use of 'manual workarounds', which are neither efficient nor scaleable, must necessarily increase the risk of compliance problems.

- Consolidation within industries has resulted in many institutions being exposed to the risks associated with the integration of business and operational processes including compliance risk. This can involve extended periods of operating parallel compliance processes and systems throughout the organisation, coupled with the migration of compliance data and management processes from pre-merger to post-merger systems. Accordingly, the potential frequency and complexity of problems must ordinarily increase.

- The extent of publicity given to both compliance and organisational failures has increased the realisation by management that compliance failures and the adverse shareholder value consequences could easily have happened in their own organisations. A scan through the press over recent years will reveal examples of compliance errors to which even the more 'robust' institutions are exposed. In some instances, these have resulted in both direct and indirect financial loss.

Building a systematic approach to compliance risk analysis and surveying

4.58 The key to developing an effective compliance risk process is the degree of consistency embedded within the process. This consistency can be achieved by systematically combining the identification of current key control weaknesses and the development of a framework to monitor the nature and extent of compliance risk and control throughout the organisation, on a continual basis. The process can be successfully applied to all types of business.

4.59 The first step in this systematic approach is to perform a current state assessment of the compliance risk and control environment. The compliance risk within each process should be identified and the key control processes analysed from both a performance and design perspective. Comparing the key control processes against industry good practice will often provide a useful benchmark when determining areas of potential control weaknesses.

4.60 In conjunction with this current state assessment, external and internal loss databases can be used to map errors and near misses against processes (providing a basis for detailed root cause analysis to identify further potential control weaknesses).

4.61 To add further value an institution could then consider the use of modelling techniques which allow management to assess a value for the risks faced by the institution. Such a model could combine the output from self-assessments with key indicator and external loss data or may simply use self-assessment information. Either way, the modelling of compliance risk data can provide a significant extension to the metrics available for the management of compliance risk.

4.62 As a result of the changes highlighted at para **4.67**, many institutions have a range of current and planned change projects. Assessing the potential impact of these initiatives on the identified compliance risks provides an insight into the residual risks not being addressed. The identification of both the residual risks and any interim risk exposures (the risk the organisation is exposed to today, and until the project addressing the risk is implemented) allows management to determine whether additional or short-term actions are required to reduce the compliance risk associated with change to an acceptable level.

4.63 The systematic approach must provide more than a 'snap shot' of the level of compliance risk in the organisation. To maintain an up-to-date assessment, there is a need to develop a framework to monitor regularly the nature and extent of risk throughout the organisation. This framework should combine a continuous assessment of the level of compliance risk by individual business areas and information from key risk indicators to continually monitor and identify the level of compliance risk within critical business processes.

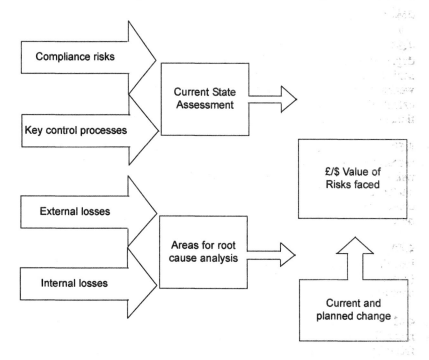

Tools to use in compliance risk analysis and surveying

4.64 There are a number of tools available for use in risk analysis and which are suitable for compliance risk analysis and surveying including:

- self-assessment;
- risk maps and process flows;
- key indicators;
- escalation triggers;
- breach logs and near miss logs; and
- internal audit reports.

4.65 Each tool is valuable in its own right although no single tool is sufficient to provide an adequate compliance analysis. Using a number of tools together will mitigate the limitations of each one.

Self-assessment

4.66 This is probably the most widely used tool and emphasises the primary responsibility which senior line management carries in relation to the proper management and mitigation of compliance risk. Self-assessment, as its name suggests, is carried out in the department giving rise to the risk. Assistance and facilitation from compliance professionals is of course also required. Surveys, questionnaires, facilitated workshops and, occasionally, independent assessments are used.

4.67 The technique can be readily used for the development of day-to-day mitigation procedures and is generally carried out on an infrequent periodic basis for bottom-up assessments. A key advantage of self-assessment is that it raises compliance awareness within the business units that are undertaking it. It enables management of the business units to identify compliance issues and it achieves, in a natural way, recognition that the business unit itself creates and should, at least initially, manage and mitigate compliance risk. The reflective technique naturally employed when using this tool is also useful in building empathy between the business unit and compliance department.

4.68 A variation on self-assessment is a top-down assessment. More frequent reviews are possible with this technique as the business unit is less involved. However, the potential remoteness of a top-down assessment from day-to-day processes must be recognised and both variations should be used in order to ensure that the assessments remain in touch with each business unit's senior management and with the everyday needs of the business.

Risk maps and process flows

4.69 These two tools are widely used by internal audit and they can be very useful for reviewing compliance risk. Given their likely existing use by internal audit it is probable that the organisation will already have a number of risk maps and process flows. Reviews of these by compliance will enable compliance risks to be identified and appropriate mitigation procedures to be implemented. Risk maps will also assist in developing suitable procedures and mitigation measures for the risks identified.

4.70 Similar methodologies to self-assessment are used for creating risk maps and process flows although the focus tends to be more on interviews and focus groups. The functional heart of the tool is centred on processes and flow of risks rather than on the business unit and it therefore covers more departments although in a narrower band. These tools are helpful at a detailed level as they define the key risk and control points as well as responsibilities and accountabilities at each step of the process. However, this is also a key disadvantage of these tools as they tend to be very detailed and therefore inappropriate for senior management reporting.

4.71 A similar increase of compliance awareness is achieved compared to self-assessment although this tends to transcend the business unit as the whole process flow is covered. Risk maps and process flows can also be alternative outputs from self-assessments.

Key risk indicators

4.72 This tool can often use existing reports and systems and is therefore easily and quickly implemented. The firm will already be measuring many key compliance indicators such as volume of trades or sales, new clients and new employees. It is possible to develop a scorecard of risk metrics that will enable the Head of Compliance or Risk to use actual figures from the organisation rather than solely relying on a qualitative assessment. Management familiarity with the indicators will also assist in developing empathy with the compliance department. Key indicators can also provide an insight on the effectiveness of compliance procedures.

4.73 The widely differing frequencies of key indicators should be borne in mind when constructing uses for them. Although compliance indicators enable trend analysis to be performed they are unlikely by themselves to yield useful procedures for mitigating compliance risk. However, they do facilitate decision-making and often enable preventative actions to take place. A detailed awareness of each business unit's sensitivities is necessary for the indicators to be fully useful as the degree of applicability of each indicator will vary with the sensitivity of each business unit.

4.74 Many institutions use a combination of key risk indicators and key control indicators to monitor operational efficiency and the effectiveness of controls. Key risk indicators (KRIs) are simply metrics that can be used to monitor risks relating to the efficiency and performance of a process or business and can include transaction turnover, staff turnover, market volumes, price movements and systems downtime. Key control indicators demonstrate the effectiveness of controls. By combining the monitoring of risk and control indicators, an organisation can establish a process to monitor key performance indicators – interpreting lagging indicators to provide a leading indicator of failure or possible breach.

Examples of KRIs in wholesale operations	**Example of KRIs in retail operations**
• Age and number of outstanding personal registrations • Age and number of unconfirmed trades • Market volumes • Price movements • Transaction turnover	• % Rejected Fact Finds • Product mix of individual's sales • Number of complaints by product, by salesperson, by product • Persistency of sales • Time for individuals to reach competent standards

Escalation triggers

4.75 These are fundamental to the reporting of potential compliance problems to higher levels of management. They can provide an early warning of an increase in compliance risk or a potential breach in regulatory requirements. A set of compliance indicators that have previously been agreed with business unit management and compliance management are a necessary prerequisite of escalation triggers. When the trigger level is reached the indicators are highlighted and given to predetermined senior management.

4.76 Escalation trigger points can be set at differing levels, which may vary over time. For example, trigger levels for a new product may initially be set at a very high level that may be decreased as the compliance department and business management gain familiarity with, and experience of, the compliance risks identified. Escalation triggers can also be set at levels that accord with a firm's compliance risk appetite. The advantage of escalation triggers is that they allow management by exception and, therefore, in theory, efficient management. However, it should be noted that it is possible for indicators to run at a level just beneath the trigger for a considerable time if too much attention is paid to the trigger levels per se.

Example: Setting trigger points for the introduction of a new retail product

- Set a high pass mark for any assessment of the training for individuals

- Set low trigger points for business review, for example you may want to review all cases during the first month decreasing the sample as results show that the product is sold correctly

---

- Set a high short-term persistency rate to ensure that a high level of cancellations in the small numbers of new products are not obscured by the mass of normal sales

---

Breach logs and near miss logs

4.77   Keeping a log of regulatory breaches and near misses can be instructive if used positively. Care must be taken to learn lessons from such logs rather than merely apportion blame. Analysis of the logs can assist assessment of current mitigation policies and controls and senior management can gain comfort on the effectiveness of the compliance risk policies. Such logs can also be helpful in identifying trends and in assisting in focusing resources. However, practitioners will have concerns that a regulator could use such logs inappropriately.

Internal audit reports

4.78   Although internal audit reports contain elements of an independent self-assessment, a breach log and a near miss log, they are themselves vital tools in surveying compliance risk. The internal audit department is perhaps the nearest department to the compliance department in having a broad functional control nature. Additionally, internal audit will often use compliance procedures and manuals as a starting point for its own risk assessment and procedures. There is therefore great value to the Head of Compliance or Risk in reviewing audit reports and extracting the relevant elements of risk from those reports.

Practical Risk Analysis

4.79   Whichever selection of tools is used there are three discrete steps in risk analysis and surveying. The first step is to formulate a framework within which the tools will be used. A coherent methodology designed in a collaborative fashion between compliance and the department or business being surveyed and analysed is essential for the successful use of the tools. Thought and time applied at this step will pay significant dividends in the subsequent steps. It is likely that a relatively small number of senior, experienced managers will be involved in this strategic design phase.

4.80   Secondly, the tool must be developed and tested in a pilot area before being fully disseminated. This allows the fine-tuning of the tool to the individual characteristics of each department/business and also allows for feedback to be easily taken into account so that the third step can be delivered efficiently. A larger but still small number of staff will be involved at this stage.

4.81 Once the development and testing in one area or unit has taken place, the tools can be rolled out to the department or business. The amount of support required should not be underestimated for this stage. Unless the tools have been constructed so that they are very intuitive, a significant amount of training may also be required. A helpdesk might be needed and e-mail support will almost certainly be required. It can be expected that a significant number of staff will be involved at this stage although most of the staff are likely to be part-time only.

4.82 The involvement of a significant number of line staff will assist the buy-in process and will disseminate the executive management's view on the identification, measuring and management of compliance risk. The advantage to the organisation of this point cannot be overstated. The process of using a risk management tool will focus the attention of large numbers of staff on potential compliance risks and will significantly increase the education and awareness of such risks in the organisation. This will considerably reinforce compliance procedures and lead directly to a more compliant organisation. A welcome by-product for executive management is likely to be a more relaxed regulatory attitude to the firm.

Risk identification

4.83 Before managing the compliance risk to an institution, its management must first identify the elements from which the institution is most at risk and then find a method of monitoring the risks. Only when an institution's compliance risk profile has been identified and is being monitored can its compliance management hope to begin serious efforts to manage and then mitigate the compliance risks.

4.84 The identification of the compliance risks facing an institution can be carried out in a variety of ways. Typically, interviews whether conducted separately or in conjunction with workshops for senior managers and compliance executives explore the compliance objectives of the institution and the possible causes that will prevent the institution from reaching those objectives. Alternatively, compliance processes may be identified and the risks to those processes considered by the managers and supervisors most familiar with the process.

4.85 Both the objectives and the process can be high-level strategic ones affecting the entire institution or can equally be part of a detailed compliance procedure specific to a department. The identification of the compliance objectives (or the process) is a necessary first step without which the risks subsequently explored will have no context. Without boundaries it is very difficult to determine at what level the risks should properly be analysed and the development of an appropriate compliance risk profile becomes much more problematic.

Risk analysis: ownership

4.86   The monitoring of compliance risks is assisted by an analysis of each risk showing the owner of the risk, the risk's impact on an organisation and the probability that it will happen. The identification of a risk owner is to ensure that a specific person (or sometimes a committee) takes responsibility for the risk and therefore for its management and mitigation, where possible. Risk owners are not identified in order to generate (or perpetuate) a blame culture and the institution's senior management must be fully committed to the responsibility approach in order for the institution to benefit from the management and mitigation of its risk. Without a commitment to the responsibility approach for risk ownership (rather than the blame approach) there will be many fewer risks identified and much less enthusiasm by management and supervisors to be conscious of the risks faced by an organisation (and the reduction of those risks).

Risk analysis: components

4.87   Typically, the impact of a risk on an organisation is initially evaluated as a high, medium or low impact. However, this analysis often rapidly translates to a monetary value and generally is viewed from a value perspective once the management of risk has been embedded in an organisation. Similarly, the probability that a risk will happen to an organisation is also often initially evaluated on a high, medium or low basis. This also tends to transform into a percentage likelihood or a time value (such as once every three months) as the managers become more familiar with risk management.

4.88   Many of the previously manual approaches to self-assessment are increasingly being automated to provide a more proactive method of monitoring compliance risk. The implementation and operation of an effective compliance control and risk self-assessment process can provide valuable management information on both the level of risk and the adequacy of the control responses to those risks. There are several critical factors that can be used to guide the success of a compliance self-assessment process including senior management sponsorship for the process, a focus on the development of action plans to address key weaknesses (rather than a focus on the existence of the weakness) and the willingness of senior and middle management to own and drive compliance risk and control accountability through the organisation.

Control identification

4.89 The same process applied to each control yields the beginnings of a tool to manage (and mitigate) compliance risk. The control owner should be identified as the person who is responsible for the control operating effectively. The control's importance and effectiveness are also assessed, during either interviews or workshops.

4.90 The importance of a control gives management the ability to judge whether a control is fundamental to mitigating the inherent compliance risk, is important to the mitigation or is one of perhaps a suite of controls, no single one of which by itself will prevent a risk from occurring. The effectiveness of a control is its ability to mitigate the risk based on the control's design and on how the control is carried out in practice.

4.91 Alternatively, the controls' design and performance could be analysed. The design of a control is the inherent mitigation of the risk by that control and often reflects the adequacy of processes and IT systems relating to the control. Its performance is the adequacy of the carrying out of the control and this is mainly reflected by the people and systems used in the control.

Example suite of controls

Compliance Risk: Mis-selling by new retail sales staff

	Control	Criteria	KPI
Level 1	Recruitment Standards	Minimum standards reached	% pass on recruitment assessment
Level 2	Induction and competence assessment	Minimum standards met	% pass internal and external exams
Level 3	Supervision	All business counter checked	% reject level for new staff
Level 4	Sign off as competent	All examinations and worksite assessments passed	Days/months to achieve sign off

Risk and control monitoring

4.92 With the above risk and control analysis an institution's senior management is equipped to start monitoring and managing its compliance risks. At an early stage the institution will probably monitor its risks once every quarter in order to begin monitoring trends in the risks. Ideally, the process of identifying the compliance risks and controls will be embedded in the institution and its compliance risk awareness will have been enhanced considerably. In these circumstances, new compliance risks to an institution and the appropriate controls will be identified as they first occur at the latest (or are first perceived at best) and will be added to the institution's compliance risk inventory (which, when displayed graphically, is sometimes called a risk map).

4.92   It is also important to review the compliance risk inventory to ensure that risks that are no longer applicable to an institution are removed and that the associated controls are not carried out (thus saving costs). However, it must be noted that a control often mitigates more than one compliance risk and, therefore, stopping a control should only be done after a full review of the design of the control (both the original design and how it works in practice).

4.93   Many varied methods are employed to monitor risk ranging from using periodic reviews of both risks and controls to the continuous real-time monitoring of both qualitative and quantitative risk indicators. A recent development in monitoring risk is the use of internal loss databases to monitor errors and near misses.

4.94   The reporting, escalation and analysis of compliance errors and breaches can be used to reinforce the diligence and thoroughness of individuals responsible for compliance risk and/or control within the business. Proactive compliance risk management functions are using these loss databases to provide a basis for detailed root cause analysis to ensure that key learning points are identified and escalated throughout the business, in order to reduce the likelihood of repeated errors.

Risk and control framework

4.95   A comprehensive compliance risk control framework is comprised of a number of different layers all working in conjunction to either prevent errors and breaches from occurring in the first place or, should a failure occur, limit either the direct or indirect exposure of the firm.

Front-line prevent controls

4.96   The first layer of control can be considered to be front-line prevent controls which are used to ensure that things go right in the first place and operate as the foundation for the business process as a whole. These commonly include: clarity of roles and responsibilities, access to accurate, timely and clear management information (e g inside information flowing into the firm) and establishing processes with minimal manual interfaces and intervention (e g automated trade generation, capture, recording and reporting mechanisms).

Processes prevent controls

4.97 A second level of prevent controls can be defined as those controls embedded within processes that are used to catch errors prior to and at the time of execution of a contract. As the name suggests the controls are designed to prevent problems and can include automated controls to prevent the entry of a prohibited trade into the firm's system.

Detect controls

4.98 Detect controls can be used to detect rather than prevent problems. Many front-line detect controls are designed to detect operational problems on the same day or, at the very least, on the next day in an effort to limit the potential impact of the problem – either operational or financial. These controls can include an end of day review. A secondary level of detect controls can be designed to detect errors on a less time critical basis (for example 2–5 days) and are particularly of use where the nature of any financial impact would not support investment in more expensive prevent type controls.

Back-stop detect controls

4.99 Back-stop detect controls can be designed to limit the financial loss associated with any errors. These controls are typically performed on a less timely basis (for example on a monthly basis).

Examples: risk and control framework

Front Line Prevent Controls	• Clear responsibility and accountability for risk areas • Prompt and pertinent MI • Clear governance for decision making affecting risk
Processsess Prevent Controls	• Automatic rejection of imperfect/incomplete applications not meeting pre-determined criteria • Pre-checking of documentation before submission
Detect Controls	• End of day balancing of trading • Manual weekly check on outstanding issues
Back stop Detect Controls	• Review of MI trends at execution meetings • Quarterly Compliance inspections

Relative cost of different controls

4.100 Placing the emphasis of control on automated front-line prevent controls and process prevent controls, with an objective of 'getting things right first time', reduces the likelihood of compliance breaches. There is, however, a price for this – preventative controls are the most expensive controls to establish and maintain as they tend to be more transaction related.

4.101 Heavy reliance on manual control processes, particularly where these processes are focused on the detection of operational errors after the point of contract execution, can increase the likelihood of delayed detection and more serious compliance problems. Not only is the organisation exposed longer to the underlying risk for which the control is designed but also to a longer period for the potential failure of the control. Untimely detection of errors can expose the organisation to adverse market movements, may exacerbate the potential financial loss and is very likely to increase the regulatory exposure. Intuitively, the timely detection of compliance errors can be a key to effective risk mitigation.

Use of technology

4.102 Leading institutions have used the implementation of new IT systems to develop a more 'straight through' process to improve efficiency where compliance risk mitigation relies on manual processes and to address key compliance risks. In many cases, enhanced process automation and the redesigning of key processes can provide the opportunity to reduce, and even eliminate, some compliance risks. In addition, it can also help to shift the emphasis of control from manual detect to automated prevent controls.

4.103 Over recent years there has been a drive to develop an organisation's capability to provide greater and more timely management information to support and enhance the control framework. Recycling management information from the administration area to the front office on a real-time basis not only ensures that decisions are based on a complete and up-to-date view but also increases the likelihood of any errors or breaches being detected quickly.

4.104 The introduction of a risk function within the compliance department, responsible for identifying and monitoring compliance risk and key indicators, can provide the firm's management with a 'dashboard' to measure compliance risk and the effectiveness of the controls in place to manage those risks. These metrics can help to shift compliance risk management from being a reactive after-the-event activity to a more predictive before-the-event activity.

Action plans

4.105 Concrete steps to reduce the institution's compliance risk profile or appetite can also be taken. Both the inherent compliance risk and the current residual risk can be evaluated when the mitigation of the relevant controls, as believed by the management, is known. Action plans can be drawn up for any control which is deemed insufficient and for any residual risk which is deemed to be beyond the institution's risk appetite. The action plans will be to enhance the existing controls, add further controls and further mitigate the risks. As a minimum, the owner of the action plan, a target date for completion and a brief description of the action plan will be drawn up. Deliverables by which the plan will be judged as completed are also often included.

4.106 It is essential that action plans are followed up on a regular basis to assess progress. The failure to do so will result in the likely event of the action plan not being followed through, with the institution losing its compliance risk momentum and requiring considerably more effort when re-evaluating its risk and control assessment in the future. However, if action plans are carried through, the institution will achieve a higher compliance risk awareness coupled with a usefully lower compliance risk profile. The natural next step in this case is to re-evaluate the compliance risks and controls for the next set of action plans, thus creating a virtuous circle of compliance risk management and mitigation. With control owners identified, it will be possible to investigate likely groupings of potential control failures and their impact on compliance risk occurrences. Groupings of risk owners can also be useful in identifying clusters of risks and therefore susceptibility to risk cascade (i e the occurrence of one risk leading to a greater likelihood of the occurrence of other risks within the risk group).

External risk data

4.107 There are a number of compliance risks that occur only infrequently and therefore, by nature, are difficult to validate and verify independently. To counter the problems of data collection, the extreme values of certain risks could be derived from external loss databases. Such collections of data are useful in allowing an institution to place a value on a risk that has not happened to it (and may be extremely unlikely to happen).

4.108 The relevance of external data needs to be questioned closely so that the risk (and the loss amount derived from the external database) is appropriate to the institution. For example, a compliance breach incurred by a commercial bank may not be relevant to a retail bank and the loss may therefore need to be multiplied by a percentage reflecting the relevance of the breach to that particular firm. A loss may also require scaling for the size of the institution wishing to use the data (against the size of the institution incurring the breach). Another area of caution with regard to external data is to ensure that the institution's view of a particular breach is the same as the database provider's view.

4.109 Subject to the above, loss data from an external database should prove useful in assisting compliance management in determining more accurate values for low likelihood risks than solely relying on management's perception of the possible loss.

Measurement

4.110 The reporting of data to the compliance department is fundamental to the proper continuing analysis of compliance risk. The reporting must be both timely and accurate. Timescales that are viewed as realistic by the supplying department as well as the compliance department should be agreed. There should also be an escalation procedure to senior management of both compliance and the supplying department if data is not supplied within the timescales. This will safeguard against circumstances where the data shows unacceptable compliance risk and the supplying department wishes, for whatever reason, to withhold such data. Additionally, it is useful to have a feedback mechanism so that unusual data can be easily and rapidly questioned and amended or actioned as appropriate.

4.111 The compliance department will wish to review different data at different intervals, for example:

- daily: trading tickets;
- weekly: temporary joiners and leavers;
- monthly: permanent joiners and leavers;
- quarterly: personal registrations; and
- annually: authorised scope of the business.

4.112 It is likely that the compliance department will wish to keep data on its management of compliance risks for a number of years in order to assist on potential investigations and to demonstrate a history of risk surveying to the regulators. However, the compliance department should also recognise that some data may be regarded as sensitive by the supplying department and clear assurances must therefore be given with regard to who will be allowed access to the data and any conclusions drawn from it. An example of sensitive data would be salaries and bonuses.

Line management of compliance risk

4.113 The tools used above will lead to the enhancement of each department's compliance policies and procedures. The review of such policies and procedures from time to time by senior management assists the executive in remaining aware of the compliance programme throughout the firm. A rolling programme of review and reporting to a committee such as the audit committee or the risk management committee will enable a senior management review process to be conducted efficiently and effectively. Detailed reviews will also be carried out periodically by the compliance department, the line department involved and possibly by internal audit.

Special areas of compliance risk

4.114 There are certain special areas of compliance risk that span a number of departments or businesses. Whilst the tools described above are just as applicable to these areas, a different approach is required. It will be necessary in the design phase to gather together specialists from the various line departments and businesses involved so that a methodology can be worked out which will cover the needs of each department or business. The special areas of compliance risk include, but are not limited to:

- insider dealing;
- money laundering;
- internal and external financial crime;
- senior management responsibility;
- training and competence;
- advertising;
- compliance fatigue/forgetfulness;
- ethical creep; and
- new staff (contract, temporary and permanent).

4.115 Although the above risks are narrower in perspective than the compliance risks applicable to an entire business or department, they are also more complex and will require considerably more input from the compliance manager. The resulting procedures following the analysis will also require much wider dissemination, typically across the entire organisation. Where compliance procedures cover a number of departments it is appropriate for an executive, or more likely a committee, that covers all those departments to provide a final review and approval before full implementation.

Risk and staff competence

4.116 The FSA rules on Training and Competence have increased the scope of the training and competence regime to encompass everyone who is involved, directly or indirectly, in regulated business. High level Principle 3 requires a firm to make 'proper arrangements for any employee associated with a regulated activity carried on by the firm to achieve, maintain and enhance competence'.

4.117 In particular, the competence of senior managers appointed to take responsibility for controlled functions, is included within the scope of these rules and evidence of their benchmark competence and continuing maintenance of those competencies is required.

4.118 Regardless of where in the organisation the responsibility sits for establishing, maintaining and supervising the scheme for the training and competence arrangements, the firm should consider two sets of risks when reviewing which rules are being met:

- Outputs from the scheme, that is the competence standards being achieved, robustness of limited sign-off of individuals as competent and the ongoing maintenance of individual employee competence; and

- Inputs to the scheme, that is the monitoring and control regime within the training area that governs the robustness of the scheme.

4.119 Common problems arise from failure to monitor the inputs, and firms have incurred disciplinary action arising where failures in the inputs to training and competence have led to activity that has been linked to a failure in staff competence. By way of example in 2003 the FSA took enforcement action against the Bank of Ireland in respect of breaches of anti-money laundering requirement[1]. In part the FSA linked those failings to the Banks staff training and said:

> 'The Bank of Ireland did not … check that its staff understood fully their anti money laundering responsibilities in relation to the recognition and reporting of suspicious transactions[2].'

Examples of areas that require attention include:

- Individuals' records can be incomplete or incorrect and under weak control which undermines the entire scheme;

- Internal assessment standards are not monitored leading to very high numbers (99%) of pass rates and question banks are not updated to reflect internal and external changes; and

• Training modules are developed without business approval and trained face to face according to the individual delivering the training without any consistency check.

---

1 FSA Final Notice 31 August 2004
2 FSA Press release 077/2004 Bank of Ireland 31 August 2004

Change

4.120 Probably the most difficult area of risk arises from change. This can range from either a fundamental shift in the strategy of the business through to a comparatively small change in an IT system on which a structure of compliance risk monitoring has been built. Sometimes changes are developed and implemented without those involved appreciating that there is any need to consider compliance. To avoid the possibility of this risk, it is appropriate for the organisation's project management procedures to contain a step that requires sign-off by compliance of the change proposals regardless of the nature of the change. Periodic reviews by compliance of all change projects underway (perhaps quarterly) are desirable.

Chapter 5

Financial Services Authority rule making, principles-based rules and its regulatory tool kit

Introduction

'... But something is seriously awry when ... the Financial Services Authority that was established to provide clear guidelines and rules for the financial services sector and to protect the consumer against the fraudulent, is seen as hugely inhibiting of efficient business by perfectly respectable companies that have never defrauded anyone ...'

The Rt Hon Tony Blair PM, Speech at the Institute of Public Policy Research 'common sense culture not compensation culture,' 26 May 2005.

5.1   This statement from the Prime Minister led to the FSA's chairman Calum McCarthy demanding an explanation for the comments made and claiming that the remarks had undermined the FSA. The financial industry however has expressed concern regarding the FSA's approach to its regulatory functions and that it on occasions operates in a heavy handed manner. The Centre for Policy Studies reported in an open letter to the John Tiner in March 2005[1] that the industry fears that the FSA is an increasingly defensive and risk-averse organisation and this has contributed to a culture of prescriptive and increasingly complex regulation. The FSA's move, to a more principles based system of rules, however, in part responds to such concerns by allowing firms to determine responses to regulatory obligations appropriate to meet the individual risks and circumstances of the business they conduct. Commenting on the move towards more principles based rules, Callum McCarthy FSA Chairman on 31 October 2006 in a speech at the Financial Skills Council 2nd Annual Conference indicated that the move would create a change in the manner of the FSA's contact with regulated firms, he stated:

'... I think that the contact between FSA and regulated firms will change, both in terms of the level of contact and the content of that contact ...The level will change towards greater contact between FSA and senior management of the firm, reflecting the increased focus on the responsibilities of senior management, away from FSA: specialist compliance function contact. And the content of those discussions will also change, away from investigation of whether evidence exists to demonstrate compliance with specific rules to discussion of broader issues and of desired outcomes: in short a move away from what is normally characterised as 'box ticking' – the comfort zone for both regulator and compliance functions ...'

---

1 'The leviathan is still at large,' an open letter to John Tiner FSA, A report by the Centre for Policy Studies review team, March 2005.

5.2   In this chapter we will consider the FSA's rules and some of its main regulatory tools. To have a full appreciation of these FSA activities it is essential that we consider both the process used by the FSA to give legal effect to its rules and the basis on which regulated firms are obliged to comply with those rules. We will also consider how the FSA uses its main regulatory tools including thematic work, information gathering and the use of skilled persons in supervising the activities of those firms it regulates.

The FSA's rules

The Process of FSA rule making

5.3   The FSA is given power in s 138 of the FSMA 2000 to make rules applying to authorised persons with respect to their carrying on of both regulated activities and activities that are not regulated. The FSA does not, however, have a completely free hand in the rules it may make with regard to regulated activities. As we have seen in Chapter 3 the influence of European legislation has a major impact on the FSA's rule book often requiring the Treasury to implement into UK law, by way of FSA rules, arrangements to ensure compliance with European Directives. Indeed, the FSA's initiative to simplify its rule book might be curtailed in certain areas necessary to meet EU legislation. Although the European commission accepts that regulation imposes costs on business and this need to be justified, a great deal of prescriptive regulation appears in EU directives which curtails the extent to which the FSA might implement such provisions of EU Directives in a principles based manner. John Tiner highlights such issue in his speech at the Apcims annual conference on 13 October 2006 when he observes,

'... it is as well to recall that some features of MiFID as well as other recent measures, such as the Insurance Mediation Directive and the Consumer Protection and Co-operation Regulation still contain high levels of prescription. These measures set requirements in the fields of monitoring and enforcement, which limit supervisors? room for exercising risk-based judgement ...'

Sections 152 to 155 of the FSMA 2000 set out the statutory requirements the FSA must follow to make rules. Contravention of those rules can lead to FSA enforcement action and also give rise to a liability for damages under s 150 for authorised persons in respect of private persons who have suffered loss as a result of the contravention of the rule.

Consultation

5.4 Where the FSA proposes to make rules, whether they are new or to be modified they are required under s 155(1) of the FSMA 2000 to publish the proposed rules so that they are brought to the attention of the public. Where, however the FSA consider that a delay caused by complying with its obligations to consult in the terms described below, would be prejudicial to the interest of consumers it may not follow those requirements. In complying with this requirement the FSA typically published proposed new or modified rules in a consultation paper. The FSA publishes all consultation papers on its website and provides copies to the practitioner panel and consumer panel (see Chapter 2). The FSA may under s 155(12) charge a fee for providing a copy of its proposed rules.

FSA consultation papers are also designed to comply with s 155(2) which requires that the draft rules are accompanied by:

- A cost benefit analysis[1]. This is described as an estimate of the costs together with the benefits that will arise if the proposed rules are made. Where, however, having made a comparison between the overall position before and after the rules having been made the FSA considers there will be no increase in cost or an increase of only minimal significance, no cost benefit is required.

- An explanation of the proposed rules.

- An explanation of the FSA's reasons for believing that making the proposed rule is compatible with its general duties in s 2 of the FSMA 2000.

- Notice of the specified time within which representations about the proposed new rules must be made to the FSA.

1 A statement of expected expenditure rather than a cost benefit analysis is required for proposed rules relating to the legal assistance scheme under the FSMA 2000, s 136(2), levies to fund the financial compensation scheme

under FSMA 2000, s 213(4), industry funding of the Ombudsman scheme under the FSMA 2000, s 234 and fees to fund the FSA under FSMA 2000, Sch 1, para 17. See FSMA 2000, s 155(3).

Considering representations and making new rules

5.5   Representations in response to the FSA consultation are submitted and collected, although each consultation will attract different types and levels of interest, usually responses will be received from the FSA panels, relevant trade associations, regulated firms and other interested groups and individuals which the FSA is obliged to have regard to under s 155(4) of the FSMA 2000 before they may make any proposed rule.

FSA rules made under this section are referred to in the Act as the FSA's general rules. Pursuant to para 1(2) of Sch 1 to the FSMA 2000 the FSA role in rule making is known as its legislative function. The FSA's legislative function must be performed by the FSA governing body (its board) and thus all FSA new rules, rule amendments or revocations must be approved by the FSA board. FSA rules must be made by written instrument. Pursuant to s 152(1) of the FSMA 2000 a copy of all new rules must be given to HM Treasury without delay. HM Treasury must be given written notification without delay of any alteration to or revocation of rules[1].

1 FSMA 2000, s 152(2).

Communicating the new rules

5.6   Under s 153(4) of the FSMA 2000, the FSA must publish its rules so as to bring them to the attention of the public. The FSA communicates all new rules in policy statements, as well as in its handbook of rules and in a monthly handbook development publication. Each of these is published on the FSA website. Under s 153(5) of the FSMA 2000, the FSA may charge a fee for providing a person with a copy of a rule making instrument.

Under s 155(5) of the FSMA 2000, an account in general terms of the representations made together with the FSA response to them must be published by the FSA and where the new rules in the FSA's opinion differ significantly from the draft published in the consultation paper then the FSA is required under s 155(6) of the FSMA 2000 to publish not only the responses to the representations but also details of the differences as well as a further cost benefit analysis.

New rule implementation

5.7   The FSA's consultation will typically set out a proposed implementation timetable. Many new FSA rules will include a proposed implementation date and a transitional period during which firms might take advantage of time to establish arrangements to implement organisational changes to comply with the new rule.

FSA Rules

5.8 The FSA rule making is in the main specified by provisions in the FSMA 2000. Section 138 of the FSMA 2000 gives the FSA general rule-making powers and ss 144–147 set out certain specific rule-making obligations. Set out below are some of the key areas of FSA rule-making obligations together with an overview of the structure of the FSA handbook.

General rules

Prudential Supervision

5.9 The viability of many firms will be determined by the financial resources of the firm and how those financial resources are managed. The firm's financial viability at a very fundamental level will be impacted by its ability to meet commercial liabilities when they fall due as well as its actual or contingent client liabilities. The extent by which a firm's viability will be affected by its financial resources will in part be determined by the type of business they conduct. Businesses at higher risk are banks and securities firms where the viability of their business will affect the financial stability of the economy as well as confidence in the financial services market.

Paragraph 4 of Sch 6 to the FSMA 2000 and FSA rule Cond 2.4.1D, known as Threshold condition 4 requires that for a firm to remain authorised its resources must, in the opinion of the FSA, be adequate in relation to the regulated activities that it seeks to carry on, or carries on. This requirement covers both financial and non-financial resources as well as how its resources are managed. In assessing the adequacy of resources the FSA may take into account whether the firm is a member of a group and if so the impact that membership will have as well as having regard for the provisions made for future or contingent liabilities. When assessing this condition the FSA will also have regard to any person that may have a relevant relationship or close links with the firm, the extent to which that person may have any influence over the firm and whether this may have an impact on the firm's resources.

Conduct of business rules

5.10 Section 138 of the FSMA 2000 provides that the FSA may make such rules applying to authorised persons with respect to the carrying on of regulated activities and the carrying on of activities that are not regulated as it appears necessary or expedient for the purpose of protecting the interest of consumers. Although not solely attending to the requirement in s 138, the FSA Conduct of Business rules set out obligations for firms when dealing with their customers.

Client money

5.11   Section 139 of the FSMA 2000 allows the FSA to make rules specifically dealing with the segregation and handling by firms of client money. Such rules are primarily designed to ensure that client money does not become merged with the firm's own money and, in the event of the firm's insolvency, client money can be identified and distributed back to clients without any prior claim by creditors of the firm. The FSA client money rules are contained in its handbook CAS.

Specific rules

Financial promotions

5.12   The Act sets out a general prohibition in s 21 restricting the issue of financial promotions to authorised persons (see Chapter 9). Section 145 of the FSMA 2000 provides that the FSA may make rules applying to authorised person's communication, invitation and inducements to engage in investment activity or participate in a collective investment scheme. The Rule made by the FSA may in particular make provision about the form and content of the communications. The FSA financial promotion rules are specifically contained in its conduct of business handbook as well as the specialist insurance and mortgage business conduct of business handbooks.

Chinese Walls

5.13   Section 147 of the FSMA 2000 allows the FSA to make rules about the control and use of information held by authorised persons. Such rules, referred to as control of information rules, provide:

* require the withholding of information which a person A would otherwise have to disclose to a person B for or with whom A does business in the course of carrying on any regulated or other activity;

* specify circumstances in which A may withhold information which he would otherwise have to disclose to B;

- require A not to use for the benefit of B information A holds which A would otherwise have to use in that way; and

- specify circumstances in which A may decide not to use for the benefit of B information A holds which A would otherwise have to use in that way.

Rules in COB 2.4 and 7.1 set out requirements for compliance with managing conflicts of interest and the maintenance of Chinese Walls, compliance with which will not expose the firm to an allegation of conflicts of interest misconduct.

Approved Person Code

5.14 A statement of principle dealing with the conduct expected of approved persons may be issued by the FSA under s 64 of the FSMA 2000. Any statement of principle must also be supported by a code of practice designed to help approved persons determine whether or not their conduct complies with the statement of principle. The FSA's code of conduct for Approved Persons is set out in its sourcebook referred to as the Statement of Principles and Code of Practice for Approved Persons (APER). Section 64(7) of the FSMA 2000 provides that the code may be relied on to establish whether or not conduct complies with a statement of principle. Under s 64(3) of the FSMA 2000, the code of practice is to specify:

- descriptions of conduct which, in the opinion of the FSA, comply with a statement of principle;

- descriptions of conduct which, in the opinion of the FSA, do not comply with a statement of principle; and

- factors which, in the opinion of the FSA, are to be taken into account in determining whether or not a person's conduct complies with a statement of principle.

Code of Market Conduct

5.15 The FSA is required under s 119 of the FSMA 2000 to issue a code containing such provisions as it considers will give appropriate guidance to those determining whether or not behaviour amounts to market abuse. The code is required to specify:

- descriptions of behaviour that, in the opinion of the FSA, amount to market abuse;

- descriptions of behaviour that, in the opinion of the FSA, do not amount to market abuse; and

- factors that, in the opinion of the FSA, are to be taken into account in determining whether or not behaviour amounts to market abuse.

Structure of the FSA rules

5.16   The FSA rules (commonly referred to as the FSA Handbook) are split into 43 parts (each part referred to as sourcebooks). The 43 sourcebooks are ordered under 10 topic headings being:

1.   The Glossary. This sets out the definition of key terms used in the Handbook.

2.   High Level Standards, including its high level principles, rules on senior management systems and controls, statement of principle and code of practice for approved persons.

3.   Prudential Standards, including the prudential sourcebooks for each of the businesses regulated by the FSA.

4.   Business Standards, including the conduct of business rules for investment, insurance and mortgage business, client money and asset rules, code of market conduct.

5.   Regulatory Processes, including the FSA authorisation, supervision, enforcement and decision-making rules.

6.   Redress, including complaint handling rules, rules relating to the Financial Services Compensation Scheme and complaints against the FSA.

7.   Specialist Sourcebooks, including rules for collective investment schemes, electronic money, Lloyd's, professional firms and recognised investment exchanges and clearing houses.

8.   Listing, Prospectus and Disclosure rule.

9.   Handbook Guides. Specialist guides for businesses such as energy and oil market participants, service companies and smaller intermediaries.

10.   Regulatory Guides. Guidance on collective investment schemes and the FSA role in policing unauthorised investment business activity.

Individual guidance

5.17   The FSA has power under s 157 of the FSMA 2000 to provide guidance in the form of information or advice relating to a wide range of matters including the operation of the FSMA 2000, any of the rules made under the Act and the FSA's functions. Section 157 provides that the guidance can be addressed to persons generally, regulated persons generally or a class of regulated persons (which is known as general guidance) or individual regulated persons. Where the FSA intends to provide general guidance it must consult on the proposed guidance complying with the same procedure as applies to proposed rules as in para **5.4**. Where the FSA provides general guidance it must provide a copy of that guidance to the Treasury.

From time to time, firms will require guidance on the interpretation or application of the FSA's rules or provisions of the FSMA 2000. Opportunities to obtain informal advice from the FSA have been significantly reduced in the FSA's drive to ensure consistent interpretation and application of its rules amongst the categories of firms it regulates. In fact the FSA does not encourage the routine publication of individual guidance to firms, which it considers would drive relationships between the FSA and firms in the direction of legalism and formalism[1]. Senior management will often experience a sense of frustration when seeking informal advice they are told that it is the firm's own responsibility to interpret FSA rules and decide how they apply to the firm's business. In these circumstances firms will often be told that they should obtain independent legal advice. Firms may, however, apply to the FSA for individual guidance under arrangements made in SUP 9. A firm should address requests for individual guidance to its usual supervisory contact at the FSA. Although the request may be made orally, the FSA will expect the details of complex or significant issues to be addressed in writing[2]. Firms need to expect that their request for guidance contains sufficient information and allows adequate time to allow the request to be properly evaluated. Firms need to appreciate that the FSA may request further information to allow the guidance to be considered or where the firm has not provided adequate information with its application. If a request is time-critical, the firm should make this clear. The FSA specifies in SUP 9.2.6G that when making a request for guidance a firm should identify the rule, general guidance, or other matter on which individual guidance is sought, and provide a description of the circumstances relating to the request. In the majority of circumstances, firms obtaining individual guidance will want to be able to rely on the guidance to demonstrate compliance with the rule in question. The extent to which a firm can rely on individual guidance given will depend on factors such as the degree of formality of the original query, the guidance given, and whether all relevant information was submitted with the request. It seems sensible, therefore, that firms deal with requests for individual guidance in a formal manner, ensuring therefore that full particulars of the issue requiring guidance together with all relevant supporting material is supplied and that the FSA's guidance is obtained in writing.

---

1 FSA Policy Statement, FSA's approach to giving guidance and waivers to firms, September 1999.

2 SUP 9.2.1G.

Rule waivers

5.18 The FSA may grant to firms, in appropriate circumstances, a direction that modifies or waives the following rules:

- Auditors and actuarial rules[1].

- Control of information rules[2].

- Financial promotion rules[3].

- General rules[4].

- Insurance business rules[5].

- Money laundering rules[6].

- Price stabilisation rules[7].

- Authorised Unit Trust Scheme rules[8].

- E-money issuers[9].

1 FSMA 2000, s 340.
2 FSMA 2000, s 147.
3 FSMA 2000, s 145.
4 FSMA 2000, s 138.
5 FSMA 2000, s 141.
6 FSMA 2000, s 146.
7 FSMA 2000, s 144.
8 FSMA 2000, ss 247–248, derived from s 250.
9 Financial Services and Markets Regulated Activities Order 2001, SI 2001/544, arts 9, 9G(1), 9H(1).

5.19 The FSA's ability to grant rule waivers and modifications is set out in s 148 of the FSMA 2000[1]. In that section rule waiver and modifications are referred to as directions. To make an application for a rule waiver, firms must follow the process set out in Chapter 8 Supervision rules (SUP8)[2]. It is sensible for firms, before formally submitting an application, to discuss with their FSA supervision team, the reasoning behind the application and the exact waiver required. The FSA also encourage firms to take independent professional advice about the basis of the waiver being sought. The FSA state a preference for the application being made by e-mail and also specify that a standard waiver application form be completed and submitted[3].

1 FSMA 2000, s 250 makes similar provision in respect of collective investment schemes and s 294 in relation to recognised investment exchanges and clearing houses.
2 FSA Policy Statement, FSA's approach to giving guidance and waivers to firms, September 1999.
3 Waiver application is available in the other publication section of the FSA website.

5.20 The FSA aims to respond to all applications within 20 business days, and where it expects that the application will take longer than this to deal with it will notify the applicant firm of the anticipated turnaround time. The exact time to deal with the application will be dependent on the extent and nature of the waiver and any further information the FSA requires to deal with the application. The firm should deal with any requests for further information as promptly and fully as possible if they wish the application to proceed without delay. Any inadequate replies to requests for further information will most likely give rise to further questions. In fact, the FSA will treat the application as having been withdrawn if they do not receive a response to their further questions within 20 business days. The processing of waiver applications is overseen by a committee of FSA staff, which operates so as to ensure that its decisions on individual applications are made promptly and that decisions are made within established precedents and policies so as to ensure that they may determine applications with substantially common characteristics in a consistent way. The FSA may make the direction subject to conditions.

Section 148 of the FSMA 2000 and SUP 8.3.1G require that before granting an application the FSA must be satisfied that the rule for which a waiver or modification is required would be unduly burdensome on the authorised firm or would not achieve the purpose for which the rules were made and the waiver would not result in undue risk to persons whose interests the rules are intended to protect. In the firm's waiver application, it must address for the FSA why it considers each of these requirements will be met as well as whether it has taken into account any previous published waivers and precedents they may have created. In addition at SUP 8.3.1A G. the FSA will also consider whether the waiver will be compatible with European law.

5.21   FSMA 2000, s 148 provides that once the FSA has determined to grant a waiver it shall publish details of the waiver (which is referred to in the Act as a direction) it so that it is brought to the attention of those likely to be affected by it, and others who may be likely to make an application for a similar direction. The FSA publishes on its website at www.fsa.gov.uk/Pages/Library/Other_publications/Waivers/index.shtml, a consolidated list of details of directions that it has made. Also, details of directions granted to individual firms are published against the firm's records on the FSA's registry.

Pursuant to FSMA 2000, s 148(7), the FSA need not, however, publish the direction where it is satisfied that it is inappropriate or unnecessary to do so taking into account whether:

●   the direction relates to rules the contravention of which would give rise to an action for damages under s 150 of the FSMA 2000;

●   the publication would prejudice to an unreasonable degree the commercial interest of the firm that applied for the direction or any person within the firm's immediate group; or

●   the publication would be contrary to an international obligation of the United Kingdom.

5.22 It is important for firms to ensure they understand the terms of the FSA waiver, both in terms of its detailed provisions and the dates within which it might apply. Firms will have to modify their own systems and controls to ensure that they are able to comply with the waiver. Furthermore a failure to comply with terms of the direction could lead to FSA enforcement action based on the terms of the direction and indeed expose the firm to an action for damages under s 150 based on the modified or conditional terms. Firms also need to ensure that the applicability of the waiver and the basis of the original application are both kept under review. If circumstances arise which could affect the continued relevance of the waiver they must notify the FSA under SUP 8.5.1R of those circumstances.

Rulebook interpretation

5.23 Each of the provisions of the FSA Handbook carry designations to assist in the interpretation of the provision or to show that the provision has a certain legal effect[1].

Interpretation of provisions of the FSA Handbook should be undertaken in the light of its purpose of the provision on question[2]. The purpose of any provision is first to be gathered from the text of the provision in question as well as its context among other relevant provisions. Rules in the Handbook, that is provisions that have a binding effect on relevant authorised persons, approved persons or listed securities, are designated by the letter R. Most of the rules in the Handbook create binding obligations and a contravention of them by the firm is open to enforcement action and in certain circumstances action for damages s 150 of the FSMA 2000 might arise. The high level principles have the same legal effect as rules although no action for damages arises from a breach of them, See prin 3.4.4R. To assist in understanding the purpose of an individual rule, guidance is often given. This will be designated with the letter G following the relevant provision. The FSA states that although any such guidance may assist the reader in assessing the purpose of the provision; it should not be taken as a complete or definitive explanation of a provision's purpose.

Certain provisions of the FSA Handbook are designated as evidential provisions and are identified with the letter E in the margin or heading. Evidential provisions are those with the characteristics specified in s 149 of the FSMA 2000, that is contravention of the provision may be relied on as tending to establish contravention of such other rule as may be specified; or that compliance may be relied on as tending to establish compliance with such other rule as may be specified. An evidential provision may be relied on as tending to establish compliance with the rule to which it relates. And when it says so, contravention of an evidential provision may be relied on as tending to establish contravention of the rule to which it relates.

Evidential provisions are also applied in relation to the Code of Practice for Approved Persons made under s 64 of the FSMA 2000 and the Code of Market Conduct made under s 119 of the FSMA 2000. Once again in relation to these codes evidential provisions may be relied upon to establish whether or not the conduct of an approved person complies with the relevant provision of the code in question. The letter C is also used[3] in the Code of Market Conduct to specify conclusive descriptions of behaviour that, in the opinion of the FSA, do not amount to market abuse.

The letter D is used to indicate directions and requirements given under various powers conferred by the FSMA 2000. Directions and requirements are binding upon the persons to whom they are addressed.

The letter P is used to indicate the Statements of Principle for approved persons[4] and as such are binding on approved persons.

---

1 For an overview of the designation given to provisions of the Handbook see FSA Readers Guide Instrument, 21 June 2001
2 GEN 2.2.1R.
3 FSMA 2000, s 119(2)(b).
4 FSMA 2000, s 64.

Principles based rules and Handbook simplification

5.24   The FSA's approach of using its rulebook as a set of principles based rules, where overarching principles set standards of behaviour within the context of the purpose behind the principle, allows the FSA as rulemaker and the regulated sector to concentrate on the spirit of the regulation rather than focusing on the detail of a prescriptive rule. Criticism of detailed rules suggests that they allow for the structuring of a firm's business arrangements so as to meet the literal requirements of the rules ignoring the intent or spirit of the standards being sought. By way of example, the US Financial Accounting Standards Board has taken steps to move towards a more principles based system of accounting standards following the collapse of Enron and other accounting irregularities. Commentators in the US have argued that detailed guidelines offer an incentive for clever companies to find a loophole. Enron had claimed that it followed FASB rules in the structuring of many of its off-balance-sheet activities, despite these being used to disguise the company's true financial standing. A principles based system of regulation does, however, present a series of challenges for both those wishing to interpret regulatory requirements and those wishing to determine whether a firm's behaviour has been compliant with the regulatory requirement. The FSA provides some guidance in ENF 11.7G on the application of the objective standard to take reasonable care. Following the example of Principle 3 which requires a firm to take 'reasonable care' to organise and control its affairs responsibly and effectively, with adequate risk management systems, the FSA states that in determining whether a firm has taken reasonable care, the FSA will consider all the circumstances of the case and take the following matters into account:

(1)   what information the firm knew at the time of the behaviour, and what information they ought to have known in all the circumstances;

(2)   what steps the firm took to comply with the rule, and what steps they ought to have taken in all the circumstances; and

(3)   the standards of the regulatory system that applied at the time of the behaviour.

5.25   The generality of the wording of principles based rules often uses provides scope for the standards of behaviour to gradually increases over time, but equally it can create a situation where issues of the past are reviewed with today's regulatory standards. This problem was of concern to the Financial Services and Market Tribunal in the matter of *Legal and General v Financial Services Authority*[1]. In the case the Tribunal had to determine standards of behaviour derived from broad requirements of 'best endeavours', 'due skill care and diligence' and the obligation to establish procedures directed at all the 'Rules and Principles' required for the selling of endowment policies at the relevant time. The Tribunal was concerned with the situation where standards changed over the course of the relevant period and ensure that the standards it applied were not those necessarily considered acceptable in 2005. It concluded that there was not a problem when a firm is being judged against an objectively measured standard or where there is explicit guidance indicating in reasonable detail what should or should not be done, but where no such detail was provided, evidence would be required to show standard practice in the industry at the relevant time. The Tribunal made clear in its written decision, that judging a past problem with today's standards was not appropriate, stating:

'... it is common ground that L&G have to be judged against the compliance standards as they applied in the Relevant Period. The fact that procedures are changed and improved as they were in the latter part of 1999 does not mean that prior conduct was necessarily inappropriate or in breach of the rules ...'

More principles based rules also provide regulated firms with the positive opportunity of shaping their response to the obligation contained in the rule in a manner that better suits their business model. This might result in a more complex approach to maintaining compliance than another firm dealing with the same rule requirement or in appropriate circumstances, a less complex approach. When one begins to appreciate the FSA's current rules, however, it is apparent that it is currently, a hybrid of high-level principles and detailed rules and guidance. Some sections are drafted in a more principles based manner, for example the Systems and controls Sourcebook's main provision at SYSC

3.1.1R allows firms the latitude to develop a system and controls response that is appropriate for their business. It states: 'A firm must take reasonable care to establish and maintain such systems and controls as are appropriate to its business.'

Conversely and by way of example, the FSA's client money rules in CASS 4.3.3R contain very specific obligations on the segregation of client money from firms' own money. For example it provides: 'A firm must, except to the extent permitted by the client money rules hold client money separate from the firm's money.'

---

1 (18 January 2005, unreferenced case number 11).

5.26   The cost of conducting investment business in the United Kingdom is greatly increased by firms' obligation to meet regulatory responsibility. In 2005 the FSA conducted a study into the cost of regulation. The key results of that study were released in June 2006 in the FSA publication 'the FSA's better Regulation Action Plan: Progress Report'. That report set out that in general it is understood that the impact and cost is more serious for small firms which have to contend with obligations that rarely distinguish between small and large firms, despite the limited resource that smaller firms have available as well as less complex business structures that do not inherently require complex systems and controls. Firms also find the technical resource to monitor and advise on compliance requirement is increased by the complexity and volume of the FSA rules themselves. The size of the FSA rulebook is partly a historical feature of the FSA having brought together the regulatory regimes of nine different regulatory organisations. However, any regime attempting to regulate so many diverse firms, investment businesses and consumer types will inevitably lead to differing rules of specificity, many attempting to deal with what is essentially the same business risk. This has led to a rulebook with significant areas of duplication and in this regard the financial services industry complains about the cost and impact of regulation on doing business in the UK.

Since 2004 the UK government has supported major initiative supporting deregulation and rule simplification. A series of government supported reviews as well as policy development put forward during the UK Presidency of the EU during 2005 have encouraged UK regulators including the FSA as well as the EU Commission to take a risk-based approach to their regulatory activities and only regulated where necessary.

The Hampton review commissioned by the Chancellor of the Exchequer in 2004 examined business-regulator interactions with certain regulators that have an enforcement function. The review report: 'Reducing administrative burdens: effective inspection and enforcement'[1] was published in March 2005 and set out a series of recommendations to improve the efficiency and reduce the adminis-trative burden of regulation. In addition, the UK government has undertaken a programme to deliver better regulation using the pre-2005 budget statement to build on changes made to strengthen systems of regulatory scrutiny and accountability by announcing a variety of measures to reform the ways in which regulations are made and enforced. Although a number of the Government's initiatives relate to government departments and agencies, the programme of reform has had an impact on the FSA's regulatory framework.

---

1 HM Treasury, Philip Hamilton, March 2005 (Crown Copyright).

Regulatory Reform Order

5.27   Section 1 of the Regulatory Reform Act 2001 gives ministers of the UK government the power by order (known as regulatory reform orders) to reform legislation which 'has the effect of imposing burdens affecting persons in the carrying on of any activity'. HM Treasury launched a consultation on 5 December 2005 entitled 'Regulatory Reform Order: on proposed changes to the Financial Services and Markets Act 2000' which is designed to provide for better-targeted and more risk-based regulation, and the removal of unnecessary or disproportionate consultation by the FSA on industry and will also enable the FSA to deregulate more freely by issuing a wider range of waivers and rule modifications. The proposals will be contained in a regulatory reform Order and are expected to come into force in around January 2007.

Legislative and Regulatory Reform Act 2006

5.28   The Legislative and Regulatory Reform Act 2000 received Royal Assent on 8 November 2006. It comes into force from 8 January 2007 and its provisions will be used to help deliver the Government's Better Regulation agenda. When introducing the Bill into Parliament the Government's aim was to make it quicker and easier to tackle unnecessary or over-complicated regulation and help bring about a risk-based approach to regulation. The 2006 Act will achieve this primarily by creating a wider law reform power than that in the Regulatory Reform Act 2001. In particular the 2006 Act requires regulators to have regard to the Better Regulation Commission's principles of good regulation.

Commenting on the new Act, William Sargent, Executive Chair of the Better Regulation Executive said:

'This Act allows out-of-date or unnecessary legislation to be removed more quickly and efficiently. It is a tremendous step forward which will allow us to reap the benefits of the simplification proposals which departments have identified. It is part of fulfilling the Government's commitment to deliver on what is the most ambitious better regulation agenda in the world.'

The Better Regulation Commission

5.29 The government announced in its 2005 Budget the establishment of a Better Regulation Commission (BRC) to take over the role of its Better Regulation Task Force to provide independent advice to government, from business and other external stakeholders, about new regulatory proposals and about the government's overall regulatory performance. The Commission terms of reference are:

'To advise the government on action to:

- reduce unnecessary regulatory and administrative burdens; and
- ensure that regulation and its enforcement are proportionate, accountable, consistent, transparent and targeted' .

The task force had established five principles of good regulation designed to embed a risk-based and proportionate approach to better regulation and encouraging effective enforcement. The five principles are:

- Proportionate: Regulators should only intervene when necessary. Remedies should be appropriate to the risk posed, and costs identified and minimised.
- Accountable: Regulators must be able to justify decisions, and be subject to public scrutiny.
- Consistent: Government rules and standards must be joined up and implemented fairly.
- Transparent: Regulators should be open, and keep regulations simple and user friendly.
- Targeted: Regulation should be focused on the problem, and minimise side effects.

Simplification by FSA

5.30 In its annual report for 2005/06 the FSA outlined an objective to simplify its rulebook. In part to make its rules more understandable for regulated businesses and secondly to allow its rules to be more flexible by removing detail and moving towards a more principled based system of regulation. The business plan set out three criteria for identifying where changes to the Handbook should be made. First where requirements in the rules are more restrictive than is needed for the FSA to achieve its statutory objectives, second, where the provisions do not deliver benefits to justify their costs; or thirdly where the provisions are not consistent with the FSA's focus on senior management responsibility.

The FSA began the process of consulting on its Handbook simplification in July 2005 with the publication of CP05/10 reviewing the FSA Handbook. In which it stated that its rulebook should reflect its visions and values, which include an approach to rule-making based as far as possible on high-level; a focus on senior management; and acting in a proportionate and risk-based way. Following concerns expressed by the financial services industry about the desirability of rulebook reform at the same time as the industry has to cope with an extensive European agenda of regulatory reform, the FSA used the consultation paper to publish a set of principles[1] to guide their work of handbook review and rule drafting. The following two principles give an insight into the FSA's approach:

- Principle 1 focusing on making changes in areas where we can have real impact and only respond to suggestions to make changes to individual Handbook provisions where the benefits are clear;
- Principle 3 adopting high-level standards where these are more appropriate than detailed rules. Benefits arise from focusing our attention on senior management responsibilities and allowing firms greater flexibility in some areas.

In that paper the FSA also said that it would bear in mind the need to:

- avoid significantly changing rules and guidance that have only recently been introduced and be sensitive to areas already undergoing significant regulatory change;
- avoid focusing on the length of the Handbook alone. We will look to shorten the Handbook only where this does not make it difficult to understand or navigate.

In December 2005 the FSA released a document entitled 'Better regulation Action Plan: What we have done and what we are doing'. In the foreword to the document John Tiner described the FSA rulebook simplification initiative in the following manner:

> '... Currently, our approach to regulation is a hybrid of high-level principles and detailed rules and guidance. While this broad structure is both necessary and desirable, we aim where we can to change the balance significantly towards a more principles-based approach. We believe this can produce better outcomes for both consumers and the financial services industry by encouraging a focus on how best to act

in a particular situation, rather than simply following a mechanistic
process. The shift towards a more principles-based approach will
take time to implement, as much care will be needed to ensure that
we retain rules which clearly add value in maintaining efficient,
orderly and fair markets or helping consumers secure a fair deal ...'

The better regulation action plan set out a variety of ways for the FSA to
improve its risk-based approach to regulation, making the FSA easier to do
business with and for the FSA to become more principles based. The plan set
out the FSA commitment to simplify and consolidate its rulebook by adopting
principles-based rules wherever possible.

In its business plan for 2006/07 the FSA sets out its continuing plan for rulebook
simplification, however, it remains to be seen whether the FSA programme will
ultimately have the effect desired by the FSA and the government. Its first
published simplified rules were those contained in Policy Statement 06/01
relating to anti-money laundering where the FSA has with effect from 31 March
2006 removed the money laundering sourcebook, replacing it with high level
anti-money laundering systems and controls requiring firms to manage money
laundering risk. See Chapter 11 on Senior Management Systems and Controls.
Although these new rules have created more generally drafted principles there
remain specific requirements and thus it seems that for the time being the FSA
rules will continue to be a hybrid of high level principles and specific requirements. Financial service and markets and products are complex, and firms with
reputations to protect will want to ensure that the arrangements they have in
place to ensure compliance will be sufficiently robust to ensure that regulatory
failure does not take place and that they do not come into conflict with their FSA
supervision team. Rules that introduce principles allowing firms to design
systems to meet the complexity and size of the firm's own business, will
necessitate firms to undertake business related risk assessments to demonstrate
that their systems are well thought out, defined and appropriate. In time the FSA
may experience a rise in the number of requests for individual guidance. There
is a linkage, moreover, between high level or simplified rules and a risk-based
system of regulation that does not invoke a zero failure regime.

There is, however, concern about the extent to which consumers and government, following the next financial failure accept a policy of risk-based regulation. Anthony Hilton in his Evening Standard City comment, 2 December 2005,
following the publication of the FSA's Better Regulation Action Plan com-
mented:

'... risk-based regulation inevitably means that some day the risk
will be misjudged and an accident will happen. Will MPs at West-
minster remember their calls for a lighter touch then or will the
relevant Select Committee of the future once again unjustly berate
the hapless regulator for being "asleep at the wheel"?...'[3]

The FSA is, however, keen to overcome such concern and establish an understanding both within the FSA and externally supporting the introduction of efficiency, productivity, no having over elaborate processes and taking risk. In an Evening Standard article 'The referee who wants fewer rules' on 1 November 2006, it was reported that John Tiner professes to being more interested in outcomes than in regulation and procedures, and that he wants to work with the industry and not against it. In particular the article highlights Tiner's determination to govern through the application of high-level principles, rather than a detailed and crippling expensive to apply rulebook.

The Financial Services Practitioners Panel in its Annual report for 2005/06 raised concern about the level of guidance that will be provided by the FSA to support compliance with principles based rules under the new regime. In the FSA business plan for 2006/07, it committed to research the extent to which it might be possible for financial firms to rely on industry drafted guidance to solve problems and define acceptable standards of behaviour. In November 2006 the FSA published Discussion Paper 06/05 'FSA Confirmation of Industry Guidance', setting out its plans to encourage the greater use of industry guidance. The paper makes clear that industry guidance will supplement FSA rules rather than replace them, and sets out a process and standard for industry guidance to be recognised by the FSA. Interestingly the paper proposes that that the FSA will not take action against a firm which has complied with recognised guidance covering the issue concerned. Whilst such plans, if introduced, will have the effect of allowing the FSA to focus its supervisory attention on the outcomes of regulation, rather than the detailed processes of compliance, it remains to be seen whether it will only serve to shift the detail of the FSA's scrutiny away from the detail of its own rule book to the extensive scrutiny of the appropriateness of specific industry guidance.

---

1 CP05/10, para 1.12.
2 John Tiner Chief Executive, Financial Services Authority Foreword to Better Regulation Action Plan, December 2005.
3 City Comment, Lighter touch on regulation needs all-round support, Anthony Hilton, Evening Standard Newspaper, 2 December 2005.

Supervision and regulatory tools

5.31 Paragraph 6(1) of Sch 1 to the FSMA 2000 requires the FSA to maintain arrangements designed to enable it to determine whether persons on whom requirements are imposed by or under the Act are complying with them. Whilst the design of the FSA's approach to supervision is shaped by its need to meet the statutory objectives, the FSA is also required to have regard to the principles of good regulation set out in s 2(3) of the FSMA 2000. The FSA states in SUP 1.1.4G that its regulatory approach aims to focus and reinforce the responsibility of the management to ensure that it takes reasonable care to organise and control the affairs of the firm's responsibly. In designing its approach to supervision the FSA has regard to the principle that a burden or restriction which is imposed on a firm should be proportionate to the benefits which are expected to result from the imposition of that burden or restriction. In part to avoid defensive regulation and fearful of legal defences from firms subject to supervision the FSA, its officers and employees receive statutory protection from damages claims under para 19 of Sch 1 to the FSMA 2000, the FSA, its members, staff and officers have statutory immunity from a liability in damages for anything done or omitted in the discharge or purported discharge of the FSA's functions (but see the tort of misfeasance in public office)[1].

The FSA's approach to supervision is also shaped by a number of international drivers including the principles of good regulation agreed at regulatory forums such as BASLE and IOSCO as well as international co-operation designed to create more efficient supervision of global investment business. The Basle Core Principles are intended to serve as a basic reference for banking regulators and other public authorities in all countries[2]. The Basle Core Principles comprise 25 basic principles that need to be in place for a supervisory system to be effective. The principles relate to:

● Preconditions for effective banking supervision – Principle 1.

● Licensing and structure – Principles 2 to 5.

● Prudential regulations and requirements – Principles 6 to 15.

● Methods of ongoing banking supervision – Principles 16 to 20.

● Information requirements – Principle 21.

● Formal powers of supervisors – Principle 22.

● Cross-border banking – Principles 23 to 25.

At para 22 the core principles address the formal powers of banking supervisors and stress that an effective banking supervisor must have at its disposal adequate supervisory measures to enable it to bring about timely corrective action either when a bank fails to meet prudential requirements, when it violates regulations, or where depositors are put at risk. An essential element of regulators supervisory powers in the core principles will allow the supervisor in extreme circumstances, the ability to revoke or recommend the revocation of the banking licence. See Chapter 5.

---

1 In relation to misfeasance in public office see the *Three Rivers* case and other legal authority.
2 Core principles for effective banking supervision, Basle committee on banking supervision, Basle September 1997.

The FSA's Regulatory Toolkit

5.32   The diversity of the FSA's objectives means that it needs to have a wider range of regulatory tools than previous regulators. Some of the tools at the

FSA's disposal are provided by provisions in the FSMA 2000 and others are set out in its supervision manual 'SUP'. Broadly, the FSA's tools can be grouped into two categories. First those intended to apply to groups at large, such as consumers, types of firms or the entire financial services industry; second, tools intended to monitor and affect the conduct of individual firms or approved persons. The FSA deploys a variety of tools to support its supervision and regulation of firms and the financial market. The FSA classifies these tools under four headings1:

- diagnostic: designed to identify, assess and measure risks;

- monitoring: to track the development of identified risks, wherever these arise;

- preventative: to limit or reduce identified risks and so prevent them crystallising or increasing; and

- remedial: to respond to risks when they have crystallised.

We have considered in Chapter 4 the FSA's risk-based approach to regulation and supervision and the tools it uses during its individual firm risk mitigation programme. In this part of the chapter we will consider other main preventative and remedial tools used by the FSA to effectively supervise regulated businesses.

---

1 SUP 1.4.2G.

Regulatory themes

5.33   The FSA complements its regulatory activities work on regulated businesses with thematic work. Its thematic activities often span many firms as well as different sectors of the financial services marketplace. Since introducing its regulatory tools in 2000 the FSA has shifted its balance towards thematic regulation and each year the FSA Board agrees new themes responding to identified and emerging risks. Where possible, details of planned thematic work are published in the FSA's annual plan and budget. This provides a useful clue to firms on what thematic work they may become involved in and potential regulatory activity that will affect how their business is conducted in future. Although we do not have space in this book to undertake a detailed analysis of each of these themes, a number of areas of thematic work has had a significant impact on both the FSA's resources and the financial services industry. The most significant thematic work that impacts the operation of every firm is the work the FSA is doing under the heading of Treating Customers Fairly. We shall now consider this area of the FSA's work and its impact on firms.

Treating Customers Fairly

5.34   The FSA's Treating Customers Fairly initiative (TCF) was first introduced by the FSA in its publication 'A new regulator for a new millennium'[1]
and has resulted in a year on year running thematic programme encouraging
firms to embed into their businesses responses for ensuring that customers
interests are regarded and they receive fair treatment. Since 2001 the FSA has
carried out both research and a series of theme visits to evaluate how firms treat
their customers. Subsequent FSA publications have provided firm's senior
management with guidance on how they should co-ordinate their internal TCF
initiatives as well as matters that have caused FSA concern. There remains,
however, no single and precise definition of the phrase 'Treating Customers
Fairly.' The FSA has sought to avoid providing an exact definition of the phrase
but rather to challenge firms and their senior management to consider how they
treat their customers and how they can ensure the fair treatment of customers
continuously throughout the operation of the firm's business as well as implementing behavioural change, through training and motivating staff, to ensure
that the firm's culture reflects the fair treatment of customers. TCF is as much
about staff behaviour and the culture and the approach of a firm, as it is about
systems and controls.

The initiative can be linked to the customer fairness high level principle, as well
as the other three customer-focused FSA Principles for Business. High Level
Principle 6 provides, 'A firm must pay due regard to the interests of its
customers and treat them fairly.'

Principle 7 provides, 'A firm must pay due regard to the information needs of its
clients, and communicate information to them in a way which is clear, fair and
not misleading.'

Principle 8 provides, 'A firm must manage conflicts of interest fairly, both
between itself and its customers and between a customer and another client.'

Principle 9 provides, 'A firm must take reasonable care to ensure the suitability
of its advice and discretionary decisions for any customer who is entitled to rely
upon its judgment.'

In addition, firms should have regard to the manner of their terms of business
and the manner in which they contract with their customers. The Unfair Terms
in Consumer Contracts Regulations 1999 provide that unfair terms in consumer
contracts are not binding on the consumer.

The FSA expect firms to consider whether they have embedded their approach
to treating their customers fairly into all aspects of their operations as well as
how they interact with customers. Although the FSA has provided guidance on
the issues that firms should address when establishing a TCF project, firms,

nonetheless, should first have regard to SYSC 3.1.1R and establish arrangements that are appropriate for their business, taking account of the nature, size and complexity of their business and the nature of the customers they deal with (see Chapter 11]). This approach will allow firms to maintain a principle-based approach allowing greater flexibility over how they can best meet their Treating Customers Fairly obligations.

---

1 Paragraph 40, A new regulator for a new millennium, January 2000.

Framework of FSA's treating customer fairly initiative

5.35 The FSA's Treating Customers Fairly work can be broken down between visits to firms, industry research, and feedback to firms on the results of its findings. As part of its research it has sought co-operation from interested industry and consumer groups and central to this is the FSA's Treating Customers Fairly consultative group. The group acts as a forum for the discussion of TCF issues, including the results of the FSA's work. The group comprises representatives of key industry trade associations, consumer groups and other interested parties. These include:

- Consumer Panel,
- Practitioner Panel,
- Smaller Businesses Practitioner Panels,
- Association of British Insurers (ABI),
- Association of Independent Financial Advisers (AIFA),
- Association of Private Client Investment Managers and Stockbrokers (APCIMS),
- British Bankers' Association (BBA),
- British Insurance Brokers' Association (BIBA),
- Building Societies Association (BSA),
- Council of Mortgage Lenders (CML),
- Investment Management Association (IMA),
- Which? and
- Financial Ombudsman Service (FOS).

During its thematic work the FSA has reviewed in particular the steps firms have taken to build TCF into the way they carry out their business. A series of publications have provided feedback to the industry. In July 2004 the FSA's publication 'Treating customers fairly – progress and next steps', set out a suggested framework for the operation of firms' TCF projects. Although the framework might not be directly applicable to all firms, the FSA views the framework as a standard approach to be adopted by firms and to the extent the discrete elements of the Framework are relevant it would expect to see them in operation. The FSA expects firms to consider TCF in respect of their activities in:

- product design;

- marketing, including the production of promotional material and disclosures;

- the sales process, including advice where that is given and the information provided to consumers as part of the sales process;

- the way that staff are remunerated;

- information and customer support after the point of sale;

- complaint handling; and

- management information.

Having considered the implications of TCF for their business, the FSA expects firms to complete a 'gap analysis' to identify any shortfalls in the treatment of customers and where shortfalls are identified to establish a programme to address any shortcomings. Firms need to set clear priorities and targets for their TCF programmes and determine how progress will be tracked to ensure that change is being successfully delivered and improves how they treat customers.

In its publication 'Treating customers fairly – building on progress', July 2005 the FSA identified a number of lessons for firms. In the main what is clear is an expectation that a firm's senior management has a key role to play in providing leadership, whether leading their TCF programmes or supporting and endorsing the work done by those accountable to them for delivering TCF. In deciding their approach to TCF firms need to take account of their strategy, the sector or sectors they operate in, the products and services they offer and their client base. Analysing how they interact with their customers by better understanding both the client and product lifecycles should be at the centre of their TCF strategy. We shall consider this type of assessment further below. FSA has also highlighted that adequate management information from both TCF programmes is essential although it remains a challenge. Firms must recognise that the outcomes from their TCF work needs to be clearly defined and obtainable. The appropriate management information must be available to the firm's management structure to enable them to track progress and monitor delivery. The FSA has expressed concern[1] that the revision of management information systems takes time and firms are finding that they have considerable analytical work to undertake to determine the management information they need. We shall consider these matters further when assessing the approaches that firms may take to managing their TCF programmes.

In its business plan for 2006/07 the FSA set out a plan for further TCF thematic activity, reflecting the progress firms are by now expected to have made and areas that continue to concern the FSA. In particular there will be work undertaken to review any feedback provided on the way in which different groups of firms have gone about it. The FSA will also, during the year, assess the progress firms are making in identifying the management information that they need to monitor their success in delivering TCF strategies. Finally the FSA will link firms' TCF programmes with the quality of advice being given to customers. This link will start to consider the interrelationship with improvements in how firms plan to deal with customers when designing and taking new products to markets and how they interact with customers. By considering the quality and standards of advice, the FSA will be able to assess the extent to which firms' TCF programmes have had an impact on advice given to clients.

Starting in the Autumn of 2005, the FSA's Arrow risk assessment process has incorporated TCF as a core component. Supervisors now, during risk assessments, identify what firms have done to assess what TCF means for their business and how they are dealing with any shortfalls that have emerged. The Arrow programme has at its core a risk-based approach to the assessment of a firm's business arrangements. This combined with the latitude given to firms to establish arrangements to most appropriately manage TCF in the context of the firm's business model will without doubt give rise to differences of view as to what approaches to TCF are acceptable. In these circumstances it is hoped that that the FSA will have regard to the rationale for a firm's own approach.

With the FSA's TCF thematic work now in place since 2001, the FSA announced in July 2006 that it expected all firms to have reached the implementing stage and as such firms will have made significant progress in embedding TCF principles within their organisation by March 2007. Firms must now accept that TCF related enforcement proceedings may be commenced by the FSA. Such actions might occur where there has been inadequate progress and thus most likely will be based on system and control failings or where there have specific customer facing compliance breaches. In reaching a decision on whether the FSA should take enforcement proceedings against a firms it has stated[2] that it will take into account whether the firm has considered the implications for TCF, and whether senior management has played the role it would expect in managing or endorsing the firm's approach to TCF. The prospect of enforcement proceedings would be heightened where a firm has not responded to indications from its own management reporting or from the FSA that there are problems, or has failed to identify shortcomings where they exist and to develop a strategy to remedy them.

1 Treating customers fairly – building on progress, July 2005.
2 See section 6 Treating customers fairly building on progress, July 2005.

How can firms approach their TCF programme?

5.36   Firms need to approach their TCF initiative in a manner that ensures that all aspects of their interaction with customers are considered as well as in a manner that is consistent with the approach taken by other firms. Firms need to be able to demonstrate to the FSA that they have a robust and well thought out programme of review and a method for implementing necessary change within their business. The FSA has provided guidance to firms on the most crucial elements of a TCF programme. This includes the following steps drawn from each of the FSA's key publications relating to TCF and in particular its TCF case studies and 'Treating customers fairly – building on progress, July 2005':

Identifying the impact of what TCF means for a firm

5.37   Firms are expected to develop a well thought out and documented strategic approach to their TCF programme. They should ensure that their approach to TCF includes not only their clients and target customer base, but also customers' likely needs, knowledge, sophistication and attitude to risk. Firms then need to ensure that their customer assessment is considered in the context of the risk and complexity of the products and services the firm offers or is planning to offer as well as the distribution channels the firms use as well as the suitability of that distribution channel for the products, services and target customers. Firms also need to consider how their commitments to customers are affected by business partners that will be involved in delivering products and services to consumers, and how they may have an impact on the risk of not treating customers fairly.

As well as considering how the firm interacts with new customers firms should also consider how they treat their existing customers including the actual or implied past promises or commitments made to customers and what is required to fulfil them. An essential part of this assessment is the need to assess the firm's interactions with its customers through the lifecycle of the products and services that it provides.

Treating customers fairly and the product lifecycle

5.38   Depending on the nature of a firm's business, applying TCF to the product lifecycle involves addressing the fair treatment of customers during product design, marketing, sales and advice, and post sales care such as claim and complaints handling. Firms must consider their targeted and actual customers in the context of, whether the products they offer them are of a type that is appropriate. The customer type should influence the style and presentation of marketing material and sales approach. Equally, the type of customer should also impact the approach the firm takes to post sales behaviour. By way of example a firm that targets sales towards vulnerable or inexperienced customers should ensure that it does not defend claims relying on highly technical contractual exclusions. The FSA has designed and published in May 2005 a good practice guide covering the need to treat customers fairly when drafting exclusion clauses. The product lifecycle assessment is straightforward when only one firm is involved in delivery to a consumer. However, in modern financial services markets this is rare. More likely are situations where a product is taken to the market by a multitude of firms each individually accountable for compliance obligations relating to part of the product design and its sale. The FSA has begun to recognise the firms that distribute and administer products through third parties introduces a dynamic to the TCF initiative that requires a more lateral approach and particular reference should be made to the FSA's Discussion paper 06/04. A firm that distributes wholly through separate intermediaries, retains responsibility for its product design and testing, ensuring that the marketing material for intermediaries is appropriate and that training on the terms of the product is available and appropriate. Firms need to consider the potential that exists for their products to be impacted by third parties when designing their products. Equally, firms that distribute or administer another's products should work with the product producer to ensure the features and operation of the product is properly and fully understood to ensure that its delivery is fair to the consumer.

Undertake a gap analysis and action planning

5.39   Firms should assess all parts of their business to understand where there is potential risk to the fair treatment of customers and to identify any areas where they may not be meeting their obligations. The gap analysis should consider the firm's operation as well as the customer and product lifecycle. Where action is needed, the FSA will expect that senior management will agree and implement a plan to set targets that will address priority areas first, and a mechanism to allow them to track that progress is being made as planned. The gap analysis and implementation plan should, where appropriate, consider the following areas, each of which has previously been identified by the FSA as integral to a firm's TCF programme:

1.   **Product and service design:** When designing new products firms should test and review the impact of a new product on consumers before launch including looking at how the product performs in adverse or unexpected market conditions and ensure that it will have the infrastructure in place to support the product after launching it. It makes sense that those designing and marketing products should each take account of the information and training needs of those selling and advising. There is also considerable value in those dealing with customers after sale (whether through complaints or otherwise) sharing information gained if after launch they find that a product does not meet consumer expectations. During the firm's design of a new product it should give consideration to the following points:

- How might future external events have an impact on the performance of a product?

- How might the product perform in very different environmental conditions?

- Which target groups of consumers would the product be suitable for – and which customer would it not be suitable for?

- How can the features and risks associated with the product be communicated to target consumers in ways they are likely to understand?

- Will the product material enable those marketing and selling the product (including intermediaries) to understand, and so explain, the product's features and its risks?

2. **Managing strategic change:** Any strategic change in a firm whether in terms of new markets, mergers and acquisitions or operational improvements, might impact the firm's current thinking and approach to TCF, thus creating risks for its products and customers. Firms need to build into any strategic change decision arrangements to ensure that customers' interests are considered as well as sufficient resource and time to ensure that it properly appreciates the changes that are to take place and the TCF responsibilities that will create for the firm's business.

3. **Financial promotions and advertising:** The FSA considers that marketing and promotional material can have a significant impact on consumers buying decisions and therefore needs to be carefully crafted to ensure it reflects the characteristics of the product and is suitable for the audience to whom it is being communicated. Central to this is that the material must enable the customer to balance potential reward against risk.

4. **Managing interfaces between providers and distributors:** The distribution of a firm's products through third parties can have major implications on the end consumers' understanding of the financial product. By way of example, when a firm is providing a product which will be distributed by others, it needs to consider whether the material it provides for distributors and their advisers clearly describes the features and risks associated with the product. This will help ensure that the distributors' understanding of the product will properly translate to accurate sales

information to the customer. A distributor's failure to adequately sell or administer a product can have a major impact on the interest of the customer which in turn could have a reputation impact on the firm. It remains to be seen whether a firm that fails to properly deal with TCF requirements when distributing its products or services through third party providers might be exposed to the risk of FSA enforcement action. The FSA published discussion paper 06/04 in September 2006 addressing the issue of providers and distributers of products. In relation to the paper John Tiner stated, "*...but we do expect providers and distributors to work together to ensure that consumers are dealt with in an effective and fair way. Providers should give more support and information to distributors of their products with a corresponding expectation that distributors should use product information effectively with consumers'.*

5. **Information and services provided after the point of sale including complaints management and handling procedures:** The manner in which a firm handles its customer complaints does have a major bearing on its fair treatment of those customers and intelligent companies will use the information it gathers from its handling of customer complaints to inform it about its strengths and weaknesses (for further information about compliant handling rules and management information see Chapter 10). The FSA will now expect firms to include complaint handling arrangements as part of their TCF initiative and review arrangements for individual complaints as well as how the firm might learn from the complaint data it gathers. The firm should ensure that the complaints arrangements it has established do not create any barriers, making it difficult for the customer to complain or for members of staff to deal with complaints. In part the firm needs to ensure that it has allocated sufficient resources to deal with complaints efficiently, but awareness and culture also have a significant bearing on whether complaints handling treats customers fairly. Firms must ensure that their staff are both trained and encouraged to recognise and record expressions of dissatisfaction from customers as complaints and that complaints are fully and fairly investigated.

    In understanding how it treats its customers a firm should establish a process of tracking complaints trends and respond to the identified themes and trends. This might include:

    *   responding quickly if volume suddenly increases;

    *   ensuring that the firm checks that it remedies the cause of complaints, in order to prevent similar problems recurring; and

    *   ensuring that the analysis extends to complaints that have been referred to the Financial Ombudsman service.

6. **Staff culture and behaviour:** The behaviour of staff and their reaction to the selling of new products are important areas for a firm to review in its

TCF work. If a firm's senior management create a culture of doing the right thing for the customer, then this can have a positive impact in the way a firm designs and distributes its products and services and its overall customer relationship. The design and structure of staff remuneration is a significant influencing factor in staff's behaviour towards customers. Issues such as basic remuneration, bonuses and sales can all have an impact. Firms, however, often overlook how remuneration can shape good standards of compliance and need to consider how they can build into their remuneration packages targets for good standards of compliance. In designing staff remuneration and rewards a firm might consider:

- Are there appropriate incentives for staff to treat complaints fairly?

- How does the firm manage risks arising from setting up incentives to encourage staff to meet particular sales targets?

- How to set targets and rewards for non-sales staff (including senior management, marketing, customer service, complaints handlers, compliance, and middle management) who can have an impact on the fair treatment of customers?

- Does the firm have the right balance between rewards for compliance and other non-sales staff and sales and marketing etc?

Management information and lessons learned

5.40   The FSA stress the importance of a firm's senior management need to ensure that it receives regular information to inform it about progress with its TCF programme. Information could logically fall into three distinct groups:

- Measures showing how the firm's TCF targets are being met.

- Lessons learned from customer experiences that will allow adjustments to the firm's TCF priorities and targets.

- Information from the TCF undertaken by the FSA to inform the firm that its own approach meets regulatory requirements.

Once firms have initiated their own programme of reform, they need to make sure they have in place a structure allowing reporting back to management sufficient to inform them that TCF performance targets are being met, identifying any areas of their programme that are not being met as well as providing information about the lessons the firm can learn from post sale customer experiences. The firm's own management structure will determine the nature and scale of reporting but firms will need to ensure that the management information they produce is both fit for purpose and is appropriately filtered and distributed so as to provide meaningful data to appropriate audiences within the firm, each of whom may have responsibility for different aspects of TCF.

Letters to Chief Executive Officers

5.41   The FSA chooses to write directly to the Chief Executive Officers of firms is increasingly used as a method of communicating directly to the senior executive of a firm to raise awareness of an important supervisory issue or a matter of regulatory risk. Such letters are used to address such matters either to a section of firms, a section of the regulated population or the financial market as a whole. In more recent years, letters to Chief Executive Officers have been used not only to draw matters to the attention of a firm's Chief Executive Officer but also to request specific actions to be taken and put in place a requirement for formal responses to the FSA on the matter in question. By way of example on 4 November 2005 the FSA wrote to all Chief Executives of insurance companies regarding the sale of payment protection insurance. The letter reported on the outcome of an FSA project into the sale of this type of insurance alongside credit arrangements. The FSA's letter explained the action the FSA were going to take and the urgent action it expected insurance firms to take that were selling this type of insurance. The letter also included an annex giving examples of what firms needed to do to comply with the FSA rules when selling payment protection insurance. The letter requested that all firms distributing and underwriting PPI undertake a review of their sales processes, systems and controls to ensure they were treating customers fairly and report to their FSA supervisor by 19 December 2005 around six weeks after the date of the letter.

Variation of business permissions

5.42   The FSA may determine that it is necessary or desirable to impose additional requirements on a firm or in some way amend or restrict the activities which the firm has permission to undertake. By waiving or modifying the requirements of a rule or imposing additional requirements or limitations the FSA can ensure that it can take full account of the firm's individual circumstances. SUP 7 sets out the process the FSA will follow in imposing individual requirements. (Chapter 12] also sets out further information regarding business permissions).

Information and use of Skilled Persons

5.43   The FSA prefers to carry out its functions with firms in the context of an open and co-operative relationship. Indeed Principle 11 requires that firms must deal with the FSA in an open and co-operative way and must disclose to the FSA anything relating to the firm of which the FSA would reasonably expect notice. When situations arise giving the FSA cause to obtain information or documents from firms it will in the first instance ask for those items and expect the firm's co-operation. Where, however, it appears that it will not be able to obtain the required information in that way it will use its statutory powers. When the FSA considers it necessary to undertake a more detailed and formal review of potential problems or risks in an individual firm, it may formally request the firm in question to provide specified information or documents, ask the firm to appoint a skilled person to provide a report on the matter to the FSA or appoint a person to conduct an investigation into the matter. Sections 165–177 of the FSMA 2000 set out the FSA's powers relating to information gathering, skilled person appointments and investigations.

Access to information

5.44   The FSA's activities with firms will give rise to situations where it will need to gather information or documents which will require the co-operation of a firm. Visits to firms may be made on a regular basis, on a sample basis, for special purposes such as theme visits. During these visits the FSA will need access to the firm's documents and information from personnel. In addition the FSA may seek information or request documents by telephone, at meetings or in writing, including by electronic communication to assist in its supervision of a firm's business or to enable it to carry out its functions. Principle 11 will apply to the firm's obligation to co-operate with the FSA's request for information and under SUP 2.3.3 G, the FSA expects a firm to:

(1)   make itself readily available for meetings as reasonably requested;

(2)   give the FSA reasonable access to or produce to the FSA any records, files, tapes or computer systems, which are within the firm's possession or control;

(3)   print information in the firm's possession or control which is held on computer or on microfilm or otherwise convert it into a readily legible document or any other record which the FSA may reasonably request;

(4)   permit the FSA to copy documents or other material on the premises of the firm at the firm's reasonable expense and to remove copies and hold them elsewhere, or provide any copies, as reasonably requested; and

(5)   answer truthfully, fully and promptly all questions which are reasonably put to it by representatives or appointees of the FSA.

Where the FSA reasonably requires information or documents in the exercise of its functions, but cannot obtain the co-operation of the firm, it may serve a written notice on an authorised person requesting specified information, information of a specified description, specified documents or documents of a specified description[1]. When the written notice has been served, the information or documents required must be provided or produced before the end of the specified period (which must be reasonable) and at the specified place[2]. As an alternative to serving a written notice, the FSA may authorise in writing an officer or agent to require an authorised person to provide him without delay with the information or documents specified in the written authorisation[3]. SUP 2.3.5R(1) requires a firm to permit representatives of the FSA or persons appointed by the FSA access with or without notice during reasonable hours to any of its business premises in relation to the discharge of the FSA's functions. Many authorised persons, however, are part of groups and will share their operational and compliance arrangements such that information and documents relating to their operation will be in the possession or under the control of another member of the group, or even in the possession of an outsourcing service provider. SUP 2.3.7R requires that firms entering into a material outsourcing agreement secure that the supplier of those services deal in an open and co-operative way with the FSA in the discharge of the arrangement. When a firm appoints or renews a material outsourcing arrangement, it should ensure that the terms of its contract with the supplier require the supplier to co-operate with the FSA to ensure access to information and provide the FSA access to its premises4. In the first instance the FSA will request the information or documents it requires directly from the firm although it reserves the right to seek it directly with the outsourcing supplier. Where it cannot obtain co-operation, s 165(7) of the FSMA 2000 provides that the FSA's powers to request information and documents can be exercised to impose the requirement on a person connected with an authorised person[5]. Furthermore where information and documents are in the possession of a third party such as a third party service provider or outsourcer s 175 of the FSMA 2000 provides the FSA with power to exercise a request for information or documents in relation to that third party.

When the FSA obtains confidential information it is obliged under Part XXIII of the Act (Public Record, Disclosure of Information and Co-operation) to treat that information as confidential.

1 FSMA 2000, s 165(1).
2 FSMA 2000, s 165(2).
3 FSMA 2000, s 165(3), (10)(b).
4 SUP 2.3.9G.
5 FSMA 2000, s 165(7) also extends to operators, trustees or depositories of collective investment schemes although not authorised and recognised investment exchanges and clearing houses.

Mystery shopping

5.45   Supervising the extent to which a firm may expose its customers to the risk of being sold inappropriate financial products can be problematic as there is difficulty in establishing after the event what a firm has said to customers or omitted to say or disclose. The FSA uses mystery shopping to help obtain information about a particular practice across a range of firms or the practices of a particular firm. Mystery shopping is often used to supplement other FSA supervision work. It may be used as part of a programme of visits or thematic activity to better understand the practice in particular areas. The FSA states at SUP 2.4.2G that, '... by recording what a firm says in discussions with a "mystery shopper", the FSA can establish a firms normal practices in a way which would not be possible by other means.' To undertake mystery shopping the FSA often appoints market research companies to approach firms in the role of a potential retail customer seeking advice or services about specific financial products. FSA requires in the appointment of market research firms that the discussion had with firms will be conducted in accordance with the Market Research Society Code of Practice including that all telephone calls or meetings held with individual the firms will be recorded.

The results from the FSA's mystery shopping exercises over a range of firms will often be published to alert firms to the FSA's findings and concerns. The publication will often be accompanied with actions that firms should take to review their own exposure to weaknesses that might have been identified. By way of example in March 2006, the FSA published the results of a mystery shopping exercise1 undertaken as an early assessment into requirements introduced in June 2005 for firms to disclose information about the services they provide and the charges that would be made to customers for packaged product services. The new rules required that an initial disclosure document and menu of charges document be given to the customer. A mystery shopping exercise was able to show that in only 75 of the 130 cases (58%) were shoppers given both of the documents. In only 55 cases (42%) were the potential customers given both documents at the correct point in the interview. In the summary to the report the FSA stated, '... The results of this research suggest low compliance with the FSA's new disclosure requirements ...' and the press release accompanying the report stated that '... the regulator will be contacting firms to ask for further information to help evaluate their compliance. It will consider the most appropriate tools to address any non-compliance that is identified, which may include referring individual firms to enforcement.'

---

1 Depolarisation disclosure: mystery shopping results, March 2006, Consumer research 48.

Skilled person reports

5.46   Where the FSA identifies during its routine supervision that a firm may have issues requiring more detailed assessment, it has to consider the availability of its own resource to undertake the necessary review and the extent to which it might rely on the authorised firm to reliably review and report further on the issue. Where its concerns relate to matters where it has required or could require the provision of documents or information under s 165 of the FSMA 2000, it can require a report from a skilled person about the concerns it has at the firm[1]. Skilled person reports are used in a variety of situations. They can be used for diagnostic purposes, enabling the FSA to identify, assess and measure risks; for monitoring purposes, enabling the tracking of how risks develop; as a preventative action, identified risks from crystallising or increasing; and as a remedial action, responding to risks when they have crystallised.

---

1 FSMA 2000, s 166(1).

Policy on using skilled person reports

5.47   The FSA's policy for the appointment of skilled persons is set out in its Supervison manual. When making the decision to require a report by a skilled person, the FSA will have regard to all relevant factors at the firm and determines each case on its own merits.

The FSA will consider the objective of its enquiry[1] and any legal and procedural issues surrounding the issues at the firm. It will have to consider the cost of using its own resource, against the cost to the firm of the FSA requesting a skilled person report, which can (depending on the skilled person used) be considerable. The FSA may conclude that the individual circumstances of the case may be better served by using alternative tools, including other statutory powers.

One of the key drivers to the FSA decision on the use of a skilled person will be circumstances relating to the firm[2]. In particular the FSA will be swayed by the attitude of the firm and its senior management to resolving and managing the identified risk or issues. If the firm and its senior management is co-operative, and the FSA has confidence about the firm's ability and willingness to provide the required information or an objective report, it is more likely to leave the firm to respond to the concerns itself. Where, however, the FSA is concerned that the subject matter of the enquiries or the report involves actual or potential misconduct, the issues might give rise to conflicts of interest, the firm lacks knowledge or expertise, or where there has been a history of similar issues within the firm which have not been dealt with timely it is likely to conclude that it is inappropriate to rely on the firm's own enquiries into the matter and its objectives are better served through the involvement of a third party skilled person.

---

1 SUP 5.3.3G.
2 SUP 5.3.4G.

Appointment process

5.48   The skilled person appointment process is set out in s 166 of the FSMA 2000: supported by SUP 5. The FSA is required to provide notice to the firm, which may be one of the following who is or was at the relevant time carrying on a business[1]:

(a)   an authorised person,

(b)   any other member of the authorised person's group,

(c)   a partnership of which the authorised person is a member,

(d)   a person who has at any relevant time been a person in (a), (b) or (c).

The notice will set out the purpose of the report, its scope, the matters which the report is required to address, any other relevant matters and the timetable for its completion. The notice will also set out requirements as to the report's format. Section 166(3) of the FSMA 2000 permits the FSA to require the report to be in such form as the FSA may specify. It is usual for the FSA, prior to formally giving the written notice, to meet the firm to discuss its decision to require a report by a skilled person, the scope of the report, who should be appointed as skilled person and the likely cost. This sometimes can present both the firm in question and the FSA with an opportunity to discuss whether there might be a more appropriate means of obtaining the information the FSA requires.

Section 166(4) of the FSMA 2000 requires that the skilled person is nominated or approved by the FSA and must have the necessary skills to report on the matter concerned. The skilled person appointment is the responsibility of the firm. It will be the firm that contracts with the skilled person for the commission of the report as well as the payment of their professional fees. The FSA will, however, need to be satisfied that the skilled person possesses the necessary skills to undertake the work required. The FSA states2 that a skilled person will most likely be an accountant, lawyer, actuary or other person with relevant business, technical or technological skills. When the FSA determines whether to nominate or approve the skilled person's appointment they will consider3:

(1)   the skills necessary to make a report on the matter concerned;

(2)   the ability to complete the report within the time expected;

(3)   any relevant specialised knowledge, for instance of the firm in question, the type of business carried on by the firm, or the matter to be reported on;

(4)   any professional difficulty or potential conflict of interest in reviewing the matters to be reported on, for instance because the matters to be reported on may involve questions reflecting on the quality or reliability of work previously carried out by the proposed skilled person; and

(5)   whether the skilled person has enough detachment, bearing in mind the closeness of an existing professional or commercial relationship, to give an objective opinion on matters.

The firm's contract with the skilled person is governed by SUP 5.5.1R. The FSA requires that the contract contains key provisions relating to the role of the skilled person as well as the firm. The contract must be governed by the laws of a part of the United Kingdom and overall must operate to give effect to the reporting requirements set out in its s 166(1) notice.

In respect of the skilled person the contract must:

(1)   require and permit the skilled person during and after the course of his appointment:

    (a)   to co-operate with the FSA in the discharge of its functions; and

    (b)   to communicate to the FSA information on, or his opinion on, matters of which he has, or had, become aware in his capacity as skilled person reporting on the firm in the following circumstances:

        (i)   where he reasonably believes that, as regards the firm concerned: there is or has been, or may be or may have been, a contravention of any relevant requirement that applies to the firm concerned; and that the contravention may be of material significance to the FSA in determining whether to exercise, in relation to the firm concerned, any functions conferred on the FSA by or under any provision of the Act other than Part VI (Official Listing); or

        (ii)   that he reasonably believes that the information on, or his opinion on, those matters may be of material significance to the FSA in determining whether the firm concerned satisfies and will continue to satisfy the threshold conditions; or

        (iii)   he reasonably believes that firm is not, may not be or may cease to be a going concern;

(2)   require the preparation of a report, as notified to the firm by the FSA, within the time specified by the FSA; and

(3)   waive any duty of confidentiality owed by the skilled person to the firm which might limit the provision of information or opinion by that skilled person to the FSA in accordance with (1) or (2).

In respect of the firm and the contract generally the contract must expressly provide[4]:

(1)   that the FSA has a right to enforce the provisions included in the contract relating to the role of the skilled person in SUP 5.5.1R and other general contractual requirements in SUP 5.5.5R(2);

(2)   that, in proceedings brought by the FSA for such enforcement, the skilled person is not to have available by way of defence, set-off or counterclaim any matter that is not relevant to those provisions;

(3)   (if the contract includes an arbitration agreement) that the FSA is not, in exercising the right in (a), to be treated as a party to, or bound by, the arbitration agreement; and

(4)   that the SUP provisions included in the contract are irrevocable and may not be varied or rescinded without the FSA's consent; and

SUP 5.5.5R also requires that the skilled person contract cannot be varied or rescinded in such a way as to extinguish or alter the provisions referred to in SUP.

---

1 FSMA 2000, s 166(2).
2 SUP 5.4.7G.
3 SUP 5.4.8G.
4 SUP 5.5.5R.

Preparation and delivery of the skilled person report

5.49   The FSA's s 166(1) notice will normally specify a time limit within which the skilled person is to deliver the report and the skilled person should take reasonable steps to achieve delivery by that time. Situations may of course frustrate and delay the preparation or delivery of the report. The FSA will expect the skilled person to raise these and discuss them as they arise. During the preparation of the report, particularly where the matters concerned are complex, the timescale for the report is lengthy or where serious issues have arisen, the FSA will expect to discuss the report's progress and matters relevant to it with the skilled person together with the firm in question. Once the report is finalised the FSA will usually wish to meet with the skilled person to discuss the report's findings. In most cases this meeting will involve senior management from the firm in question, although the FSA may decide to exclude the firm.

Operational consequences for firms

5.50   The costs incurred by firms having to instruct skilled persons is often far in excess of the cost of deploying their own staff to undertake the same review. Firms subject to skilled person work often experience a major disruption to the operation of their business as the skilled person's review work progresses. Senior management often find they are required to manage and direct the skilled person's staff as well as attend for interview and respond to enquiries relating to the matter under review. SUP 5.5.9R requires that the firm must provide all reasonable co-operation to the skilled person. Ultimately the skilled person's report is to be submitted to the FSA although most skilled persons will provide the firm and its management with an opportunity to comment on the report. The extent to which the firm is able to influence the report content is limited to factual inaccuracies. The fundamental views and findings expressed in the report are to be those of the skilled person and not the firm. Inevitably, any part of a firm's business operation that is subjected to scrutiny will display weaknesses. Indeed, where the FSA has identified issues or risk within a firm, the scrutiny of the skilled person is more likely to confirm the FSA's concerns.

Powers of investigation

5.51 Sections 167–169 of the FSMA 2000 empower the FSA and HM Treasury to appoint persons to conduct an investigation into either general matters, specific areas of concern or to support an overseas regulator. The FSA will consider utilising its formal investigation powers either where immediate risks are identified and the FSA believed that a firm will not take the appropriate action or in its preparation of enforcement proceedings against a firm.

International co-operation and supervision of global firms

5.52 Where a firm undertakes business internationally (whether directly or where it is part of an international group), the FSA will, dependent on the nature and scope of the regulation to which the firm or group is subject in the other jurisdictions in which it operates as well as the country in which its head office is based, usually seek some degree of co-operation including the exchange of intelligence with those other overseas regulators1. The FSA has entered into a series of arrangements with other regulators each designed to enhance cooperation when dealing with multi-jurisdiction firms. By way of example on 14 March 2006, the FSA signed a Memorandum of Understanding (MoU) with the United States' Securities and Exchange Commission (SEC) to strengthen co-operation in oversight and supervision of global firms. The arrangement will support the exchange of supervisory information when undertaking consolidated supervision of major UK and US firms. In announcing the MOU John Tiner said:

'This arrangement builds upon the existing framework for exchanging information between our two institutions, when this is necessary, as part of our day-to-day supervision of firms operating in both the

US and UK. We already work closely with the SEC; this MoU will
facilitate that process by setting out the basis on which we will do
this.'

---

1 SUP 1.2.2G.

Enforcement and discipline

5.53   In this section the key stages in the FSA's enforcement process will be
considered. Regulator enforcement is an essential element of ensuring satisfactory standards of compliance by firms and approved persons. As part of its
regulatory toolkit the FSA has available a number of enforcement based tools,
each designed to secure a particular outcome. The FSA's enforcement powers
range from compelling or prohibiting a firm in relation to a desired outcome;
suspending or withdrawing authorisation through to punishing a firm for past
misconduct. The imposition of disciplinary action such as financial penalties
and public censures illustrates that regulatory standards are being upheld and
helps to maintain market confidence and promote public awareness of regulatory standards; it can also act as a deterrent to others from committing regulatory misconduct1. In a speech on 11 April 2006 Margaret Cole, the FSA's head
of enforcement, said:

> '... Enforcement activity generates more publicity (whether positive
> or negative) about the FSA than any other single issue. Enforcement
> outcomes can therefore play a very significant role in educating the
> industry and consumers about issues of concern and the FSA's
> approach to them. It can also be a very powerful way of changing
> behaviour. Obviously we want to encourage and promote high
> standards of behaviour, both in terms of our market integrity and our
> protection of consumers' objectives ...'

In strict terms the FSA's disciplinary measures refer to public statements and
public censures2, and financial penalties3. Each of these powers available to the
FSA is contained within Part V of the Act in relation to approved persons and
Part XIV of the Act (disciplinary measures in relation to authorised and
regulated firms). In broader terms, however, the FSA has available a number of
enforcement measures it can take as an alternative to disciplinary action. Such
additional measures may be taken where the FSA considers it is necessary to
take remedial action or ensure that the market is protected. In addition the FSA
may take specific action to suspend, vary or prohibit activities where, for
example, a firm's continuing ability to meet the threshold conditions or where
an approved person's fitness and propriety to perform the controlled functions
to which his approval relates, is called into question. ENF 11.2.3G set out the
following three alternative measures:

(1)   the variation or cancellation of permission and the withdrawal of a firm's authorisation4;

(2)   the withdrawal of an individual's status as an approved person5; and

(3)   the prohibition of an individual from performing a specified function in relation to a regulated activity6.

1 For a more detailed review of the FSA enforcement process see Freshfields' Guide to FSA Enforcement and Investigations (Second edn) Tottel publishing 2006.
2 Described in ENF 12.
3 Described in ENF 13.
4 Described in ENF 3 and ENF 5.
5 Described in ENF 7.
6 Described in ENF 8.

Approved Person's Enforcement

5.54   The FSA enforcement regime allows the FSA to take action against individuals as well as authorised firms. An individual faces greater risks from a successful enforcement action, arising from damage to reputation and livelihood. It is the FSA's experience that cases against individuals are harder to prove, take longer to resolve and are less likely to be settled. The FSA has, however, stressed the role that a firm's senior management have and that in appropriate cases it will take enforcement action against individuals. Margaret Cole, the FSA's head of enforcement, stated on 11 April 2006:

> '… Failure to manage risks properly is now, more then ever, likely to result in disciplinary action being brought against individuals as well as firms. Senior managers need to understand this and ensure that they are taking appropriate action to identify and mitigate risks to protect their firm, and increasingly, themselves …'

Under s 66 of the FSMA 2000 action may be taken against an approved person if it appears to the FSA that he is guilty of misconduct and the FSA is satisfied that it is appropriate in all the circumstances to take action against him. Section 66(2) of the FSMA 2000 specifies that a person is guilty of misconduct if while an approved person:

(a)   he has failed to comply with a statement of principle issued under s 64, or

(b)   he has been knowingly concerned in a contravention by the relevant authorised person of a requirement imposed on that authorised person by or under this Act.

Section 66(4) of the FSMA 2000 provides a de facto limitation period restricting the time in which the FSA may take action against approved persons. The FSA may not take s 66 action after the end of two years from the day on which the FSA knew of the misconduct, save where proceedings in respect of the misconduct began before the end of the period.

Authorised and regulated persons

5.55   Where the FSA considers that an authorised person has contravened a requirement imposed by or under the Act then it may publish a public censure under s 205 of the FSMA 2000 and a financial penalty of such amount as it considers appropriate under s 206. Financial penalties, may not, however, be imposed where the FSA determines to withdraw a person's authorisation1. To ensure the right enforcement outcome the FSA disciplinary policy towards firms seeks to ensure that regulatory fines are not simply regarded as just another cost of doing business.

The Act sets out a series of formal steps the FSA must follow once they have determined to commence enforcement proceedings. Each of these steps are designed to ensure that the person against whom the proceedings are begun is aware of the allegations made, the time within which they can respond and in which the action will be taken and of their rights in appropriate cases to refer the matter to the Financial Services and Markets Tribunal.

---

1 FSMA 2000, s 33.

When does the FSA decide to take enforcement action?

5.56   The FSA is required under ss 206 (in respect of authorised persons) and 66 (in respect of approved persons) of the FSMA 2000 to publish its policy towards enforcement and discipline. This policy statement provides a useful insight into the factors that will determine whether enforcement or disciplinary action will be taken in response to allegations of misconduct or rule breaches. The FSA sets out in ENF 11.4.1G criteria for the taking of enforcement proceedings. And in the introduction to these criteria the FSA states:

'In determining whether to take disciplinary action in respect of conduct appearing to the FSA to be a breach, the FSA will consider the full circumstances of each case. A number of factors may be relevant for this purpose. The following list is not exhaustive: not all of these factors may be relevant in a particular case, and there may be other factors that are relevant.'

Although each individual's or firm's case has to be treated on its own merits, the FSA will use these criteria to ensure that their own disciplinary actions are conducted consistently and that an individual sanction can be justified against predetermined standards. It is important to stress the FSA point that the list is not an exhaustive one and although it is a useful tool for firms to judge the seriousness with which the FSA will view the firm's misconduct, the FSA will take into account factors relevant to each individual case. The criteria are:

(1)   The nature and seriousness of the suspected breach

(a)   whether the breach was deliberate or reckless;

(b)   the duration and frequency of the breach (including, in relation to a firm, when the breach was identified by those exercising significant influence functions in the firm);

(c)   the amount of any benefit gained or loss avoided as a result of the breach;

(d)   whether the breach reveals serious or systemic weaknesses of the management systems or internal controls relating to all or part of a firm's business;

(e)   the impact of the breach on the orderliness of financial markets, including whether public confidence in those markets has been damaged;

(f)   the loss or risk of loss caused to consumers or other market users;

(g)   the nature and extent of any financial crime facilitated, occasioned or otherwise attributable to the breach; and

(h)   whether there are a number of smaller issues, which individually may not justify disciplinary action, but which do so when taken collectively.

(2)   The conduct of the firm or the approved person after the breach

(a)   how quickly, effectively and completely the firm or approved person brought the breach to the attention of the FSA or another relevant regulatory authority;

(b)   the degree of co-operation the firm or approved person showed during the investigation of the breach;

(c)   any remedial steps the firm or approved person has taken since the breach was identified, including: identifying whether consumers have suffered loss and compensating them; taking disciplinary action against staff involved (where appropriate); addressing any systemic failures; and taking action designed to ensure that similar problems do not arise in future; and

(d)   the likelihood that the same type of contravention (whether on the part of the firm or approved person concerned or others) will recur if no disciplinary action is taken.

(3)   The previous regulatory record of the firm or approved person

(a)   whether the FSA (or any previous regulator) has taken any previous disciplinary action resulting in adverse findings against the firm or approved person;

(b)   whether the firm or approved person has previously given any undertakings to the FSA (or any previous regulator) not to do a particular act or engage in particular behaviour;

(c)   whether the FSA (or any previous regulator) has previously taken protective action in respect of a firm, using its own-initiative powers, by means of a variation of a Part IV permission (see ENF 3) or otherwise, or has previously requested the firm to take remedial action, and the extent to which such action has been taken; and

(d)   the general compliance history of the firm or approved person, such as previous private warnings or the type of correspondence referred to in ENF11.3.9G.

(4)   Guidance given by the FSA

The FSA will take into account whether any guidance has been issued relating to the behaviour in question and if so the extent to which the firm or approved person has sought to follow that guidance – see the Reader's Guide part of the Handbook.

(5)   Action taken by the FSA in previous similar cases

The FSA will take account of action which it has taken previously in cases where the breach has been the same or similar.

(6)   Action taken by other regulatory authorities

Where other regulatory authorities propose to take action in respect of the breach which is under consideration by the FSA , or one similar to it, the FSA will consider whether their action would be adequate to address the FSA's concerns, or whether it would be appropriate for the FSA to take its own action (see ENF 11.8).

Settlement

5.57   It is important for the FSA to achieve early settlements in its enforcement cases, to enable it to secure prompt redress where consumers have been affected and also to efficiently utilise its resource and move on to the next important case. Many firms that experience enforcement prefer to settle the case against them as quickly as possible and save management time by concentrating on the resolution of the matter and effective future management of their business. Although early settlement is in the main in the interest of both the FSA and the regulated person the FSA stresses that it is not prepared to compromise the integrity of its enforcement decision made by rushing to reach a settlement on bases which are inappropriate. Margaret Cole in a speech on Enforcement priorities and issues for 2006 on 11 April 2006 has said:

'... And you should not approach settlement discussions as if you are trying to resolve a commercial transaction. There will be limits beyond which we will not go and we will not engage in pure horse trading ...'

Settlement decisions are now made on behalf of the FSA by two decision makers of at least Director status. To assist in certain disciplinary cases the FSA operates a mediation scheme designed to promote settlement. Mediation is not available in criminal cases or where injunctions are necessary to stop a course of action. Full details of the mediation scheme are set out in the FSA's Handbook DEC.

Although the RDC and FSA Enforcement Division are separate, it is important that the FSA is seen to achieve consistency in approach between contentious matters dealt with by the RDC decisions and cases settled by the FSA executive. To achieve such consistency there is regular liaison to ensure consistency of approach and briefings to the RDC to ensure awareness of factors the FSA considers are important when setting financial penalties.

Warning notice

5.58 Where the FSA proposes to take disciplinary action it must provide the approved person or authorised person a warning notice[1]. The content of a warning notice is prescribed under s 387(1) of the FSMA 2000 and must:

(a)   state the action which the FSA Authority proposes to take;

(b)   be in writing;

(c)   give reasons for the proposed action;

(d)   state whether s 394 applies (access to evidence); and

(e)   if that section applies, describe its effect and state whether any secondary material exists to which the person concerned must be allowed access under it.

Although in many cases an authorised firm or approved person would have informally been made aware by the FSA that disciplinary action was contemplated, the warning notice acts as the formal trigger for a response, any settlement negotiations and making of formal representations to the FSA regulatory decisions committee.

---

1 For approved persons see the FSMA 2000, s 66(3)(a) and (b). For authorised persons see the FSMA 2000, ss 207 and 208.

Decision notice

5.59 Where the FSA decides to publish a statement or impose a financial penalty it is required to give the approved person[1] or authorised person[2] a decision notice containing details of the public statement or financial penalty. The content of the decision notice is prescribed by s 388 of the FSMA 2000 which requires that:

(a)   it be in writing;

(b)   it give the Authority's reasons for the decision to take the action to which the notice relates;

(c)   it state whether s 394 applies;

(d)   if that section applies, it describe its effect and state whether any second-ary material exists to which the person concerned must be allowed access under it; and

(e)   it give an indication of;

    (i)   any right to have the matter referred to the Tribunal which is given by this Act; and

    (ii)   the procedure on such a reference.

An FSA decision notice, in practical terms is the communication of the regula-tory decision committee's determination of the matter and indicates that the disciplinary action set out in the notice will take effect unless the approved or authorised person refers the matter to the Tribunal (see Chapter 13).

---

1 FSMA 2000, s 67(5) and (6).
2 FSMA 2000, s 208.

Final notice

5.60 After giving a person a decision notice and provided the matter has not been referred to the Tribunal, the FSA having taken the action set out in the decision notice is required by s 390 of the FSMA 2000 to give the person concerned a Final Notice. The contents of the Final Notice are prescribed in s 390 and will vary depending on the matter in question. In relation to public censures the content required is:

(a)   the terms of the public statement; and

(b)   details of the manner in which the statement will be published and the date of publication.

And in relation to financial penalties the Final Notice is required to state:

(a)   the amount of the penalty;

(b)   the manner in which and the period within which the penalty is to be paid; and

(c)   details of the way in which the penalty will be recovered if not paid by the date stated in the notice.

The FSA publishes copies of Final notices on its website.

Private warnings

5.61   In certain cases, despite having concerns about the behaviour of a firm or approved person, the FSA may consider it more appropriate to make a firm or person aware that it or they came close to being subject to formal disciplinary action rather than commence formal disciplinary proceedings. ENF 11.3.2G gives two examples of circumstances in which a private warning will be given in preference to formal disciplinary action:

(a)   if the matter of concern is 'minor in nature or degree'; or

(b)   the firm has taken 'full and immediate remedial action'.

A private warning is considered by the FSA as a serious form of reprimand, identifies and explains to the firm or individual the areas that concern the FSA and that formal disciplinary proceedings had been considered. There is no provision in the FSMA 2000 for the giving of private warnings although an explanation of their meaning and impact is set out in ENF 11.3. Although a private warning is only considered a reprimand ENF 11.3 makes clear that it will have an influence on the FSA's response to any future rule breach and the question of whether to start disciplinary action in relation to any future breaches. The FSA may not, however, rely on a past private warning as evidence that new possible rule breaches have taken place or when determining the level of penalty to impose.

Internal FSA procedures

5.62   Schedule 1, para 6(3) of the FSMA 2000 provides that the FSA must maintain arrangements for enforcing the provisions of, or made under, this Act.

The FSA's Enforcement Manual describes the policies and procedures for the exercise of the enforcement powers granted to the FSA and FSA rules in DEC sets out the steps the FSA take in reaching enforcement decisions. During the Financial Service and Markets Act's passage through parliament, there was considerable time spent on the question of the FSA enforcement process and concern about the FSA being given power to create rules, monitor compliance with its rules and where it determined that a firm was not acting in compliance take enforcement action. Parliament considered that such powers would create conflict within the FSA and be prejudicial for firms. As a result steps were taken to establish a structure within the FSA to separate the FSA rule making and monitoring function from its enforcement function (see further Chapter 2). Section 395(2) of the FSMA 2000 requires that the FSA procedures in relation to supervisory, warning and decision notices must be designed to secure that the decision which gives rise to the obligation to give any such notice is taken by a person not directly involved in establishing the evidence on which that decision is based. The FSA Regulatory Decision Committee (RDC) is established as an independent and objective committee to take administrative decisions in respect of enforcement actions proposed by the FSA. The RDC's members are appointed by the FSA Board and comprises practitioners and non-practitioners all of who can represent the public interest. The current Chairman is Tim Herrington a solicitor who was appointed on 1 February 2005.

Although the RDC is separate from the FSA Executive it is accountable to the FSA Board. The RDC is the committee through which the FSA makes disciplinary decisions and its decisions are those of the FSA. The RDC's approach to dealing with matters is informal and although it will allow firms and the FSA to make oral representations about cases, it is not intended to resemble a Court or a Tribunal or to have a quasi-judicial function. Indeed the RDC will reach its decisions having considered the papers presented and any legal representations made by either the person subject to enforcement or the FSA party. The RDC's decisions, however, will be based on the FSA's interpretation of the law and if there is an irreconcilable difference between the parties on a point of law then, it will be for the firm or approved person to refer the matter to the Financial Services and Markets Tribunal.

Enforcement process review

5.63 Since 2001 many firms in the financial service industry affected by enforcement actions had doubts about the fairness of the FSA's process. Moreover, in 2005 the FSA's attempt to impose a financial penalty on Legal and General Assurance Society for the mis-selling of endowment polices, and failing to have adequate systems and controls, led to criticism by the Financial Services and Markets Tribunal of the FSA's enforcement process. Although the Tribunal stopped short of making recommendations to the FSA under s 133(8) of the FSMA 2000, the FSA Board responded to the criticism by undertaking a full review of its enforcement process. The outcome of that review led to fundamental changes to the way FSA manages its enforcement work and further developed the independence and objectivity of the FSA's Regulatory Decision Committee. In particular the FSA have put in place arrangements to have a distinct separation of the preparation of an enforcement case from those who make decisions. The RDC now has its own dedicated legal function in place and the FSA Enforcement Division no longer gives legal advice to the RDC, although it does make submissions about the case which are also automatically disclosed to the firm or individual under enforcement. A series of other changes to the process have been made including:

- Legal reviews are now carried out on all cases before the RDC stage by lawyers who have not been part of the investigation team.

- Straightforward uncontested cases are now dealt with by an RDC panel of fewer than three members.

- Introduction of a scheme to give a discount on financial penalties where there has been early settlement.

FSA executive now agrees settled cases, leaving the RDC to decide contested cases.

Chapter 6

The role of compliance and fashioning compliance systems

6.1

'Because of the nature and levels of risks inherent to their business activities, complex ...organizations should have in place a compliance-risk management framework that makes is possible to identify, monitor, and effectively control the compliance risks facing their entire organization. Of course, such a framework needs to be commensurate with the nature and level of the organization's compliance risk. It should evolve with the ever changing product lines and business activities of any growth orientated organization. And, of course it needs to stay on top of regulatory developments.'

Mark W Olson: Member of the Board of the US Federal Reserve, 16 May 2006

Introduction

6.2   The Basel Committee explain internal risk-based compliance as being:

'An independent function that identifies, assesses, advises on, monitors and reports on the bank's compliance risk, that is, the risk of legal or regulatory sanctions, financial loss, or loss to reputation a bank may suffer as a result of its failure to comply with all applicable laws, regulations, codes of conduct and standards of good practice.[1]'

1 Basel Committee, The Compliance Function in banks, 31 January 2004 at 10, www.bis.org/publ/bcbs103.pdf.

6.3   For 'banks' it could more accurately read 'financial services firms'. This is now seen as best achieved by managing the risks associated with these issues rather than simply by complying with a set of rules issued by a regulator. This culture of risk-based compliance is one that is being widely adopted through the financial world. It partly evolved from the conclusions of the Basel

Committee[1] and a range of other bodies and has emerged as a methodology in areas other than just financial services. As a result major national regulators whose work has international ramifications, now adopt an approach that is consistent with this. In any event, it is an approach that they regard as desirable. The FSA is a good case in point. Their regulatory approach is based on the premise that a financial services business poses risks to the regulator's objectives. The regulations passed are thus a means to making sure that these risks are being managed in an appropriate way. So the days of 'compliance', where maintaining a satisfactory set of systems was determined by whether a set of rules were being complied with, are gone. What it has been replaced with is a system of risk-based compliance which involves satisfying a series of principles and rules in the course of managing the necessary risks. In some areas, such as mainstream conduct of business, the consequences of this should not be too great. In others, such as market abuse, it will be fundamental.

---

1. Basel Committee, Core Principles for effective Banking Supervision, September 1997, www.bis.org/publ/bcbs61.pdf.

The role of the regulator

6.4 The regulator itself operates by a combination of regulation, persuasion[1] and, where necessary, discipline. To quote Callum McCarthy[2] the FSA is:

> '... not an enforcement led regulator. Indeed, one of the challenges of any enforcement policy is to make sure that it does not disturb the openness and candour which are essential for day- to-day supervision ...But there can be no doubt that enforcement action is necessary from time to time.'

---

1. N. Reichman 'Moving Backstage: Uncovering the Role of Compliance Practices in Shaping Regulatory Policy' in 'Reader in Regulation,' Oxford University Press, 1998, p328.
2. FSA Enforcement Policy, International Financial Services, London, 29 June 2004, http://www.fsa.gov.uk/pubs/speeches/sp184.hml.

6.5 When enforcement action is taken '... its principal purpose is to change behaviour.'[1]

This is put into effect by a regulator in the UK that also licenses the participants in the market, drafts the regulations and also takes enforcement and disciplinary action against malfeasants. This is a consequence of the Financial Services and Markets Act 2000 which imposes on the regulator[2] the obligations to:

- maintain confidence in the UK financial system;

- promote public understanding;

- protect consumers; and

- reduce the opportunities for financial crime.

---

1 McCarthy, supra.
2 FSMA 2000, ss 3–6.

6.6   The first and third of these may prove to create a conflict of interests. Other areas of regulation – the oil industry for example, have seen a reduction in protection where the same regulatory body is required to police market efficiency[1]. In that instance the Department of Energy was required to regulate both oil rig safety and energy output, with an obvious reduction in safety standards resulting. There are few risks to the regulator given its exemption from negligence actions[2] and the difficulties in proving misfeasance[3], which is the only action left an injured party could rely on, apart from (where appropriate) one under s 61 of the Human Rights Act 1998. In any event the primary driving force in maintaining standards in this regard must be inside the regulated firm itself.

---

1 See, for example, Carson W G 'The Other Price of Britain's Oil', Oxford, 1981, p 145 and also Sangha, PhD thesis 'The role of the regulator, auditor and banker. The limits of regulation'.
2 FSMA 2000, s 102.
3 *Three Rivers District Council v Bank of England* [2000] 2 WLR 15.

6.7   The regulators themselves have become increasingly focused on: '... assessing the safety and soundness ... based less on the strength of the balance sheet today, and more on the strength of the controls that will safeguard (the firm's) financial health tomorrow.[1]' Such assessments will focus on both the risks that could threaten the institution itself, and in the case of larger institutions, those that could cause a knock-on effect and damage the financial conglomerate of which the firm may be a part. This is called 'systemic risk' and can on occasion be extremely complicated. It also becomes more likely that the standard risk regulations may not work well in some of these cases. As a result the regulators will often be prepared to allow a different approach, provided they are satisfied that the risks concerned are still being effectively managed. This can also happen with smaller firms, but it is only likely to occur in specialised businesses. 'Whilst regulators wish to see the regulations complied with it is the satisfactory management of risk rather than the existence of the rules that will be the overriding factor.[2]'

---

1 William J McDonough in 'Risk Management, Supervision and the New Basel Accord.' At the Bond Market Association, New York City, 4 February 2003.
2 Bazley, Haynes and Blunden, *ibid* at p2.

Compliance risk analysis

6.8   Compliance risk analysis and surveying has developed significantly in recent years with a number of approaches becoming commonplace with methodologies for identifying risks and their associated mitigating controls now being used by compliance managers. Frameworks for managing compliance risk and the use of action plans to improve the framework elements are also increasingly employed. However, the specialised needs of compliance managers must continue to be taken into account and the issues raised embraced by the board and line management.

6.9 Managing and mitigating the compliance risk of an organisation is probably the most difficult challenge facing compliance managers. Compliance risk can be a consequence of employee misbehaviour, external shock or systemic risk. In addition, compliance risks have become more and more prominent partly as a result of changes in many sectors of the financial services industry, for example: the boundaries of existing business processes have been stretched by a continuing need to innovate through new product launches, the use of more complex investment instruments and the use of increasingly complicated structures. The compliance responses to these have ranged from increasing compliance awareness through training to changes to existing processes.

6.10 Consolidation within industries and across different sections of the financial services industry has resulted in many institutions being exposed to the risks associated with the integration of business and operational processes including compliance risk. This can involve extended periods of operating parallel compliance processes and systems throughout the organisation, coupled with the migration of compliance data and management processes from pre-merger to post-merger systems. Accordingly, the potential frequency and complexity of problems must increase. There may also be problems for a period of maintaining disparate risk-based compliance systems across the post-merger group which may not be suited to covering the risks associated with the post-merger organisation.

6.11 The extent of publicity given to both compliance and organisational failures has increased the realisation by management that compliance failures and consequential costs could have happened in their own organisations. A scan through the press over recent years reveals examples of compliance errors to which even the better managed institutions are exposed. In some instances, these have resulted in both direct and indirect financial loss. That said, most of the recent fines imposed by the FSA in the United Kingdom have not resulted in a drop in share price. What it has tended to result in is the firms affected engaging in large-scale and expensive advertising campaigns to try and reduce the damage to their reputation.

The relationship between the Compliance Department, other departments and external agents

6.12 It should be borne in mind that the different departments in a financial services firm have dissimilar points of focus and are prone to having disparate key values. This is something that compliance personnel have to both manage and combat. Those in sales and marketing for example will tend to have an aggressive approach to marketing and selling new products, whereas the risk-based compliance focal point is that of managing this in the context of the legal and regulatory issues arising. A message that has to be communicated to all parties is what the potential dangers are to the firm and the personnel concerned if these risks are not successfully handled. This can only be done if everyone adopts the values concerned. Risk-based compliance cannot succeed if it is seen as the job of one department. It has to be seen as part of the function of all of them. One of the threats potentially obstructing a common misconception in management that the compliance department is the conscience of the firm[1].

---

1 Bob Moritz in 'Compliance: A gap at the heart of risk management,' PriceWaterhouse Coopers and the Economist Intelligence Unit, 2004, www.pwcglobal.com.

6.13   These issues can be exacerbated by the relationship of the compliance department with the other control departments in the firm. There is the potential for considerable overlap with the legal, internal audit and risk management departments. Additional issues can arise when interrelating with external agents such as external auditors, rating agencies, regulators and clients. These are examined below along with other relevant departments.

Legal department

6.14   The legal department's role is essentially advisory, examining relevant laws and regulations and giving an opinion on their meaning. Although risk-based compliance has its roots in legislation, regulation and sometimes common law and equity, the spirit of implementing these rules and guidelines is sometimes a step removed from the legal content. Thus, whereas the legal department's role will involve a legal interpretation of the precise meaning of words, that of risk-based compliance involves assessing how those will potentially impact on the firm's business operations, and what steps need to be taken to make sure that they do not do so in a negative way.

Internal auditors

6.15   It is vital that internal audit and the risk-based compliance department remain independent of each other. If internal audit starts to operate as a management consultancy it loses its independence. One of the tasks of internal audit is to carry out independent reviews of the effectiveness of the compliance process[1]. Indeed that is one of the Basel Committee's Principles[2]. Key issues which should be checked include:

●   assurance of the quality of information in the compliance reports;

- suitability and effectiveness of training programmes;

- success at correcting deficiencies;

- how effectively product managers implement risk-based compliance; and

- whether sufficient resources are available.

---

1 Susan S Bies. Member of the Board of Governors of the US Federal Reserve, speaking at the Annual Regulatory Compliance Conference, Washington, 11 June 2003.

2 Draft Principle 10. See also Singh 'Basel Committee on banking Supervision: the compliance function in banks,' JIBR vol 5, no 2 pp110–112.

6.16 Although internal audit should operate as an independent review and verification function, there is a possibility that it is viewed by management as an additional oversight and review operation. When this mistake occurs there is a real likelihood of significant conflict with the compliance department, one of whose main functions is to review and oversee the compliance of the firm with the regulations imposed on it. The relationship of internal audit to the compliance department should be one where internal audit independently reviews the processes undertaken and the risks controlled by compliance.

6.17 In addition: 'Is the internal audit function robust enough to challenge senior management?[1]' If it is not it will have little impact. It must be able to effect those who make operational decisions or risk-based compliance will lose a key operational element.

---

1 John Tiner, Chief Executive, IIA, Conference speech, 22 September 2005.

Risk management department

6.18 Confusion can arise in the relationship with risk management, indeed in some institutions the division between the two functions seems to become blurred. The risk management function should, *inter alia*, provide the compliance department with subject matter and expertise in terms of identifying risks and controls for managing and mitigating those risks. This can be utilised by the compliance department in the latter's assessment of the compliance risks facing the firm and the appropriateness and effectiveness of the controls over those risks.

6.19 Risk-based compliance is broader than risk management. In involves 'an enhanced role in counselling top management, and a leading part in the unlocking of new possibilities and market opportunities. In short, compliance should be regarded as more than risk management. It can serve as an enabler, or catalyst, for significant value creation[1].' Thus the departments' roles should function as follows:

- **Risk Management** assess the extent of the risks facing the business in current and prospective activities > make sure loss control or hedging mechanisms are in place (or decide the risk is too high to carry) > advise other departments of the firm accordingly.

- **Risk Based Compliance** assess the issues arising that threaten the firm's ability to satisfy compliance related demands in both current and prospective activities> make sure the firm is functioning in a manner that incorporates these into the business in a cost effective way.

---

1 Andrew Podd 'Best Practice and Delivering Value – The Future for Compliance', PriceWaterhouse Coopers 2002, www.pwcglobal.com.

6.20   This presupposes that there is an effective risk management process taking place. A recent survey in the United States[1] revealed that 45% of directors said that their organisations did not have a formal enterprise risk-management process and 19% said they did not know whether their company had a process for identifying risks! In financial services firms these figures will hopefully be much lower but they remain sobering statistics, and should be borne in mind by those in compliance in smaller, non-specialised financial institutions.

---

1 The Internal Auditors and the National Association of Corporate Directors, 2002.

External auditors

6.21   External auditors can provide an additional line of defence to the compliance department that compliance policies and procedures are being followed. However, it should be remembered that, in the words of Lord Justice Lopes[1], external auditors function as a watchdog, not a bloodhound. Cases of major failure in major institutions never seem to have been brought to the fore as a result of external auditors having spotted the failures. Examples include BCCI, Barings, Sumitomo, ABI, Maxwell Group Enterprises, Worldcom and, for different reasons, Enron and Parmalat. It is therefore important not to over rely on them and assume they will pick matters up that the firm's own procedures have not.

---

1 *Re Kingston Cotton Mills Co* (1896) 2 Ch 279.

6.22   Causes of external auditors not noticing findings include the members of external audit teams being inexperienced and not fully understanding the business they are looking at, and issues being skillfully hidden so that auditors cannot see them. It should be borne in mind, however, that the cases mentioned above are not typical and that generally, external audit will be thorough and effective. It will also, as part of its process have involved interviewing those in risk-based compliance and examining parts of their work.

Credit department

6.23 The analysis of clients and prospective clients by this department will need to be more penetrating than anything carried out for money laundering checks as part of the compliance procedures. It will give the credit department an insight into the financial strengths and weaknesses of the clients which extends to being able to assess the risk they pose to a bank dealing with them.

6.24 The benefits that the credit department can offer compliance are amplified by the fact that it is a department which has an increasing range of software, databases, models and risk rating systems which provide detailed and useful material. To quote the Chief Executive Officer of the US Federal Reserve Bank:

> 'Our examiners have noted growing sophistication in banks' ... risk rating processes, portfolio management methodologies and the use of stress testing. As you know, all of these new tools and processes were developed and refined to promote a bank's competitiveness and to protect it against loss – and not just to respond to a regulatory mandate.[1]'

For these reasons it makes sense for the compliance department in financial services firms (not just banks) to access the information that exists as a result of this process.

---

1 William J McDonough, *ibid.*

Front office departments: trading and sales

6.25 There is an obvious difference of focus between compliance on one hand and sales and trading on the other. The need of those in sales and trading to hit targets can make them cavalier about the requirements that compliance seeks to impose on them and in some cases to see them as a barrier to success. Staff training and clear direction from the top can ameliorate the position, though it is always an area where compliance will need to maintain attention.

6.26 It is an area that has seen considerable change over the years. In earlier times compliance was focused in the back office and was often focused on after trading[1]. As a reaction to problems that have arisen in this aspect of risk management it has tended to migrate to a more proactive and front office focused relationship with the rest of the firm:

'Compliance has to be proactive, and must be involved in newly
sought acquisitions, new products and services as they come on
stream.[2]' After all the main aim of compliance is to stop people
breaking the rules rather than manage the consequences when they
fail to.

---

1 Frances Maguire, 'Mind the Gap' in Compliance & Technology Review, issue No 1, p 8.
2 Brian Harte, Group Head of Compliance, Barclays Bank quoted in Maguire, *supra*.

Research department

6.27   This is an important area for compliance. In part this is because the
laws which have emerged, and are emerging on market abuse[1], insider dealing
and financial promotions pose a considerable threat to firms. Those involved in
research may not always be conscious of the potential impact that their release
of information could have on the markets. Nor may they always be aware of the
complexity and subtlety of some of the relevant law and regulation. The
response to this has to be dealt with in part by compliance and in part by
in-house training. The role of compliance will be particularly important in that
there can be very short time frames between information coming into the
possession of the firm, and a potential offence being committed.

---

1 See the new Market Abuse Directive and also recent FSA disciplinary cases on market abuse and insider dealing
such as Middlemiss, Bracken and Shell at www.fsa.gov.uk.

Corporate finance department

6.28   This is an obvious area of concern for compliance, most obviously
because of the insider dealing risk. This could arise through deliberate misbehaviour, but more probably by a careless remark being made by a member of
corporate finance which could be an offence in itself, or at least trigger one[1].
Such sensitive information will often relate to clients but may also relate to
target companies on whom clients are considering a takeover bid.

---

1 Criminal Justice Act 1993, s 52.

6.29   There is one advantage, and that is that for many years banks have been
very conscious of the risks posed to them. Chinese walls are standard procedure
and their strict observance tends to be the order of the day due to their protective

effect[1]. This does need to be reinforced, however, by periodic training and reviews.

---

1 *R v Swiss Bank Corporation* (unreported).

Litigation risk

6.30   Litigation risk is a potentially expensive area and one that can lead to serious damage to reputation. This can arise as a result of misleading communication with clients, but there may also be further evidence in the form of records or tapes of phone calls with the clients and also in house, particularly amongst dealers which might cast a light on the behaviour of the firm. Matters can become more problematic when the financial arrangements are particularly complex, and it is no coincidence that much of the US litigation has focused on complex derivatives cases.

6.31   The greatest compliance risk to a firm often lies in this area through misunderstanding by a past client, especially when now contracting as a counterparty. In some cases the scale of the financial losses that have accrued will tend to give rise to litigation as the firm's counterparty tries to find a way to avoid liability. Cases in point can be found in the US where clients tried arguing that a 'banker – customer' relationship existed on the grounds that the counterparty to a client was their banker[1]. Here the bankers found protection in advertising content, pre-contract correspondence and the terms of the standard ISDA contract which had been used. They still settled out of court for very large amounts of money as a result of evidence of a failure to satisfy internal compliance procedures in the dealing room.

---

1 *Gibson Greetings v Bankers Trust Co* (CV No C-1-94-620 Ohio), *Proctor & Gamble v Bankers Trust* (CV No C-1-94-735 SD Ohio), *PT Adimitra Rayapratama (AR) v Bankers Trust & BTI* (1995 Southern District of New York). By way of comparison see also the English case of *PD Adimitri v Bankers Trust* (1995) (unreported).

6.32   Another area of concern can be pricing models. In complex derivatives experts can differ on the correct way pricing should be calculated. Matters are complicated by the fact that such models are commercially sensitive – and valuable. The bank may not wish to release them to counterparties.

The key compliance issues here are going to relate to communication with clients: initially advertising, then pre contract documentation and finally the contracts themselves. Here the legal department may also be involved in giving advice on what should or should not be said.

Regulators

6.33   The FSA have already made clear that firms who are open and co-operative about failings will be treated more leniently than equivalent firms who are not[1]. However, the regulatee's behaviour will not be the only issue in determining the regulator's attitude. Fines may be imposed, but this is potentially a small part of the picture. Such fines may trigger expensive advertising campaigns by such firms to try and repair damaged reputations. Of greater importance, and potentially scale, the regulator may require compensation to be paid. 'Lloyds TSB was fined £1.9 million for mis-selling precipice bonds, but agreed to compensation of over £100 million; Lincoln Assurance was fined £485,000 for mis-selling of 10-year savings plans by a representative, but provided £8.8million in compensation. In fact, over the last 18 months a total of £135 million has been paid or set aside in compensation as a result of FSA action.[2]' It is important to remember that keeping the regulator happy is not the limit of risk-based compliance. It must seek to '... improve the quality of its management and to reap the benefits of being seen to be at the leading edge of good governance. Confidence stems from competence not compliance.[3]'

---

1 See Final Notices 12/12/02 Royal Bank of Scotland, 9/12/03 Abbey National and 12/1/04 Bank of Scotland, www.fsa.gov.uk.
2 McCarthy, *ibid.*
3 PriceWaterhouse Coopers survey April 2004, www.pwcglobal.com.

6.34 Hopefully, regulatory reviews will give the firm a clean bill of health. Even positive reviews may flag up small areas of concern and it is important that compliance communicate to the board and senior managers that, within limits, such regulatory observations are not a sign that people are not doing their jobs properly.

Rating agencies

6.35 The role of such agencies has grown in importance over the years and in the case of large firms the agencies may well wish to meet key personnel, so as to formulate a clearer view of the bank's operations. Compliance has a role to play here in making sure that the rating agencies get a view of the skill with which the bank is engaging in the management of the risks associated with the compliance operation.

IT department

6.36 The relationship between compliance and IT can be a crucial one. According to a court report by PriceWaterhouse Coopers[1] this is an area that tends to be weakest at the lower levels of strategic monitoring. Where senior managers used the firm's intranet and workflow technology to raise awareness of the effect of regulation on the firm's business, the relationship between IT and compliance became strained. Compliance should therefore seek to manage the relationship with this department in a way that is mutually constructive.

1 PriceWaterhouse Coopers: 'The Future of Compliance – Using technology to deliver value', 2004, www.pwc-global.com.

The Board and Chief Executive Officer

6.37   Clearly it is vital that the Board and the Chief Executive Officer have a good, ongoing working relationship with compliance and are fully aware of the legal and regulatory obligations imposed on them by the current regulatory regime. This can assist in tying the firm's development in with compliance necessities. For example, the PWC Report cited above found that banks virtually never consulted the head of compliance about which trading systems to buy. Many compliance departments had no IT budget themselves at all!

6.38   The key issue here, however, is that the buck stops at the top. To quote Susan S Bies[1]: 'The board of directors and senior management cannot delegate the responsibility for having an effective system of compliance. Certain portions of the implementation of the compliance process may be conducted by more junior management, but this does not relieve the board and senior management of responsibility for the design and effectiveness of the system.'

1 PriceWaterhouse Coopers: 'The Future of Compliance – Using technology to deliver value', 2004, www.pwc-global.com.

6.39   The Basel Committee go further and state:

'The bank's board of directors has the responsibility for overseeing the management of the bank's compliance risk. The board should approve the bank's compliance policy, including a charter or other formal document establishing a permanent compliance function. At least once a year, the board or committee of the board should review the bank's compliance policy and its ongoing implementation to assess the extent to which the bank is managing the compliance risk effectively.[1]'

1 The Compliance Function in Banks, 31 January 2004 at Principle 1, www.bis.org/publ/bcbs103.pdf.

6.40   The FSA Principles for Business for Approved Persons take this a step further and create personal liability for senior Approved Persons such as board members and senior executives stating they must:

'take reasonable steps to ensure that the business of the firm for which he is responsible in his controlled function complies with the regulatory requirements imposed on that business.[1]'

1 FSA Principle for Approved Persons 7, www.fsa.gov.uk.

6.41   Another issue is whether changes need to be made in the light of events such as Worldcom and Enron. Since the Worldcom fiasco a number of parties have suggested separating the roles of Chairman and CEO, requiring all directors other than the CEO to be independent, requiring the full board to meet eight times a year and substantially raising directors' compensation. One American state has even gone so far as to create a director's duty of care of ensuring that corporate information and reporting systems exist[1]. It is an area that warrants full board attention and in some cases a board subcommittee fully focused on the issue.

---

1 *Re Caremark International Inc Derivative Litigation* 698 A.2d 959 (Del. Ch. 1996).

Factors affecting risk

Independence

6.42   For reasons that must be apparent from the above analysis of the various departments that compliance must deal with, the compliance function can only operate effectively if it is independent. The person in charge must both have a suitably senior position inside the firm and also have a strong enough personality to withstand pressures to operate in a way he finds inappropriate. He must also be capable of forcing through the policies he believes to be appropriate and be able to make certain that such policies operate effectively. The relationship is not made any easier by the need for compliance to make reports to the regulator where necessary. The department therefore sometimes tends to be seen to be operating as both in-house operatives and outsiders. This tends to be exacerbated by the severity with which the regulators sometimes act.

Restrictions on compliance staff

6.43   As a result of this relationship it is crucial that compliance personnel themselves maintain the highest personal standards and comply with all internal rules and relevant external ones. All personnel must be 'fit and proper' but those in personnel must be seen as being above reproach. Many firms do not allow personal account dealing by personnel in compliance and those who do should make it subject to careful review. There will usually be room for slightly more flexibility when dealing with most of the rest of the firm's personnel.

Access to senior management and audit committees

6.44   There must be easy access to the highest levels of the management structure, eg, the Chief Executive Officer or the Audit Committee Chairman, who will very likely be a member of the Board of Directors. The wide perception of unfettered access to senior management is as important as actual access. The audit committee itself is of increasing importance. In the US for example, it is now necessary for companies to disclose whether the audit committee has at least one financial expert, and if not, why not[1]. 'Financial expert' in this context is a defined term and means someone with:

- 'an understanding of GAAP (Generally Accepted Accounting Principles);

- the ability to assess the general application of GAAP in connection with accounting for estimates, accruals and reserves;

- experience of either preparing, auditing or analysing financial statements that present a breadth and level of complexity of accounting issues that are reasonably comparable to those that the issuer's financial statements can reasonably be expected to reach or actively supervising individuals engaged in these activities.[2]'

It is inconceivable that a financial institution of any size would put itself in a position where this requirement was not satisfied in any event.

---

1 Sarbanes-Oxley Act 2002, s 407.
2 Editorial 'Legal requirements and responsibilities of the audit committee under Sarbanes-Oxley,' International Journal of Disclosure and Governance, Vol 1, No 1, p 6.

Compliance policy drift

6.45   Any policy has the potential to gradually migrate from its place of origin. The most obvious is that of a general relaxation of standards, where people stop obeying the regulations strictly and gradually become more and more cavalier. A less obvious process can occur where new products appear as a result of product innovation, or more complex ones evolve from simpler, existing ones. Where such developments are incremental, it is likely that any compliance slippage will be as well, thus making it more difficult to spot. It is partly the job of compliance to pick these matters up, but internal audit checks may be more likely to show them. It is better caught at this stage rather than by the external auditors, as in serious cases they may feel the need to mention it in the audit report. Worst of all is it not being noticed at all until a regulatory inspection or proposed litigation suddenly reveals the problem.

Regulatory ability

6.46   The capacity of a regulator to fully understand the firm's business can be a factor. This tends to arise where a subsidiary or branch of a large complex multinational operation is functioning in a small state with an unsophisticated regulator. This tends to occur in developing countries where there is sufficient wealth to attract the selling of complex financial products. The local regulators will then be starting from scratch in attempting to supervise matters. They may also find themselves running one step behind as the sophistication of the products being marketed continues to develop. Matters can be further complicated by cultural, religious and political issues colouring the view the regulator wishes to take.

Size of a regulated entity

6.47   The size of a firm can be a factor in determining its capacity to handle compliance related issues. Small firms sometimes find it difficult to provide sufficient resources, skills or knowledge to ensure full compliance, especially if they operate in the retail market where compliance demands can be heavy. For such firms it can be a struggle balancing the business needs of generating money with the compliance needs for monitoring and record keeping. As a result small businesses tend to use firms of compliance specialists who provide part- time periodic compliance reviews. This can be appropriate provided it is a case of experts coming in to help the firm, rather than the job being seen as contracted out.

6.48   On the other hand large firms can face different problems. There may be less tolerance of large firms by some regulators who see major players as role models for the industry for whom there can be no excuse for failing to meet the highest standards. In some states there may not be a level playing field with the home regulator being prepared to deal with infractions by national champions by private admonition, but taking more serious steps if a subsidiary or branch of an overseas operation does the same thing.

Training risk

6.49   This is a crucial area, whether for new arrivals, those who have been promoted and existing staff. Without suitable training it is improbable that staff will be sufficiently up to date with new laws and regulations, or changes to the firm's compliance procedures. It facilitates the effectiveness of the training if the logic and reasoning behind the requirements are made clear. In the case of new arrivals, some may not come from a financial services background and therefore have little awareness of compliance, or even a clear idea how the firm functions. On the other hand a new employee may have worked in financial services but have worked in a firm with a different compliance culture. The problem here can be more subtle and in some cases more intractable. Careful training and ongoing follow up will be necessary to make sure that the person adapts.

Risk-based compliance framework

6.50 The firm's risk-based compliance approach, together with its reasons and effects must be fully understood and applied by all relevant parties, such as the Board of Directors, external auditors, regulators, shareholders and customers. 'Reference to the compliance culture in all external documents, eg, the annual report and product sales leaflets, is helpful in making clear the firm's position with regard to compliance. Internally, the inclusion of a compliance report in regular Audit Committee or Risk Committee documents helps to ensure the widespread dissemination of compliance information at a senior level.[1]'

---

1 Bazley, Haynes and Blunden, *ibid.*

Meeting attendance

6.51 Part of a successfully functioning risk-based compliance system is that of its rationale, contents, processes and objectives being successfully communicated to relevant personnel and then acted upon. Partly this will be done by training, but training alone will be insufficient to achieve these things. Existing meetings within the organisation need to have a compliance element. This is not limited to meetings with an obvious compliance ingredient such as internal and external auditor's meetings, but also sales, research and departmental/interdepartmental meetings. If compliance issues are raised and resolved in this way it assists in compliance being seen throughout the firm as a useful solution to the firm's problems rather than as an irritating distraction from them.

Differing views of risk

6.52 As has been discussed above under 'risk-based management' not all the departments in the firm have the same aspects of risk to manage, and even where the same risk issue arises it will be looked at from a different vantage point and in many cases with a view to achieving a different aim. Obvious examples are: the legal department, the credit department, the internal audit department and risk management. What is important is to make sure that the risk-based compliance nexus in the firm recognises the necessity of this.

Secure area within compliance

6.53 Important and sensitive compliance related issues may need to be handled by a limited number of people, and kept confidential to them. Thus, within compliance there can be an inner compliance unit, sometimes called the control room or conflicts room. In large multinational banks this will need to be a 24 hour a day, 365 days a year operation to deal with emergencies. Problems can arise when a crisis does erupt as the numbers of people needed to handle this can suddenly increase. In such cases it will be necessary to co-opt additional staff with appropriate expertise for the duration of the resolution of the crisis.

Building and shaping compliance systems

Vision

6.54 There needs to be a starting point from which the risk-based compliance structure emerges and to which it seeks to measure up. This vision must set out the aims of compliance, the principles to be followed and what is currently termed a 'mission statement'. This is the background against which the framework must be constructed.

Framework

6.55 How this fits in with the other risk issues the firm faces has already been examined, but this does need to be articulated as a coherent structure, be clearly understood and spelt out in written form. It also needs to be agreed to and supported by the Board and communicated to all those in the firm whose job functions mean they need to be conscious of the compliance aspects of the firm's operation. The framework must include responsibilities of the Board of Directors and senior management as well as staff responsibilities. Without this it will not be possible to keep the entire firm operating on the desired basis.

Oversight structure

6.56 The roles and responsibilities of each of the control departments within the firm with respect to compliance will have been spelt out in the framework but there also needs to be a structure for spelling out exactly how the framework will be overseen. Other key factors have been spelled out as follows: 'Reporting processes and escalation triggers need to be detailed. How the compliance department will achieve quality assurance and quality control will also be articulated. The staffing and management of the department together with its interaction and integration with other departments of the firm will be mentioned.[1]'

---

1 Bazley, Haynes and Blunden, *ibid*.

Change management

6.57   Managing change is always a difficult and subtle problem. In the context of risk-based compliance it can arise as an issue due to: changes in technology, changes in the firm's structure, takeovers and mergers, new products and moving into new markets. It can also arise because of changes required by the law or a regulator. If the vision, framework and oversight structures all operate as they should the task will be made much easier. Even so, changing existing habits can be hard work, and require sustained management, supervision and training to make sure the new approach takes hold.

Common language

6.58   There are two issues here. The use of specific terminology and, in the case of large multinationals, of which country's language to use. In the case of the former it is vital that the key terminology is understood by all relevant staff. This is particularly true of words and phrases that are given key meanings by the law or by a regulator. A failure to retain these words and phrases in compliance documentation and procedures can lead to the compliance slippage that was discussed above as a consequence of a change in wording leading to a subtle but critical change in staff behaviour.

6.59   In the case of large multinationals it may well be the case that a number of languages have to be used in the firm, but that a certain managerial and oversight level the strategic issues have to be done in one language. This is clearly critical for compliance where the translation of words and sometimes transliteration of them can lead to a change in meaning. What will be appropriate will depend on the geographical split of the firm's operations and which regulators become involved. Ideally though the compliance issues need to be kept in one language as far as possible.

What risks should be covered?

6.60   The defining of compliance risk within a financial services firm needs to be carefully done. If it is too narrow issues may be missed by the other departments they have been left to. On the other hand if it is too wide damage may be caused to relationships with other departments. There is also the separate issue of the manner in which the risks are classified. This can be done in different ways. The following table sets out the key risks from three vantage points. The first of these risk listing approaches deals with the risks by examining the relevant processes, people, systems and external risks[1]. These can be worked through to cover all relevant risks. On the other hand the same result could be achieved by looking at the strategic risks involved, by examining the various activities the firm must engage in and then work through these to make sure that the risks associated with each of these are covered[2]. Finally, the risks could be structured by approaching them as a set of procedures and standards[3]. These can be listed and then worked through to provide a coherent list of the risks to be managed. This is the approach adopted in the US Federal Sentencing Guidelines which are further discussed below. The biggest problem with these lists is the broad nature of many of the categories, though this does have the advantage of clarity at a strategic level.

The compliance risk approach chosen must be appropriate for the nature of the business concerned and be suited to functioning successfully given the structural realities of the business.

---

1 Supra at p 33, 34.
2 Supra at p 34, 35.
3 US Federal Sentencing Guidelines, due diligence criteria, 1991.

6.61

RISK LISTING	STRATEGIC RISK-BASED APPROACH	DUE DILIGENCE CRITERIA
Processes		
third party risks, eg *laundering* business reputation risks, *e g insurance* client risks, eg *suitability, capacity, sales practices and client identification* employee risks, *wrongful trading, market abuse, insider dealing, collusion, trading limits and delegation of duties* management risks, *e g control valuation and audit* product risks, *e g complexity, internal disclosure, external disclosure* strategic risks, *corporate governance, reputation, new markets, acquisition and disposal*	Authorisation and registration risk Client money and assets risk Customer risk, *e g insolvency, fraud, laundering* Advertising/promotion risk. *Differs from state to state and is regulated on a host state basis* Packaged product risk, *i e extensive consumer protection regulations apply* Order execution risk Market abuse risk (including insider dealing), *differs in many jurisdictions. Can thus be a problem for multi-jurisdictional organisations and transactions.* Stabilisation risk Transaction reporting and record keeping risk Personal account dealing Complaints Regulator risk	Compliance standards. *Are they appropriate? Are they being met?* Compliance procedures. *As above* High level officers. *Do they have appropriate knowledge, experience and understanding of relevant risk?* Due care in delegating authority Effective communication (*best done in writing for evidential purposes*) Monitoring auditing and reporting Consistent discipline Process modification
People		
Employee failure, *e g malice, fraud, negligence, information misuse* employee proficiency, *e g competence and training* inappropriate culture risk conflict of interest risk		

Systems		
communication risks, *e g availability* data risks, *e g quality, integrity and model risk.* hardware risks, *e g failure, integrity and security* software risks, *e g programming errors, security and capacity*		
External risk		
governmental risk, *e g change in political environment, military coups* industry-related risk, *e g change in regulatory standards and practices* physical risk, *e g physical security, internet security and natural disasters* terrorism risk		

Relationships and lines of communication

6.62   The division of responsibility inside the firm is a crucial issue. As discussed above the ultimate responsibility rests with the Chief Executive Officer and Board of Directors. In reality the operation of compliance is delegated to the compliance department, though it is important that the framework discussed above sets out clearly where one person's responsibilities start and another's end. Appropriate line management[1] coupled with suitable reporting lines can then keep this in place. The various departments discussed above must also be made to understand that the handling of the relevant part of the risk-based compliance issues rests within their department. They can look to the compliance department for guidance and assistance but cannot abrogate the job to them.

---

1 Required by FSA Principle for Approved Persons 5.

6.63   To facilitate line management and to leave a clear record of what has happened it is vital that suitable reporting systems are put into place. These should include agreed and acceptable timescales within which the reports must be submitted and the minimum amount of information required that enables the compliance department to perform its functions efficiently.

Enforcing compliance obligations

6.64 This chapter concentrates on internal arrangements and mechanisms that a firm should have in place to ensure that its staff comply with regulatory obligations. In the United States the Federal Sentencing Guidelines, first introduced in 1991, provide a set of due diligence criteria to managing the compliance risks discussed. These are set out in column three of the above table. They provide a basic common-sense approach to getting things done. If firms can show that they have satisfied these guidelines it reduces their 'culpability score'. If there is a failure in the bank the sanctions imposed by the regulator would normally then be reduced. For firms outside the US it provides a useful series of yardsticks. However, if risk-based compliance is to work to full effectiveness it must work as '..a broad based, proactive compliance programme that is fully integrated into a company's business.[1] ' Indeed it has been argued[2] that reducing a checklist approach can result in compliance failure. The key issue therefore is to make sure that it does not lead to over simplification.

1 Christopher Michaelson 'What is Effective Compliance?' in re: Business, December 2001.
2 Michaelson, *supra*.

Regulatory principles for business

6.65 In the UK the rules imposed by the regulator operate under the umbrella of a list of eleven general Principles for firms and seven Principles for Approved Persons (see Chapter). Whilst these do not create civil liability to private clients in the way that the rules themselves do, it makes it easier for the regulator to stamp on unacceptable behaviour. The argument that there is a loophole in the rules, or something behind which improper behaviour can be hidden will be defeated if the regulator can point to a general principle that has been broken. FSA Principle for Business 3 dictates that an authorised firm must take reasonable care to organise and control its affairs responsibly and effectively, with adequate risk management systems. It can apply not only to procedures that firms should have in place, but also to the methods they undertake to ensure that their staff comply with those procedures. As mentioned above, Approved Person's Principle 7 states that 'An Approved Person performing a significant influence function must take reasonable steps to ensure that the business of the firm for which he is responsible in his controlled function complies with the regulatory requirements imposed on that business.' Thus, in the UK at least, there is now personal responsibility imposed on senior figures in a financial institution to make sure that compliance functions as it should.

6.66   There are two schools of thought as to how compliance can be integrated within the firm's business. The top down approach, where a firm establishes a dictatorial compliance department, and a bottom up approach. The latter involves integrating the compliance requirements within the work patterns of each relevant department. The former approach has the advantage of instilling a sense of discipline but it can create an atmosphere of threat. A bottom up approach works on the premise that compliance will happen automatically as a member of staff is not able to distinguish between a business process and a distinct regulatory requirement and so satisfies both.

6.67   Which is most appropriate depends not only on the firm but also the circumstances. The top down approach is more likely to be suitable where there is an immediate issue to be handled, such as a regulator taking disciplinary steps or a major change to the compliance model being put into effect.

Conclusions

6.68   Key issues to consider are[1]:

- is management support for compliance evident in its values, as they are stated and practised;

- is there cross functional support for compliance? Is it put into action through effective project management;

- is the approach to compliance rooted in consistent ethical values;

- does the compliance programme utilise technology effectively;

- is there a balance of rewards for promoting compliance and consequences for misconduct or disengagement;

- are regulators and other stakeholders constructively engaged; and

- is compliance managed by an appropriate mix of thinkers and doers?

---

1 See Michaelson, *ibid.*

6.69   Achieving this can be sought by a single centralised compliance office or by way of a decentralised compliance function, with the compliance staff being located in different business areas[1]. Either may be appropriate according to the bank concerned. What is crucial is that the responsibilities of the compliance function are clearly defined and that it should be independent from the business activities of the bank.

---

1 The Compliance Function in Banks, 31 January 2004, www.bis.org/publ/bcbs103.pdf.

6.70   Some other key issues can be highlighted. It is vital that the risk-based compliance function remains engaged in the firm as an element in its planning and development and does not function in a way that is negative. Its function is not purely to '… spend time warding off disasters rather than making positive contributions to the firm.[1]' As well as the right approach being needed to achieve this it also involves having sufficient resources. This issue has already been cited as a problem in one major regulatory failure[2]. From the point of view of risk- based compliance '… it is no longer about sitting in an ivory tower or ensuring that you have a monitoring plan. Effective compliance is about helping the business when a department or … individual …floats an idea for a new product.[3]' Perhaps above all else the compliance function is in reality part of everyone's job, not just those with it as part of their job title. In this day and age compliance has to function effectively throughout the firm or the firm may not have a future. On a positive side large institutions operating risk-based compliance in an effective way can influence the regulators in their approach to that market sector[4]. On the other hand the consequences to a firm of a failure of its risk-based compliance function can be catastrophic.

The author wishes to acknowledge the input of Stuart Bazley & Tony Blunden through their contributions to 'Risk Based Compliance' on which parts of this paper are based[5].

---

1 Pete Malcolm in 'Who would want to be a compliance officer?' in Compliance & Technology Review, issue No 1, p 22.
2 FSA investigation into market rigging at ABN AMRO Equities (UK) 2003, www.fsa.gov.uk.
3 Simon Elvidge, deputy head of compliance, Fimat, Compliance & Technology Review, issue No 1, p 24.
4 Pieth and Aiolfi, 'The Private Sector becomes Active: The Wolfsberg Process. In a Practitioner's Guide to International Money Laundering Law and Regulation, City and Financial, 2003 at pp 273, 274.
5 Bazley, Haynes & Blunden 'Risk Based Compliance', Butterworths, London 2001.

Chapter 7

Special compliance obligations: money laundering

'We expect firms to manage their financial crime risk as they manage other business risks. That means resourcing that activity adequately and putting resources where there is most marginal benefit, against the backdrop of their legal obligations .....Firms ...need to play their part ever more effectively.'

Philip Robinson, Crime Sector Leader, FSA

Introduction

7.1   This chapter examines the legal and regulatory position concerning money laundering. It covers the position under the Terrorism Act 2000 and the Proceeds of Crime Act 2002, as amended, plus the relevant delegated legislation. Coupled with this the chapter looks at the FSA regulatory position which applies to FSA regulated firms. The issues arising from the civil law are looked at and finally the Wolfsberg Principles are analysed.

7.2   Laundering is the process of hiding and moving money to make it appear that illegal funds have been honestly earned and possibly to also appear to have nothing to do with the real owner. In the case of terrorist funds the money may be honestly earned and the criminal event be planned at the end of the money trail. For this reason it has a separate definition.

Money laundering has been defined as[1]:

'... the process by which criminals attempt to conceal the true origin and ownership of their criminal activities. If undertaken successfully, it also allows them to maintain control over those proceeds and, ultimately, to provide a legitimate cover for their source of income'.

---

1 Joint Money Laundering Steering Group *Guidance Notes for the Financial Sector*, at 1.03.

7.3   Another, briefer definition[1] was:

'rendering the proceeds of crime unrecognisable as such.'

However, the Joint Money Laundering Steering Committee Guidelines adopt a common mistake which provides false security in many of the larger laundering operations, ie:

'Criminally earned money is invariably transient in nature.'

---

1 Simon Gleeson 'The Involuntary Launderer 'in *Laundering and Tracing* 1995.

7.4   This will often be the case as the criminal concerned will be in need of the funds as soon as possible. However, the vast increases in wealth available to the larger organised crime groups in recent years, and possibly some of the smaller ones, means that it may be possible for them to tie up some of their funds for significant periods of time as part of the laundering process.

7.5   The range of methods that can be utilised to launder money are enormous and anyone needing to have a clear understanding of the subject needs to read widely and keep abreast of changes in laundering patterns. The commonest vehicles for laundering are those where large amounts of cash, liquid investments or assets are handled. In the financial markets banks and investment business firms are the most heavily used. In the commercial field are businesses dealing in high value goods who can prove attractive as they provide the opportunity for moving money by dealing in expensive items, often across international boundaries. Another development, and one that has become more heavily utilised as banks and other financial businesses have attempted to tighten their anti-money laundering operations is to include a firm of solicitors, accountants or other professionals in what appears to be a bona fide scheme to invest or transact money. This provides the attraction of feeding money through a professional's client account to mask the arrangement with a veneer of respectability. A particular problem in spotting laundering is that most of those with large amounts of money to launder can construct their operations intelligently enough to avoid it looking suspicious. In almost all instances of large movements of laundered money the criminals will be employing experts to advise and assist them.

7.6   The legislation and guidelines focus primarily on laundering the proceeds of crime. A consequence of this is that they are not of great assistance in picking up terrorist monies. In the UK in particular a dissimilarity arises between the patterns of terrorist money and many of the other laundering schemes. There is also a dissimilarity in the legislation in that it is necessary to report the movement of monies which may be utilised to commit a criminal act by a proscribed organisation rather than just money being moved after a crime. This issue is examined more closely below.

7.7   The imposition of money laundering obligations on financial institutions and certain professionals has created a situation where those parties must ascertain whether a particular transaction is 'suspicious' and, if so, potential reporting issues arise. This chapter will consider what circumstances should arouse suspicion, what reporting issues then arise and what to do in borderline situations.

The criminal offences 1 – Laundering Drug Proceeds and the Profits of Crime

7.8   The law is mainly found in the Proceeds of Crime Act 2002 which creates three principal laundering offences in ss 327 to 329. This Act has been amended by the Serious Organised Crime and Police Act 2005 and the Proceeds of Crime Act 2002 and Money Laundering Regulations 2006[1]. This statute is being introduced in stages and some subsections will be issued by statutory instrument. It is important therefore to check from time to time to ascertain whether additional amendments have not been made. In addition there are two other statutes, the Terrorism Act 2000 and the Anti-terrorism, Crime and Security Act 2001, which together with the Terrorism (United Nations) Order 2001[2] determine the position with relation to funds that are suspected of being used to further the ends of terrorism. In addition, the Money Laundering Regulations 2003[3] govern many of the detailed issues relating to the day-to-day requirements imposed on those caught by the law relating to money laundering.

---

1 SI 2006/308.
2 SI 2001/3365.
3 SI 2003/3075.

Concealing etc the proceeds of crime

7.9   It is an offence under s 327 to conceal, disguise, convert, transfer or remove criminal property from the jurisdiction. This extends to concealing etc its nature, source, location, disposition, movement, ownership or any rights in relation to it. There are defences in as much that it is not an offence if the person concerned has made a protected disclosure under s 338, usually to the Serious Organised Crime Agency (SOCA), and has been given consent to continue to act. Likewise, if he was going to make such a disclosure but there was 'a reasonable excuse' for not doing so. Finally there is a third defence where the act that has been done consists of carrying out a function he has in relation to enforcing any provision of the Proceeds of Crime Act 2002 or of any other statute relating to criminal conduct or benefiting therefrom. 'Criminal property' is defined by s 340(3) as being someone's benefit from criminal conduct where the alleged offender knows or suspects that it represents such a benefit.

199

7.10 Under s 327(2C) a deposit taking body that converts or transfers criminal property does not commit an offence provided it does the act concerned in operating an account which it maintains and the value of the criminal property concerned does not exceed the threshold amount. At present the threshold amount has been set at £250. This exception is a very limited one as it only applies to those carrying on deposit taking business.

Arrangements

7.11 It is an offence under s 328 to enter into or become concerned in an arrangement which that person knows, or suspects, facilitates the retention, use or control of criminal property. There are three defences which are the same as those in **7.9** above. The same exception for deposit taking bodies that exists for s 327 also applies here.

Acquisition use and possession

7.12 It is an offence under s 329 for someone to acquire, use or have possession of criminal property. The three defences to s 327 apply here. There is also a fourth, namely where the person acquiring, using or having possession obtained the property for adequate consideration. This is to protect traders who buy goods and are not therefore under a duty to question the source of the money. It would not extend to a situation where the goods or services were being knowingly provided to assist in the carrying out of a crime, or where there was suspicion. The deposit taking exception applies. It should be noted that the definition of 'property' includes money and therefore this section will cover someone in possession of funds that are being or are to be laundered.

Failure to disclose

7.13 It is an offence under s 330 to fail to make a report where someone knows or suspects (or has reasonable grounds for so doing) that someone else is engaged in money laundering where the knowledge or suspicion came into that person's possession in the course of their business in the regulated sector. The person on whom this legal obligation rests must either be able to identify the person concerned or the whereabouts of the laundered property. The report should be made to the firm's nominated officer or the person authorised for this purpose by the Director General of the Serious Organised Crime Agency. This disclosure should consist of the person's identity, the whereabouts of the laundered property concerned and any information or other matter on which this knowledge is based which came to him in the course of his business. Such a disclosure must be made as soon as reasonably practicable once the information is in that person's possession.

7.14   There is a defence[1] where the person concerned has a reasonable excuse for not making the required disclosure or where he is a professional legal adviser and if he knows the relevant information because of facts coming into his hands in privileged circumstances. There is a further defence that would apply where the person concerned does not know or suspect that the other person is engaged in money laundering and had not been provided with money laundering training by their employer. There is also the possibility[2] that a professional legal adviser can make a communication to the money laundering reporting officer for the purpose of obtaining an opinion regarding the situation. Any information made for such a purpose is not regarded as a disclosure. It is useful where the legal adviser is less *au fait* than the money laundering reporting officer as to the relevant legal position. Often such information will have come into the firm's possession in privileged circumstances where a professional legal adviser has been provided with it in connection with his giving legal advice or in connection with legal proceedings. However, this exception does not apply where the communication has been made with the purpose of furthering a criminal purpose.

1 Proceeds of Crime Act 2002, s 330(6).
2 Proceeds of Crime Act 2002, s 330(9A).

Failure to report

7.15   It is an offence under s 331 where a money laundering reporting officer who receives a report which gives them grounds to know or suspect that laundering is taking place does not then make a report to the SOCA. The report that he has received should have stated the identity of the suspected person, the location of the laundered property or why he believes (or it is reasonable to expect him to believe) that the information will assist in identifying the person or location of the laundered property. An offence is not committed if he has a 'reasonable excuse'[1] for not making the required disclosure. Unfortunately this is not a defined term and pending judicial interpretation it would be wise to interpret it very narrowly.

The same offence and defence apply under s 332 to nominated officers outside the 'regulated sector'. This is defined in Sch 9 and covers virtually all financial services business.

1 Proceeds of Crime Act 2002, s 331(6).

Tipping off and prejudicing an investigation

7.16   It is an offence under s 333 where someone knows or suspects that a report to the SOCA or other appropriate person along the lines set out above has been made and the person then makes a disclosure which is likely to prejudice an investigation which might follow. It is a defence where the person who has done this did not know or suspect that the disclosure was likely to be prejudicial. There is a second defence where the disclosure is made in carrying out a function that person has relating to the enforcement of the Proceeds of Crime Act 2002, or a similar statute. Finally it is a defence where the person who has tipped off is a professional legal adviser and the disclosure was to a client of the adviser in connection with giving legal advice or to anyone in connection with legal proceedings. This last defence would not apply where the disclosure was made for the purposes of furthering a crime.

7.17   There is a separate offence under s 342 of prejudicing an investigation. It is committed if someone knows or suspects that someone is acting or proposing to act in connection with a confiscation investigation or a money laundering investigation. To commit the offence they must make a disclosure that is likely to prejudice the investigation or falsify, conceal, destroy or otherwise dispose of documents relevant to an investigation, or cause or permit that to happen. There are defences[1] where the person concerned does not know or suspect the disclosure will prejudice an investigation, where disclosure is made in the exercise of a function under the Proceeds of Crime Act 2002 (or any other relevant Act) or he is a professional legal adviser acting under privilege.

---

1 Proceeds of Crime Act 2002, s 342(3).

Appropriate consent

7.18   An individual within a firm may be provided with appropriate consent by the money laundering reporting officer, the SOCA, or where appropriate HM Customs and Excise. In the last two instances appropriate consent will exist: where it has been granted, where seven working days have elapsed without permission being refused and where permission is refused but thirty one days have elapsed[1]. In practice this is not particularly helpful because in many instances a quick decision will be needed. For example, a solicitor who has a client arrive at his office for a completion meeting in a conveyancing transaction wishing to hand over the balance of the purchase price in cash, will need a quick decision. In such instances a faxed report can be sent to the SOCA marked 'urgent' and a follow up phone call be made. It will normally be possible to get a decision very quickly and if the money is not leaving the jurisdiction as a result of the transaction there is a high likelihood that consent to proceed will be granted.

The money laundering reporting officer must not give consent to a member of staff unless appropriate consent has been obtained from the SOCA or another appropriate person[2].

1 Proceeds of Crime Act 2002, s 335(3)–(6).
2 Proceeds of Crime Act 2002, s 336.

Protected disclosures

7.19   A disclosure which satisfies the conditions that it came into a person's profession in the course of his trade, profession, business or employment, that it caused him to know or suspect that a person is engaged in money laundering, and that it is made to the SOCA, HM Customs or a money laundering officer as appropriate does not breach any restriction on the disclosure of information[1]. This covers both common law restrictions and those found in statute, in particular the Data Protection Act 1998.

1 Proceeds of Crime Act 2002, s 337.

Authorised disclosures

7.20   A disclosure should be made before acting. However, no offence is committed if the act is still taking place without it being known that laundering was taking place and the disclosure was made as soon as practicable after the person first knows or suspects that laundering is taking place[1].

1 Proceeds of Crime Act 2002, s 338.

Form and manner of disclosure

7.21   It is an offence unless any report made is not on the prescribed form unless there is a 'reasonable excuse'. Unfortunately, this is not defined[1].

1 Proceeds of Crime Act 2002, s 339(1A), (1B).

Prejudicing an investigation

7.22   Where a person knows or suspects that there is going to be: a confiscation investigation, a civil recovery investigation or a money laundering investigation, they commit an offence if they make a disclosure which is likely to prejudice that investigation or they falsify, conceal, destroy or dispose of relevant documents. A defence exists where they do not know or suspect that the disclosure made is likely to prejudice the investigation, the disclosure is required by a relevant statute, or he is a professional legal adviser giving advice in relation to legal proceedings. This last exception does not apply where the disclosure is made with the intention of furthering a criminal purpose. A second defence exists where the person destroying documents does not know or suspect that they are relevant to an investigation or does not intend to conceal any facts contained in the documents[1].

---

1 Proceeds of Crime Act 2002, s 342.

Penalties

7.23   Anyone convicted under ss 327 to 329 is liable on summary conviction to up to six months in prison and/or a fine. On indictment this rises to prison for up to 14 years and/or a fine. A conviction under ss 330 to 333, breach of the law on appropriate consent by a money laundering reporting officer and prejudicing an investigation are all liable for up to six months in prison and/or a fine on summary conviction. On indictment this rises to five years and/or a fine[1].

---

1 Proceeds of Crime Act 2002, ss 334 and 336(6).

The Criminal Offences 2 – Terrorist Funds

7.24   There are a separate set of laws that apply to terrorist money. Primarily, separate laws are needed as terrorist funds are often not the proceeds of crime but are utilised with a view to committing a criminal offence afterwards. These are determined by the Terrorism Act 2000 which, *inter alia*, creates a series of criminal offences relating to handling terrorist money. They are:

● to receive money or other property with the intention that it be used, or where there is reasonable cause to believe it will be used for the purposes of terrorism[1].

● to become concerned in an arrangement which facilitates the retention or control of terrorist property by or on behalf of another whether this be done by concealment, removal from the jurisdiction, transfer to nominees or in any other way[2].

● To fail to report to the police (in practice the SOCA) as soon as is reasonably practicable a suspicion that someone has committed a financial offence in relation to laundering where this information has come into their possession as part of their trade, profession, business or employment. They must also report the information on which their suspicion is based. There is a defence of having a 'reasonable excuse' for not making the disclosure. Information obtained by a professional legal adviser is exempt if it is obtained in privileged circumstances[3].

- To disclose information to another which is likely to prejudice an investigation or interfere with material which is relevant to such an investigation where there are reasonable grounds to suppose that the police are conducting, or proposing to conduct a terrorist investigation[4].

1 Terrorism Act 2000, s 15(2).
2 Terrorism Act 2000, s 18.
3 Terrorism Act 2000, s 19(2).
4 Terrorism Act 2000, s 19(5).

7.25   Terrorist offences by their nature related to terrorist organisations and the Act provides a list of 14 who are all parties involved in the conflict in Northern Ireland[1]. Since then a statutory instrument has added a rather more cosmopolitan list of 21 additional organisations whose activities relate to overseas conflicts in the Terrorism Act (Proscribed Organisations) (Amendment) Order 2001. Updated information is added to the Bank of England website warning of persons and organisations whose accounts must be frozen and of whom a report must be made.

The penalties for non compliance are a fine or up to six months' imprisonment on summary conviction and a fine or up to fourteen years on indictment[2].

1 Terrorism Act 2000, Sch 2.
2 Terrorism Act 2000, s 22.

7.26   There is a new disclosure requirement added by the Anti-terrorism, Crime and Security Act 2001 that a firm must disclose to the Treasury any knowledge or suspicion that a customer is in one of the categories of proscribed organisations. The Treasury can also direct anyone to provide them with any information in their possession or control or to produce any document in their possession which the Treasury requires to secure compliance with the statutory instrument.

7.27   As a result of the terrorist attack on the world trade centre there was an urgent reassessment of legislation relating to terrorism. The result was the Anti-terrorism, Crime and Security Act 2001 and the Terrorism (United Nations Measures) Order 2001[1]. The main issue arising in the context of laundering being the seizing of terrorist funds. The Act allows the forfeiture of funds in civil proceedings in a magistrates court[2] where the monies concerned are:

- intended for use for terrorist purposes; or

- which consists of the resources of a proscribed organisation; or

- which amounts to property obtained through terrorism.

1 SI 2001/3365.
2 Anti-terrorism, Crime and Security Act 2001, s 1.

7.28   An authorised officer is permitted to seize cash if he has reasonable grounds for believing it to be terrorist cash. This extends to seizing cash, only part of which is believed to be terrorist cash where it is not practicable to seize only the relevant part. Seizure is for an initial period of 48 hours, though this can be extended by up to three months from the date of the order, or in the case of a subsequent order for up to two years. If it is held for more than 48 hours it must be placed in an interest bearing account. The application must be made by the Customs and Excise, or in Scotland the Procurator Fiscal.

The Treasury may also make a freezing order if they reasonably believe that:

- action that is of detriment to the UK economy has been, or is to be taken; or

- action which constitutes a threat to the life or property is likely to be taken. The person responsible for that act must be an overseas government or resident.

7.29   The statutory instrument mentioned above widens these powers of seizure. It states that where the Treasury has reasonable grounds for supposing that someone on whose behalf funds are being held is directly or indirectly involved in acts of terrorism, it may require that those funds are not released without Treasury consent. The holder of the funds must then immediately notify their owner of the seizure order. It is also an offence to make funds or related services directly or indirectly available to such people.

7.30   There is a disclosure requirement that a firm must disclose to the Treasury any knowledge or suspicion that a customer is in one of the categories of proscribed organisations. The Treasury can also direct anyone to provide them with any information in their possession or control or to produce any document in their possession which the Treasury requires to secure compliance with the statutory instrument.

The Money Laundering Regulations 2003

7.31   The Money Laundering Regulations 2003[1] greatly extend the range of those caught by the laundering laws to those carrying on 'relevant business'. This is defined as the following regulated activities:

- accepting deposits;
- effecting and carrying out contracts for long-term life assurance;
- dealing in investments;
- arranging deals in investments;
- managing investments;
- safeguarding and administering assets;
- sending dematerialised instructions;
- establishing etc collective investment schemes;
- advising on investments; or
- issuing electronic money.

1 SI 2003/3075.

7.32 In addition it also catches:

- the activities of the National Savings Bank;
- raising money under the National Loans Act 1986;
- bureaux de change;
- banking activities;
- estate agency work;
- casinos;
- insolvency practitioners;
- tax advisers;
- accountants;
- auditors;
- those providing legal services which involves participating in a financial or real property transaction
- business services involving the formation, operation or management of companies or trusts;
- dealing in goods whenever the value exceeds €15,000.

7.33 It does not apply to:

- the issue of withdrawable share capital under the Industrial and Provident Societies Act 1965;

- accepting deposits under that Act;

- issuing withdrawable share capital under the Industrial and Provident Societies Act (Northern Ireland) 1969;

- accepting deposits under that Act;

- activities carried on by the Bank of England;

- an activity in respect of an exemption order, Proceeds of Crime Act 2000, s 38;

- an activity which would have been caught by s 45 of the Financial Services Act 1986 before it was repealed;

- arranging and advising on regulated mortgage contracts;

- dealing, arranging, managing or advising in relation to an insurance arrangement which is not a qualifying one; or

- the Official Solicitor when acting as trustee in his official capacity.

Requirements of the Regulations

7.34 Part II of the Regulations requires those caught by them to engage in certain activities.

Identification procedures

7.35 The Regulations require that the identity of a new client be checked in any of the following situations:

- where it has been decided that a business relationship should be formed with them;

- when the person dealing with the client has reason to suspect that a one-off transaction could be part of a money laundering operation;

- where a one-off transaction exceeds €15,000; and

- where there are a series of connected transactions exceeding €15,000 in total value.

7.36 It would be wise for most affected firms of solicitors to require that all new clients have their identity checked at the outset, not just those carrying on a financial or real property transaction. Failure to do so could give rise to the risk of someone using the firm on a non-financial or real property matter and then getting round the identity checking requirement because staff do not remember to check later. Alternately, a client might initially use the firm on a matter below the financial limit of €15,000 and later use the firm on a larger matter with the same results. Generally speaking the client's identity should be checked at the outset but the regulations do permit some variation in this, where the nature of the contact with the client may make this impossible, eg, where they are in another country. In any event it should always be done at the first reasonably possible time. If the person dealing with the financial institution appears to be acting for someone else, that person's identity must also be checked in the same way.

7.37　The regulations require that identity be checked by an approach that is 'reasonably capable of establishing that the applicant is the person he claims to be.' This means seeing original documents that prove that the person is who he claims to be and also that they live at the address they have provided. This will generally mean seeing more than one document. Ideally one should include a photograph and the person's name and the other should include their name and address. Documents that are useful to prove identity are:

- passport;
- driving licence;
- identity card (if from a country that has them); or
- references.

7.38　To prove that the person is resident where they claim to be it is useful to see:

- utility bills;
- a bank statement;
- check the electoral roll; or
- check the telephone directory.

7.39　Once both of these have been carried out and a photocopy of the document concerned has been placed on file the identity checking requirements have been met. However, it should be borne in mind that any criminal seeking to launder money will have no difficulty at all in satisfying the requirement that they produce such documents. They will either have fake or real documents in the name they are using. This is not a reason for being cavalier about checking identity, but it does mean that possession of 'proof' is not a reason to lower a firm's guard when it comes to suspicious activity by a client.

7.40　In the case of corporate clients a company search will have to be done to ascertain the owners and directors of the company. The position regarding corporate groups is not fully clear. The safest approach is to also check a controlling company and any company in the same group with which the client company is intimately connected, eg, if it trades heavily with it.

7.41   A problem can arise where the client is foreign and as a result the relevant documents are not written in a language that anyone in the firm can read. Here the documents should be translated by a certified notary who offers translation from that language. Their certified translation has the same legal status as the original.

Know your client

7.42   Clearly it will not be possible to spot a suspicious transaction unless the solicitor understands the nature of clients' business activities. Suspicions will normally be aroused by a transaction being incongruous given what is known of the client concerned, or incongruous for businesses of that type. Banks, financial institutions, solicitors, accountants etc are thus required to know their customer.

7.43   The Proceeds of Crime Act 2002 requires that a suspicious transaction report be made as soon as possible once a person acting in the course of their trade, profession or business knows or suspects that someone is engaged in drug money laundering. Unfortunately, the Act gives no guidance on what this state of mind means. 'Knows' presents no problems beyond those of proof: 'suspect' is less clear. The test is now an objective one. The Law Society Guidance Notes at 6.39 suggest that it should arise when:

> '... where there are certain factual circumstances, from which an honest and reasonable person engaged in a business in the regulated sector would have inferred knowledge or formed the suspicion that another was engaged in money laundering.'

7.44   A useful interpretation has been provided by AUSTRAC[1], the Australian suspicious transaction reporting agency. Their view as to the cause of the suspicion is that it should relate to apprehension or mistrust considering:

- its unusual nature or circumstances, or
- the person or group of persons with whom they are dealing.

The nature of suspicion is analysed in greater detail at **7.50** to **7.52** below.

---

1 The Australian Transaction Reports and Analysis Centre.

Systems to prevent money laundering

7.45   Employees must be trained so that they are capable of spotting transactions that are suspicious and to this end they must know the relevant law.

Internal reporting procedures

7.46   It is necessary for firms to have in place systems whereby suspicious transactions are reported to 'the nominated officer', in normal parlance, the money laundering reporting officer. That person has the responsibility of ascertaining whether or not the report made to them really does give rise to suspicion and if so they must make a report to the SOCA as soon as is practicable.

7.47   When a disclosure is made the party making the report is immune from being sued for breach of confidentiality by the client concerned[1]. It will also be necessary for the party making the suspicious transaction report to enquire of the SOCA whether it is acceptable to continue with the transaction. In practice they will normally give consent for the transaction to continue, as they will wish to observe the transaction and compile evidence as to what may be going on. Without such consent, the party who has become suspicious may well be committing an offence such as aiding and abetting a criminal offence or being an accessory after the fact.

---

1 Proceeds of Crime Act 2002, s 337.

7.48   Problems have arisen where the grounds for suspicion arise at the moment of completion of an arrangement, eg, where the purchaser suddenly indicates that they wish to pay in cash. In such cases the report should be made to the SOCA and highlighted as urgent. A follow-up call could also be made. The SOCA have indicated that in such cases they will do what they can to expedite a response.

Staff training

7.49   The Regulations also require that a firm should engage in appropriate staff training, have systems in place to facilitate the spotting and reporting of laundering and also to have a money laundering reporting officer to organise this.

Additional regulations will come into effect in 2007 applying the third EU Directive on money laundering.

What is 'suspicion'?

7.50   Unfortunately the statutes mentioned above give no guidance on what 'suspicion' means. It probably relates to apprehension or mistrust considering the unusual nature or circumstances of the transaction or the person or group of persons with whom they are dealing. Whilst there is no case law in this country in the context of the legislation, there is case law on the nature of suspicion. In *Hussein v Chong Fook Kam*[1] Lord Devlin stated that:

> 'Suspicion in its ordinary meaning is a state of conjecture or surmise where proof is lacking.' He added that 'Suspicion can take into account matters that could not be put in evidence ....Suspicion can take into account matters which, though admissible, could not form part of a prima facie case.'

---

1 [1970] AC 942, [1969] 3 All ER 1626, [1970] 2 WLR 441, 114 Sol Jo 55, PC.

7.51 The Money Laundering Guidance Notes reinforce this[1]. '*Suspicion ... falls far short of proof based on firm evidence.*' It goes on to say that '*a suspicious transaction will often be one which is inconsistent with a customer's known, legitimate business or personal activities or with the normal business for that type of account.*'

The guidance above provides assistance as to what can be regarded as suspicious. In part however there is also an element of common sense as to what looks unusual or abnormal.

---

1 At 6.01.

7.52 Issues to consider would include:

● the speed with which cash is being transferred to another form of money and to another place. In particular is money, and in particular cash paid into an account and then paid out at unusual speed?

● Does the routing of the funds involve a country with close contacts to drug production, processing or the laundering of proceeds?

● Is the arrangement one which does not make sense from a business point of view? In particular is it an arrangement that did not appear to be designed to make a profit? This is not always an element however. Many criminal organisations now attempt to utilise the laundering process to make a profit, eg, by utilising funds to buy goods which are then resold at a mark up.

● Does the arrangement involve offshore shell companies, trusts and tax haven banks when the purpose of their involvement does not fit in with normal business practice for the type of transaction taking place. Unfortunately it often will as the criminals will have constructed their finances to optimise their tax position on an international basis after taking legal and financial advice. In reality their transactions will tend to replicate legitimate ones.

- Does the transaction involve cash flows in and out of countries where the banking system is heavily permeated by organised crime, eg, Russia? If it does careful note should be made of the exchange rates at which the currency concerned changes from one currency to another. If these appear to be other than market rates, the transaction should be regarded as particularly suspicious.

- Note should be taken of structures that seem to be designed to make it difficult for outsiders to ascertain exactly what is going on. An abnormally complex structure of companies should arouse suspicion.

- There may be issues relating to the client that raise suspicion. This is only likely to occur with the less professional criminals. The rest will have little difficulty in maintaining a credible appearance.

Making a suspicious transaction report

7.53   Once a suspicious transaction report has been submitted, the SOCA will then inform the person who has made the report whether it is acceptable to continue with the transaction. The SOCA normally prefer the transaction to continue to facilitate their observation of the transaction and to provide them with the opportunity to analyse the events concerned. It is necessary to obtain consent to act otherwise the party who made the report will almost certainly be committing a criminal offence such as aiding and abetting or being an accessory after the fact. On the other hand if the firm refused to continue to act for the client they could effectively be 'tipping off[1]' because the client will then realise that the firm is suspicious and assume that a report has been filed. (See also 'Suspicious transaction reports and civil liability' at **7.92** and **7.93** below.)

---

1 See Proceeds of Crime Act 2002, s 333 discussed above at **7.16**.

7.54   In cases where there are slight grounds for suspicion but the person concerned does not feel there is sufficient evidence to make a suspicious transaction report, it is a good idea to make a file note of the reasons for concern. It may be that as time goes by a succession of other minor issues may arise and eventually there will be sufficient grounds for making a report.

The third EU Laundering Directive

7.55   A Third EU Directive has been passed and in due course a statutory instrument will be put in place to take effect in 2007. The exact contents of the statutory instrument remain unclear at the time of writing. The Treasury website at www.hm-treasury.gov.uk under 'Financial Services' and then 'Money Laundering' will provide a draft statutory instrument once available.

Case law

7.56   There have been recent cases which have clarified how the relevant law operates.

Bowman v Fels[1]

7.57   This case arose as a result of a property dispute between ex-cohabitees. Shortly before a hearing in the county court the solicitor for one party submitted a suspicious transaction report concerning the other. The legal adviser to that party then requested an adjournment because 'appropriate consent' was not anticipated. The Law Society intervened seeking clarification on the meaning of 'arrangements' under the Proceeds of Crime Act 2002, s 328. The Bar Council and NCIS also became involved.

---

1 [2005] EWC Civ 226.

7.58   The case was settled between the original parties but the resulting Court of Appeal decision arose from the court wishing to provide clarification on how the Proceeds of Crime Act 2002 impacted on litigation. The key point was that certain activities are excluded from the scope of proceedings related to s 328. The ruling appears to relate to:

- litigation from the issue of proceedings;
- securing injunctive relief;
- a freezing order up to its final disposal; or
- the final division of assets in accordance with a judgment or settlement including the handling of assets which are criminal property.

7.59   The decision extends to Alternative Dispute Resolution.

The effect of this is that those involved in litigation and related settlements are not involved in 'arrangements' under s 328. This appears to imply they could not be acting within ss 327 or 329 either. The only exception to this would be where it appears that false litigation is taking place so that the party defending could settle out of court to launder money to the plaintiff.

7.60   Any property however dealt with after the judgment could still be criminal property under s 340(3). As a result suspicious transaction reports may have to be made at that stage. Information governed by professional privilege may not be disclosed unless the solicitor has grounds to suppose that the client is abusing privilege to involve the solicitor in the commission of a criminal offence.

7.61   This fits in with the minority opinion of Lord Hope in *Taylor v Serious Fraud Office*[1] where he stated that absolute privilege should apply and *Mahon v Rahn (No 2)*[2] where the principle of absolute privilege was extended to reports to regulatory authorities, in this case the now defunct SFA[3].

---

1 [1999] 2 AC 177, [1998] 4 All ER 801.
2 [2000] 4 All ER 41, [2001] WLR 2150. See also *Amalgamated Metal Trading Ltd v City of London Police Financial Investigation Unit* [2003] 1 WLR 2711.
3 For a more detailed discussion of this point see Alexander. R PhD thesis: *'The regulation of insider dealing and money laundering in the European Unio,'* Institute of Advanced Legal Studies, University of London, 2005, p 329.

Squirrel Ltd v National Westminster Bank Ltd[1]

7.62   The Chancery Division of the High Court heard this decision which involved a bank account that the bank said it was forced to block because of s 340(3). It regarded the arrangements as reportable under s 328. The bank made a report and then blocked the account but felt it could not explain the reasons to the account holder because of the tipping off provision in s 333.

---

1 (2005) Times, 25 May.

7.63   The Court held that were the bank to have operated the account once they were suspicious they might be committing an offence under s 328. The meaning of the word 'suspicious' was considered and it was held that in this situation a bank did not have powers of investigation and therefore the suspicion did not need any wider justification to be reasonable.

7.64   The combined effect of ss 328, 335 and 338 was to force a bank that made a suspicious transaction report to report suspicions and then not move the funds or property concerned for either seven working days or if notice of refusal was sent, 31 working days from receipt of that refusal. The customer could not be told. Squirrel Ltd who had brought the case for an explanation as to why their account was frozen could not be informed.

7.65   This followed the two cases of *C v S*[1] and *Bank of Scotland v A Ltd*[2] on the earlier legislation. In the latter case the Court of Appeal provided five key guidelines governing the steps a firm or bank should take in dealing with its client's money:

- freezing orders would not normally be granted;

- where there is a dispute over whether a payment can be made out of the account or a disclosure be made to a client the firm or bank should discuss the matter with the Serious Fraud Office. If this does not lead to resolution an application should be made for interim declaratory relief;

- the bank should consider whether it is worth contesting actions brought by clients in such cases;

- where such a claim is contested consideration should be given as to whether the judge who hears the proceedings should also be the one from whom guidance is sought; and

- if the firm or bank follows the court's guidelines it should not be at risk of being in breach of the criminal law.

---

1 [1999] 2 All ER 343.
2 [2001] EWCA Civ 52.

7.66 In the vast majority of cases this should not be necessary. The firm or bank will be able to make a report to the SOCA and then act according to its instructions. If this leads to instructions not to release the funds or a response cannot be obtained from the SOCA in time and the client then objects, the firm or bank will be unable to inform them as to why. It will then normally be up to the client to decide on the next step.

FSA Rules

7.67 Until the end of August 2006 the FSA had a detailed and prescriptive set of rules governing money laundering. However, it was accepted by the FSA that they were over detailed and in line with the FSA's 'light touch' approach a new set of rules were brought into effect from that date. To quote Philip Robinson, the FSA's Financial Crime Sector Leader[1]:

'The risk-based approach has always been part of our financial crime strategy, and has increasingly become the driver of all we do ...it is clear ...that an overwhelming majority want us to focus on principle not prescription, stressing the importance of senior management and risk assessment and mitigation ....We expect firms to manage their financial crime risk as they manage other business risks.'

---

1 Speech at the BBA Conference, 6 December 2005.

7.68 The FSA rules on Systems and Controls (SYSC) starts off by stating that: *A firm must take reasonable care to establish and maintain such systems and controls as are appropriate to its business.*[1]' (See Chapters 4 and 11 for a further discussion of systems and controls). As well as this having a general scope which will catch money laundering, along with other business areas, there are SYSC rules that deal specifically with laundering. At **3.2.6** the rules state that: 'A firm must take reasonable care to establish and maintain effective systems and controls for compliance with applicable requirements and stand-

ards under the regulatory system and for countering the risk that the firm might be used to further financial crime.' Such systems must make sure that the firm can identify, assess, monitor and manage money laundering risk and are comprehensive enough given the nature, scale and complexity of the firm's activities[2]. These systems must be checked on a regular basis to make sure that they remain sufficient to comply with the laundering threat. The risk areas need to be identified and are likely to include:

- customers, products and activities engaged in;
- distribution channels;
- the complexity and volume of the transactions engaged in;
- the processes and systems; and
- the operating environment[3].

1 SYSC 3.1.1R.
2 SYSC 3.2.6AR.
3 SYSC 3.2.6FG.

7.69 As far as the FSA are concerned a key element will be whether the firm has satisfied the Joint Money Laundering Steering Group Guidelines. An analysis of these is beyond the remit of the text, however the latest version can be accessed online at www.jmlsg.org.uk. The guidance falls into two main parts. Part 1, which covers laundering generally, and Part 2 which provides sectoral guidance. The website is open access and firms should make sure that appropriate personnel are cognisant of the relevant parts.

7.70 The systems and controls need to cover: training for employees, information for directors and senior management, appropriate documentation of the policies adopted and suitable measures to make sure that money laundering risk is taken into account in the running of the business. This needs to extend to new products, new customers and the firm's business profile[1]. There is one allowance, which is that identity checking requirements for new customers should not unreasonably deny access to customers who cannot produce detailed evidence of identity.

1 SYSC 3.2.6G G.

7.71 Firms must appoint someone to be responsible for anti-money laundering risk assessment. This person should be a director or senior manager, with both enough seniority and independence to make sure the systems are effected properly. They should be based in the UK. Someone should also be appointed to fulfil the money laundering reporting functions. This may be the same person, and in smaller firms normally will be. In larger and more complex operations it may be a separate person. In addition the money laundering reporting officer should produce an annual report to the directors on the operation and effectiveness of the systems and controls concerned[1].

---

1 SYSC 3.2.6I G and J G.

Civil Law issues

Introduction

7.72   It is not only the criminal law and regulatory issues that pose a threat when an institution launders funds, there is also the potential threat of civil proceedings to recover them. For this to occur there must be a real owner of the money acting in pursuit of it. Two problems occur: the concept of real owner is widely defined and the area of law concerned is unclear.

7.73   The position is complicated by the doctrine of constructive trusts. These occur where a court decides to determine after the event that a state of affairs shall be treated as though the parties had set up a trust. Thus, the obligations of a trustee can be imposed on someone who had not thought of themselves as being in that position. This was traditionally done where someone was behaving in an illegal or immoral fashion. It has also been used to create liability by creating a situation where the trustee is then held to have knowingly assisted in breaching the trust or having knowingly been in receipt of funds from one who has.

7.74   This issue often arises because of the doctrine of tracing. This is an old rule of law that permits someone to pursue money they have lost through the wrongful behaviour of another into the place where it now resides. The common law rule of tracing is of limited use because of old case law that said that once money that had been taken from someone had been mixed by a recipient with their own money in a purse, the true owner could no longer use tracing because it was no longer possible to tell which money was which. However, equitable tracing got round this problem by applying relevant maxims of equity which resulted in the court assuming that anyone in possession of the property of another would act to try and repay it. Thus, any money they still had would be treated as the injured party's funds. Likewise, if they spent all the money, the first money received back would be held for the benefit of the injured person. The only situation that defeated equitable tracing was where the money had been paid through an overdrawn bank account as there the bank would have been a creditor for the overdraft.

7.75   To obtain equitable tracing it is necessary to prove that the funds were subject to a trust or that there was a fiduciary relationship. Thus those who have lost funds usually wish to try and obtain a court declaration that the money was subject to a constructive trust as it was not subject to one in an ordinary sense.

7.76   There is also a jurisdictional problem in that, generally speaking, only those jurisdictions that recognise trusts will allow equitable tracing into their jurisdiction. That said it is normally possible to trace through such a jurisdiction into one that does recognise trusts. As a general rule it is the common law countries (generally ex British Empire states) together with some others that recognise the concept of trusts.

Grounds for constructive trusteeship

7.77   There are two basic grounds used by the courts:

- knowing receipt; and
- knowing assistance.

7.78   The classic exposition of English law on the point was stated by Selborone LC in *Barnes v Addy*[1]:

> 'strangers are not to be made constructive trustees ...... unless (they) receive and become chargeable with some part of the trust property or unless they assist with knowledge that it is a dishonest and fraudulent design on the part of the trustees.'

---

1 (1874) 9 Ch App 244, 43 LJ Ch 513, 22 WR 505, 30 LT 4.

7.79   Unfortunately the cases that have followed have left this area of law in an unclear state. Perhaps the crucial case is *Royal Brunei Airlines Sdn Bhd v Tan*[1]. Here the airline had appointed Borneo Leisure Travel as its agent for selling seats and cargo space on the airline. The contract stated that Borneo Leisure was to hold any money received on trust for the airline. However, instead of paying these funds into a trust account for their principal Borneo Leisure paid funds received into their own account. The person controlling Borneo Leisure then allowed the company to use the money for its own purposes. Eventually the firm became insolvent and the airline appeared to have lost its money. It then brought legal proceedings against the managing director and main owner of Borneo Leisure alleging that he had knowingly assisted in breach of trust. He claimed that there was only mismanagement, which did not give rise to personal liability. The Privy Council stated that there were certain key issues:

(1)   the liability of an accessory should apply regardless of whether the trustee and the third party have both displayed dishonesty or whether the trustee was innocent;

(2) that liability could be imposed regardless of whether the third party had procured the breach or dishonestly assisted in it; and

(3) that the key issue is the state of mind of the third party not the trustee.

1 [1995] 2 AC 378, [1995] 3 All ER 97, [1995] WLR 64, [1995] BCC 899, [1995] 27 LS Gas R 33, [1995] NLJR 888, PC.

7.80 In other words, where someone interferes with a trust and deprives the beneficiary of some or all of their property, they should be able to get it back.

7.81 The Privy Council also approved some earlier cases which could be of particular concern for financial institutions who have laundered funds. One of these cases was *Fyler v Fyler*[1]. Here a firm of solicitors had put funds from a trust into an investment which was unauthorised. They were held liable even though they had believed that the investment would be of benefit to the beneficiary. The other was *Eaves v Hickson*[2]. Here the trustees made a payment on the basis of a forged document that was presented to them and which according to the judge would have fooled anyone not looking for forgery. The person who had produced the forgery was made liable to repay the money in priority to any claim being made against the trustees. However, had they not got the resources to pay the trustees would then have been liable.

1 (1841) 3 Beav 550, 5 Jur 187.
2 (1861) 30 Beav 136, 7 Jur NS 1297, 132 RR 213, 10 WR 29, 5 LT 598.

7.82 Liability was stated to arise where the person concerned was dishonest rather than unconscionable in their conduct. This consisted of not acting as an honest person would and the test was objective. Interestingly, negligence was held to be insufficient to create liability.

Knowing receipt

7.83 There is a dichotomy between two legal issues in many of the cases. This arises between knowing receipt of funds and liability for breach of fiduciary duty. Knowing receipt occurs when property has been received knowingly in breach of trust. Fiduciary duty is a generic term to cover one of a number of situations that occur where someone is held to have particular obligations to another party because of their relationship with them. There does not need to be a trust (though a trust does give rise to a fiduciary relationship) but similar obligations then occur. Again a party who had laundered funds when a fiduciary relationship arose could find themselves faced with a civil claim. To provide such a right the courts have stretched the doctrine further and further over recent years, although surprisingly a thief is not automatically a fiduciary of the true owner.

7.84 The legal consequences of the two states of affairs are different. In cases of knowing receipt an action in equity can be brought to recover the full amount including any capital growth that has occurred since the recipient received it. On the other hand in cases of knowing assistance the liability is for the total amount lost plus simple interest.

7.85 Many of the issues were considered in *Lipkin Gorman v Karpnale Ltd*[1] where a solicitor became an obsessive gambler. He started gambling with clients' money. The firm's bank noticed that client account cheques were being paid to a casino but did nothing about it. A claim was brought for constructive trust, quasi-contract, negligence and conversion. The House of Lords held that a recipient of stolen money who was unjustly enriched was under an obligation to pay the same amount back to the victim. There is however a degree of protection for the recipient if he can show that his position had changed as a result of the arrangements and that he would lose out by having to pay the money back. This defence is of value to the financial extent of the change of position that has taken place. Unfortunately the only issue that was considered on appeal to the House of Lords was a claim for money had and received. However, the Court of Appeal stated that a bank could not be liable to its customer as a constructive trustee unless it was in breach of its contractual duty of care to that customer.

---

1 [1992] 4 All ER 409.

7.86 In *Agip (Africa) Ltd v Jackson*[1] a firm of accountants had been acting for a fraudulent client. The accountants received funds from their clients and then passed them on as per instructions received. The true owners eventually appeared and claimed the funds back. As there was no financial sense in pursuing the clients the wronged parties sued the accountants. It was held that they were not liable as they had not received the funds for their own benefit. However, it was stated that were a bank to receive funds to reduce an overdraft it would be receiving the funds for their own benefit.

---

1 [1992] 4 All ER 385.

7.87 In *Polly Peck International plc v Nadir and others (No 2)*[1] a claim for knowing receipt and knowing assistance was brought against Asil Nadir and the Central Bank of Northern Cyprus claiming that a huge amount of money had been wrongly transferred out of the company concerned. The Bank had received the funds for foreign currency contracts and in the course of this had not made enquiries about the source of the funds. The Turkish Cypriot bank concerned had £45 million on deposit with Midland Bank in London. The company's administrator sought an order freezing the bank account. The court held that the key issue was whether or not the bank had been involved in any dishonesty or want of probity in that they had actual or constructive notice that they were receiving misapplied funds. The bank did not need to be shown to have been acting fraudulently. One of the judges felt that it was a case of knowing assistance and that the bank would only be liable if they received the money for their own use and benefit. As they received the money as agents and accounted for it to their principals he did not believe that this requirement had been satisfied. Another of the judges however believed that most of the funds had been received as banker because the bank received the funds in their own right as a result of a currency transfer and therefore the issue was one of knowing receipt. The appropriate measure to apply was therefore whether there was knowledge that trust funds had been misapplied.

---

1 [1992] 4 All ER 769, [1992] 2 Lloyd's Rep 238, [1992] NLJR 671, CA.

Holding property to the order of another

7.88   Sometimes called 'holding in a ministerial capacity' this arises when one person holds property belonging to someone else and mixes it with their own property. This is beyond 'knowing receipt' as discussed above unless an agent is setting up their own title to the funds. Two issues arise here. The first is the principle that an agent who uses their principle's money in good faith to pay off a debt owed by the principal can raise the defence of 'payment over'. In *Holland v Russell*[1] an agent paid money to another as agent for a ship owner whose ship had sunk. It later transpired that the policy was void for non disclosure. By then the agent of the ship owner had paid some of the money over to his principal. The court held that the action would lie against the principal not the agent for this sum as the money had been properly paid over.

---

1 (1861) 1 B & S 424; affd B & S 14, 32 LJQB 297, 2 New Rep 188, 11 WR 757, 8 LT 468.

7.89   However, in *Springfield Acres (in liquidation) v Abacus (Hong Kong) Ltd*[1] the defence failed. A company had successfully sued Springfield Acres for a large sum. Whilst the claim was waiting to be settled Springfield's assets were transferred to another company outside the jurisdiction. This money was then advanced to another company via a solicitor's trust account. These funds were then transferred to the defendants who in turn paid them on to other parties. In reality these transactions were for the benefit of one man who was the major shareholder of Springfield and whose family were the beneficiaries of the trusts where the money ended up. The claim succeeded as the defendants were knowingly involved.

---

1 [1994] NZLR 502.

7.90   In *El Ajou v Dollar Land Holdings plc (No 2)*[1] the plaintiff had been defrauded of money. The money concerned ended up being used as part finance for a building project in England and a claim was then brought against the building company claiming knowing receipt. It was held that a claim could only succeed if enquiry was not made in a situation where an honest and reasonable man would have done so.

1 [1995] 2 All ER 213.

7.91   In *Cowan de Groot Properties Ltd v Eagle Trust plc*[1] a claim was brought following an allegation that the directors of a company had sold some of its property at an undervalue. The purchaser was alleged to have been in knowing receipt. The case is not entirely in line with the others but it does appear to accept the doctrine that a defendant's knowledge will be determined on the basis of what a reasonable person would have learned.

1 [1992] 4 All ER 700, [1991] BCLC 1045.

Suspicious transaction reports and civil liability

7.92   When deciding on how to interpret suspicious behaviour there are problems in the context of civil liability. In theory it can depend on the party concerned failing to carry out a professional level of 'knowing their client' or failing to report suspicious transactions. In practice we seem dangerously close to being in a situation where the courts impose a constructive trust wherever it suits them in order to recover illicit funds. The solution is for firms to be scrupulous in maintaining the requirements of the law and their professional bodies as minimum. Wherever they are in doubt as to whether to make a suspicious transaction report they should do so. From the point of view of both criminal liability and constructive trusteeship they should be safe. However this last issue can then arise in a secondary way.

7.93   A suspicious transaction report may be made internally in a firm to its money laundering reporting officer, or an appropriate report made to the SOCA. Once this is done it could be argued that the firm is knowingly in receipt of illegal funds. Once a report has been made the firm will normally request permission from the body to whom they made that report before they act further. In most cases this will be the course of action which the criminal law enforcement bodies will prefer, so that they have the opportunity to observe the transaction and the client. There is no risk to the firm from the criminal courts in such cases, but neither is there a guarantee that the knowing receipt issue will cease to be a problem. It is possible that such a firm could still be held to be a constructive trustee, a risk exacerbated by the firm potentially ending up in a catch 22 situation. If they refuse to act on the client's instructions whilst waiting for confirmation from the criminal authorities that they can continue, they may be effectively tipping off the client. If however they act on such instructions there may be fear that they could be held to be a constructive trustee. This now seems to be an over cautious interpretation of the position. One High Court judge, Coleman J stated that *it* was wholly unrealistic that an institution which had followed the *C v S* guidelines and *Bank of Scotland v A* approach (see **7.62** to **7.65** above) would find itself held a constructive trustee[1].

---

1 *Hosni Tayeb v HSBC and Al Farsan International* [2004] EWHC 1529 Comm.

The Wolfsberg Principles

Why were they created?

7.94   Without pressure from regulators or prompting governments a group of international banks created a set of codes which they have publicly issued and to which they have publicly sworn allegiance. The first step occurred in late 2000 when a number of leading banks[1], acting in co-ordination with Transparency International, agreed to take on board a set of general principles to facilitate improving the standards applied in combating money laundering where private banking relationships are concerned. They also accepted as a formal principle that the responsibility for this rested with the management of the banks.

---

1 ABN Amro Bank NV, Santander Central Hispano SA, Bank of Tokyo-Mitsubishi, Barclays, Citigroup, Credit Suisse Group, Deutsche Bank AG, Goldman Sachs, HSBC, J P Morgan Chase, Société Générale and UBS AG.

7.95   The background to these banks acting as they did arose in part because of the influence of the Basel Committee of Banking Supervisors[1] and the Working Group on Bribery at the OECD. This was taken further by a specialised group within the Financial Stability Forum[2]. Transparency International also became involved by enlisting the support of a small number of banks in a programme to prevent the abuse of financial centres by launderers. Concerns were also developing amongst some of the banks that money laundering could damage their reputation[3]. As a result of this two of the banks who were later to make up the Wolfsberg Group exchanged their internal compliance regulations. This led to a larger meeting of banks to take matters a step further.

---

1 Bank for International Settlements: Basel Committee on Banking Supervision: Prevention of Criminal Use of the Banking System for the Purpose of Money Laundering, Statement of Principles, December 1988.
2 Financial Stability Forum, Working Group on Offshore Financial Centres Report, April 2000.
3 Minority Staff Report for Permanent Subcommittee on Investigations; Hearings on Private Banking and Money Laundering: A Case Study of Opportunities and Vulnerabilities.

7.96   The resulting Principles (named after the castle in Switzerland where the working sessions took place) were then publicised in the hope that other financial institutions will follow them. Since then the original Principles were amended in 2002 and a second set of Principles issued to deal with the potential abuse of correspondent banking relationships. Finally, early in 2003 a further set of Principles were issued with the view to suppressing terrorist finances.

7.97 One reason for the creation of the Principles was to create a common standard to reduce the uncertainties and complexities resulting from running multinational banks across disparate laundering regimes. This is facilitated by the fact that the banks concerned make up over 60% of the world market in private banking and around 50% of the market share in each of the key offshore financial centres[1]. A set of common requirements operated across the jurisdictions in which an international bank operates, even though more onerous than that imposed in any of the states in which the banks concerned carry on business, makes the running of the banks much simpler and thus reduces risk management costs. In part the Principles were also driven by the belief that the standards required in the US were insufficient, particularly after the Congress threw out one Presidential attempt to tighten up the law[2].

1 See Peith and Aiolfi, '*The Private Sector becomes Active: The Wolfsberg Process*' in A Practitioner's Guide to International Money Laundering Law and Regulation, Ed Clark and Burrell, City and Financial 2003 at p 273.
2 International Money Laundering and Foreign Anti-Corruption Act 2000, House of Representatives Report 106/2728, Committee on Banking and Financial Services, Chairman, Senator Leach.

7.98 The banks involved had become increasingly concerned that the enormous quantities of money laundering currently taking place could pose a threat to them. This could come about as a result of it becoming public knowledge that a bank has laundered money. If the bank concerned has maintained good standards there is still likely to be damage to reputation, even where the regulator does not believe that disciplinary steps are warranted. In many cases however they will. There are clear signs that the regulators had been becoming both more assertive and proactive in this field[1]. As the Basel Committee pointed out[2]:

'Reputational risk poses a major threat to banks, since the nature of their business requires maintaining the confidence of depositors, creditors and the general marketplace. Reputational risk is defined as the potential that adverse publicity regarding a bank's business ... will cause a loss of confidence in the integrity of the institution ...... They need to protect themselves by means of continual vigilence through an effective know your client programme.'

1 (2001) Financial Times, March 24, p 3.
2 '*Customer Due Diligence for Banks*,' October 2001.

7.99 However, paradoxically the Basel Committee have excluded reputational risk from CAD III, the argument being that there is no accurate way of quantifying it. It can be countered however[1] that there is no real evidence of banks suffering measurable financial loss as a result of damage to reputation being caused by a money laundering scandal. UK examples include a number of leading banks being fined for money laundering failings only to see their share price rise! In the longer run though there could be the danger of a systemic consequence where the general damage to the image of banks starts to reflect such crises.

---

1 See, for example, Emma Codd 'Reputational Risk' in 'A Practitioner's Guide ...' supra, see footnote 1 above.

7.100   In the UK the FSA have adopted a similar approach to that seen in the Wolfsberg principles. In Consultation Paper 142 it stated:

'... a firm must take reasonable care to establish and maintain effective systems and controls for compliance with the applicable requirements and standards under the regulatory system and for countering the risk that the firm might be used to perpetrate financial crime.'

7.101   Rather worryingly in this context was an FSA investigation into banks[1]. Four of the main deficiencies that were found related to this. They were:

● inadequate supervision by senior management of account opening procedures by higher risk customers;

● insufficient checks on the identity of the beneficial owners of companies;

● too much reliance on introductions by existing customers; and

● insufficient understanding of the source of customers' wealth.

---

1 FSA Press Release, March 2001.

7.102   Another key element in the formation of the Wolfsberg Principles has been the perceived threat of formal regulation on the subject. Traditionally, when faced with this banks have tended to adopt self imposed codes. This way they provide the government or regulator concerned with enough of what they require for imposed regulation to cease being a political imperative. The Code is then drafted in a way that the banks find acceptable. In the United Kingdom the Code of Banking Practice adopted at the time of the Jack Report and the more recent Mortgage Code of Practice are cases in point[1].

---

1 Though this was superseded by events as a result of lending and administering in relation to mortgages on residential property becoming covered by the FSA regime.

7.103   There is also an element of safety in numbers. If the banks in general agree on an approach that appears to satisfy or exceed what regulators are asking for, it provides evidence that the banks taking part are engaged in good practice. This inevitably creates pressure for others to join in.

The Wolfsberg Principles – private banking

Client acceptance: general guidelines

1.1 General

7.104 *Bank policy will be to prevent the use of its worldwide operations for criminal purposes. The bank will endeavour to accept only those clients whose source of wealth and funds can be reasonably established to be legitimate. The primary responsibility for this lies with the private banker who sponsors the client for acceptance. Mere fulfilment of internal review procedures does not relieve the private banker of this basic responsibility.*

One aim of this is to deal with the issue of criminals in government who steal and then launder the assets of their country and hide them as a personal investment fund. In addition there are others, particularly criminals involved in the drug trade, illegal arms dealing and people smuggling; to name the biggest operators. Principle 1.1 has the weakness of only being aimed at private clients. In most instances those wishing to launder large amounts will have no difficulty in establishing a network of companies throughout the world and then get the payments that enter the western banking system to be made out to companies in that group. In the case of corrupt government officials receiving bribes, the bribe will often be paid into a corporate bank account which appears to have no connection with the official in any event. The person receiving the bribe will nominate the account signatories and thus be able to indirectly access the account.

1.2 Identification

7.105 *The bank will take reasonable measures to establish the identity of its clients and beneficial owners and will only accept clients when this process has been completed.*

This is perhaps all that can be reasonably be expected of a bank, but the effectiveness of such checks is rather limited due to the relative ease with which false documents and real documents in false names can be obtained. (See 7.39 above). In addition, how does a bank ascertain that the beneficial owner is who they appear to be? It is a relatively straightforward matter for one person to create a false identity or to hide behind the identity of another. A bank cannot become, nor be expected to become a detective agency. The consequence of this is that Principle 1.2 may give a false sense of security to the bank which has taken this step and to others which deal with it.

1.2.1 Client

7.106 *Natural persons: identity will be established to the bank's satisfaction by reference to official identity papers or such other evidence as may be appropriate under the circumstances.*

The problem here is the general availability of good forged documents and the relative ease in which it is possible to obtain documents in the wrong name. Apparently safe identity documents such as passports, national identity cards and driving licences are no real guide to identity. To give an idea of the scale of the problem, in the United Kingdom there are also estimated to be between one and a half million more national insurance numbers being used than should be the case.

7.107 *Corporations, partnerships, foundations: the bank will receive documentary evidence of the due organisation and existence.*

This will tend to reduce the number of off-the-shelf companies created specifically to launder money. However, it may well also accelerate the market in buying small, relatively dormant companies that are a number of years old and less likely to attract suspicion. There is evidence that this has been happening in the West Indies. Recent changes in ownership and radical changes in the financial behaviour of a company following acquisition should thus attract close investigation.

7.108 *Trusts: the bank will receive appropriate evidence of formation and existence along with identity of the trustees.*

This is going to cause particular problems. It is never going to be possible to be certain whether the trustees are running the trust themselves or as a front for others. In some cases, for example the blind trusts available in Cyprus, the vehicle itself seems to have been designed to facilitate this very state of affairs.

Identification documents must be current at the time of opening.

1.2.2 Beneficial owner

7.109 *Beneficial ownership must be established for all accounts. Due diligence must be done on all principal beneficial owners identified in accordance with the following principles:*

- Natural persons: when the account is in the name of an individual, the private banker must establish whether the client is acting on his/her own behalf. If doubt exists, the bank will establish the capacity in which and on whose behalf the account holder is acting.

While this is an admirable sentiment it seems difficult to see how this is going to be achieved. Those with large amounts to launder should not find it difficult to hire people to front the transactions they need to engage in. Many of the points made above will also apply here.

7.110

- *Legal entities: where the client is a company, such as a private investment company, the private banker will understand the structure of the company sufficiently to determine the provider of funds, principal owner(s) of the shares and those who have control over the funds, e.g. the directors and those with the power to give direction to the directors of the company. With regard to other shareholders the private banker will make a reasonable judgement as to the need for further due diligence. This principle applies regardless of whether the share capital is in registered or bearer form.*

Clearly this is an area where experience and staff training could make a vital difference. Does the client's corporate group structure make sense in terms of the business transactions being carried on? If not, may it be explicable in terms of the historical development of the corporate group. If neither is the case then the reaction should be one of suspicion and the banker concerned should contact the money laundering reporting officer.

A more difficult problem will apply with investment companies. Namely, whose money is being invested? In the case of well-known fund managers and investment companies, 'know your client' provisions will normally suffice. However, in cases of firms who are not already known, 'know your client' is going to involve knowing your client's client; or at least being satisfied as to the intermediary's identity checking requirements.

7.111

- *Trusts: where the client is a trustee, the private banker will understand the structure of the trust sufficiently to determine the provider of funds (e g settlor) those who have control over the funds (e g trustees) and any persons or entities who have the power to remove the trustees. The private banker will make a reasonable judgement as to the need for further due diligence.*

The points made above in relation to beneficial owners will apply here as well.

7.112

● *Unincorporated associations: the above principles apply to unincorporated associations.*

This turns to the issues raised above concerning ascertaining who may be standing behind the party dealing with the bank. No guidance is given as to how this should be done. Indeed, the author has yet to come across guidelines issued by any state that have yet satisfactorily done this. It is perhaps a noble sentiment rather than a realisable objective.

1.2.3 Accounts held in the name of money managers and similar intermediaries

7.113 *The private banker will perform due diligence on the intermediary and establish that the intermediary has a due diligence process for its clients, or a regulatory obligation to conduct such due diligence, that is satisfactory to the bank.*

The comments made above in relation to investment companies will also apply here.

1.2.4 Powers of attorney/Authorised signers

7.114 *Where the holder of a power of attorney or another authorised signer is appointed by a client, it is generally sufficient to do due diligence on the client.*

1.2.5 Practices for walk-in clients and electronic banking relationships

7.115 *A bank will determine whether walk-in clients or relationships initiated through electronic channels require a higher degree of due diligence prior to account opening.*

This remains a rather vague suggestion. It might be helpful if the banks could agree a clarification to this Principle to reach an agreed minimum standard. There are a number of variables here. How clearly can the proposed customer prove their identity? In regulatory terms how safe is the country they are based in? In short the fact that they contacted the bank by walking into the branch or by electronic contact is not of importance in itself. The key issue is the context and whether this explains the manner of contact. If it does then the degree of due diligence should not need to be higher than for other customers.

1.3 Due diligence

7.116 *It is essential to collect and record information covering the following categories:*

- Purpose and reasons for opening the account;
- Anticipated account activity;
- Source of wealth (description of the economic activity which has generated the net worth);
- Estimated net worth;
- Source of funds (description of the origin and the means of transfer for monies that are accepted for the account opening);
- References or other sources to corroborate reputation information where available;
- Unless other measures reasonably suffice to do the due diligence on a client (e g favourable and reliable references), a client will be met prior to account opening.

7.117 This could prove particularly helpful. It is unlikely to assist in spotting suspicious clients or funds at the outset unless the launderers are unusually obtuse. However, it will provide the bank concerned with a context into which to place the client's financial activities. It may well be that in the longer term apparently incongruous payments will be made and thus draw the bank's attention. 'Know your customer' has considerably more potential to lead to laundering being spotted than identity checking on opening an account.

1.4 Oversight responsibility

7.118 *There will be a requirement that all new clients and new accounts be approved by at least one person other than the private banker.*

This is a useful step. It will reduce the risk of a private client banker being too enthusiastic about getting a new, apparently wealthy client who will presumably be helping him hit his financial targets. It will also reduce the risk of corruption, as a new client wishing to subvert a bank into laundering his funds will not be able to achieve this by bribing just one person. Even so, there is evidence that suggests that a greater number of bankers than one might hope will be willing to engage in illegal activity.

Client acceptance: situations requiring additional diligence/ attention

2.1 Numbered or alternate name accounts

7.119 *Numbered or alternate name accounts will only be accepted if the bank has established the identity of the client and the beneficial owner.*

2.2 High-risk countries

7.120 *The bank will apply heightened scrutiny to clients and beneficial owners resident in and funds sourced from countries identified by credible sources as having inadequate anti-money-laundering standards or representing high-risk for crime and corruption.*

This is a useful step and it has been assisted by the FATF and Transparency International both placing on their websites the information to assist firms in making such assessments.

2.3 Offshore jurisdictions

7.121 *Risks associated with entities organised in offshore jurisdictions are covered by due diligence procedures laid out in these guidelines.*

2.4 High-risk activities

7.122 *Clients and beneficial owners whose source of wealth emanates from activities known to be susceptible to money laundering will be subject to heightened scrutiny.*

2.5 Public officials

7.123 *Individuals who have or have had positions of public trust such as government officials, senior executives of government corporations, politicians, important political party officials, etc. and their families and close associates require heightened scrutiny.*

This is a particularly important addition given the unfortunate tendency of political leaders in certain parts of the world to regard their country's national wealth as a personal piggy bank from which monies can be removed at will. It will also make it more complicated for such people to launder such monies, though there are no shortage of methods that they could adopt to disguise what was going on. For example, by utilising fake trading transactions involving state entities.

Updating client files

7.124 *The private banker is responsible for updating the client file on a defined basis and/or when there are major changes. The private banker's supervisor or an independent control person will review relevant portions of client files on a regular basis to ensure consistency and completeness. The frequency of the reviews depends on the size, complexity and risk posed of the relationship.*

Practices when identifying unusual or suspicious activities

4.1 Definition of unusual or suspicious activities

7.125 *The bank will have a written policy on the identification of and follow-up on unusual or suspicious activities. This policy will include a definition of what is considered to be suspicious or unusual and give examples thereof.*

- Unusual or suspicious activities may include:

  — Account transactions or other activities which are not consistent with the due diligence file

  — Cash transactions over a certain amount

  — Pass-through/in-and-out-transactions.

4.2 Identification of unusual or suspicious activities

7.126 *Unusual or suspicious activities can be identified through:*

- Monitoring of transactions

- Client contacts (meetings, discussions, in-country visits etc.)

- Third party information (e g newspapers, Reuters, internet)

- Private banker's internal knowledge of the client's environment (e g political situation in his/her country)

4.3 Follow-up on unusual or suspicious activities

7.127   The private banker, management and/or the control function will carry out an analysis of the background of any unusual or suspicious activity. If there is no plausible explanation a decision will be made involving the control function:

- To continue the business relationship with increased monitoring
- To cancel the business relationship
- To report the business relationship to the authorities.
- The report to the authorities is made by the control function and senior management may need to be notified (e g Senior Compliance Officer, CEO, Chief Auditor, General Counsel). As required by local laws and regulations the assets may be blocked and transactions may be subject to approval by the control function.

7.128   These guidelines are very useful. The one troubling element is the suggestion that one of the options is to cancel the business relationship. This will simply warn the client that they have aroused suspicion. Their reaction will be to take their business elsewhere and do a better job of disguising it. If the bank is suspicious it should instead be reporting the matter to the relevant authority and taking their guidance as to whether to continue to act. The regulators will normally want the bank to continue acting, thus giving them the opportunity of watching what is taking place. The only potential outstanding issue that could then arise is where the bank suspected it to be a situation where a true owner might later arrive in pursuit of the funds. This is a distinct possibility where large amounts of funds have been pillaged from a state. The bank's fear will be that they may then be made liable to repay the funds even if they have parted company with them. As discussed above at **7.93** the safest course of action in such circumstances is to seek a closed sitting at the appropriate civil court, seeking an order that having made a suspicious transaction report the bank can continue to act.

Monitoring

7.129   *A sufficient monitoring program must be in place. The primary responsibility for monitoring account activities lies with the private banker. The private banker will be familiar with significant transactions and increased activity in the account and will be especially aware of unusual or suspicious activities (see 4.1). The bank will decide to what extent fulfilment of these responsibilities will need to be supported through the use of automated systems or other means.*

Control responsibilities

7.130 *A written control policy will be in place establishing standard control procedures to be undertaken by the various 'control layers' (private banker, independent operations unit, Compliance, Internal Audit). The control policy will cover issues of timing, degree of control, areas to be controlled, responsibilities and follow-up etc.*

Reporting

7.131 *There will be regular management reporting established on money laundering issues (e g number of reports to authorities, monitoring tools, changes in applicable laws and regulations, the number and scope of training sessions provided to employees).*

Education, training and information

7.132 *The bank will establish a training program on the identification and prevention of money laundering for employees who have client contact and for compliance personnel. Regular training (e g annually) will also include how to identify and follow up on unusual or suspicious activities. In addition, employees will be informed about any major changes in anti-money-laundering laws and regulations. All new employees will be provided with guidelines on the anti-money-laundering procedures.*

Record retention requirements

7.133 *The bank will establish record retention requirements for all anti-money-laundering related documents. The documents must be kept for a minimum of five years.*

Exceptions and deviations

7.134 *The bank will establish an exception and deviation procedure that requires risk assessment and approval by an independent unit.*

Anti-money-laundering organisation

7.135 *The bank will establish an adequately staffed and independent department responsible for the prevention of money laundering (e g Compliance, independent control unit, Legal).*

In some respects the emergence of the Principles represents a triumph of risk over rule-based management[1]. Indeed there have been conflicting interpretations as to whether the message being sent by the banks involved is a reaction against further regulation or a move to facilitate it[2]. It can also be seen as an attempt to shape its future form[3]. Whichever is the case the Principles should result in a more precise, practice based, focused and appropriately crafted set of regulations than would emerge from the traditional rule-based, regulator led, compliance approach. The problem that this potentially opens up is that it leaves it in the hands of the banks concerned to change the rules when they believe it to be appropriate. It thus becomes an internal matter for banks rather than a policy matter for regulators and therefore depends on those engaged in risk-based compliance, laundering and risk management in those banks having sufficient power vis a vis sales, new products and marketing to hold the most suitable line. Perhaps it is a positive sign that the creation of the Wolfsberg Principles means that for the banks concerned, at least, such matters should now be more visible. A weakness however[4] is that there is no enforcement procedure should one of the banks fail to maintain the Principles. It will be interesting to see the response of the relevant national supervisor should such a failure occur.

1 Peith and Aiolfi, *'The Private Sector becomes Active: The Wolfsberg Process'* in A Practitioner's Guide etc.
2 Examples being the New York Times, editorial, 11 June 2000; American Banker, 11 June 2000; Financial Times, 23 October 2000 and The Banker, 1 October 2001.
3 Peith and Aiolfi supra
4 See Peith and Aiolfi, supra 274.

7.136 In the words of Dr Peter Eigen[1]:

'We fully expect that other banks will recognise these guidelines and volunteer to accept them ... We believe it is essential that internationally active investment firms, brokerage houses, insurance companies, property and asset management firms, fully embrace standards similar to those being announced by the banks.'

Eigen has gone on to make the point that the Principles involve facing up to five essential points. The first is that they have been drafted to avoid ambiguity. The second is the voluntary nature of the Principles, it being anticipated that banks will engage more fully with the process if they have volunteered in the first place rather than having been coerced. Thirdly, there is the expectation that there will be a systemic spread of the Principles and that they will become the norm. This overlaps with the fourth, which is that non-bank financial institutions should adopt similar principles as well. The final one is that they are designed to catch the full range of laundering.

1 Chairman, Transparency International, 30 October 2000: http://www.transparency.org

7.137 Reinout van Lennep, head of ABN Amro private banking, recently went on record as saying[1]: *'These principles reflect decent and adequate*

standards; we neither expect nor wish to see the standards being raised higher.'
The experience of banks since statutory requirements were first brought in
during the mid-1980s, suggests that this may be optimistic. Having opted to
create principles to manage an ongoing and intractable problem, the banks have
already had to amend and develop them. It would be surprising if it were to stop
there. Indeed the banks involved in the process are engaged in ongoing monitoring meetings that may facilitate exactly such a process.

---

1 http://www.moneuunlimited.co.uk

7.138   There could also be market pressures for other banks to join in. Winer
has suggested[1] that international financial institutions should only be prepared
to distribute funds via banks that maintain the highest standards. The Wolfsberg
Principles would be one of the factors that could be used to measure this. If this
were to happen all major banks would find themselves corralled into adopting
the Wolfsberg approach.

---

1 Jonathan Winer, Globalization, Terrorist Finance and Global Conflict, Time for a White List? EJLR 2002.

Chapter 8

Special compliance obligations: market abuse, insider dealing and misleading statements

'..confidence in the financial system and consumer protection will be seriously undermined if the financial system and individual institutions are abused for criminal purposes.'

Howard Davies, FSA

Introduction

8.1   Market abuse was first introduced as part of the extensive programme of developments that were brought in to the financial services regulatory regime by the Financial Services and Markets Act 2000 ('the Act'). Since then market abuse has seen significant change as a result of the Market Abuse Directive which in turn led to changes to the relevant UK legislation[1]. This Directive is a part of the EU's Financial Services Action Plan which has been created to try and develop a pan EU financial market and to enhance market integrity[2]. Problems had arisen with regard to market abuse because member states had different laws. This meant that if a company in one member state were to mount a takeover bid for a company in another, and that second company had subsidiaries in other member states, the takeover would have to be designed not to fall foul of the market abuse regulations in all those states. By having a single EU approach this problem is hopefully avoided. However, the UK government has already 'gold plated' the Directive, with the result that slightly different rules survive.

---

1 Financial Services and Markets Act 2000 (Market Abuse) Regulations 2005, SI 2005/381.

2 Of specific reference to market abuse/insider dealing are Directive 2003/6/EC on insider dealing and market abuse, Directive 2003/124/EC which established criteria for determining when inside information is precise and price sensitive, Directive 2003/125/EC creating standards for presenting investment recommendations and disclosing conflicts of interest, Commission Regulation 2273/2003 providing technical conditions for share buy-backs and price stabilisation, and Directive 2004/72/EC regarding accepted market practices, inside information, insider lists and notification requirements.

8.2   The key element of the Directive is that it applies to all transactions involving financial instruments that have been admitted to trading on at least one prescribed market in the EU regardless of whether that market is regulated. More than one state may be involved in the matter as the regime results in the state in which the market abuse occurs and that in which the relevant financial instrument is admitted both having jurisdiction. In most instances though both activities will occur in the same state. The regime extends to cover insider dealing and to reduce the risk of this occurring a requirement was introduced for disclosure by issuers of inside information, on the basis that once this is done the information is in the public domain and insider dealing should cease to be a risk. A requirement that is new to the UK is the need to create an 'insider list' of people who have access to inside information. In addition there is an obligation to make sure that those producing or disseminating research make sure that it is fairly presented and any conflicts of interest disclosed. The previous safe harbours have disappeared but two are added: these relate to share buy backs and stabilisation. Powers are also provided to the relevant authorities, in the UK the FSA, to provide guidance on 'accepted market practices'. This is assistance in ascertaining whether a particular trade will give false or misleading impression and whether particular information is inside information. There remains some debate about the precise legal status of such guidance but in practice its status will make little difference. The rules are drafted by the FSA and they are also the body who will determine whether to take steps against someone believed to be in breach of the law. The issue is only likely to arise if FSA guidance is cited in the defence of a criminal prosecution or in an FSA Tribunal hearing.

8.3   The essence of the regime however has remained the same since the passing of the Act which is that certain types of behaviour are deemed to be in breach of the Act. This does not necessarily mean that the behaviour will amount to a criminal offence – though in some cases it undoubtedly will. What it does mean is that the behaviour will give rise to the Financial Services Authority (FSA) having the power to take steps against FSA authorised persons and firms together with anyone else who has committed market abuse[1]. This will result in potential fines and in the case of authorised firms also the possibility of loss of licences[2]. A complication arises here because if the FSA decide to fine someone '*... they may not in respect of any contravention both require a person to pay a penalty ...and withdraw his authorisation under section 33.*'[3] What they can do if the person agrees to co-operate with the FSA is to include an agreement to not work in the financial services sector as part of the settlement. The taking of steps against non FSA regulated people is most likely to impact on commodity companies whose involvement in that sector can have an impact on prices. Indeed one of the cases examined below[4] involved a major oil company. This chapter will consider 'market abuse' itself and also insider dealing which comes within the remit of market abuse. Finally there will be a consideration of the relevant law relating to misleading statements[5].

1 FSMA 2000, s 123.
2 FSMA 2000, s 123.
3 FSMA 2000, s 206(2).
4 *Shell Petroleum and Trading Co plc and The Royal Dutch Petroleum Co NV*, FSA enforcement action, 24 August 2004.
5 FSMA 2000, s 397.

8.4   One issue that arises here is that of the nature of a civil offence. It is not an approach that has been a significant part of English law. Essentially there is a civil burden of proof coupled with a potentially unlimited fine[1]. There have been suggestions[2] that the courts will regard market abuse as a criminal offence but the view of the majority is that[3] the power to fine is only unlimited because some of those who might potentially be fined are large financial institutions for whom a fine would have to be large to make any impact. However, a common misconception is that as it is a civil offence the burden of proof simply operates as the balance of probabilities:

> '*A civil court, when considering a charge of fraud, will naturally require a higher degree of probability that that which it would require if considering whether negligence were established. It does not adopt so high a degree as a criminal court, even when it is considering a charge of a criminal nature, but still it does require a degree of probability which is commensurate with the occasion.*[4]'

> '*The case, like any civil case, may be proved by a preponderance of probability, but the degree of probability depends on the subject-matter. In proportion as the offence is grave, so ought the proof be clear.*[5]'

1 FSMA 2000, 123(1).
2 Joint Committee on Financial Services and Markets '*Draft Financial Services and Markets Bill: Parts V, VI and XII in relation to the European Convention on Human Rights*', 27 May 1999, HC 415, p 82.
3 House of Commons research paper, 99/68 p 61–3.
4 Denning LJ in *Bater v Bater* [1951] 35
5 Lord Denning in *Blyth v Blyth* [1966] AC 643.

8.5   Leaving aside certain technical situations where the burden of poof in a civil matter is beyond all reasonable doubt (eg, antisocial behaviour orders, disciplinary proceedings concerning the legal profession and situations where the circumstances are tantamount to a criminal offence[1]) the remaining situations see the civil burden of proof as flexible. Technically, the burden remains the balance of probabilities, but the more serious the allegation and the more serious the consequences, then the stronger must be the evidence before the court will find the matter proved. Although there remains a distinction in principle between the civil standard and the criminal standard, the practical application of the flexible approach means that they are likely to produce the same or similar results[2]. Therefore, in those cases where the market abuse alleged would also be a criminal offence then the stronger the evidence that will be required in the FSA Tribunal. In most cases this has not become an issue as those facing market abuse charges have co-operated and accepted disciplinary action. This is perhaps the true measure of success of the new regime. Few if any would be likely to have so co-operated with a criminal prosecution because of the potential consequences.

---

1 Lord Lane in *Re a Solicitor* [1993] QB 69.
2 Richards LJ in *R v Mental Health Review Tribunal* (December 2005, unreported).

8.6   For market abuse the key issues relate to FSMA 2000, ss 73, 96 and 118 to 131 (as amended) together with the FSA Market Abuse Handbook and some parts of the FSA Conduct of Business rules. For insider dealing much of the relevant law is still to be found in the Criminal Justice Act 1993, though the FSA Handbook at MAR 1.3 impacts on the treatment of insider dealing as a category of market abuse rather than as a criminal offence. Misleading statements are dealt with in the FSMA and can also be affected by MAR 1.5.

8.7   Inevitably, the recent developments in this area of law raise the issue of how common market abuse and insider dealing are. The FSA themselves have published an analysis[1] which measured the extent to which share prices moved ahead of the regulatory announcements that companies are required to make. The analysis focused on two areas; those relating to takeover bids and announcements about trading performance made by FTSE 350 companies. An assessment was then made of the proportion of these that were preceded by abnormal share price movements. The research did not prove how much market abuse was taking place but it did suggest that 28.9% of takeover announcements and 21.7% of trading announcements were preceded by transactions that were probably based on inside information.

---

1 Dubow B and Monteiro N '*FSA publishes measure of scale of market abuse*' March 2005, FSA.

Market abuse

The offences

8.8   Market abuse is defined as

'... *behaviour (whether by one person alone or by two or more persons jointly or in concert) which –*

(*a*)   *occurs in relation to –*

    (*i*)   *qualifying investments admitted to trading on a prescribed market,*

   (ii)   *qualifying investments in respect of which a request for admission to trading on such a market has been made, or*

   (iii) *in the case of subsection (2) or (3) behaviour, investments which are rated investments in relation to such qualifying investments, and*

  (b) *falls within one or more of the types of behaviour set out in subsection (2) to (8).' From 30 June 2008 the 'regular user' definition in s.130A(3) disappears and this subsection will have its impact affected accordingly.[1]'*

This does not require the person concerned to have intended to commit market abuse[2].

The categories of behaviour which amount to market abuse are examined below.

1 FSMA 2000, s 118(9).
2 MAR 1.2.3G.

Insider dealing

8.9 Insider dealing where '... *an insider deals, or attempts to deal, in a qualifying investment on the basis of inside information relating to the investment in question.[1]'*.

1 FSMA 2000, s 118(2).

Disclosure of inside information

8.10 *'where an insider discloses inside information to another person otherwise than in the proper exercise of is employment, profession or duties.[1]'*

1 FSMA 2000, s 118(3).

Failure to observe proper standards of behaviour

8.11 In any other case where the behaviour concerned is '... *based on information which is not generally available to those using the market but which, if available to a regular user of the market, would be, or would be likely to be, regarded by him as relevant when deciding the terms on which transactions in qualifying investments should be effected, and ...is likely to be regarded* *by a regular used of the market as a failure on the part of the person concerned to observe the standard of behaviour reasonably expected of a person in his position in relation to the market.[1]'*

This follows the previous wording of s 118(1)(c) and (2)(a).

---

1 FSMA 2000, s 118(4)(a), (b).

Giving a false or misleading impression

8.12   Where transactions are carried out other than for legitimate reasons and in line with '*... accepted market practices ...*' on the market concerned which '*... give, or are likely to give, a false or misleading impression as to the supply of, or demand for, or as to the price of, one or more qualifying investments, or ... secure the price of one or more such investments at an abnormal or artificial level.[1]'*

This follows the wording of the previous version of s 118(2)(b).

---

1 FSMA 2000, s 118(5)(a), (b).

Fictitious devices

8.13   Carrying out transactions which employ fictitious devices or deception[1].

---

1 FSMA 2000, s 118(6).

Disseminating misleading information

8.14   Disseminating information which '*... gives, or is likely to give, a false or misleading impression as to the supply of, or demand for, or as to the price of ... qualifying investments, or ... secure the price of one or more such investments at an abnormal or artificial level.[1]'*

---

1 FSMA 2000, s 118(7).

Market distortion

8.15   Where not already covered above such behaviour as is likely '*... to give a regular user of the market a false or misleading impression as to the* *supply of, demand for, or value of, qualifying investments or ... would be ... regarded by a regular user of the market as behaviour that would distort, or would be likely to distort, the market ... and the behaviour is likely to be regarded by a regular user of the market as a failure on the part of the person concerned to observe the standard of behaviour reasonably expected of a person in his position in relation to the market.[1]'*

These two subsections develop the wording of the previous version of s 118(2)(c).

1 FSMA 2000, s 118(8)(a), (b).

Encouraging others

8.16 There is also a secondary offence[1] of taking or refraining from taking any action which requires or encourages another person to engage in market abuse.

1 FSMA 2000, s 123(1)(b).

Inside information

8.17 This leads us to the question of what exactly 'inside information' is. It is[1] information of a precise nature relating to qualifying investments (see below) which are not commodity derivatives, which is not generally available, relates directly or indirectly to the issuer of a qualifying investment and would if generally available be likely to have a significant effect on the price of the investment concerned or of a related one. Where commodity derivatives are concerned inside information is that which is of a precise nature which is not generally available and relates directly or indirectly to such derivatives, and users of the relevant markets would expect to be provided with it in line with accepted market practice. This may be because such information is routinely made available to users on that market or because it is required by statute, the rules of the market concerned or custom either on the derivatives market or that of the underlying commodity[2]. General availability in either instance extends to information that is obtainable by research or analysis[3].

1 FSMA 2000, s 118C.
2 FSMA 2000, s 118C(7).
3 FSMA 2000, s 118C(8).

8.18 There is a different definition of 'inside information' in relation to anyone charged with executing orders concerning qualifying or related investments. Here it includes information received from a client in relation to a pending order. The information must be of a precise nature, not be generally available and relate directly or indirectly to an issuer of qualifying investments. If it were generally available it must be likely to have a significant effect on the price of the qualifying investments, or related ones.

8.19 The concept of 'precision' crops up in these definitions. It means[1] information which indicates circumstances or an event that exists or is reasonably likely to and is specific enough to enable conclusions to be drawn as to the effect on the price of qualifying investments or related ones. This is likely to be the case only if it is information which a reasonable investor would be likely to use as part of the basis of his investment decisions.

---

1 FSMA 2000, s 118C(5).

Protected disclosures

8.20 Information can be disclosed without being in breach of any restrictions provided it causes the person making the disclosure to know or suspect that someone else is engaging in market abuse. That information must have come to them in the course of their trade profession, business or employment and it must have been made to the FSA or the appropriate internal officer as soon as reasonably practicable after it was obtained[1].

---

1 FSMA 2000, s 131A.

8.21 Certain key issues arise from all this: what is an insider, what should be done by firms to highlight who these people are, to which investments does the regime apply and which markets are affected?

Insiders

8.22 Clearly a key focus point is the nature of an 'insider'. This is defined[1] as anyone who has inside information:

- as a result of their membership of a company whether as an administrator or manager or a supervisory body;

- as a result of them holding capital issued by a company;

- as a result of them having access to the information concerned through carrying out their employment or professional duties;

- as a result of criminal activities; or

- which they obtained by other methods which they know, or could reasonably be expected to know would be inside information.

---

1 FSMA 2000, s 118B.

Insider lists

8.23 Lists must be kept which, at the least, must state:

- the identity of anyone having access to inside information;
- the reason why any person named is on the list; and
- the date on which the list was created and updated.

8.24 On any occasion when the list is updated, and when necessary this must be done promptly, there must be a statement as to:

- why there is a change when someone is already on the list;
- why anyone has been added; and
- when anyone previously on the list no longer has access to inside information.

8.25 This list must be kept for a minimum of five years. The people responsible for creating these lists must also make sure that anyone who has access to inside information acknowledges the legal and regulatory requirements and that they are aware of the potential consequences should they be breached.

Qualifying investments

8.26 These are defined[1] as:

- transferable securities;
- units in collective investment schemes;
- money market instruments;
- financial futures contracts including equivalent cash settled instruments;
- forward rate agreements;
- interest rate, currency and equity swaps;
- options;

- commodity derivatives;

- any other instrument admitted to trading on a regulated market in a member state or for which a request for admission has been made.

---

1 See Directive 2003/6/EC, art 1(3).

Prescribed markets

8.27   These are defined by statutory instrument[1] as all markets that are established under the rules of a UK recognised investment exchange and all other regulated markets. For the purposes of all types of market abuse other than insider dealing, relying on information not generally available[2] and behaviour likely to give a misleading impression and to distort a market[3] The investment exchanges also include OFEX.

---

1 Prescribed Markets and Qualifying Investments Order 2001, SI 2001/996, as amended by the Financial Services and Markets Act 2000 (Market Abuse) Regulations 2005, SI 2005/381, art 4.
2 FSMA 2000, s 118(4).
3 FSMA 2000, s 118(8).

Transparency standards

8.28   Those engaged in research and the recommendation of investments to the public or distribution channels must disclose their relevant interests. This is mainly aimed at financial analysts and journalists who profit from this activity.

Reporting requirements

8.29   There are reporting requirements for managers and those closely associated with them. The latter category covers spouses, dependent children and other relatives in the household. The reports must be made within five working days to the FSA covering:

- the name of the person concerned;

- the reason why there is a need to notify;

- the name of the relevant issuer;

- a description of the financial instrument;

- the nature of the transaction;

- the date and place of the transaction; and

- the price and volume of the transaction

8.30   If a transaction is suspicious a report must be made to the FSA and if money laundering is possibly a factor also the Serious Organised Crimes Agency and in either event stating:

- a description of the transaction including the type of order concerned;

- the reasons for believing that the transaction might amount to market abuse;

- the means for identifying the person concerned and anyone else involved;

- the capacity in which the person subject to the notification operates; and

- any other relevant information.

Notices

8.31   The FSA is required by s 124 to issue statements when penalties are imposed providing the relevant details and also whether the behaviour concerned had caused an adverse effect on the market. They should also indicate circumstances in which the person concerned should be taken to have had a reasonable belief that their behaviour did not amount to market abuse or that they had taken all reasonable precautions and exercised due diligence to avoid market abuse.

8.32   There are a range of other notices required under FSMA 2000, ss 92, 126,127, 205, 207–209, 387–390 and 393. FSMA 2000, s 92 requires that a notice be given if the FSA is to take steps against someone under s 91 for breach of the listing rules, s 126 requires that a warning notice must be given to someone against whom it proposes to take action setting out any proposed penalty and warning notice. If it is then decided to take action a decision notice must be sent in similar terms. Section 205 enables the FSA to publish a statement where they believe that an authorised person has contravened a requirement under the FSMA 2000, s 207 extends this to situations where the FSA proposes to issue a s 205 notice or to take steps under s 206 (imposition of a financial penalty on an authorised person). It must give the person concerned a warning notice setting out the terms of any statement and the penalty. Once the decision has been made so to act a decision notice must be issued under s 208 again setting out the terms of any statement to be published and any fine. If a s 205 statement is issued a copy should also be sent to anyone else to whom notice was given. Section 387 determines the content of warning notices, s 388 of decision notices, s 389 requires that a notice of discontinuance be issued if they decide not to proceed and s 390 requires a final notice where the action set out in a decision notice has been taken. Finally, s 393 requires that third parties are identified where the FSA think they will be affected prejudicially and that person should then receive a copy of the relevant notice unless they have already received a separate warning notice in relation to the same matter.

8.33   This was the subject of the dispute in *Watts v FSA*[1], a case concerning the Chairman of the Dutch/Shell group. This matter concerned s 393(4) of the FSMA 2000, which provides a right to anyone who is a third party under a 'notice procedure', ie, someone who is prejudicially identified, to be given a copy of relevant notices and a reasonable period in which to make representations to the FSA. If action is proposed on the basis of market abuse and breach of the Listing Rules (as it was here) any person concerned should be given a warning notice under FSMA 2000, ss 126(1) and 92(1). In the absence of a reference to the Tribunal, in this case because matters were proceeding consensually, a final notice has to be issued under s 390(1). Sir Philip Watts had not been explicitly identified in the FSA notice, but as a result of it he had been subject to considerable adverse media coverage. He therefore believed that he had been implicitly identified and that notifying a company or accusing it of misconduct is a legal fiction[2] as it can only act through individuals. His challenge under s 393(11) was also partly based on his belief that the FSA investigation was incomplete and flawed. The FSA disagreed that Sir Philip Watts was a third party for these purposes and also felt that if it were required to give notice in all cases such as his it would face a 'potentially massive and administratively impractical task'[3]. It was therefore necessary for the Tribunal to consider the meaning and purpose of such notices. Clearly the key element was to ensure fairness. The Tribunal were influenced by the House of Lords debate in which the relevant amendment was introduced:

'The new clause on third party rights ...rationalises the existing provisions dealing with the rights of third parties identified in warning or decision notices in a way that is prejudicial to them. These provisions were designed to deal with cases where there is some wrongdoing alleged on the part of the third party who is not himself the subject of action by the FSA. For instance, in disciplinary cases under Part XIV, it was felt that action might be taken against a firm for reasons which implied that there has been some failing by one of its directors or employees; or in market abuse cases, where other parties might well be involved in the transactions giving rise to the allegation that market abuse has been engaged in.

The provisions give third parties, who are identified in prejudicial terms in the reasons for a warning or decision notice, the right to receive a copy of the notice, and to make representations or refer the matter to the tribunal in the same way as the person who is the subject of the FSA's proposed action. We took the view that although these rights create an administrative burden for the FSA, they are necessary to give the third party the right to defend himself against any implied blame arising from the reasons given for the action.' per Lord Bach.

---

1 FSA Tribunal, 25 July 2005.

2 See *Lennards Carrying Company Ltd v Asiatic Petroleum Co Ltd* [1915] AC 705 at 713 per Viscount Haldane LC.
3 FSA Tribunal, 25 July 2005 at 42

8.34 It was held that although it was not always the case that courts would refer to Hansard[1] it was appropriate here because of the novel nature of the issue being contested. It was also pointed out that there were parallels with DTI procedures[2] where it is required that the investigating body acts fairly and provides the opportunity to anyone who has allegations made against them to have a fair opportunity to answer.

1 See *Pepper v Hart* [1993] AC 593; *R v Sec of State for the Environment, ex p Spath Holme Ltd* [2001] 2 AC 349, and *Robinson v Sec of State for Northern Ireland* [2002] NI 390.
2 See *Re Pergamon Press Ltd* [1971] 1 Ch 388.

8.35 Overall the Tribunal rejected Sir Philip Watts's claims and held that s 393(4) afforded third party rights to anyone identified in 'the decision' not 'the matter'. The former did not extend to Sir Philip. This is in line with other uses of 'matter' in the FSMA 2000[1]. There was also a precedent on this point of interpretation in *Parker v FSA*[2]. In addition s 393(4) refers to the FSA issuing a decision notice as the same time that it issues '... the decision notice which identifies him.' In addition s 393(12) refers to the material relating '... to the matter which identifies the third party.' It was also stated that an allegation against a company would not necessarily imply criticism of particular individuals. The whole point of the notices in this context was to give a right of reply to someone who was identified in the FSA notice. It would have been different had Sir Philip been identified by name or job description.

1 FSMA 2000, see ss 92(7), 127(4), 133(4), 205, 208(4), 388(1)(e) and 390(1).
2 See FSA Tribunal, 13 October 2004.

FSA Regulations

8.36 The FSA Principles (see Chapter 1 at **1.24**) will be relevant here. In addition the FSA have published the Code of Market Conduct pursuant to s 119 to provide guidelines as to what behaviour the FSA will regard as market abuse. Section 122 makes clear that if behaviour takes place that does not amount to market abuse under the Code, then it is not market abuse for the purposes of the FSMA. Thus, if the Code were found to be in error it would need to be amended before anyone could have civil proceedings taken against them. However, in serious cases the option of a criminal prosecution for insider dealing, issuing misleading statements or certain other criminal offences would remain.

8.37 As far as the FSA are concerned behaviour will be carried out '*in relation to*' investments prior to an admission for trading or the commencement of trading if the act is in relation to them and it continues to have an effect once the application has been made or it has been admitted to trading[1]. Refraining from action might amount to market abuse if the behaviour satisfies s 118(1)(a) and the person concerned has not carried out a legal or regulatory requirement or if they gave rise to the impression that he would correct previous statements where necessary and he has not done so[2]. When determining whether or not someone could reasonably be expected to know that information in their possession was inside information the FSA are guided by whether or not a normal and reasonable person with inside information would or should have known that the person they received it from was an insider and if a normal and reasonable person in the position of the person holding inside information would or should have known that it was inside information[3].

---

1 MAR 1.2.5 E.
2 MAR 1.2.6 E.
3 MAR 1.2.8 E.

8.38   The FSA will consider the following factors in determining whether information is generally available and therefore not inside information where information is available within the UK:

- whether the information has been disclosed on a prescribed market through a regulatory information service or in any other way in line with the rules of the market concerned;

- whether the information can be obtained from records available to the public;

- whether the information is otherwise generally available or can be derived from such information even if it is only available on the payment of a fee;

- whether the information can be obtained by observation without infringing confidentiality;

- the extent to which such information can be obtained by analysis of information which is generally available even if that analysis requires abnormal skill or expertise[1].

---

1 MAR 1.2.12 E.

8.39   As mentioned above particular problems arise in relation to commodity derivatives. In particular, what amounts to inside information in this context is in part determined by what information market participants expect to be provided with.

8.40   The FSA also has its own view on what will amount to insider dealing for market abuse purposes. It falls into four main groupings:

●   dealing on the basis of inside information that is not trading information;

●   front running (ie, trading on a person's own behalf ahead of a client order whilst in possession of inside information to take advantage of the expected price change in the investment concerned);

●   when a takeover is taking place, an offeror entering into a transaction in a qualifying investment on the basis of inside information concerning that takeover which involves exposure to a price movement in the target company's shares. This would cover not only dealing in those shares but also derivatives;

●   when a takeover is taking place, acting on one's own behalf on the basis of inside information when acting for the offeror[1].

---

1 MAR 1.3.2 E.

8.41   In determining whether someone's behaviour amounts to acting 'on the basis of' inside information the FSA will have regard to whether the decision to deal was made before the person possessed the relevant inside information, if they dealt to satisfy a regulatory requirement or legal obligation that came into existence before they obtained the inside information and whether the individuals in possession of the inside information had any involvement with the decision to deal or behaved in a way to influence it or had any contact with those who were dealing[1]. In any event if the FSA believes that the person did or did not act in line with a regulatory requirement, this will be a factor in shaping their view as to whether or not the behaviour amounted to market abuse[2].

---

1 MAR 1.3.3 E.
2 MAR 1.3.11 E.

8.42   One piece of good news for firms with effective compliance systems is that the existence of effective Chinese walls separating those who deal and who influence them from those in possession of the inside information will be regarded by the FSA as an indication that insider dealing cannot have been taking place[1].

---

1 MAR 1.3.5 E.

8.43   Market makers also have the capacity to engage in legitimate business when dealing and underwriting even if they are in possession of inside information. However, a factor here will be whether the inside information is limited to trading information. If not this will suggest the trading was not legitimate. This does not extend to underwriting[1].

1 MAR 1.3.7 C to 1.3.9 E.

8.44   The FSA's view on whether a person's behaviour represents legitimate business is shaped by four key issues:

- the extent to which the relevant trading is carried out to hedge a risk arising out of their business and the extent to which that risk is neutralised;

- where a transaction is carried out on the basis of inside information concerning a client transaction that has been executed, that information has not yet been required to be published by the exchange concerned or relevant regulations;

- if the trading is connected with a client transaction and has no impact on the price, or that there has been adequate disclosure to the client who has not objected; or

- whether the person's behaviour was reasonable by the proper standards of the market concerned bearing in mind any relevant legal or regulatory requirements and whether the transaction was carried out in a way that reflected the need for the market concerned to operate fairly and efficiently[1].

1 MAR 1.3.10 E.

8.45   What then does not amount to market abuse? Certainly the dutiful carrying out of client orders or the arranging of the same on behalf of someone else will not be market abuse. It will very probably also be safe if the person acting possesses inside information that is not limited to trading information. Factors to consider are: whether the person has complied with the FSA Conduct of Business Rules and Code of Market Conduct (or overseas the equivalent), whether the person agreed with a client to behave in a particular way, whether the person's behaviour appears to have been the effective carrying out of a client order, the extent to which the behaviour was reasonable by the standards of the market or whether the trading was connected with a client and the trading had no impact on the price. Alternately, there was adequate disclosure to the client that the deal would occur and they did not object[1]. Where takeover and merger activity is occurring there is an obvious risk of market abuse in general and insider dealing in particular. However, trading whilst in possession of inside information as part of a public takeover or merger does not of itself amount to market abuse. Likewise, arranging an issue of securities to be offered as consideration in a takeover or merger or making a cash offer[2]. In addition the

FSA are influenced by whether transactions are in the target company's shares and are for the sole purpose of carrying out a takeover or merger. If so it will not be market abuse.

---

1 MAR 1.3.15 E.
2 MAR 1.3.17 C.

8.46 In the case of whether or not behaviour is improper disclosure amounting to market abuse the FSA view the following as determining factors: whether the behaviour is permitted by the rules of market concerned or the Takeover Code or whether the disclosure is accompanied by the imposition of confidentiality requirements on the person to whom the disclosure was made. In this instance it must be reasonable to enable the person concerned to perform their proper functions, or is needed by a professional adviser to give advice on a transaction, or is reasonable to facilitate a transaction, or is reasonable and for the purpose of obtaining a commitment or expression of support or finally that it is in fulfilment of a legal obligation[1].

---

1 MAR 1.4.5 E.

8.47 When determining whether there is misuse of information amounting to market abuse the FSA are influenced by the extent to which the information is reliable, the closeness to its source of the person passing the information on and its reliability. In addition, whether the information differs from that which is generally available or, where it relates to possible future developments that will require a disclosure in the future and the certainty that the development will happen. Finally, if there is no other material information generally available. In determining whether a regular user of the market would reasonably expect information to be disclosed or announced the FSA are influenced by whether the information was disclosed in line with legal or regulatory requirements or if the information is routinely the subject of public announcements. Finally, is the behaviour based on information leading to possible future developments where it is reasonable to believe that the information in question will become one of these categories?[1]

---

1 MAR 1.5.6 E – 1.5.7 E.

8.48 The FSA will regard behaviour as amounting to market abuse by way of market distortion where deals are done at the close of a market to mislead people as to the real value, wash trading (where the trade does not reflect a change in beneficial interest or market risk, or where there is but the deal is between parties acting in collusion), painting the tape (entering into transactions that are shown on public display to give the impression of activity) and entering orders into an electronic trading system at prices that are higher than the previous bid or lower than the previous offer and then withdrawing them before they are executed to give a misleading impression of demand or supply. Examples of behaviour that the FSA will regard as amounting to market abuse through manipulating transactions by way of price positioning are:

- transactions by people acting in collusion to secure a dominant position over the demand or supply of a qualifying investment to fix the price or create unfair trading conditions;

- transactions where both buy and sell orders are entered into at the same time with the same price, quantity and party (or different but colluding parties) for non-legitimate reasons. Sometimes this can be acceptable if the trades are in line with those of the trading platform concerned such as cross trades;

- entering small orders into an electronic trading system at higher prices than previous bids or lower ones than previous offers to move the price;

- abusive squeezes (where someone has a significant influence over the supply or demand or delivery mechanisms of a qualifying investment or the underlying product of a derivative contact and also has a position in an investment under which such investments are deliverable and engages in behaviour which distorts the price);

- parties subject to a primary offering colluding in buying further amounts when trading commences to raise the price;

- transactions or orders used to stop the price falling below a certain level; and

- trading on a market or platform to improperly influence the price of the same or a related investment on another prescribed market[1].

---

1 MAR 1.6.4 E.

8.49 In this context the issues the FSA will take into account in determining whether the behaviour concerned is legitimate are as follows. Is the person motivated by a desire to induce others to trade or to move the price of a qualifying investment? Do they have another illegitimate reason to trade and was the transaction executed in a particular way with the purpose of creating a false or misleading impression? Factors that are indications that behaviour is legitimate are: is the transaction entered into pursuant to a prior legal or regulatory obligation, is it executed in a way which takes into account the need for the market to operate fairly and efficiently, the extent to which the transaction opens a new position increasing exposure to market risk and if the transaction complied with the rules of the relevant market. It is unlikely that market users when trading in a manner and on a scale most beneficial to them will be distorting the market and therefore be committing market abuse. Trading on prices outside the normal range will not always be an indication of market abuse. This can happen as a normal part of trading[1].

1 MAR 1.6.5 E, 1.6.6 E, 1.6.7 G and 1.6.8 G.

8.50   Key factors in determining whether market abuse by way of giving a false or misleading impression has taken place are:

- the extent to which the orders to trade are given or transactions undertaken represent a significant volume of transactions in the relevant investment, especially when the trading leads to a significant change in price;

- the extent to which orders to trade given or transactions undertaken by someone with a significant buying or selling position leads to a significant change in the price of the underlying investment, related derivative or underlying investment;

- whether the transactions lead to a change in beneficial ownership;

- the extent to which orders to trade given or transactions undertaken include position reversals over a short period, a significant proportion of the daily volume of transactions in the relevant investment and might be associated with significant changes in the price;

- the extent to which orders to trade given or transactions undertaken are concentrated within a short time span leading to a price change which is subsequently reversed;

- the extent to which orders to trade given change the representation of the best bid or the representation of the order book available to market participants and are removed before they are executed; and

- the extent to which orders to trade are given or transactions are undertaken at or around a specific time when reference prices, settlement prices and valuations are calculated and lead to price changes which have an effect on this type of price and valuation[1].

1 MAR 1.6.9 E.

8.51   In determining whether behaviour amounts to securing an abnormal or artificial price level the FSA consider three key factors. The extent to which the person has an interest whether direct or indirect, in the price or value of the investment, the extent to which price, rate or option volatility movements and the volatility of these factors for the investment in question, are outside their normal range and whether a person has successively and consistently increased or decreased the bid offer he has made[1].

1 MAR 1.6.10 E.

8.52 As far as ascertaining whether abusive squeezes have taken place the FSA will consider the extent to which the person has been willing to limit their control or influence in order to help maintain an orderly market and the price at which they are willing to do so. If the person was willing to lend the investment there is less likelihood of it being an abusive squeeze. The extent to which the person's activity has caused settlement default on a bilateral or multilateral basis will also be a factor. The more widespread the risk of multilateral default the greater the risk that it is an abusive squeeze. The extent to which prices under the delivery mechanisms of the market diverge from the prices for delivery will be a factor. There is a direct correlation between the divergence and the risk. Finally, the extent to which the spot or immediate market is unusually expensive compared with the forward market will correlate with the risk of an abusive squeeze. It should be borne in mind that squeezes will occur in the markets on a non-abusive basis. Having a significant degree of control of a market through ownership does not necessarily mean an abusive squeeze has occurred[1].

---

1 MAR 1.6.11 E – 1.6.12 E.

8.53 Market abuse through manipulating transactions may occur if a trader buys and sells at the same time, ie, trades with himself to give the impression of trading taking place outside the normal price range to benefit financially from an option. It can also occur where a trader buys a large volume of commodity futures just before close of trading to create a false price. Alternately it could occur where a trader holds a short position in an investment that will show a profit if it falls out of an index in which it is currently quoted and he then places a large order to sell just before the close of trading. The manipulation here will be the attempt to create a false market causing the investment to fall out of the index. A fund manager would be engaging in manipulation if at the end of a quarter he places a large buy order or relatively illiquid shares which are a component of his portfolio to be executed just before market close to create a false price. Another example would be where a trader with a long position in bond futures borrows a large amount of the cheapest and then either will not re-lend them or only does so to those he believes will not re-lend to the market. The aim here will be to force those with short positions to have to deliver to satisfy their obligations at a higher level, resulting in the trader making a profit[1].

---

1 MAR 1.6.15 E – 1.6.16 E.

8.54 Market abuse by manipulating devices can occur in a number of ways. Perhaps the most obvious would be to take a position in an investment and then by access to the media voice opinions about the investment or its issuer and profit from the subsequent price movement. Another would be to enter into a transaction, or a series of them, to conceal the ownership of an investment by hiding the real owner to get round disclosure requirements. (Nominee holdings do not fall foul of this unless done for illicit purposes). One method is known as 'pump and dump' ie, taking a long position and then putting out misleading information to increase its price, following which the investment is sold at an artificially high price. Another is known as 'trash and cash'. This consists of taking a short position in an investment and then putting out negative information to force down the price to make a profit[1].

---

1 MAR 1.7.2 E.

8.55 Factors the FSA will take into account in determining whether manipulating devices have been used will include whether, if orders to trade are given or transactions undertaken following the dissemination of false or misleading information by those people or others linked to them. Another would be where orders to trade are given or transactions undertaken by people before or after those same people disseminate research which is biased in favour of their investments[1].

---

1 MAR 1.7.3 E.

8.56 Market abuse by dissemination consists of behaviour such as knowingly or recklessly spreading false or misleading information about an investment through the media. Alternately it might consist of undertaking a course of business to give a false or misleading impression of an investment. Another example would be where a person puts false or misleading information on the internet or where someone responsible for submitting information to a regulatory information service provides information that is false or misleading. The FSA will consider whether a normal and reasonable person should have known that the information was false or misleading or whether the person concerned actually did know. They will also form an opinion on whether the individuals responsible for disseminating information could only have known that the information was false or misleading if they had access to information the other side of a Chinese wall. If this is the case it is only going to amount to abuse by dissemination if there is evidence the wall may have been breached. This is an area where good compliance can provide protection[1].

---

1 MAR 1.8.3 E – 1.8.6 E.

8.57 Market abuse by misleading behaviour or distortion occurs where the movement of physical commodity shares might create a misleading impression as to the supply of or demand for a commodity or futures contract or the price of the same. The FSA will consider the following behaviour in determining whether this type of market abuse has occurred. These are: the experience and knowledge of the people concerned, the structure of the market including reporting notification and transparency requirements, the legal and regulatory requirements that are applicable, the identity and position of the person concerned and the extent and nature of the visibility of the activity. The FSA will take into account whether the transaction was carried out pursuant to a pre-existing legal or regulatory obligation, whether it was executed in a way that took into account the need for the market to operate fairly and efficiently and the characteristics of the market in question. This will take into account any relevant law, rules and code of conduct. In addition the position of the person concerned and the standards that can be expected from someone with that level of skill and knowledge will be considered. It would protect the person under suspicion if it transpired that the transaction complied with the rules of the market concerned. Finally, the protection provided where the necessary information was the other side of a Chinese wall from the person under suspicion will apply here as well[1].

---

1 MAR 1.9.1 E – 1.9.5 E.

FSA Regulations – Conduct of Business

Investment research – conflicts of interest

8.58   CoB 7.16 applies to all types of investment research. The FSA recognise the reality that if research is being carried out for a firm's internal use there is little danger of conflicts of interest arising. However, CoB 7.16.3 makes it clear that the FSA think it inappropriate for internal research papers to be used for the firm's own advantage and then to be given to clients where it is reasonable to suppose it might influence their decisions.

8.59   Where conflicts of interest arise there is senior management responsibility for resolving the matter. For this reason there are normally internal compliance rules on the point. The FSA believe that conflicts of interest arise if matters can be resolved entirely by disclosure.

When a firm distributes investment research and holds this out as being impartial or that is how it is going to be seen by those to whom it has been distributed the firm must:

● have a policy to manage conflicts of interest which might affect the impartiality of the research;

● keep a record of the policy;

● take reasonable steps to make sure employees comply with it;

● make it available externally on request; and

● take reasonable steps to make sure it stays appropriate and effective.

8.60   The firm's policy must make clear to what extent it relies on the firm's Chinese walls policy. It must:

- identify conflicts of interest which could affect the impartiality of the research;
- the investments analyst's payment method;
- the extent to which analyst might become involved in other matters;
- the extent to which inducements issued by issuers might be accepted by analysts;
- who might influence research papers before publication;
- the nature, timing and manner of publication;
- what information and disclosures it might be appropriate to include.

8.61   The firm's policy documents can reasonably be influenced by:

- the firm's size and structure;
- the nature of those to whom the research is circulated;
- the nature of the investment to which it relates; and
- the nature of its business.

8.62   A party other than the analyst should not be able to engage in day-to-day supervision of that analyst, decide on the subject matter or date of publication of research or determine his remuneration if they have responsibilities that conflict with the interests of the clients to whom the research is distributed. They could however check on the accuracy of his facts.

8.63   Those with commercial interests that might conflict with those of clients should not be given editorial control of research. Only investment analysts should approve research before publication. Persons outside the firm should only be able to see it for the purposes of checking information.

8.64   The nature of analysts' remuneration should not create an unreasonable incentive by being inconsistent with impartial assessment or be linked to a specific transaction or recommendation. Firms should also prohibit their analysts from accepting inducements to favour firms or investments.

8.65   An analyst should not appear to be representing the interests of the firm or a client if this looks inconsistent with an impartial assessment of the investments. Nor for the same reason should he be used in pitches to solicit business where this would make him appear lacking in impartiality, or to be representing the issuer of a security.

8.66   There should be a policy to determine when analysis should be given to clients and how this is to be done. An employee should not communicate it in any other manner. It is appropriate to consider limits on research publication around the time of a public offering. The firm should also have a policy on the disclosures that might be made when research is published.

Investment research recommendations – required disclosures

8.67   The Conduct of Business Rules provide specific requirements to those engaged in research analysis at CoB 7.17. They apply when a firm engages in preparing or disseminating 'research recommendations'. This is fairly narrowly defined and does not apply to internal research recommendations unless they are then more widely used. The definition of research recommendations[1] is:

'(a)   *concerning one or several financial instruments admitted to trading on regulated markets, or in relation to which an application for admission to trading has been made, or issuers of such financial instruments;*

(b)   *intended for distribution so that it is, or is likely to become accessible by large numbers of persons, or for the public, but not including:*

(i)   *an informal short-term investment personal recommendation expressed to clients, which originates from inside the sales or trading department, and which is not likely to become publicly available to a large umber of persons; or*

(ii)   *advice given by a firm to a body corporate in the context of takeover bid and disclosed only as a result of compliance with a legal or regulatory obligation, including rule 3 of the Takeover Code or its equivalents outside the UK; and*

(c)   *which:*

(i)   *explicitly or implicitly, recommends or suggests an investment strategy; or*

(ii)   *directly or indirectly, expresses a particular investment recommendation; or*

(iii)   *expresses an opinion as to the present or future value or price of such investments'.*

Therefore not all research is caught by these rules, it depends on the use that is put to it. There are also exceptions for the media[2].

---

1 Market Abuse Directive Instrument 2005, SI 2005/15.
2 Investment Recommendation (Media) Regulations 2005, SI 2005 and parts of CoB 7.12 – 7.17.

Chinese walls

8.68   There is no requirement that those who produce research recommendations follow the rules set out below where this will result in a Chinese wall being breached.

Fair representation

8.69   Firms must make sure that research recommendations are fairly presented and interests must be disclosed. A firm must also make sure that where a research recommendation is made the identity of the person responsible for its production is provided and their job title together with any necessary status disclosure. In the case of non-written research recommendations it is sufficient that there is a reference to a place where this information can be accessed by the public, eg, an internet site. Firms must take reasonable steps to make sure that facts in a research recommendation are distinguished from interpretation, estimates, opinions and other types of non-factual information. They should also make sure that the sources are reliable and any doubt on this point must be flagged up. All projections, forecasts and price targets must be clearly labelled as such and any material presumptions made should be indicated. The FSA can require that the substance of any research recommendations be substantiated. Relevant records must also be kept.

8.70   In research recommendations a firm must:

(a)   make sure all substantial material sources are indicated including the issuer and whether the research has been disclosed to the issuer. If the latter it must also be made clear if any alteration was made prior to it being put out. *

(b)   Make sure any basis of valuation or methodology used to evaluate a security, derivative or an issuer or to set a price target for a security or derivative is set out. *

(c)   Make sure any recommendations made are explained as must any time horizon together with any risk warning or sensitivity analysis. *

(d)   Make reference to the planned frequency of any updates to the research recommendations.

(e)   The date at which the research recommendation was first released for distribution is clearly indicated as well as the date and time for any security mentioned; and

(f)   Make clear if a research recommendation differs significantly from an earlier one relating to the same investment in the previous year and if so the nature of the change and the date of the earlier recommendation.

* If in any of these cases this would be disproportionate the firm can make reference to a place where this may be found.

Disclosure of interests and conflicts of interest

8.71   A firm must disclose any relationship that might impair the research objectivity of its research recommendations. Obvious matters will be investments and issuers. It must also include the details of who was working for the firm doing this and whether their income is related to the performance of the firm's investment banking transactions or those of an affiliated company.

8.72   If the firm is a company or LLP, the information to be disclosed must include any conflicts of interest of the firm that are potentially accessible to the researcher and any conflicts of interest known to others who could reasonably be expected to have access to the research prior to its dissemination. (This does not extend to those in compliance). The disproportionality rule mentioned at **8.70** also applies here.

8.73   A research recommendation produced by a firm must show clearly:

- major shareholdings between the firm or any affiliated company on one hand and a relevant issue on the other where these exceed 5% of the relevant issuer's share capital;

- any other financial interests held by the company or an affiliate in relation to the relevant issuer that might be relevant to the research;

- a statement if the firm or an affiliate is a market maker or liquidity supplier in the securities of the issuer or in related derivatives;

- a statement if the firm has been lead manager in the last 12 months of a publicly disclosed offer;

- a statement if the firm is party to any other agreement with the relevant issuer relating to investment banking services provided this does not result in confidential information being disclosed. The agreement concerned must have been in effect over the previous year or there must have been a payment or obligation during that time;

- a statement if the firm is party to an agreement with the issuer relating to research recommendations.

8.74   The research recommendation must show the organisational and administrative arrangements to prevent conflicts of interest, including information barriers. Investment firms and credit institutions who have a researcher obtaining shares in an issuer at a public offering must know at what price were they obtained at and what was the date?

8.75 Investment firms and credit institutions must disclose in their research recommendations and also quarterly the proportion of research recommendations published during the relevant quarter that are buy, hold or sell and the proportion of relevant investments in these categories issued by issuers the firm has supplied investment banking services to in the previous year. The disproportionality rule at **8.70** applies here again.

Third party recommendations

8.76 If the firm disseminates a research recommendation produced by a third party that firm must be clearly identified. If such material is substantially altered the alteration must be described in detail and if the change is a reversal of a recommendation the requirements above apply to the firm to the extent of the alteration. If a firm is to disseminate substantially altered recommendations it must have a formal policy to govern those receiving the recommendations where they can determine its producer and any conflicts of interest that person might have. If the firm disseminates a summary of a third party's research recommendation, it must make sure the summary is clear, fair and not misleading, have its source identified and state any publicly available third party disclosures relevant to the source of the material. In this context investment firms and credit institutions must also disclose their status on the material, provide the conflict of interest disclosure described above as though they had produced the material, and if the firm has substantially altered the recommendations the fair representation and disclosure rules above apply to the firm itself.

Other FSA Conduct of Business rules

8.77 In addition to rules passed pursuant to the Market Abuse Directive there are other FSA rules that can impact. Of particular relevance here are a number of sections:

ENF 14.8 Market Abuse and breaches of FSA Principles

8.78 This rule highlights the fact that a breach of the market abuse legislation will also be a breach of FSA Principle 5 which requires firms to observe proper standards of market conduct. However, the converse does not necessarily hold as the Principle is wider than the legislation. In appropriate cases the FSA can take enforcement action for a breach of the Principle.

CoB 2.1 Clear, fair and not misleading communication

8.79 FSA Principle 7 requires firms to communicate with clients in a manner that is clear, fair and not misleading. CoB 2.1.3 restates this, the main effect of which is that a private client affected by a failure to meet this rule will have a right of action under s 150 for any loss resulting.

CoB 2.4 Chinese walls

8.80   A consequence of FSA Principle 8 (that a firm must manage conflicts of interest fairly, both between itself and its customers and between one customer and another) is that firms must create Chinese walls. Under CoB 2.4.4 this may require a firm to avoid passing certain information from one person to another. Acting in conformity with this provides a defence against charges of market abuse, misleading statements[1] (see below), against FSA enforcement actions and s 150 claims by private clients. Likewise, when a firm is required to act with knowledge the effect of a Chinese wall in stopping someone from being in possession of that knowledge will not be an offence.

1 FSMA 2000, s 397(2), (3).

CoB 5.10 Corporate finance business issues

8.81   Firms engaged in corporate finance business must have in place systems, controls and procedures suitable to the nature of their work. Provided they do this and act in line with CoB 5.10 they should not end up in breach of the market abuse laws.

CoB 7.1 Conflicts of interest and material interest

8.82   If firms act in line with FSA Principle 8 and CoB rule 7.1 on conflict of interest they should avoid committing market abuse.

CoB 7.3 Dealing ahead of investment research

8.83   Firms may use research papers for their own use but the FSA considers it inappropriate that they should use them internally and then circulate them to clients[1]. Likewise, when material is circulated to clients the firm should not deal ahead of the clients until they have had a reasonable opportunity to act on it.

1 FSA Conduct of Business Rule 7.3.2A G.

CoB 7.13 Personal account dealing

8.84 Firms must take reasonable steps to make sure that they have restrictions on own account dealing by relevant staff to avoid a conflict of interest with clients in line with CoB 7.13. Again, this should minimise the risk of market abuse being committed.

Case law

8.85 There have been a number of relevant cases, most of which have been FSA enforcement actions, though some have involved the accused taking the matter to the FSA Tribunal. There have also been a small number of cases where criminal prosecutions have been brought. Between them they provide some useful illumination of the law and regulations discussed above.

8.86 *Middlemiss*[1] was the first FSA relevant enforcement action. Like the other cases below it turned on the earlier wording of s 118. However, there can be no doubt that the new wording would still catch such cases. It concerned a company secretary who became aware that the company, which was listed on AIM, was going to see a significant reduction in its revenue. He therefore sold 70,000 shares he owned in the company to avoid a loss. Following a trading statement released by the company the share price fell significantly and Mr Middlemiss avoided a loss. He was fined £15,000. *Bracken*[2] concerned a Group Head of Communications who became aware that a negative trading statement was in the offing. He therefore short sold shares in the company and made a profit. He was also fined £15,000. In *Davies*[3] the person concerned had helped to prepare the interim results which showed healthy profits. He also knew that exceptional items in the previous year's results would not be recurring. He then purchased shares prior to the results being released and sold them at a profit shortly afterwards. He was given a small fine, its size being influenced by his co-operation.

1 FSA Enforcement action, 10 February 2004.
2 FSA Enforcement action, 7 July 2004.
3 FSA Enforcement action, 28 July 2004.

8.87 In *Shell and Royal Dutch Petroleum*[1] it was held that misleading statements in the annual accounts overstating the size of the oil reserves held by the companies over a number of years amounted to market abuse. This was information which the companies knew, or should have known to be inaccurate. This is an unusual case as it is the only one so far where the matter has not involved an FSA regulated firm or person. They were fined £17 million.

1 FSA Enforcement notice, 24 August 2004.

8.88 *Evolution Beeston Gregory Ltd and Potts*[1].Here the company, an investment bank, short sold shares through Potts in Room Service Group plc. At one point the volume of shares being short sold exceeded 100% of Room Service's share capital. This was done in the expectation that Room Service would engage in a new share issue which would cover the position, which as it transpired did not occur. The behaviour was determined to be market distortion amounting to market abuse as a result of which 250 investors did not receive their shares in a timely manner. The company was fined £500,000 and Mr Potts £75,000.

1 FSA Enforcement action, 12 November 2004.

8.89 *Hutchings and Smith*[1] concerned a fairly straightforward insider dealing case. Hutchings and Smith were fined £18,000 and £15,000 respectively for illegal trading in the shares of Feel Good (Holdings) plc. Smith provided inside information to Hutchings who traded on the basis of it.

1 FSA Enforcement action, 13 December 2004.

8.90 *Isaacs*[1] concerned the misuse of dishonestly obtained information. Isaacs was an experienced private investor who memorised confidential information he saw lying around on a visit to a friend's house. The nature of the information was firstly in relation to the company's products, the second to better than expected sales figures. This would clearly have been regarded by a regular user of the market as being relevant when deciding on the terms of a transaction. He put this information on an internet bulletin board under a pseudonym to try and raise the price of that company's shares. This was behaviour which a regular user of the market would regard as a failure to observe the standard of behaviour that was appropriate. He was fined £15,000.

1 FSA Enforcement action, 28 February 2005.

8.91 In *Arif Mohammed v FSA*[1] an audit manager was fined £10,000 for market abuse. Mr Mohammed traded in the shares of Delta plc on the basis of information he had acquired that it was going to sell its electrical division. He had acquired this information as the firm was an audit client of his employers PwC, and he had worked on the audit.

1 FSA Tribunal, 7th – 9th March 2005.

8.92 *Malins*[1] concerned market abuse by misusing relevant information. Malins was fined £25,000. He was co-founder of a company, Cambrian which was listed on the AIM. He was also its sole UK director and finance director. He bought 50,000 ordinary shares ahead of an announcement concerning a placement by the company later that day. Later the same day he chaired a meeting discussing the placement at which he requested the company's broker to release the announcement as soon as possible. He did not sell the shares once the market price had risen as a result of the placement but continued to hold them. He later purchased another 20,000 shares ahead of the announcement of the interim results. He also gave a presentation in the City without having checked that the interim results had been released. Due to unforeseen formatting problems they did not come out until an hour after the normal time. He thus committed the offence.

---

1 FSA Enforcement action, 20 December 2005.

8.93 *Bonnier and Indigo Capital*[1] concerned the issuance of materially inaccurate statements which created a false or misleading impression amounting to market abuse. Bonnier was managing director of ICL, a New York company providing financial advisory services and capital investment assistance in North and Latin America. The second company involved in the matter was Regus plc, a UK listed firm. Mr Bonnier traded in Regus shares and in contracts for differences in relation to them through Cantors. They in turn took up a position in Regus shares to hedge their position. They retained the voting rights under these shares and the right to transfer them. As a result Mr Bonnier did not have an obligation to report the transaction to Regus. He later contracted with Cantors for the transfer of their voting rights to ICL. Regus' registrar then sent Bonnier a request for clarification of the share holding. He disclosed the shareholdings but not the contracts for differences. In total he made 12 misleading notifications. It gave the impression that ICL's holding in Regus had risen from 3.51% to 15.12% when in fact it had decreased from 2.3% to 0.07%. Regus' registrar deduced the position and informed Regus. ICL later made an inaccurate statement regarding its beneficial interest in Regus. Bonnier was fined £290,000 and ICL £65,000.

---

1 FSA Enforcement action, 21 December 2004.

8.94 *Baldwin and WRT Investments Ltd v FSA*[1] concerned Baldwin's investment vehicle, WRT Ltd. It was alleged by the FSA that as a result of a telephone conversation with the chief executive officer of another company he discovered that the company concerned had news likely to increase its profits. This was not news that was publicly available. The Tribunal ruled against the FSA on the ground that the evidence did not support the allegation that Baldwin traded as a result of receiving inside information. The evidence was too vague and Baldwin could provide a reasonable alternative explanation for his trading behaviour.

---

1 FSA Tribunal, 19–21 December 2005.

8.95 *Davidson and Tatham v FSA*[1] was a Tribunal decision that attracted a great deal of media attention. The case concerned Mr Davidson, who was a majority shareholder in, though not a director of Cyprotex Ltd. This company was to be admitted to trading on the AIM. The take up of shares was slow and the idea emerged that a spread bet could taken in the shares and in turn the counterparty could enter into a contract for differences and then hedge that contract for differences by purchasing shares in the placing. The company who accepted the spread bet were City Index and they in turn entered into a contract for differences with Dresdner Kleinwort Wasserstein Securities Ltd. They in turn took up shares in Cyprotx Ltd.

---

1 FSA Tribunal decision, March 2006.

8.96 The FSA issued a Decision Notice in respect of these events and fined Mr Davidson, Mr Howe, an employee of the nominated broker in charge of the placing and Mr Tatham, executive director of trading at City Index. This was challenged by Mr Davison and Mr Tatham and the FSA Tribunal held in their favour. The Tribunal held that the scheme concerned was likely to give a false impression as to the demand for and the value of shares in Cyprotex Ltd. However, there appeared to be no regulatory obligation to disclose the spread bet or the contract for differences in the Prospectus. Therefore any failure to disclose was not market abuse within s 118 FSMA. Even if there had been an obligation to disclose, appropriate disclose was made to the nominated broker. It was the responsibility of that broker to make full disclosure to the board of Cyprotex so that the Prospectus could contain all relevant information. As a result the behaviour or Mr Davidson and Mr Tatham would still not have created a false and misleading impression. Nor did the Tribunal believe that they had failed to observe the standards of behaviour reasonably expected of them.

8.97 In *Tebbutt*[1] the FSA fined the chief executive of a firm of financial advisers for providing misleading information to the FSA in connection with his firm's application to merge with another financial adviser. The misleading information related to a guarantee that had to be provided by the directors of his firm (Millfield Partnership Ltd) which was an important part of the FSA's decision to approve the merger.

---

1 FSA Enforcement action, 10 April 2006.

8.98 The FSA also imposed sanctions on *Deutsche Bank* and their former Head of European Cash Trading *David Maslen*[1]. This case concerned a book build in the shares of Scania AB and the stabilisation of Cytos Biotechnology. The first transaction concerned a 'book build', ie, an arrangement where a bank may try to sell a parcel of shares to a number of investors at one time by selling within a marketing range price. The share price in the company whose shares were to be offered fell below the marketing range. Deutsche, through Mr Maslen got an internally based trader to purchase shares in Scania. This was done through two Swedish brokers and the scale of this trading represented 90%

of the trading in those shares. This was not transparent to the market and forced the share price back within the marketing rage.

---

1 FSA Enforcement action, 10 April 2006.

8.99 The second matter concerned stabilised shares in Cytox which Deutsche offered whilst not making sure the trader followed the appropriate stabilisation rules on the relevant exchange (Zurich). Both matters were dealt with by the FSA imposing fines, the level of which took into account that Deutsche Bank had brought the matter to the FSA's attention, taking internal disciplinary action, undertaking an internal review and bringing in new senior management to the area. Deutsche Bank were fined £6,363,643 and Mr Maslen £350,000.

Safe harbours

8.100 There are safe harbours which apply where:

- the behaviour conforms with a rule which makes it clear that such behaviour is not market abuse;
- the behaviour conforms with the EU Regulation[1] implementing the Directive[2] regarding exemptions for buy-back programmes and stabilisation rules;
- it is carried out by someone acting on behalf of a public authority in pursuit of monetary authorities or policies with regard to exchange rates or managing public debt or foreign exchange[3].

---

1 EC Regulation 2273/2003.
2 Directive 2003/6/EC.
3 FSMA 2000, s 118A(5).

8.101 In addition FSMA 2000, s 123(2) states that a penalty should not be imposed if having considered the response to a warning notice there are reasonable grounds for the FSA to be satisfied that the person concerned had reasonable grounds to believe he had not committed market abuse and had taken all reasonable precautions. In such cases the FSA does have the option of announcing that such behaviour is market abuse[1]. This would then make it possible to punish anyone who in the future engaged in that behaviour.

---

1 FSMA 2000, s 123(3).

Jurisdiction

8.102 The jurisdictional elements limit the offence to acts carried out in the United Kingdom, or in relation to investments traded on a prescribed market in the United Kingdom or for which a request for admission has been made and related investments in either case[1].

1 FSMA 2000, s 118A(1)(b)(i)–(iii).

Insider dealing as a criminal offence

Introduction

8.103   Since the new regime came into force there has only been one criminal prosecution for insider dealing, the rest having been dealt with under the civil regime described above. Nonetheless, there will be future cases where it is believed the insider dealing is so serious that it warrants criminal prosecution. For these purposes the law created by the Criminal Justice Act 1993 (CJA)[1] still applies. This is very similar to the civil offence of insider dealing but the criminal offence is slightly narrower in that it does not extend to related derivative contracts and off market transactions. It is not likely that someone would face both criminal proceedings under the Criminal Justice Act and a market abuse action under the Financial Services and Markets Act 2000. It would not fall the wrong side of the double jeopardy rule as the market abuse action would be civil, but the FSA have recognised the unsatisfactory nature of permitting something that is so close to double jeopardy and announced that they would not bring proceedings if a criminal prosecution were taking place. It has to be said that the utilisation of criminal law has been so unsuccessful that it was the primary reason for the development of the civil offence discussed above. There have been very few successful criminal prosecutions since insider dealing became a statutory criminal offence in 1980 and hardly any of these resulted in custodial sentences. The previous law, that of conspiracy to defraud, still exists but proved even less useful[2].

1 Which put into effect Directive 89/592.
2 See *R v de Berenger* (1814) 105 ER 536, for a rare success.

The nature of the offences in the Criminal Justice Act

8.104   There are three potential offences.

Insider dealing

8.105   This occurs when a party who is able to access information relating to the company concerned deals in securities whilst in possession of such information, which must be unpublished and likely to affect the price of the securities concerned. They need not have accessed the information directly.

271

Encouraging others to deal

8.106 This offence is committed where someone encourages another to deal in securities whose price is likely to be affected by inside information in their possession. The insider will be committing an offence even if the person being encouraged does not know that the person concerned is an insider or that unpublished price sensitive information is involved. A transaction need not actually take place. It is sufficient that encouragement takes place.

Disclosure

8.107 This consists of someone disclosing inside information outside the proper performance of their duties. It is not necessary for a conviction for there to be evidence that the party disclosing intended it to be acted upon.

In any of these instances a prosecution can only be brought by or with the consent of the Secretary of State for Trade and Industry or the Director of Public Prosecutions[1].

---

1 Criminal Justice Act 1993, s 61(1).

Key elements

8.108 What then is an 'insider'? Section 57 defines this as someone who has inside information from an inside source and knows that this is the case. The person concerned will need to have acquired the information as a result of being an employee, a director or a shareholder of an issuer of securities; though it is not necessary for the crime to relate to shares in that company. Thus, the 'insider' might be a professional adviser or someone doing unrelated work for the firm on a temporary basis, eg, a decorator. However, the access to the information concerned should have arisen as a result of that person's employment, office or protection. There are however two statutory limitations which stop this catching those who as a part of their business or professional activities are rightfully involved in price analysis:

● Section 58 which states that information is not inside information if it can be either readily acquired by those likely to deal in securities or be acquired by those exercising due diligence.

● The possibility of interpreting the description of information being accessed by virtue of the insider's employment to exclude situations where an expert accesses information by virtue of his employment. There is no direct case on the point but either *Grey v Pearson*[1] (golden rule) or *Heydon's Case*[2] (mischief rule) would assist.

1 (1857) 6 HL Cas 61.
2 (1584) 3 Co Rep 74.

8.109   Secondary insiders are also caught as are parties they pass the information on to, subject to this not extending to situations where the act of passing on the information has made it public. There is no requirement for the secondary insider to have taken any active steps to acquire the information. It is sufficient that they know that it was inside information and was obtained from an inside source and then acted on it.

8.110   What then is 'inside information'? It is 'specific information' that must relate either to specific securities or a specific issuer of securities. If made public it would have a 'significant effect' on the price of any securities. This is not defined but the relevant Stock Exchange Guidance Note stated: *'it is not feasible to define any theoretical percentage movement in a share price that will make a piece of information price sensitive'*. The Takeover Panel suggested a 10% price movement in a day.

8.111   The information concerned need not be precise. The crucial element is that it must not be publicly available information. Section 58 provides guidance by providing a non-exhaustive list. It provides two categories:

(1)   Those where information must be treated as publicly available.

(a)   Where it is published in accordance with the rules of a regulated market to inform investors and their advisers.

(b)   Where the information is publicly available as a result of being set out in public records, eg, Companies House.

(c)   Where the information can already be readily acquired.

(d)   Where it is derivable from publicly available information.

(2)   Those where information may be treated as publicly available even though:

(a)   it can only be worked out by experts or analysts.

(b)   Communication has only been to a section of the public.

(c)   The information can only be found by observation.

(d)   Money has to be paid to get the information.

(e)   The information is published abroad.

Such information must in any case be price sensitive. This means that the price or value of the securities concerned is likely to be significantly affected[1].

1 Criminal Justice Act 1993, s 56.

Securities

8.112 Securities themselves have a definition which is idiosyncratic to the CJA. Schedule 2 lists them as:

Shares

Shares and stock in the value of a company.

Debt securities

Any instrument creating or acknowledging indebtedness which is issued by a company or public sector body, including, in particular, debentures, debenture stock, loan stock, bonds and certificates of deposit.

Warrants

Any right (whether conferred by warrant or otherwise) to subscribe for shares or debt securities.

Depositary receipts

(1)   The rights under any depositary receipt.

(2)   For the purposes of sub-paragraph (1) a 'depositary receipt' means a certificate or other record (whether or not in the form of a document) -

    (a)   which is issued by or on behalf of any person who holds any relevant securities of a particular issuer; and

    (b)   which acknowledges that another person is entitled to rights in relation to the relevant securities or relevant securities of the same kind.

(3)   In sub-paragraph (2) 'relevant securities' means shares, debt securities and warrants.

Options

Any option to acquire or dispose of any security falling within any other paragraph in this Schedule.

Futures

(1)   Rights under a contract for the acquisition or disposal of relevant securities under which delivery is to be made at a future date and at a price agreed when the contract is made.

(2)   In sub-paragraph (1):

    (a)   the references to a future date and to a price agreed when the contract is made include references to a date and a price determined in accordance with terms of the contract; and

    (b)   'relevant securities' means any security falling within any other paragraph of this Schedule.

Contracts for differences

(1)   Rights under a contract which does not provide for the delivery of securities but whose purpose or pretended purpose is to secure a profit or avoid a loss by reference to fluctuations in:

    (a)   a share index or other similar factor connected with relevant securities;

    (b)   the price of particular relevant securities; or

    (c)   the interest rate offered on money placed on deposit.

(2)   In sub-paragraph (1) 'relevant securities' means any security falling within any other paragraph of this Schedule.

The securities concerned must either:

(1)   be listed on an official exchange of a State within the European Economic Area; or

(2)   be admitted to dealing on, or have their price quoted on, a regulated market.

The Stock Exchange Guidance Note suggested:

(1)   develop a consistent procedure for determining what is price sensitive and for releasing that information to the market;

(2)   ensure price sensitive information is kept confidential until the moment of announcement;

(3)   consider whether unaudited quarterly statements or announcements updating the market at the end of a financial period are appropriate;

(4)   brief employees who meet analysts visiting the company's premises as to the extent and nature of information that can be communicated;

(5)   obtain and record the consent of parties attending a meeting at which price sensitive information is to be given to the effect that they will not deal in the company's securities before the information is made public.

Dealing

8.113   Section 55 provides three categories.

(1)   Acquiring securities. This may be as principal or agent.

(2)   Disposing of securities. This may also be as principal or agent.

(3)   Procuring another party to acquire or dispose of the securities. This may be done directly or indirectly.

AG's Reference (No1 of 1975)[1] held that 'procure' means 'to produce by endeavour'.

In none of these cases need the insider be proven to have benefited from the deal, though in practice this is obviously the normal motive.

---

1 [1975] QB 773.

Defences

8.114   Once the offence has been shown to have satisfied the elements of their definition (as shown above) the burden of proof shifts to the accused to show that there is a valid defence. The defences fall into two categories, General and Specific.

General defences

(1)   Where the accused did not expect to make a profit or avoid a loss[1].

(2)   Where the accused reasonably believed that the information concerned was widely distributed enough to avoid prejudicing the interests of anyone else involved in the deal[2].

(3)   Where the accused can show that they would have entered into the arrangement in any event[3].

---

1 Criminal Justice Act 1993, s 53(6).
2 Criminal Justice Act 1993, s 53(1)(b), (2)(b).
3 Criminal Justice Act 1993, s 53(1)(c), (2)(c).

8.115   In the event of the accused being charged with disclosing price sensitive information there are two general defences:

●   that the accused did not expect anyone to deal in securities as a result of his disclosure[1]; or

- that the accused did not expect anyone to deal at a profit or avoid a loss as a result of the disclosure[2].

---

1 Criminal Justice Act 1993, s 53(3)(a).
2 Criminal Justice Act 1993, s 53(3)(b).

8.116 Specific defences

(1) Market makers and dealers can plead that they were acting in good faith in the course of their business[1]. A market maker is someone who holds themselves out as operating in compliance with the rules of a regulated exchange or under those of a prescribed market or Treasury approved organisation.

(2) Where it was market information and it was reasonable of the accused to act as they did[2]. Market information is that securities are to be traded, or at least that this is being considered or negotiated, and includes information on a number of securities, their prices and the persons involved.

(3) If it was market information which the insider acquired as a result of being involved in buying or selling securities[3].

(4) If the insider can show that they acted in line with the FSA's Price Stabilisation Rules[4].

---

1 Criminal Justice Act 1993, Sch 1, para 1.
2 Criminal Justice Act 1993, Sch 1, para 2.
3 Criminal Justice Act 1993, Sch 1, para 3.
4 Criminal Justice Act 1993, Sch 1, para 5.

Jurisdiction

8.117 The territorial limit for the crimes concerned is the United Kingdom. Thus the accused must either have been within the United Kingdom when the act concerned was committed, the market concerned must have been situated in the United Kingdom, the crime must have involved an intermediary who was situated in the United Kingdom, or either the disclosure must have been made by the accused when they were situated in the United Kingdom or that the recipient of the information or of the encouragement to deal was so situated.

Penalties

8.118 On summary conviction, a maximum fine of £5,000 or imprisonment of up to six months, or both[1]. On indictment, an unlimited fine or imprisonment of up to seven years, or both[2]. Directors may be disqualified as the crime is one which shows sufficient connection with corporate management: *R v Goodman*[3].

1 Criminal Justice Act 1993, s 61(1)(a).
2 Criminal Justice Act 1993, s 61(1)(b).
3 [1994] 1 BCLC 349.

8.119 Any profits may also potentially be seized under the Proceeds of Crime Act 2002. This permits[1] the Crown Court to order confiscation where two conditions are satisfied. The first is that the defendant has been convicted by the Crown Court or committed to the Crown Court for sentencing because of the seriousness of the offence and the prosecutor or the Director of the Assets Recovery Agency has asked the court to so proceed and the Court thinks it appropriate. Factors the court will take into account are: whether the defendant had a criminal lifestyle, if so whether he benefited from his criminal conduct and whether he has so benefited even if he does not have a criminal lifestyle. This last caveat could be crucial in enabling the seizure of funds from insider dealing as the person so acting will normally have had a respectable lifestyle in all other respects. If the court decides to proceed they must then decide on the recoverable amount and make a confiscation order to that level. There is a statutory requirement[2] that the court should take into account whether a victim of the conduct intends to start proceedings against the defendant, because if this is the case a confiscation order should not be used if it would render the defendant incapable of compensating the victim. It will be interesting to see whether this would apply if an action were brought by the firm employing the defendant for recovery of money made by insider dealing (see below) as here the firm would not have been a victim.

1 Proceeds of Crime Act 2002, s 6.
2 Proceeds of Crime Act 2002, s 6(6).

Dealing in directors' options

8.120 It is a criminal offence for a director to buy a call option in shares or debentures or buy a put option in shares or debentures or to buy the right, at the director's election, to call for or make sale of a specified number of quoted shares or debentures at an agreed price at an agreed date in the future[1]. This extends to shadow directors, spouses, and infant children unless they can show they did not have reason to know of the directorship. It does not extend to unquoted securities, rights to buy shares or the purchase of convertible debentures. There is however a right for a director of a public company to buy call options on its own treasury shares or those of its parent or a subsidiary[2].

1 Companies Act 1985, s 323(1)(a)–(c).
2 Companies Act 1985, s 323(6), (7).

Penalties

8.121   On summary conviction, a fine of up to £1,000 or up to six months' imprisonment, or both. On indictment, an unlimited fine, or up to two years' imprisonment, or both.

Civil law issues other than the Market Abuse regime

8.122   Contracts that amount to market abuse could well be unenforceable under the principle in *Mackender v Feldia*[1]. However, this does not appear to be the case with the main offences of insider dealing which are specifically stated not to be void or unenforceable: Criminal Justice Act 1993, s 62(2).

---

1 [1967] 2 QB 590.

8.123   Any profit wrongly made by a director will belong to the company of which he is a director[1]. This is a consequence of his owing a fiduciary duty when he is held to have acted as a constructive trustee: *Boardman v Phipps*[2] and *AG for Hong Kong v Reid*[3]. See also *Nanus Asia Co Inc v Standard Chartered Bank*[4] where confidential information obtained in breach of an employee's duty of fidelity gave rise to a constructive trust over profits resulting from its use. If a third party in receipt of information should realise that the information was given to them in breach of a fiduciary duty then the same principle will apply. If the information is given in breach of confidence then an action will lie on that basis. This will extend to employees.

---

1 *Walsh v Deloitte and Touche* [2001] UKPC 58.
2 [1967] 2 AC 46, HL.
3 [1994] AC 324, PC.
4 [1990] HKLR 396.

8.124   Beyond the position stated at **8.123** directors do not normally have a fiduciary obligation to the company or shareholders, but *Coleman v Myers*[1] suggests that they can acquire one where they are dominant directors in a small company. They must however declare secret profits: *Regal (Hastings) v Gulliver*[2]. However, there does not appear to be a basis for shareholders or other dealers in securities claiming compensation because they traded with the insider dealer at what they may later believe to have been an unfair price. In theory a criminal court could consider a compensation payment under s 130 of the Powers of Criminal Courts Act 2000.

---

1 [1977] 2 NZLR 225.
2 [1942] 1 All ER 378 HL.

Relevant Codes

8.125   *Rule 2.1 of the City Code on Takeovers and Mergers* states that anyone who is in possession of confidential information relating to offers must only make it available when it is necessary. Rule 4.1 goes on to bar dealing in the securities of an offeror or offeree prior to the information relating to the deal becoming publicly available.

8.126   *The Model Code for Securities Transactions by Directors of Listed Companies* requires the directors to notify an appointed party on his board of directors before dealing in any of the company's securities. Clearance should not be given for dealing during a close period, ie, the 60 days prior to the company's annual results or half-yearly report and 30 days prior to the quarterly results[1]. He is debarred from dealing if he is in possession of unpublished price sensitive information. Nor should clearance be given whilst any inside information is available. Nor should the dealing be on the basis of short-term interests[2].

---

[1] Para 8.
[2] Paras 8 and 20.

Misleading statements

8.127   This is also an area where a criminal conviction could be the result of improper behaviour rather than just civil proceedings under the FSMA. The specific offence is set out in s 397 and states that it is an offence where someone:

'(1)(a)   *makes a statement, promise or forecast which he knows to be misleading, false or deceptive in a material particular;*

(b)   *dishonestly conceals any material facts whether in connection with a statement, promise or forecast made by him or otherwise; or*

(c)   *recklessly makes (dishonestly or otherwise) a statement, promise or forecast which is misleading, false or deceptive in a material particular.*

(2)   *A person to whom subsection (1) applies is guilty of an offence if he makes the statement, promise or forecast or conceals the facts for the purpose of inducing, or is reckless as to whether it may induce, another person (whether or not the person to whom the statement, promise or forecast is made)-*

(a)   *to enter or offer to enter into, or refrain from entering into, a relevant agreement; or* (*b*) to exercise, or refrain from exercising, any rights conferred by a relevant instrument.

(*3*) Any person who does any act or engages in any course of conduct which creates a false or misleading impression as to the market in or the price or value of any relevant investments is guilty of an offence if he does so for the purpose of creating that impression and of thereby inducing another person to acquire, dispose of or subscribe for or underwrite those investments or to refrain from doing so or to exercise, or refrain from exercising, any rights conferred by those investments.'

8.128   It is a defence to a charge under s 397(2) in relation to behaviour under s 397(1)(a) to show that the statement, promise or forecast was made in conformity with price stabilising rules or control of information rules. A further defence is available under s 397(5) where the accused can show that he reasonably believed that his act or conduct would not create an impression that was false or misleading, that he engaged in the conduct for the purpose of stabilising the price of investments in conformity with price stabilisation rules, or that he acted in conformity with control of information rules.

The offence can be punished on summary conviction by up to six months in prison and/or a fine, or on indictment by up to seven years in prison and/or a fine.

8.129   There has been one conviction recently, *R v Rigby, Bailey and Rowley*[1] which involved the criminal conviction of three men; Rigby for recklessly making a statement to the market which was misleading, false or deceptive in a material particular contrary to s 397(1)(c), Bailey for making a statement, promise or forecast which was misleading, false or deceptive in a material particular contrary to s 397(c) and Rowley on both counts. Rigby and Bailey had stated that both turnover and profit were in line with expectations. For this to have been true the revenue from three contracts totalling £4.8 million had to be included. These contracts did not exist. Just under a month later an update was issued stating that one of these contracts had not been confirmed and that there was a shortfall of £1.1 million. A cash shortfall was also highlighted. Two weeks later a further statement was issued announcing that their preliminary results would not be published that day because of issues arising in the audit. A further shortfall in revenue and profit was forecast on the grounds that the company had failed to satisfy the terms of a licensing agreement worth £2.5 million. This was the second of the three contracts referred to above. The first two accused were sentenced to 31/2 years, and 2 years respectively and also disqualified from being a director for 6 and 4 years. The prison sentence was reduced by the Court of Appeal.

---

1 (2005) Unreported.

Misleading the Financial Services Authority

8.130   There is an additional offence in FSMA 2000, s 398 where someone knowingly or recklessly gives false or misleading information to the FSA in purported compliance with a requirement imposed by the FSMA. It can be punished by a fine.

Chapter 9

Promotional and advisory activities

'I'll sweep the chamber soon at night, and set a dish of water o' the hearth. A fairy may come in and bring a pearl, or a diamond …Why might we two rise up early I' the morning …afore anyone is up, and find a jewel i' the streets, worth a hundred pounds? May not some great court-lady as she comes from revels at midnight, look out of her coach, as 'tis running, and lose such a jewel, and we find it? Ha?' Jonson, Marston and Chapman.

'Eastward Ho' 1605

Introduction

9.1   Sadly, the passing of the centuries has not greatly altered the degree of credulity with which some will enter into contracts that offer the apparent opportunity to make money. For this reason, and the others given in Chapter 1, a whole range of investment activities are regulated by the FSA. Some of these, relating to promoting an investment or investment activity are particularly at issue as the advertising of a product and the main communications in relation to it have the potential to lure inappropriate investors. Additionally advising a customer once they are in touch with an adviser is also an area requiring regulation for the same reason. An inherent part of this is the suitability of advice given to investors; an area covered by the FSA rules. These will all be discussed in turn.

Financial promotions

Introduction

9.2   The issuing of adverts, or promotions as they are now termed, is a key part of any pursuit of new financial services clients. However, this is territory where there is a clear potential risk to the public, who may receive such a promotion and then be misled into investing in a product that is unsuitable for them. As a result s 21 FSMA states that an *'invitation or inducement to engage* *in investment activity'* can only be issued by an authorised person or where the content has been approved by an authorised person. *'Investment activity'* is defined by s 21(8) as entering into or offering to enter into an agreement concerning a controlled activity, or exercising rights under a controlled investment. Section 21(9) states that a *'controlled activity'* is an activity of a specified kind or which falls within a specified class of activity. An *'inducement'* is a controlled investment if it is of a specified kind or falls within a specified class[1]. The meaning of these has been detailed by the Financial Promotion Order 2005 and is examined below[2].

---

1 FSMA 2000, s 21(10).
2 SI 2005/1529.

9.3   The contravention of this section is an offence which on summary conviction can lead to six months in prison and/or a fine, or in indictment up to two years and/or a fine[1]. There is however a defence where the person concerned believed on reasonable grounds that the content had been properly prepared by an authorised person or that they had exercised all due diligence to avoid breaching s 21[2]. Further, there is an enforceability issue in that if a contract is entered into as a result of a communication that breaches s 21 that contract cannot be enforced against the customer (unless a court believe it is just and equitable[3]) and yet the customer is entitled to any money or property paid over under the agreement and compensation for any loss they suffered[4]. Further, any rights that may have been exercised in this situation do not lead on to enforceable obligations being imposed on the customer[5]. The utilisation of terminology such as 'financial promotion' is a consequence of the law being drafted to catch electronic communication and websites as well as the more traditional types of advertising.

---

1 FSMA 2000, s 25(1).
2 FSMA 2000, s 25(2).
3 FSMA 2000, s 30(4).
4 FSMA 2000, s 30(2).
5 FSMA 2000, s 30(3).

9.4   The content of s 21 is for the most part fairly straightforward. The communication concerned must have been entered into in the course of business, though this is not limited to financial services business. 'Communicate' includes causing a communication to be made[1]. One area that causes problems arises where firms wish to communicate details to employees of employee share schemes. For this reason the Treasury has drafted a statutory instrument to come into effect during 2007[2]. This states that:

'If an employer offers to his employees membership of a group personal pension scheme or stakeholder pension scheme …the financial promotion restriction does not apply to any communication which is made to an employee in relation to the scheme.'

---

1 FSMA, s 21(13).
2 Financial Services and Markets Act 2000 (Financial Promotion) (Amendment) Order 2007.

9.5 There are certain provisos[1] and in addition, in the event of an employee becoming a member of the scheme the employer must be making a contribution towards it.

In addition employers will be able to communicate to employees without the financial promotion regulations applying where it applies to rights under a contract of insurance. The employer must not be receiving any commission should the employee take up an insurance policy and in the case of a non real time communication it must contain or be accompanied by a statement informing the employee of their right to seek advice from an IFA or appointed representative.

---

1 Financial Services and Markets Act 2000 (Financial Promotion) (Amendment) Order 2007, art 3(4).

9.6 This does not exhaust the situations where those in non-financial services businesses might wish to engage in communications concerning investments. Care should always be taken in such cases to ascertain whether the financial promotion rules apply. If they do, there is the opportunity presented by s 21(2)(b) that the bar on issuing investment advertisements other than by an authorised person can be circumvented if the content of the communication is approved by an authorised person.

9.7 The section refers to *'an invitation or inducement'* and whilst the FSMA nowhere defines these terms Watkins[1] has pointed out that there is a dichotomy between the Oxford English Dictionary definition of these words and the interpretation placed on them by H.M.Treasury and in Parliamentary debate. The former states that a communication will be an inducement if the recipient acts on it regardless of the intent of the representor. The latter's position is that:

'... the Government do not believe that "inducement"... will catch communications where the effect has been to prompt an investment decision regardless of the motivation of the communication. We are convinced that "inducement"... already incorporates an element of design or purpose on the pat of the person making the communication.

... Inevitably, in determining whether a particular communication constitutes an inducement, much will depend on the context. Something that would not be considered an inducement in one set of circumstances could well be an inducement in another. Very often the difference will depend on the actual or perceived intent behind the communication. [2]'

---

1 Owen Watkins, 'Financial Promotion' in 'Financial Services Law Guide, 3rd edition' Tottel, Haynes, 2006 at p75.
2 Lord McIntosh of Haringey, HL 613, 18 May 2000.

9.8   There will be no certainty until there has been judicial interpretation on the point.

In any event s 21(6) reserves the right to the Treasury to draft regulations clarifying the point. Section 21(7) even allows them to repeal it. The main regulations that have been passed pursuant to s 21 will now be considered.

Financial Promotion Order 2005

Methods of communication

9.9   This statutory instrument[1] specifies the types of activities and investments that are controlled activities and controlled investments for the purposes of financial promotion. The categories of 'communications' in the context of a financial promotion are also dealt with here and are divided into three types:

- unsolicited real time communications;
- solicited real time communications; and
- non real time communications.

---

1 Which repeals SI 2001/1335, as amended.

9.10   Real time communications are:

'... any communication made in the course of a personal visit, telephone conversation or other interactive dialogue.[1]'

---

1 SI 2005/1529, art 7.

9.11   If a communication does not satisfy this definition it is a non real time communication and specifically this will include letters, e-mails and publications. Factors that will also categorise a communication as non real time are:

- that the communication is directed at more than one recipient in identical terms;

- that the communication is made in a way that provides the recipient with a record of it at a later date; or

- that the communication is made or directed by way of a system that does not enable the recipient to respond immediately to it.

9.12   The second issue that arises is the difference between solicited and unsolicited real time communications. A communication is regarded as solicited where:

'... it is made in the course of a personal visit, telephone call or other interactive dialogue if that call ...

(a)   was initiated by the recipient of the communication, or

(b)   takes pace in response to an express request from the recipient of the communication.[1]'

1 SI 2005/1529, art 8(1).

9.13   However, there were concerns that firms would seek to unfairly have communications categorised as solicited real time communications by requiring recipients of earlier communications to tick a box if they did not wish to have future communications regarded as being unsolicited. Thus the wording *'expressly requested'* was used to remove this possibility. The statutory instrument continues at art 8(3):

'(a) person is not to be treated as expressly requesting a call, visit or dialogue-

(i)   because he omits to indicate that he does not wish to receive any further visits or calls or to engage in any further dialogue;

(ii)   because he agrees to standard terms that state that such visits, call or dialogue will take place, unless he has signified clearly that, in addition to agreeing to the terms, he is willing for them to take place.

(b) a communication is solicited only if it is clear from all the circumstances when the call, visit or dialogue is initiated or requested that during the course of the call, visit or dialogue communication will be made concerning the kind of controlled activities or investments to which the communication in fact made relate.'

9.14   A communication which is only solicited in this way is therefore treated as a solicited communication. If a communication really is solicited the solicited real time communication may also be made at the same time to a close relative of the person soliciting or to someone with whom they are going to jointly invest.

Exempt communications

9.15   Leaving aside those communications that are exempt for reasons of jurisdiction (see below) there are a number of exempt communications, that is they are exempt from the requirement in s 21 discussed above. A firm can rely on more than one exemption if they are available[1]. The most important is that communications only made to intermediates or market counterparties are exempt[2].

In the following instances all the exemptions in the Financial Promotion Order apply, except as listed:

---

1 COB 3.2.6 R.
2 COB 3.2.6 R, 3.5.6 R and 3.5.7R.

Unsolicited real time communications

9.16   The exemptions in the statutory instrument all apply apart from the following:

Article 16(2)

9.17   The restriction does not apply to an unsolicited real time communication made by an appointed representative in carrying out business for which his principal has accepted responsibility and in relation to which the appointed representative is exempt.

Article 17A

9.18   Real time communications caused to be made or directed by an unauthorised person which are made or directed by an authorised person who prepared the content are exempt.

Article 20A

9.19   A promotional broadcast by a company director or employee is exempt where it induces the recipient to acquire a controlled investment (i e shares or options, futures or contracts for differences in relation to shares) issued by an undertaking in the same group as the director or employee's company. The communication should normally be made other than as part of an organised marketing campaign and not reduced to words. It can however be put in writing as part of an interactive dialogue to which the person making the communication is a party.

Article 23

9.20   Real time communications relating to deposit taking are excluded.

Article 26

9.21   Real time communications relating to insurance activity are excluded

Article 28A

9.22   A one-off unsolicited real time communication is excluded from the restriction provided the sender believes the recipient to understand the risks associated with the investment activity concerned and the sender has reasonable grounds for supposing that the recipient expects to be contacted regarding that type of investment business.

Article 28B

9.23   Real time communications relating to qualifying credit agreements are exempt where they are made to introduce the representee to an authorised person, an appointed representative or an overseas person. There are disclosure requirements on the receipt of money by the party making the representation.

Article 32

9.24   In addition, unsolicited real time communications are excluded if made to previous overseas customers. The basis of the previous business must have been such that the customer would expect to be contacted and that they have been previously informed that they will not receive the protections of the FSMA regime may not apply. Likewise, they must be informed as to whether the contract will fall within any dispute resolution or compensation scheme.

Article 33

9.25   Unsolicited real time communications to knowledgeable customers are excluded if made from outside the UK in the course of carrying on investment business outside the UK. The representor must have reasonable grounds for supposing that the recipient is sufficiently knowledgeable to understand the risks and that they have been previously informed that they will not receive the protections of the FSMA regime. Likewise, it must have been pointed out to them whether the contract will fall within any dispute resolution or compensation scheme.

Article 55

9.26   The restriction does not apply to a real time communication which is made by someone carrying on a regulated activity permitted by FSMA 2000, s 327 (i e the activities categorised as exempt regulated activities) and it is made to a recipient who has already engaged the representor to act on their behalf. The service referred to in the communication must be incidental to the professional service being offered.

Solicited real time communications

9.27   The exemptions in the statutory instrument all apply except in the following cases:

Article 14

9.28   If a communication is exempt because of the provisions of this statutory instrument then a subsequent communication made within 12 months by the same person to the same recipient relating to the same controlled activity and investment is also exempt.

Article 16(1)

9.29   The restriction does not apply to non real time or solicited real time communications made directly by an exempt person provided it relates to the exempt person's business of carrying on a controlled activity which is also a regulated activity in relation to which he is an exempt person.

Article 17A

9.30   See above under unsolicited real time communications.

Article 18A

9.31 See above under unsolicited real time communications.

Article 20A

9.32 See above under unsolicited real time communications.

Article 23

9.33 Real time communications relating to deposit taking are excluded.

Article 26

9.34 Real time communications relating to insurance activity are excluded

Article 28

9.35 The restriction does not apply to a one off communication which is either solicited real time or non real time communication provided:

- the communication is made to a single individual or group of recipients;
- the identity of the product or service is determined; and
- the communication is not part of an organised marketing campaign

Article 28B

9.36

See above under unsolicited real time communications.

Article 30

9.37 The restriction does not apply to solicited real time communications made by an overseas communication from outside the UK in the course of the recipient carrying on investment business outside the UK. This is limited to communications relating to:

- dealing in securities and contractually based investments;
- arranging;
- managing;
- safeguarding and administering;
- advising;
- providing qualifying credit;
- arranging qualifying credit;
- advising on qualifying credit; and

agreeing to carry on specified ativities.

Article 34

9.38   There is an exemption for any financial promotion that is a solicited real time or non real time communication and is communicated by and relates only to controlled interests issued by a government, local authority, international organisation, the Bank of England, the European Central Bank or any other overseas central bank.

Article 35

9.39   The restriction does not apply to a communication which is a non real time or solicited real time communication, communicated by an industrial and provident society and relates only to instruments creating or acknowledging indebtedness.

Article 36

9.40   Nor does the restriction apply to a communication which is a non real time communication or solicited real time communication by a national of an EEA state other than the UK, issued in the course of a controlled activity lawfully carried on there, provided the communication conforms with any relevant FSA rules.

Article 37

9.41   The financial promotion restriction does not apply to a non real time communication or a solicited real time communication which is communicated by a relevant market in Jersey, Guernsey, the Isle of Man, Pennsylvania or Iowa.

However, this is limited to communications concerning facilities provided by the market concerned that do not identify any particular investment issued from an identified person that can be traded on that market.

Article 40

9.42 The restriction does not apply to non real time or solicited real time communications made by someone who is an operator of a regulated collective investment scheme to people in the UK who participate in such a scheme the representor is operating.

Articles 41 and 42

9.43 The restriction does not apply to non real time or solicited real time communications made by a company (other than an open ended investment company) regarding its bearer instruments when such a communication is required by the rules of a relevant market or where it is a promotion to an existing holder. It is also permissible if they are issued by its holding company or a subsidiary. In this context *bearer instruments* means shares, bonds, warrants and certificates representing securities.

Article 43

9.44 The restriction does not apply to non real time or solicited real time communications by a company (other than an open ended investment company) to a creditor of that company or one in the same group, or to someone who is entitled to become a member of such a company by being entitled to a share, bond, warrant or certificate representing securities.

Article 44

9.45 Nor does the restriction apply to a non real time or solicited real time communication communicated by a company (other than a open ended investment company) to a creditor or someone entitled to bonds, instruments entitling the holder to investments or units in collective investment schemes to be issued by the company making the communication.

Article 48

9.46 It does not apply to non real time or solicited real time communications to a certified high net worth individual concerning shares, bonds, instruments entitling the holder to investments, certificates representing securities, units in collective investment schemes that invest primarily in shares and bonds together with options, futures and contracts for differences in the above. For this exemption to apply it must not be an investment under which a person can acquire a liability in excess of the amount invested.

Article 51

9.47   The restriction does not apply to non real time or solicited real time communications made to an association which the representor has reasonable grounds to suppose is made up wholly or predominantly of certified or self-certified high net worth individuals or sophisticated investors. It must not be an investment under which a person can acquire a liability in excess of the amount invested.

Article 52

9.48   The restriction does not apply to a non real time or solicited real time communication regarding shares or bonds made to a common interest group. This is an identified group of people who might be reasonably regarded as having a common interest with each other and the company making the communication.

Article 55

9.49   See above under unsolicited real time communications.

Article 58

9.50   Non real time and solicited real time communications are not covered by the restriction when made by management companies for the purposes of managing the building concerned or issuing shares.

Article 61

9.51   The exclusion does not cover non real time and solicited real time communications made by a supplier of goods and services to a customer provided the communication does not relate to insurance, units in a regulated collective investment scheme or rights or interests in investments.

Article 67

9.52 The exclusion does not cover non real time and solicited real time communications relating to shares, bonds, gilts, instruments giving entitlement to investments or certificates representing securities which are required to be communicated by the market they are traded on.

Article 68

9.53 The restriction does not apply to non real time or solicited real time communication which a relevant EEA market requires to be made before an investment can be admitted to trading on that market. It should not contain other material than that required by those rules.

Article 69

9.54 The restriction does not apply to non real time or solicited real time communications made by a company (other than an open ended investment company) and relating to shares, bonds, warrants or certificates representing securities when either of the last two relate to shares in that company or another company in the same group. The communication must not be accompanied by an invitation to engage in investment activity which refers to the price of relevant investments in the past or the yield thereon unless accompanied by a statement that past performance cannot be relied on as a guide to future performance.

Non real time communications

9.55 The exemptions in the statutory instrument all apply except in the following cases:

Article 14

9.56 See above under solicited real time communications

Article 16(1)

9.57 The restriction does not apply to non real time or solicited real time communications made directly by an exempt person provided it relates to the exempt person's business of carrying on a controlled activity which is also a regulated activity in relation to which he is an exempt person.

Article 18A

9.58 The restriction does not apply to an electronic commerce communication where it consists of providing information society advice within the Electronic Commerce Directive 12(1), 13(1) or 14(1).

Article 20

9.59 Communications made by journalists are exempt from the restriction where certain criteria are met:

- it is in a qualifying publication as defined in the Regulated Activities Order[1];

- the content is devised by a journalist; and

- where the communication requires disclosure an indication is included of the author's financial interest.

The publication concerned must fall within the remit of one of the named codes of practice.

---

1 Art 54, SI 2001/544

Article 20A

9.60 A promotional broadcast by a company director or employee is exempt where it induces the recipient to acquire a controlled investment (i.e., shares or options, futures or contracts for differences in relation to shares) issued by an undertaking in the same group as the director or employee's company. The communication should normally be made other than as part of an organised marketing campaign and not be reduced to writing. It can however be put in writing as part of an interactive dialogue to which the person making the communication is a party.

Article 20B

9.61 The restriction does not apply to an incoming electronic commerce communication unless it amounts to:

- an advert by the operator of a UCITS directive scheme regarding units in the scheme;

- an invitation to enter into a contract of life assurance as covered by any of the insurance directives; or

- unsolicited communications by e-mail.

Article 22

9.62   Non real time communications are not caught by the restriction if it relates to deposit taking, provided the deposit taker provides key information, such as their name, country of location, regulator and any applicable dispute resolution and deposit guarantee scheme.

Article 24

9.63   Non real time communications issued in relation to an insurance contract are excluded from the restriction provided certain criteria are met in the communication's contents, namely:

- the name of the recipient;
- the country in which the insurer is situated and if different the state of the insurer's principal place of business;
- whether the insurer is regulated and if so by whom; and
- whether there is an applicable dispute resolution scheme or compensation scheme.

Article 25

9.64   Non real time communications relating to reinsurance and large risk insurance are excluded subject to certain requirements concerning the figures in the most recent accounts.

Article 28

9.65   See above under solicited real time communications.

Article 31

9.66   There is an exception where the restrictions do not apply to non real time communications sent from outside the UK to someone who was a former overseas customer in the previous 12 months.

Article 34

9.67 There is an exemption for any financial promotion that is a solicited real time or non real time communication and is communicated by and relates only to controlled interests issued by a government, local authority, international organisation, the Bank of England, the European Central Bank or any other overseas central bank.

Article 35

9.68 The restriction does not apply to a communication which is a non real time or solicited real time communication, communicated by an industrial and provident society and relates only to instruments creating or acknowledging indebtedness.

Article 36

9.69 Nor does the restriction apply to a communication which is a non real time communication or solicited real time communication by a national of an EEA state other than the UK, issued in the course of a controlled activity lawfully carried on there, provided the communication conforms with any relevant FSA rules.

Article 37

9.70 The financial promotion restriction does not apply to a non real time communication or a solicited real time communication which is communicated by a relevant market in Jersey, Guernsey, the Isle of Man, Pennsylvania or Iowa. However, this is limited to communications concerning facilities provided by the market concerned that do not identify any particular investment issued from an identified person that can be traded on that market.

Article 40

9.71 The restriction does not apply to non real time or solicited real time communications made by someone who is an operator of a regulated collective investment scheme to people in the UK who participate in such a scheme the representor is operating.

Articles 41 and 42

9.72 The restriction does not apply to non real time or solicited real time communications made by a company (other than an open ended investment company) regarding its bearer instruments when such a communication is required by the rules of a relevant market or where it is a promotion to an existing holder. It is also permissible if they are issued by its holding company or a subsidiary. In this context *bearer instruments* means shares, bonds, warrants and certificates representing securities.

Article 43

9.73   The restriction does not apply to non real time or solicited real time communications by a company (other than an open ended investment company) to a creditor of that company or one in the same group, or to someone who is entitled to become a member of such a company by being entitled to a share, bond, warrant or certificate representing securities.

Article 44

9.74   Nor does the restriction apply to a non real time or solicited real time communication communicated by a company (other than an open ended investment company) to a creditor or someone entitled to bonds, instruments entitling the holder to investments or units in collective investment schemes to be issued by the company making the communication.

Article 48

9.75   It does not apply to non real time or solicited real time communications to a certified high net worth individual concerning shares, bonds, instruments entitling the holder to investments, certificates representing securities, units in collective investment schemes that invest primarily in shares and bonds together with options, futures and contracts for differences in the above. For this exemption to apply it must not be an investment under which a person can acquire a liability in excess of the amount invested.

Article 51

9.76   The restriction does not apply to non real time or solicited real time communications made to an association which the representor has reasonable grounds to suppose is made up wholly or predominantly of certified or self-certified high net worth individuals or sophisticated investors. It must not be an investment under which a person can acquire a liability in excess of the amount invested.

Article 52

9.77   The restriction does not apply to a non real time or solicited real time communication regarding shares or bonds made to a common interest group. This is an identified group of people who might be reasonably regarded as having a common interest with each other and the company making the communication.

Article 55

9.78   The restriction does not apply to solicited or unsolicited real time communications made by professionals (ie, solicitors, chartered accountants, certified accountants or actuaries) to clients. The communication must relate to incidental elements of financial business which need to be carried out to perform the professional task in hand, as permitted under FSMA 2000, s 327.

Article 55A

9.79   Non real time communications by members of a profession (in effect solicitors, chartered accountants, certified accountants and actuaries) are not covered by the restriction provided the communication is made in the prescribed form. Essentially it states that the firm is permitted to carry on a very limited range of investment activities under FSMA 2000, s 327 even though not regulated by the FSA.

Article 58

9.80   Non real time and solicited real time communications are not covered by the restriction when made by management companies for the purposes of managing the building concerned or issuing shares.

Article 61

9.81   The exclusion does not cover non real time and solicited real time communications made by a supplier of goods and services to a customer provided the communication does not relate to insurance, units in a regulated collective investment scheme or rights or interests in investments.

Article 67

9.82   The exclusion does not cover non real time and solicited real time communications relating to shares, bonds, gilts, instruments giving entitlement to investments or certificates representing securities which are required to be communicated by the market they are traded on.

Article 68

9.83   The restriction does not apply to non real time or solicited real time communication which a relevant EEA market requires to be made before an investment can be admitted to trading on that market. It should not contain other material than that required by those rules.

Article 69

9.84   The restriction does not apply to non real time or solicited real time communications made by a company (other than an open ended investment company) and relating to shares, bonds, warrants or certificates representing securities when either of the last two relate to shares in that company or another company in the same group. The communication must not be accompanied by an invitation to engage in investment activity which refers to the price of relevant investments in the past or the yield thereon unless accompanied by a statement that past performance cannot be relied on as a guide to future performance.

Article 70

9.85   The restriction does not apply to non real time communications in listing particulars, prospectuses or supplementary prospectuses or other similar documents required by the listing or prospectus rules.

Article 71

9.86   Non real time communications in the form of a prospectus or supplementary prospectus are not covered by the restriction provided it states the name of the transferee, the number, nature and nominal value of the transferable securities concerned and gives instructions for obtaining the prospectus.

All communications are excluded from the restriction in the following cases

Article 13

9.87   Communications made by a customer to a supplier when it is made to get information about an investment.

Article 15

9.88 A communication made with regard to introducing the recipient to an authorised or exempt person is excluded from the restriction. However, the person making the communication must not be to a close relative or member of the same group as the person to whom the introduction was made. The maker of the communication must not receive any financial benefit other than that received from the recipient. The recipient must also not be someone who has sought investment advice from the person who made the communication, or if it was sought it must have been refused.

Article 17

9.89 The restriction does not apply to a communication which does not identify the person who provides the controlled investment to which the communication relates and does not identify anyone who carries on a controlled activity in relation to that investment.

Article 18

9.90 The restriction does not apply where a comunication is made by someone who acts as a mere conduit for it as part of the business of communicating which primarily consists of transmitting information received from others.

Article 19

9.91 The restriction does not apply to promotions made only to recipients where the person making it reasonably believes them to be investment professionals.

Article 29

9.92 The restriction does not apply to a communication required by statute – apart from the FSMA 2000. This does not extend to communications relating to controlled activities in relation to providing, arranging or advising on qualifying credit or agreeing to carry on specified kinds of activity.

Article 38

9.93 The restriction does not apply to communications made to someone whose business consists of placing or arranging the placing of promotional material where it is made for that purpose.

Article 39

9.94   Nor does it apply to communications made to a participant in a joint exercise by another participant where it relates to the joint exercise.

Article 45

9.95   The restriction does not apply to any communication made by one company in a group to another.

Article 46

9.96   It does not apply to communications relating to qualifying credit if only directed at companies or if it is directed at an individual with a warning in an approved form given at the outset orally and confirmed in writing. This should state:

> 'The content of this promotion has not been approved by an authorised person within the meaning of the Financial Services and Markets Act 2000. Reliance on this promotion for the purpose of engaging in any investment activity may expose an individual to a significant risk of losing all of the property or other assets invested.'

Article 47

9.97   The restriction does not apply to a communication to people who the communicant reasonably believes to be a director, officer or employee of a firm and where the communication is through a publication of information concerning controlled activities which that firm carries out.

Article 49

9.98   The restriction does not apply to communications made to a company which has (or is part of a group with a company that has) over 20 members or is a subsidiary of an undertaking with more than 20 members and has a called-up share capital or net assets of over £500,000. Otherwise it must have a called-up share capital or its net assets must exceed £5 million. If the communication is made to an unincorporated association it must have net assts of not less than £5 million, or if it is a communication made to the trustees of a high value trust or anyone to whom it could have been lawfully made. This extends to directors, officers and employees of those companies who are involved in the company's investment activity. A *high value trust* is one where the aggregate value of the cash and investments which form the trust's assets exceed £10 million or more at any time during the year preceding the date on which the communication was made.

Article 50

9.99   If the self-certification requirement is met the restriction does not apply to any communication which is made to a certified sophisticated investor provided it does not engage the investor with the person who has signed the certificate and relates only to an investment to which the certificate relates. The certificate itself should be worded:

> 'I make this statement so that I am able to receive promotions which are exempt from the restrictions on financial promotion in the Financial Services and Markets Act 2000. The exemption relates to certified sophisticated investors and I declare that I qualify as such in relation to investments of the following kind ....I accept that the contents of promotions and other material that I receive may not have been approved by an authorised person and that their content may not therefore be subject to controls which would apply if the promotion were made or approved by an authorised person. I am aware that it is open to me to seek advice from someone who specialises in advising on this kind of investment.'

Article 50A

9.100   The restriction does not apply where a communication is made to someone who the person making the communication believes on reasonable grounds to be a self-certified sophisticated investor. This is someone who has, in the previous 12 months signed a statement in line with the Order[1]. There must also be a warning provided to the recipient in the following form prior to the communication that precedes any other written matter:

> 'The content of this promotion has not been approved by an authorised person within the meaning of the Financial Services and Markets Act 2000. Reliance on this promotion for the purpose of engaging in any investment activity may expose an individual to a significant risk of losing all of the property or other assets invested.'

---

1. Set out in Pt II of Sch 5.

9.101   There should also be a statement that the communication is exempt from the general prohibition because it is made to a self-certified sophisticated investor and that if they are in any doubt they should see an appropriate authorised person.

9.102 This exclusion only applies to shares, bonds, warrants, certificates representing certain securities, units in a collective investment scheme, options, futures or contracts for differences provided in any case the investor cannot incur a liability or obligation to pay more than he has committed by way of investment.

Article 53

9.103 The restriction does not apply to a communication made between a settler or grantor of a trust, a trustee or a personal representative and a trustée, fellow trustee or fellow personal representative where that communication relates to the purpose of the trust or estate.

Article 54

9.104 The restriction does not apply to a communication made between a settler or grantor of a trust, trustee or personal representative and a beneficiary under the trust, will or intestacy provided the communication relates to the management or distribution of the trust fund or estate.

Article 56

9.105 The restriction does not apply to any communication made or directed by someone for the purpose of enabling any injustice stated by the Parliamentary Commissioner for Adminsitration in a report under s 10 of the Parliamentary Commissioner Act.

Article 57

9.106 The restriction does not apply to a communication received by someone who receives the publication containing it because he has placed an advert there.

Article 59

9.107 The restriction does not apply to a communication by a body corporate (other than an open ended investment company) which consists of, or is accompanied by, a company's annual accounts or a report prepared by the directors under ss 234 and 234A of the Companies Act 1985 or the equivalent law of an EEA state. However, the communication must not contain an invitation to subscribe for, underwrite or otherwise acquire or dispose of a controlled investment or advice in that regard. Nor should the communication invite people to transact with the company in relation to dealing in securities and contractually-based investments, arranging, managing, safeguarding and administering, advising, advising on syndicate participation at Lloyd's, providing funeral plan contracts, providing arranging or advising on qualifying credit or agreeing to carry on specified kinds of activity. Nor should the communication contain an inducement relating to an investment (other than one issued by the company or a group company itself) which relates to shares, bonds, warrants or certificates representing securities. In addition the communication should not contain references to the price at which investments issued by the company have been traded in the past or their yield unless it is accompanied by a statement that past performance cannot be relied on as a guide to the future. Oddly, in this context *yield* does not mean earnings, dividend or nominal rate of interest.

Article 60

9.108 The restriction does not apply to communications made by a member or trustee of an employee share scheme for the benefit of employees, former employees or family members where the communication relates to:

- shares;
- bonds
- share or bond warrants;
- certificates representing shares or bonds;
- share or bond options; or
- rights or interests in bonds or warrants.

Article 62

9.109 The restriction does not apply to a communication by or on behalf of a company, partnership, individual or group of individuals if it relates to acquiring or selling shares in a company (other than an open ended investment company) and day-to-day control of the company concerned is being transferred. Normally this would be evidenced by 50% or more of the voting shares being transferred or that amount being reached when aggregated with previous transfers. The transfer must be between parties each of whom is a company, a partnership, an individual or a group of connected individuals.

Article 64

9.110 The restriction does not apply to a communication made in connection with the takeover of an unlisted company. The communication must be accompanied by stated material[1.]

---

1 SI 2005/1529, Pt I, Sch 4.

Article 65

9.111   Nor does the restriction apply to a communication made at the same time or after a takeover offer is made for an unlisted company if it relates to warrants or certificates representing securities which relate to shares or bonds in the company concerned.

Article 66

9.112   The restriction does not apply to a communication made in connection with a takeover offer for an unlisted company when it is a form of application for shares or bonds issued by the company or warrants or certificates representing securities relating to the shares or bonds issued by that company.

Article 72

9.113   The restriction does not apply to any communication made by an employer to an employee in relation to a group personal pension scheme or a stakeholder pension scheme. However, the employer must be going to make a contribution to the scheme and the employee must be informed of this and of the amount. The employer must not receive any direct benefit from the scheme and in the case of a non real time communication there must be a statement informing the employee of their right to seek advice from a financial adviser, whether independent or otherwise.

Article 73

9.114   Communications made by advisors to or employees of advice centres are excluded where the communication is made as part of their duties. However, this exclusion only extends to statements concerning qualifying credits, rights under contracts of insurance relating to the needs of the advice centre and child trust funds.

Certified high net worth individuals and sophisticated investors

9.115   These two categories of people are perceived as being generally less at risk than the public at large. The former because they can afford to pay for good quality expert advice and the latter because they are sophisticated in assessing the risks inherent in the investment concerned. Nonetheless in the response to the Treasury Consultation paper[1] on the Financial Promotions Order this was an area that elicited a number of responses. As has been seen in the discussion of arts 48, 50, 50A and 51 above special provision was made for such people being exempt from the financial promotions restriction. A leading expert Charles Abrams[2] raised the point that there was no register of qualifying certified high net worth individuals which those proposing to make communications could inspect. This would be useful as wealthy individuals have shown a propensity for refusing to reveal details about themselves until they know what investment opportunity is being proposed to them. The City of London Law Society in their response[3] also raised the issue that there was a risk with the self-certification scheme as unscrupulous advisers might advise inappropriate people to sign themselves off, a point reiterated by the Financial Services Consumer Panel[4]. The City of London Law Society also raised the issue that the reasonable belief element was inappropriate. If the self-certification document had been seen the reasonable belief element is irrelevant and if it has not been, how can the reasonable belief exist?

1 H M Treasury, Consultation Paper, (January 2004).
2 Comments on the Treasury's Consultation Document of January 2004.
3 Letter to H M Treasury dated 7 June 2004.
4 Letter to H M Treasury dated 14 April 2003.

Jurisdiction

9.116 One issue that arises in any area of financial regulation is that of jurisdiction. It is of particular importance in the context of financial promotions as they may be issued out of the UK or into the UK as well as being purely domestic. The issue of the jurisdictional element is dealt with in FSMA 2000, s 21(3). It states that:

> 'In the case of a communication originating outside the United
> Kingdom (the law) applies only if the communication is capable of
> having an effect in the United Kingdom.'

9.117 The wording is unfortunate as in theory almost any communication could have such an effect. What presumably is meant is that a communication will be caught if it is placed in a manner and a language which render it reasonably likely that it will be acted on in the United Kingdom. It would be absurd if an advert in a newspaper in Chile to sell local investments which happens in one instance to be responded to by an investor in the UK should give rise to the UK law applying. As a result art 12 of the Financial Promotion Order states that the restriction does not apply to a communication:

(a) which is made (whether inside or outside the United Kingdom) to a person who receives the communication outside the United Kingdom; or

(b) which is directed (whether from inside or outside the United Kingdom) only at persons outside the United Kingdom'

9.118 This however does not extend to unsolicited real time communications unless they are made from a place outside the UK and it is made for the purposes of a business carried on outside the UK and not in it. As far as communications directed only at people outside the UK are concerned; the statutory instrument provides further clarification[1]. These are that:

- the communication is accompanied by an indication that it is only directed at people outside the UK;

- the communication is accompanied by an indication that it must not be acted on by people in the UK;

- the communication is not referred to in or accessible from any other communication directed at people in the UK by the person directing the communication;

- there are proper procedures in place to prevent recipients in the UK engaging in the investment activity the communication relates to with the person directing the communication or a connected person;

- the communication is included in a website, newspaper, journal or similar periodical principally directed at readers outside the UK or a tv or radio broadcast directed mainly for reception outside the UK; or

- the communication can be treated as directed at people outside the UK if it is directed at investment professionals or high net worth parties outside the UK, provided it contains an indication that it cannot be acted on by someone in the UK apart from those of sufficient professional experience in matters relating to investments or high net worth parties.

---

1 SI 2005/1529, art 12(4).

Collective Investment Schemes

9.119 Collective investment schemes are already separately regulated and this extends to the manner in which they are promoted. Whilst a detailed examination of these schemes is beyond the scope of the text such schemes are normally authorised or recognised. If they fall into neither category it is not normally possible to promote them. If they do fall into one of these categories then s 21 applies. In such cases the Financial Services and Market Act (Promotion of Collective Investment Schemes) (Exemptions) Order 2001 applies[1]. In essence its approach is similar to that in the Financial Promotion Order, utilising the same categories of communication – unsolicited real time, solicited real time and non real time together with the same overall approach to categorising exclusions to the general prohibition

---

1 SI 2001/1060.

FSA financial promotion rules

9.120 There are a few parts of the FSA rule book which are directly relevant, the most important general rules being COB 3.2.4 – 5 and 3.8.4, 5, 8 – 11 and 13 and MCOB 3 and ICOB 3. In addition COB 3.11.2 is applicable to collective investment schemes. It is clear from the content that the FSA has not sought to change the regime in the Financial Promotions Order, and indeed any attempt to do so would inevitably cause friction between the FSA and the Treasury.

9.121 Chapter 3.2 COB states at the outset that 'The rules in this chapter adopt various concepts from the restriction on financial promotion by unauthorised persons in s 21(1) of the Act.' The guidance at 3.2.2G also provides a useful discussion on the various types of communication that are caught. The key issue arises at 3.2.5 where it states that the chapter does not apply to any of the following:

- financial promotions to a market counterparty or an intermediate customer (or at least to those who the party making the communication has taken reasonable steps to so establish their status or where they may reasonably be so regarded). In the case of an expert private customer who has been classified as an intermediate the exemption only applies to a communication relating to the investment or investment activity in which he is an expert. This is to stop someone who may be classified as an expert in say equities, then being vulnerable to approaches to engage in investments that may be beyond their expertise, e.g., complex derivatives.

- Financial promotions that can be lawfully communicated to an unauthorised person without first being approved.

- A communication from outside the UK which would be exempt under arts 30–33 Financial Promotion Order if the office from which the communication is made is a separate unauthorised business.

- One-off non real time communications and one-off solicited real time communications where communicated to a single group of recipients in the expectation that they would jointly engage in that investment activity, the identity of the product to which the communication relates has been chosen bearing in mind the circumstances of the recipient and the communication is not part of an organised marketing campaign.

- Financial promotions that only contain the following: the firm's name, the investment, a contact point, a logo, a brief factual description of the firm's activities (or those of its appointed representatives), a brief description of the investment products and the price or yields of the investments and any charges.

- Personal quotations and illustrations.

- Financial promotions subject to the Takeover Code or equivalent EEA requirements.

- Finally, communications in the form of a decision tree for a stakeholder pension scheme subject to certain restrictions on the content.

9.122 The main significance of this is the first one. Many investment banks and other large investment businesses will only be dealing with people in these categories. Many do not have a private client base and as this part of the rules functions as a consumer protection measure for private customers it will not be relevant to their activities. The other is the third, the effect of which is less obvious. This type of communication was already exempt from the restriction in all cases except those where the communication applied to deposit taking and insurance contracts. The FSA rules include these as well.

9.123 Many financial promotions must be in a specific form and these are dealt with in COB 3.8. COB 3.8.4 deals with non real time financial promotions and requires that firms should take reasonable steps to make sure that communications are clear, fair and not misleading. If a comparison is included it must be a comparison of investments meeting the same needs or purpose, ie, in this sense like must be compared with like. Care must also be taken to make sure that there is no confusion between firms, investments or services. Statements of opinion are required to be honestly held[1] and therefore it is good compliance procedure to make sure there is evidence on file as to why the opinion was held. Guidance[2] suggests that the minimum and maximum amounts that can be invested and the investment period should be stated, as should the likelihood that there will be a time delay before there is a return on the investment and whether the investment is likely to be tied up for more than one month. If the investment relates to securities or an investment trust savings scheme investing in securities the risks must be properly explained as, where applicable, should the fact that gearing is to be engaged in. There must also be a general warning that the securities are likely to face significant fluctuations in value.

---

1 COB 3.8.5 E.
2 COB 3.8.9 G.

9.124 If a specific non real time communication relates to an investment, service or person other than the issuer there must be a description of the nature of the investment or service, the commitment required and the inherent risks. In addition, the name and contact details of the firm on whose behalf it has been issued must be included.

9.125 Where a specific non real time promotion relates to investments other than packaged products it must state whether the firm making the promotion or its associate holds a position or material interest in that investment or that it is the only market maker dealing in that security.

9.126 That past performance is not a guide to future conduct must be clearly stated on the text of the promotion[1]. No such comparison can be made unless the period of past performance has existed for over 12 months. Care should be taken when presenting information in Euros if the prior performance was measured in a different currency to make sure that readers are not misled. In the case of unit linked policies and schemes the compared period must be the previous five years unless it is less than this in which case it must be the whole period.

---

1 COB 3.8.11 R.

9.127 MCOB 3 (mortgages) and ICOB 3 (non investment insurance products) largely parallel the COB rules though they only apply to non real time communications. They also parallel the Financial Promotion Rules including the requirement that promotions be clear, fair and not misleading. A detailed examination of these rules is however beyond the scope of the book.

9.128 There are also separate Conduct of Business rules relating to distance marketing. COB 2.6.2 R requires that firms must make sure that information provided to a retail customer before a distance contract is entered into conforms with the obligations that are imposed on the firm under the law applying where the contract is concluded. If the customer wants the terms in writing this must be provided at no extra cost. There are additional rules that also apply to distance customers regarding supplying services and enforcing obligations[1].

---

1 COB 2.6.3 R.

Conclusions

9.129 One conclusion that will occur to many is that the current regime is over complicated. As has been suggested[1] one option would be to replace the current regime made up of '... *a* blanket prohibition, subject to narrow exemptions' with '..regulation targeted at identified consumer protection issues.'

---

1 City of London Law Society letter to H M Treasury dated 7 June 2004.

9.130 The relevant case law provides some illumination as to how the relevant law and regulations are interpreted. The FSA Enforcement Action against *The Ancient Order of Foresters Friendly Society Ltd*[1] concerned financial promotions failings. Specifically, the Order of Foresters were held to be in breach of FSA Principles 3 and 7, Senior Management Systems and Controls 3.2.6R, 3.6.1R, 3.6.2R and Conduct of Business rule 3 relating to financial promotions and retaining appropriate records, specifically 3.1.1R and 3.7.1R.

---

1 23 August 2006.

9.131 Foresters is a mutual authorised friendly society which is permitted to carry out contracts of insurance, limited to long-term insurance. For historical reasons the Committee of Management was made up entirely of non-executive directors. The constitution debarred employees from serving on the Management Committee. This is now being changed. Its products include with profits whole of life assurance policies, one of which at the time was 'Autumn Gold'. This restricted cover in the first two years but after that provided the premiums were kept up then their estate would receive a guaranteed sum plus a declared bonus from the with profits fund on the customer's death. There was a maximum contribution of £25 per month.

9.132 In 2003 the government created a child trust fund for the benefit of children born after 1 September 2002 who received a state contribution to such accounts, to which additional contributions could be made to by others. A key caveat is that the fund is not accessible until the child reaches 18.

Foresters also had a plan called a tax exempt policy which could be taken out for up to £300 per year available to both children and adults.

9.133 These products were marketed by Foresters as the 'Teddy Trust', the CTF, a tax exempt policy for older children and 'Autumn Gold'. The promotion of the products was done by television, newspaper and magazine advertisements to which those who responded were sent a direct offer pack. There was also advertising material on their website. No advice was given by Foresters themselves. Legal advice was never taken by the firm on the content of the advertisements concerning regulatory issues. Appropriate risk warnings were never given. There was no statement regarding Autumn Gold policies that the amount paid out at the end could be less than the premiums paid. There was no statement that during the first two years the plan had no value at all and no warning that the guaranteed cover provided was not inflation proofed; nor were there inflation risk warnings. The promotion referred to a 'guaranteed tax-free lump sum' but failed to refer to the potential inheritance tax liability. In addition Foresters failed to keep a record of the version of the promotion that was issued. In addition there were failures of systems and controls in that reasonable care was not taken, there was no effective procedure for monitoring issued promotions or keeping records of them. Nor was there a proper review of the compliance department.

9.134 Autumn Gold policy holders were later sent a letter by Foresters pointing out that the reference to it being a funeral plan was inaccurate. The policyholders were given the right to review their options. This type of correction was later done with the other policy holders.

9.135 A warning letter was sent out by the FSA to all friendly societies warning them that they should pay particular regard to the financial promotions rules and gave specific warnings about the content of investments for children; providing examples which Foresters should have noted raised issues concerning the promotion of some of their products.

9.136 The reasons for the FSA action were: that Foresters did not pay due regard to the information needs of its customers and potential customers and information was communicated to them in a way that failed to be clear, fair and not misleading. It also did not take reasonable care to organise its financial promotions properly resulting in inadequate risk management systems.

9.137 The FSA stated that:

'One of the FSA's three strategic aims is to help retail customers achieve a fair deal. Ensuring that financial promotions are clear, fair and not misleading is a key part of that strategy as the FSA aims to ensure that customers have access to clear, simple and understandable information to help them make financial decisions.'

9.138 It was taken into account in Forester's favour that they had and were continuing to improve their systems, the fact that their behaviour was not deliberate or reckless and that it co-operated with the FSA enquiry and took steps to remedy some of the financial promotions breaches. Foresters were fined £55,000

9.139 Finally, the FSA have published an evaluation[1] on the effectives of the financial promotion regime over the preceding two years. They evaluated almost 1,000 financial promotions and concluded that the proportion of promotions falling below regulatory standards fell to 32% in 2006 from 52% in 2004. The weakest areas appeared to be the insurance sector and sub prime mortgages. During that period the FSA also examined 4,500 promotions and found 820 cases where standards fell below regulatory standards. 55 firms were visited to enable the FSA to assess their systems and controls and in these cases they intervened to change or withdraw promotions.

---

1 1 August 2006.

9.140 The key factors that the FSA raised were:

● to what extent is the financial promotion strategy overseen by senior management;

- how is the requirement to treat customers fairly taken into account when financial promotions are designed;

- to what extent do those signing off promotions challenging the content to make sure they are balanced, fair, clear and not misleading;

- how is the relationship between marketing and compliance managed;

- what management information is produced on financial promotions and to what extent is this used to identify emerging risks and to facilitate remedial action; and

- how are approvals staff trained and how are they assessed?

9.141 Tellingly for those involved in issuing financial promotions the FSA have said[1]:

> '... we must see further progress. Responsibility for ensuring that customers are given clear fair and straightforward descriptions of financial products and services lies squarely with the senior management of the firms selling them. So while our shift away from detailed rules towards a more principles based approach will allow firms the freedom they need to market effectively, senior management also needs to put in place the right checks and balances to ensure that customers are being treated fairly.[2]'

---

1 Vernon Everitt, FSA Retail Themes Director.
2 FSA Business Plan 2006/7, p 26.

Advising

9.142 This covers giving advice to an investor or prospective investor on the merits of buying, selling, subscribing for or underwriting an investment which is a security or a contractually-based investment or exercising any right conferred by such an investment. It applies whether the advice is given to someone in their own capacity or as agent or another. However, generic advice is not covered, so for example it is possible to advise on the relative merits of direct and indirect investments or of investments of a particular nature. Advising is an area that the FSA see as one of its core activities:

> 'One of our key priorities is to make the market in retail financial services function more effectively and, as a consequence, help retail customers get a fair deal ...In order to achieve this aim, we focus on what we consider to be the four main features of an effective and efficient retail market:
>
> - capable and confident consumers;

- clear, simple and understandable information for, and used by, consumers from the industry and the FSA;

- responsible firms who treat their customers fairly and are soundly managed and adequately capitalised; and

- risk-based regulation, through firm-specific and thematic supervision and policy.[1]'

---

1 FSA Business Plan 2006/7, p 25.

Investment suitability

9.143 In essence, an adviser who provides advice to a new customer must make certain that they have carried out a fact find into the customer's financial provision. This will normally be done by filling in a standard form that provides details of the customer's income, projected income, assets, liabilities, other investments, future plans and in the case of a spouse or partner, the equivalent information from them. Other family issues such as dependants also need to be looked into. It is only once all this has been done that it will be possible to ascertain what investments are suitable for the customer concerned. It will not be sufficient to simply provide advice on the basis of a new customer asking for information on a particular type of product as this may not be a suitable investment. This does not preclude the customer instructing an adviser on an execution only basis but in that instance no advice will be provided. If there are any risks associated with a particular investment these must also be spelt out.

9.144 It should be noted that an adviser's responsibilities do not stop there. The FSA aims to encourage firms to consider the needs of consumers at all stages of the product lifecycle, including *'product design; marketing; the sales and advice processes and after-sales care (including complaints handling). We also encourage firms to ensure that there is a joined-up approach across these functions, even if they are spread across different corporate entities.'*

9.145 Some of these issues arose in *Legal & General Assurance Society Ltd v FSA*[1] which dealt with alleged breaches of the old SIB Principle 2 and Rules 7.1.2(1). It was claimed by the FSA that Legal & General had made certain failures in the identification of risk averse customers who did not wish to accept the risk of capital shortfall. Legal & General's procedures did not require their advisers to find out whether customers were prepared to accept the risk of a shortfall. Where third party customers advised taking out an interest only mortgage the procedures at Legal & General did not require confirmation that the customer understood and was prepared to accept the risk of a capital shortfall. The allegation was that Legal & General's procedures were inadequate in that they drew no distinction between low risk and risk averse customers. The definition of *low risk* referred to customers who were not prepared to take risks with investments. Inadequate guidance was given to advisers concerning the risk of with-profit endowments, risk warnings were inadequate and review procedures failed to pick up unsuitable sales.

---

1 Financial Services and Markets Tribunal, 18 January 2005.

9.146 Legal & General disputed this: they stated that their customers were provided with the risk warnings required by the rules then in force (the old PIA rules) including the risk of capital shortfall. Advisers were required to explain each document and the customers had to sign a confirmation that this had been done. A second copy of the explanation was sent with a right to cancel before the contract was entered into. Their procedures did require advisers to explain the advantages and disadvantages of interest only mortgages and that customers should be advised that they were unsuitable unless the customer was prepared to accept the risk of capital shortfall. The risk of shortfall also had to be explained where the advice was given by a third party and steps taken to make sure the customer understood the risk.

9.147 Legal & General also argued that its documentation had been approved by the relevant regulator, the risk categories referred to the risk associated with selecting an investment fund not shortfall risk and they had provided advisers with comprehensive training and guidance. There was also ongoing maintenance to make sure that standards were maintained. Full risk warnings had to be provided and explained to each customer and there was no evidence that this had not been done. Finally, their review procedures were claimed to be sufficient.

9.148 The issue arising under rule 7.1.2 was over its interpretation. Legal & General's view was that it was not an absolute obligation, but required reasonably effective procedures designed to prevent non compliance. It was impossible to make sure that no representative ever acted in breach. The FSA's interpretation was that the rules required firms to have in place systems that were effective in ensuring that its representatives complied with the rules, though there may be isolated instances where individual sales personnel made an error. They also believed that adequate steps had not been taken to make sure that sales personnel followed the rules in practice.

9.149 The conclusions reached by the Tribunal were that:

(1) The written sales procedures did not ensure that the practice of advisers explaining shortfall risk to customers was followed. There was a deficiency in the Personal Finance Review procedure in that it did not require the adviser to record whether the customer understood and was prepared to accept the capital shortfall risk. Had this been done it would have left the adviser with no option but to have an informed discussion with the customer about the risk concerned.

(2) The definition of *low risk* in the same document was inappropriate in that it was the lowest of the risk levels set out and therefore gave the impression to customers that this was a suitable position for those adverse to risk.

(3) The recommendation section of the same form was not completed so as to take proper account of shortfall risk. The utilisation of sample wordings led to a masking of the customers' attitude to risk, prevented sufficiently thorough checking of customers' attitudes prior to them choosing the type of mortgage they wanted. This was not offset by the accuracy of the Key Features Document and the illustrations provided, even though they complied with regulatory requirements.

(4) The above three points were qualified by the fact that the regulator at the time, the PIA, had not criticised any of these points in their Personal Finance Review. The other defects picked up by the PIA in 1999 were not seen as sufficiently serious to warrant disciplinary action. Legal & General had agreed to put them right over a period of 18 months and had done so. During the intervening period after that the FSA had changed its position regarding with profit low cost endowments as it realised the scale of the problem.

(5) The scale of mis-selling was low. Out of 250 cases sampled, 8 were instances of mis-selling with 14 further potential ones; 13 possible further cases and 25 too unclear to decide.

9.150 The question of an appropriate penalty was left to a later decision. This determined that certain factors had to be considered:

- the investments concerned were likely to be the most important financial decision to be made by many of the customers;

- the breaches continued over a three-year period;

- there were two significant weaknesses in Legal & General's selling techniques that could lead to customers failing to appreciate the risk of loss;

- Legal & General had been warned about the problem some time earlier and had done nothing;

- Legal & General were a very large business with 41,000 customers potentially facing loss;

- they also had very large financial resources;

- they had co-operated with the regulator but had not provided such *'extensive proactive co-operaton'* as would result in a discount to any penalty;

- Legal & General had a better than average compliance history;

- the Tribunal did not believe that any damage to Legal & General's reputation caused by the publicity should be taken into account in mitigation;

- there had been extensive delays in the FSA's investigative process, most of which was the responsibility of the FSA; and

- the breaches had now ceased and customers who have suffered loss were to be compensated.

9.151   As a result a penalty of £575,000 was imposed with no order for costs. There was no recommendation made as to the FSA's regulatory provisions or its procedures[1] as the FSA had already announced that it was making its own review of the enforcement process.

---

1 FSMA 2000, s 133(8).

9.152   A more recent case was that of the FSA enforcement action against *Rainbow Homeloans Ltd*[1] concerning systems and controls failings that resulted in approximately 1,000 people being sold unsuitable products. The bases of the problem were that:

(1)   the directors of Rainbow had not discharged their responsibilities regarding monitoring and controlling the business but had relied to an inappropriate extent on an outside consultant.

(2)   The firm did have a management structure and oversight arrangements but it did not ensure that it had an appropriate governing body in the form of FSA approved directors performing the controlled function of directors.

(3)   Certain key decisions relating to the firm's business relevant to the treatment of customers were taken by the two individual controllers of the company who lived outside the UK rather than by the firm's directors as should have been the case.

(4)   The firm also used an unauthorised marketing company to gather information concerning customers' financial circumstances on the basis of which the firm's staff would make initial product recommendations prior to the customer seeing a qualified adviser, never mind filling out an appropriate questionnaire concerning their circumstances. The firm thus failed to take reasonable steps to make sure that advice given was suitable in that the mortgages taken out were affordable, appropriate to the needs of the customers and the most suitable.

(5)   The firm did not provide customers with appropriate product information in the form of a key facts illustration before completing the mortgage applications. This was a particular problem because a significant propor-

tion of the customers were consolidating debts into a new mortgage because they faced repayment difficulties.

(6) Nor did the firm have an adequate complaints handling procedure in place.

---

1 26 June 2006.

9.153 In addition certain of the FSA rules were relevant: 2.1.1R, 3.1.1R of Senior Management Systems and Controls, 4.7.2R, 4.7.4R, 4.7.6R and 5.5.1R in Mortgages: Conduct of Business, and 1.2.1R and 1.2.22R in Dispute Resolution Complaints.

9.154 Rainbow's situation was however mitigated by their behaviour:

- the firm accepted that its systems and controls were inadequate and therefore ceased carrying on any further regulated activities;

- the FSA's investigation showed that none of the customers approached were unhappy with the service they had been provided with;

- the firm had agreed to carry out a review of mortgage business transacted within the period and to provide redress where appropriate; and

- they had fully co-operated with the FSA.

As a result of these factors they received a 30% discount on the penalty and were fined £30,000.

9.155 The most recent case at the time of writing was the FSA enforcement action against *Hoodless Brennan plc*[1]. The basis of the action was the firm had acted in breach of FSA Principles 2, 6 and 7 together with COB 2.1.3R relating to communications with customers being clear, fair and not misleading and COB 5.4.3R. In essence their behaviour was at fault in that:

1 they did not deal appropriately with the issue of whether information about the price information service they had contracted to offer to its customers was in the public domain;

2 they did not take sufficient steps to make sure broking staff were fully aware of the contract entered into in this regard, nor were they briefed as to whether they could mention it to customers when it was not in the public domain;

3 they did consider whether the firm they had agreed to purchase the price information from might have to make a public announcement but took no professional advice and made assumptions;

4 broking staff engaged in unacceptable selling practices such as persuading customers to buy stock when they were not ready to do so and to take

more stock than they appeared to want, though only a small number of customers were affected and no complaints received;

5   when retailing broking staff retailed shares in the company they provided personal opinions and used the existence of the contract as an inappropriate sales aid despite having had no guidance or training on it;

6   a lack of specific information was provided in some instances when investing in penny shares in the firm the price information was being purchased from.

Hoodless Brennan were fined £90,000.

---

1 FSA Enforcement Action 16 August 2006.

Conduct of Business rules

9.156   The FSA COB rules deal with the subject of advice, primarily at COB 5.1. Two of the FSA Principles, 6 on customers' interests and 7 on communication with clients are also relevant.

Much of the concern in COB 5 focuses on the need to make sure the private customers are adequately informed about the nature of the advice they may receive in relation to packaged products. The advisers must also make clear the scope and range of the products and product providers on which their advice is based.

9.157   Where packaged products are concerned the FSA have concerns due to the risks to consumers. (Packaged products are life policies, units in a regulated collective investment scheme, an interest in an investment trust savings scheme or a stakeholder pension scheme, whether or not held in an Independent Savings Account or Child Trust Fund and whether or not the packaged product is also a stakeholder product). These concerns arise because some of the investment vehicles are complex, some have the risk that the capital amount available at the end will be less than the amounts paid in and some may involve time delays in drawing down the money and yet others may face complications arising from the product being designed to reduce a tax liability. These are not exclusive and many will combine some or all of these elements. As a result COB 5 requires that those advising in this area take on board certain requirements. COB 5.1 states that a firm giving advice to private customers on packaged products must take reasonable steps to make sure that the advice given is based on one of:

•   the whole relevant market;

•   a limited number of product providers; or

321

● a single company or group of companies.

9.158 This is because some financial advisers are tied to one product provider and are therefore only in a position to advise on their products. Others are independent and are therefore supposed to advise on the full product range available. For many years these were the only two possibilities (called 'polarisation') but larger financial institutions repeatedly lobbied for a middle approach to be permitted where an adviser could advise between a range of products from a small range of suitable providers. The current rules reflect this state of affairs. It is vital that which of these situations the adviser is operating in must be made clear at the outset to the customer[1].

1 COB 5.1.6B.

9.159 To make sure that advisers only advise within the scope of their expertise and licences firms must keep an up-to-date, written record of appointed representatives including the range of packaged products on which they can advise. Records must also be kept of the scope of the advice given and be retained for six years. The record for distribution to customers must set out the range of packaged products which is appropriate for the service provided to the customer and include details of the identity of the product providers whose products the firm may sell and a list of the categories of products. There must also be a record of the range of packaged products on which its advice to customers is based and this must also be kept for a minimum of six years.

9.160 There is also protection for customers in terms of being sure who is providing a packaged product. Rule 5.1.6F requires that if a firm advises a private customer on a packaged product produced by someone else they must make sure that they do not hold themselves out as being the producer. Advice on packaged products can in any event only be given provided the product is within the range that the firm's licence permits it to advise on[1]. If advice is held out as being independent then it must either consist of advice given across the whole market, or a sector of it.

1 COB 5.1.7R.

9.161 To stop customers having to pay by commission, and therefore in some cases end up paying an excessive amount for the work provided, rule 5.1.11A requires a firm to offer the alternative of fee based advice. Coupled with this is the risk that advisers become blinded by the commissions that are available from certain products and recommend them in inappropriate circumstances. For this reason firms must make sure none of their representatives are compensated excessively in proportion to the commission they bring in. The bulk of their remuneration should therefore be by way of salary.

9.162 The core suitability rule is COB 5.3 which requires that when an adviser makes a recommendation to a private customer[1], (unless it is a stakeholder product) reasonable care must be taken to ensure the suitability of the advice. This is also a requirement of Principle 9. Specifically it applies to personal recommendations to buy sell, subscribe for or underwrite investments, to elect to make income withdrawals or buy a short-term annuity, enter into a pension transfer or opt out from an occupational pension scheme, or effect a discretionary transaction, or where a recommendation is made to an intermediate client or a market counterparty to take out a life policy. In the case of packaged products the one recommended must be the most suitable from the range on which advice is given. If there is not one no recommendation should be made. It is also possible to go 'out of range' and recommend a packaged product outside the range of those on which the firm provided advice to that client provided it would have been at least as suitable as the most appropriate one inside the range[2]. The analysis carried out prior to the recommendation must in any case consist of analysing a sufficiently large number of packaged products which are generally available on the market, or where appropriate from the relevant sector[3].

1 This does not apply to a financial promotion other than one promoting a personal pension scheme. COB 5.3.2G.
2 COB 5.3.8A R.
3 COB 5.3.10A R.

9.163 If a customer has pooled his funds with others with a view to obtaining common discretionary management instructions, the firm must take reasonable steps to make sure the transaction being considered is suitable for the fund bearing in mind its stated investment objectives[1].

1 COB 5.3.5(5).

9.164 Suitability letters must also be provided to a customer prior to the conclusion of the matter in hand where the matter consists of:

● buying, selling, surrendering, converting, cancelling or suspending premiums to a pension or stakeholder pension scheme;

● making income withdrawals or buying a short-term annuity;

● acquiring a holding in or selling part of the holding in a scheme; or

● entering into a pension transfer or pension opt out from an occupational pension scheme[1].

1 COB 5.3.14 R.

9.165 This letter must explain why the firm decided that the transaction was suitable and contain a summary of the main consequences of it and any disadvantages to the transaction. The individual who advised the customer must be identified. There are specific requirements in 5.3.16 that where the matter concerned a personal pension scheme or a free-standing AVC and where the recommended product is from a product provider or its immediate group, the disclosure information given in the original disclosure document must be repeated. If a recommendation has been made out of the firm's normal product range the reasons for its recommendation and suitability must be set out. In the case of intermediate customers and market counterparties the reasons for the recommendation of any life policy must be set out. Suitability letters must be kept for three years unless it relates to a life policy, pension contract or stakeholder pension scheme in which case it is six years. In the case of letters relating to pension transfers, pension opt outs or free-standing AVCs they must be kept indefinitely[1].

---

1 COB 5.3.19A R.

9.166 A suitability letter is not needed where:

- the firm is acting as an investment manager for a private customer and makes a recommendation relating to a regulated collective investment scheme.;

- the firm is not acting as an outgoing ECA provider and the customer is habitually resident in another EEA state at the time they consent to the recommendation;

- if the customer is habitually resident outside the EEA and the customer is not present in the UK when they acknowledge consent to the recommendation;

- a small policies exemption applies where it is a personal recommendation by a friendly society for a life policy with a premium not exceeding £50 per year or £52 if payable weekly;

- it is a personal recommendation to increase a regular premium to an existing contract; and

- it is a personal recommendation to make additional contributions to an existing packaged product[1].

---

1 COB 5.3.19 R.

Chapter 10

Complaint rules and the Financial Ombudsman Service

10.1   The Financial Ombudsman Services acts as an independent complaint ombudsman services for consumers of the financial industry and in the five years since 2001 has seen complaint references rise to 110,000 cases per year. However, the true volume of complaints in the financial services industry is not clear because most firms resolve the majority of the complaints they receive internally only a small proportion of complaints made by consumers find their way to the Ombudsman Service. The FSA-led endowment policy review has alone led to an increase in complaint numbers and complaints of this type accounted for 2/3rds of the FOS workload in 2005 and to keep pace with demand and an increasing workload staff levels at FOS have increased from around 350 in 2001 to 1,000 in 2005. In addition to the complaints it handles, the FOS also handles 615,000 enquiries a year and predicts this will increase to 690,000 enquiries a year in 2006/07.

10.2   Although the FOS predicts that overall complaint numbers will decrease slightly over the next few years, without further analysis that does not provide a true picture of the level of complaints in the industry. The scope of the FOS jurisdiction is likely to widen and the decrease in endowment complaint volumes is likely to be filled with complaints arising from consumers of products currently outside of the FOS scope. By way of example in October 2004 the FSMA was extended to cover Mortgage business and General Insurance in January 2005. Further amending provisions are proposed that will cause the regulation of Self Invested Personal Pensions Schemes and Equity Release Schemes and Islamic Home finance products in 2006. Moreover to meet EU legislation, the government is considering the feasibility of extending the FSA's role in regulating sectors such as money service business, trust and company service providers and firms providing consumer credit. This extension to the FSA's role is likely to provide challenges to consumer protection and the role of the Financial Ombudsman Service.

10.3   The FOS's role in adjudicating on complaints, should, however not be viewed as a litigation service for firms. FSA rules make it clear that regulated business must have in place arrangements for dealing with complaints from their customers and the FSA's expects that all complaints that can be reasonably identified as legitimate must be fully investigated and settled by the firm with the customer.

10.4   In the Chairman's foreword to the FOS annual report for 2004/05, Sir Christopher Kelly KCB stated:

> 'the last year has seen another significant increase in the workload of the ombudsman service, caused entirely by the continuing flood of mortgage endowment complaints. Meeting the demands that this has involved has posed considerable operational challenges. Complaints-handling resource is not a tap that can just be turned on and off. We have mounted an intensive – and successful – recruitment and training programme, and our staff have responded magnificently at all levels. But the stresses this imposes on the organisation are considerable. If we are to continue to provide a fair and effective service – resolving disputes within reasonable timescales – complaints-handling by some financial firms must improve, so that a smaller proportion of disputes need to be referred to the ombudsman service, or better still, so that the causes of disputes can be reduced.'

10.5   In this chapter we will consider the obligations placed on firms to have procedures for dealing with Investor complaints together with the arrangements under ss 225–234 of the Financial Services and Markets Act 2000 (FSMA 2000) for the establishment and operation of the Financial Ombudsman Service. In particular this chapter will address, the legal basis for the Financial Ombudsman scheme and the FSA rules relating to complaint handling. It will go on to consider standard approaches for internal complaint handling and system and controls including the consequences for firms when dealing with complaints referred by a complaints management company, together with standard approaches for dealing with complaints referred to the FOS.

Why do consumers complain and why have an ombudsman system?

10.6   Greater numbers of people are aware of their rights as consumers and are prepared to ensure their rights are respected. Consumers regularly resort to the law wherever they consider use of the legal system is the best method to uphold their rights. As a result, case numbers in the courts are high which, in turn, can contribute towards delay. By way of example, in 2005, 1,610,347 money claims were issued in county courts in England and Wales (a rise of 17% over the previous year) and the average waiting period for a trial was 52[1] weeks. For consumers that have suffered a disadvantage at the hands of a financial adviser or an investment firm, resorting to law can be a costly and time consuming exercise. In addition, the tactics of delay often encountered during a litigation can cause anxiety and distress and even consumers with good prospects of success will give up their case, or settle their claims at a level they ultimately feel unsatisfied with.

---

1 Department of Constitutional Affairs, Judicial Statistics Annual report (Revised) 2005, August 2006, Section 4 County Courts Table 4.1.

10.7   Understanding the standard and level of service to expect of a financial services firm can be problematic for the non-professional investor. The nature of intangible products such as stocks, bonds and packaged products cause difficulties for the investor wishing to determine whether an acceptable level of service has or has not been received. Compare this to a consumer purchasing a new domestic appliance. The consumer will know very soon whether the item is defective. It may not operate at all or only in part, and the consumer will be in a position to develop an appreciation of what to expect from the product by reference to whether it does the job it is described as being able to perform. Consumers will carry out their own immediate assessment of the product in comparison to this information and use their own knowledge and experience to determine the value of what they have received.

10.8   Investment products, however, can be complex. Whilst consumers may be able to calculate the value of certain investments this may not always be possible and in the case of many packaged products, investors may not always be in a position to determine easily whether they have received suitable advice if the investment has been sold as part of a complex financial planning exercise. For example, following the availability of personal pensions as an alternative to occupational pensions, investors were generally unable to determine whether they had been appropriately advised, wether to opt out or not join their employers' occupational pension schemes in preference to a personal pension.

10.9   A variety of factors also determine the cause for investor complaints and it doesn't always seem to be the case that a high level of complaints offers a direct correlation to the standards or quality of the advice or service provided by a firm although a high propensity of complaints can be a good indicator of the standard of service offered by a firm. The performance of the financial markets affects investment returns and upturns and downturn in the stock market affect the behaviour of consumers. As a general rule the financial industry will experience an increase in complaints about the mis-selling of investments when the market goes down in value. Consumers tend not to complain about their investments, even if they are mis-sold, when investment performance is good. Campaigns directed at consumers by the Financial Services Authority, consumer bodies, the financial press or even claims management companies may give rise to an increase in consumer complaints about their investment: by way of example the Financial Ombudsman Service, in its annual review of 1 April to 31 March 2005, it reported that it had received 5,500 split capital complaints following the collapse of these types of investments. The impact of regulation or regulatory initiatives may lead to a rise in complaint numbers. A change in FSA rules may increase consumers expectations and the improvement in financial education might affect the consumers' view on investment already made or raise their propensity to complain. The FOS also report in their corporate plan and budget for 2006/07 a concern that changes in firms' complaint management can also directly affect the number of complaints that are referred to the FOS. They suggest that a small change in a firm's approach can have a significant effect on the number of complaints referred to them and they provide the following example:

- if a firm satisfactorily resolves 95 in 100 complaints, 5 in 100 of these complaints may be brought to the Ombudsman Service;

- if a firm satisfactorily resolves only 90 in 100 complaints (about 5% fewer), 10 in 100 of these complaints may be brought to the ombudsman service (100% more)[1].

The Financial Ombudsman Service was established to provide an impartial, fair, accessible, timely, informal, efficient and free to consumer method of resolving complaints awarding compensation or redress where it is appropriate. The system was specifically established to encourage complaints to be resolved by firms before they reach the Ombudsman service.

---

1 Financial Ombudsman Service Corporate Plan & 2006/07 Budget. Section 2 a demand-led service.

The legal basis for the Financial Ombudsman Service

10.10   The FSMA 2000 makes provision for the establishment of a single complaints resolution scheme covering all authorised activities under the Act. The statutory framework for the scheme is contained within FSMA 2000, ss 225–234 and Appendix 17 to the Act which sets out the detailed provisions for the scheme's constitution and jurisdiction. FSMA 2000, s 225(1) sets out the general objective for the scheme, as follows: '... *a scheme under which certain disputes may be resolved quickly and with minimum formality by an independent person*'. Section 225(2) to the Act also specifies that the scheme administration must be undertaken by a scheme operator which must be a corporate body. Appendix 17, Part 2 sets out the legislative and constitutional requirements for the scheme operator and specifies matters relating to the scheme's consitution, appointment of a panel of ombudsman the roel and duties of a chief ombudsmen, the requirement of an annual report and the budget and fees for the running of the scheme. It is the scheme operator that is known as the Financial Ombudsman Service.

Constitution

10.11   The scheme operator is required to have a Chairman and board (being the scheme operator's directors). The Chairman and scheme board members are appointed and removed by the FSA and in the case of the Chairman his appointment and removal must also be approved by the Treasury. Despite the FSA's critical role in the appointment of both board members and the scheme chairman, the terms of their appointment must under para 3(3) of Sch 17 be such as to secure their independence from the FSA in the operation of the scheme. The board members are essentially non-executive directors as they have no role in dealing with individual complaint cases. Their formal role and powers are provided in the scheme's memorandum and articles of association.

The current scheme Chairman is Sir Christopher Kelly and the Scheme Operator has a further eight board members.

Panel of Ombudsmen

10.12   The scheme operator is required to maintain a panel of ombudsmen each of whom must have qualifications and experience appropriate to act as ombudsman under the scheme[1]. The Ombudsmens' appointments are required to be made on terms that are considered by the scheme operator to be consistent with the notion of the independence of the persons role. The scheme currently has a panel of 8 Principal Ombudsmen and 24 Ombudsmen each responsible for and covering specific areas of investment and financial services business.

---

1 FSMA 2000, Sch 17, para 4(1).

Chief Ombudsman

10.13   FSMA 2000, Sch 17, para 5 requires that the scheme operator appoint one member of the panel of Ombudsmen as Chief Ombudsman. The Chief Ombudsman's responsibilities include reporting each year to the FSA on the discharge of his functions. The current Chief Ombudsman is Walter Merricks.

Annual scheme report

10.14   Each year the scheme operator is required to make an annual report to the FSA on how it has discharged its functions, separating out in its report matters relating to its voluntary jurisdiction from the compulsory jurisdiction (further details relating to the Ombudsman Jurisdiction is set out in paragraphs

10.19 – 10.25 below). The annual report must also include a report from the Chief Ombudsman on the discharge of his functions.

Typically the FOS report is published in June on the FOS website.

10.15 In its report for the year 2004/05 the Chief Ombudsman's report included a statement concerning the rise in complaints referred to the scheme. He stated:

'... This year alone, the number of new complaints reaching the Ombudsman Service increased by 57% on the previous year (which itself saw a 44% annual increase).

This significant rise has been driven by the flood of mortgage endowment complaints – from under 15,000 last year to over 50,000 this year. Neither we nor the financial services industry – which we consult on our workload estimates – had forecast a surge on such a major scale. It has meant that this has been a year of dealing with big numbers and big operational challenges ...'

Funding, fees and budget

10.16 The operation of the scheme is funded in part by an industry levy (known as the general levy) paid by all authorised persons together with individual case fees charged to the respondent authorised persons in respect of each complaint about them concluded by the Ombudsman Service. For the financial year running from 1 April 2006 to 31 March 2007, the scheme is budgeting to collect £15.8m by way of general levy and £43.2m by way of case fees[1]. In respect of the general levy, FSMA 2000, s 234 allows the FSA to make rules requiring authorised persons to make payment to cover the cost of both the establishment and operation of the scheme. FSA sourcebook rules at FEES 5.3.6R requires an authorised firm to pay to the FSA the general levy which goes toward the cost of operating the scheme's compulsory jurisdiction. The general levy is calculated by way of a system of fee tariffs by reference to industry classification (known as industry blocks). To arrive at each firm's general levy payment for a year, an authorised person is first classified by reference to the appropriate industry block (it is possible for a business to fall into more than one block). Secondly the tariff for each block is then used to calculate the fee to be paid for each block a firm's businesses falls into. Tariffs for each block are either fixed fees or represent a firm's business volumes or number of certain categories of approved persons within the firm. The industry blocks and tariff bases are set out in FEES 5, Annex 1R, Part 2.

---

1 Financial Ombudsman Service Corporate Plan and 2006/07 budget, section 8.

10.17   The general levy is collected each year by the FSA. To enable it to collect the correct amount from each firm rule FEES 5.4.1R (1) requires all authorised firms (save those paying the general levy on a flat fee basis) to file with the FSA by the end of February each year a statement of the total amount of business it conducted in the year or as at 31 December in the previous year. A failure to file the appropriate statement on time results in a fixed penalty administrative charge and may expose the authorised person to further disciplinary action[1].

---

1 FSA rule FEES 5.4.1(5) R.

10.18   In respect of individual case fees Sch 17, para 15 (in relation to the compulsory jurisdiction) and para 18(2) (in relation to the voluntary jurisdiction), state that the scheme rules are permitted to require a respondent to a complaint to pay a fee in relation to that case. This ability is confirmed in FSA rules FEES 5.5.1R. which requires firms to pay a case fee in respect of a chargeable case, defined as a case referred to the FOS except where the Ombudsman considers the complaint should not proceed because either the complainant is not eligible or the compliant does not fall within the FOS jurisdiction or the FOS considers the complaint should be dismissed without consideration of its merits or on grounds that it is frivolous or vexatious[1]. The FSA have, however, adopted a more sophisticated approach to the calculation of fees for individual complaint cases recognising first that the majority of authorised persons have very little exposure to the operation of the scheme, whereas the majority of the scheme's complaints work is derived from a small number of large businesses and second that complaints from consumers that are themselves small businesses[2] tend to be by their very nature more complex[3]. Under rule FEES 5.5.15 R firms are only liable to pay a standard of special case fee in respect or the third and any subsequent case in the year. The level of fees is £360 in respect of the standard case fee and £475 in respect of the special case fee.

Rules have been made to allow any unpaid case fees to be collected by the FSA.

---

1 See FSA Glossary definition of chargeable complaint.
2 Small businesses as eligible complainants as defined in DISP 2.4.3R (1)(b), (c) or (d).
3 Under Rule FEES 5.5.3R applying to Credit Unions and 5.5.4R applying to cash plan health providers and small friendly societies there is no obligation to pay the standard case fee in relation to those industry blocks. These businesses (save where they may conduct business in other industry blocks) contribute to the operation of the scheme through the general levy only.

Jurisdiction and scope

10.19   The FSMA provides for two parts to the scheme. The first relating to complaints over which the FOS has compulsory jurisdiction and the second to complaints over which it has voluntary jurisdiction. In essence, the compulsory jurisdiction requires authorised forms to submit to the jurisdiction of the scheme for resolution of any complaints made against it by its customers. The voluntary jurisdiction allows firms to participate in the ombudsman scheme where they are not authorised by the FSA, or in respect of activities falling outside the compulsory scheme.

10.20   The FOS only has jurisdiction to consider complaints made in relation to activities carried on by a firm or its appointed representative from an establishment in the United Kingdom[1]. The FOS therefore does not have jurisdiction in its compulsory scheme to consider complaints concerning business conducted by branches of firms outside of the United Kingdom or by EEA firms operating on a services basis from outside of the United Kingdom.

---

1 DISP 2.7.1R.

The compulsory scheme

10.21   The compulsory scheme has jurisdiction to deal with eligible complaints relating to regulated activities of authorised persons. The Statutory provisions relating to the scheme's compulsory jurisdiction scheme are contained in FSMA 2000, ss 226, 228 and Part III, Sch 17.

10.22   The main thrust of the compulsory elements relate only to complaints where certain conditions apply. These conditions, contained in FSMA 2000, s 226 are:

- the complainant is an eligible complainant, that is he falls within a class of person specified in the rules (the meaning of eligible complainant is considered further in **10.28** below);

- the complainant wishes to have their complaint dealt with under the scheme;

- the respondent to the complainant is an authorised person at the time of the act or omission complained of;

- the act or omission occurred at a time when the compulsory jurisdiction rules were in force in relation to the activity complained of; and

- only regulated activities specified in the scheme rules may be the subject of the complaint.

10.23   The scheme operator is required under Sch 17, para 14 to make rules relating to its compulsory jurisdiction setting out the procedure for the reference of complaints, their investigation, consideration and determination. The scheme operator must publish any draft of scheme rules that it proposes and within a time limit that it may specify take into any representations about its proposals[1].

The scheme's compulsory jurisdiction rules are set out in FSA rules DISP. Specific key provisions relating to the scheme's compulsory jurisdiction rules are set out in **10.26** below.

---

1 FSMA 2000, Sch 17, para 14(4)–(7).

The voluntary scheme

10.24 The voluntary scheme has jurisdiction in dealing with complaints from persons who are either not authorised persons or where the subject of the complaint is not a regulated investment and cannot be dealt with under the compulsory scheme. The fundamental precondition for a complaint being dealt with under the voluntary jurisdiction is that the respondent to the complaint is participating in the scheme.

10.25 The Statutory provisions relating to the scheme's Voluntary Jurisdiction are contained in FSMA 2000, s 227 and Pt IV, Sch 17. The main thrust of the voluntary elements relate only to complaints where certain conditions apply. These conditions, contained in FSMA 2000, s 227 are:

- the complainant must be an eligible complainant as defined in the voluntary scheme rules (see **10.28** for further discussion on the definition of the term Eligible Compainant);
- the complainant wishes to have their complaint dealt with under the Voluntary Scheme;
- at the time of the act or omission complained of, the respondent was participating in the scheme;
- the respondent has not withdrawn from the scheme at the time the complaint is made;
- the act or omission complained of occurred at a time when the voluntary jurisdiction rules were in force in relation to the activity in question; and the complaint can not be dealt with under the scheme's compulsory jurisdiction.

The scheme's voluntary jurisdiction rules are set out in DISP. Specific key provisions relating to the schemes Voluntary Jurisdiction rules are set out in **10.31** below.

FOS complaint rules

10.26 The scheme rules set out the procedure for the investigation, consideration and determination of complaints and are designed to ensure that the scheme's objective of providing an independent, informal and quick complaint resolution service is met.

10.27 Although the provisions relating to the compulsory and voluntary jurisdiction schemes derive from different sections of FSMA 2000, the FSA complaint rules have attempted to unify the two different scheme rules wherever possible so as to provide for a single process for consumers when dealing with the Financial Ombudsman Service no matter whether they are raising a compulsory or voluntary jurisdiction complaint. A five-step basic test must be applied to determine whether FOS has jurisdicion to deal with any individual complaint. (further steps are also necessary in relation to complaints made in relation to activities occurring before FOS jurisdiction came into effect and also certain mortgage and general insurance matters). Each of the following steps must be satisfied:

Eligible Complainants

10.28 **Step 1:** Is the complaint made by an Eligible Complainant? The term Eligible Complainant is a defined term in DISP 2.4 and is a critical term throughout both the legislation and rules underpinning the Ombudsman Scheme. The process of determining whether someone is an Eligible Complainant is in itself a complex process requiring two key issues to be satisfied. The first test is whether the complainant is within a certain class of person described in DISP 2.4.3R. The second test is whether the complainant has either:

(a) a customer or potential customer relationship with the firm complained of. To determine whether a customer relationship exists, assistance is provided by DISP 2.4.7R 'customers' and 2.4.8R 'potential customers'. Unfortunately both definitions are somewhat circular as they both rely on the unprecisely defined use of the word customer. It is therefore sensible to assume that a customer is someone that has used or currently uses the investment services of the firm. The scheme rules define a customer as someone that is or has been a customer of the firm and whose complaint arises out of matters relevant to his being or having been a customer of the firm and is in one of the classes of person in DISP 2.4.3(1)R. The definition of a Potential customer once again receives a limited definition and the attempt to define the term should be viewed more as a qualification of the term. A potential customer is defined as someone whose complaint arises out of the firm's actions or failure to act for the complainant in his capacity as a potential customer of the firm and who falls into one of the classes of persons in DISP 2.4.3(1)R. The FSA attempt to qualify the definition by providing an example, at DISP 2.4.4G, of the type of situation that would give rise to a potential customer complaint. They suggest that it would apply where a firm is alleged to have caused financial loss, material inconvenience or material distress arising out of its maladministration or illegal discrimination leading to its services not being provided. By way of example this situation could occur where a

Stockbroker firm dealing with a person who instructs that he wants to sell securities he holds, fails to open an account for the person despite having all necessary information to enable it to and in the meantime the value of the securities falls. Without determining the merits of the complaint the FOS would have to be satisfied that the facts of the consumer's dealings with the firms were such that it gave rise to a potential customer situation. Classes of persons which are essentially private individuals and small businesses are defined in DISP 2.4.3(1)R as:

(a)   a private individual; or

(b)   a business, which has a group annual turnover of less than £1million at the time the complainant refers the complaint to the firm, or

(c)   a charity which has an annual income of less than £1million at the time the complainant refers the complaint to the firm, or

(d)   a trustee of a trust which has a net asset value of less than £1million at the time the complainant refers the complaint to the firm

Certain types of persons are, however, specifically excluded by DISP 2.4.3 (2) R from the specified classes of persons:

(a)   an individual, business, charity or trustee, who was an intermediate customer or market counterparty in relation to the firm in question at the time of the act or omission, and in respect of the activity, which is the subject of the complaint;

(b)   a firm whose complaint relates in any way to an activity which the firm itself has permission to carry on or which the Voluntary Jurisdiction participant itself conducts, and which is subject to the Compulsory Jurisdiction or the Voluntary Jurisdiction of the FOS.

(b)   an indirect relationship with the firm that is the subject of the complaint[1].

---

1 Transitional rules apply to relevant complaints from eligible customers of mortgage and general insurance that became regulated by the FSA in October 2004 and January 2005 respectively. See the Ombudsman Transitional Order and Mortgage and General Insurance Transitional Order.

FOS Jurisdiction

10.29   **Step 2:** Is the firm complained of subject to the compulsory or voluntary jurisdiction of the scheme? All authorised firms and authorised professional firms and Voluntary scheme participants are subject to the jurisdiction of FOS. A series of provisions relate to eligible complaints about unauthorised persons who were authorised at the time the matter complained of arose[1].

---

1 FSMA 2000, s 226.

10.30 **Step 3:** Does the activity complained of fall within the compulsory or voluntary scheme? The Ombudsman can consider a complaint under the Compulsory Jurisdiction relating to an act or omission by a firm in the carrying on of one or more of the following activities:

- Regulated activities;

- Lending money secured by a charge on land;

- Lending money (other than restricted credit which is a loan for which, the customer's application to the firm is submitted through a supplier and the terms of the loan require that it be paid to the supplier for goods or services supplied to the customer);

- Paying money by plastic card (other than a store card);

- Provision of ancillary banking services.

The compulsory jurisdiction also includes any activities ancillary to the items above, which would in the main include advice provided by a firm in relation to them.

The voluntary scheme

10.31 The Ombudsman can consider a complaint under the Voluntary Jurisdiction only if it is not covered by the Compulsory Jurisdiction and it relates to an act or omission in the carrying on of one or more of the following activities by a Voluntary Jurisdiction participant. This would for example be non-regulated activities by authorised firms and the specified activities below by firms that are not-authorised.

- Accepting deposits;

- Lending money (other than restricted credit);

- Paying money by a plastic card (not a store card);

- Provision of ancillary banking services;

- National savings and investments business;

- Together with provisions relating to business covered by any former schemes that the Voluntary Jurisdiction participant was a member in respect of activity before 30 November 2001 and any activities that were regulated at the time the Voluntary Jurisdiction participant joined the scheme but was not a regulated activity at the time of the act or omission complained of.

The Voluntary Jurisdiction also includes any activities that are ancillary to those listed above. This would include for example advice provided on the listed activities.

Firm's internal investigation

10.32   **Step 4:** Has the firm failed to resolve the complaint to the satisfaction of the complainant within eight weeks of receiving it?

The FOS will generally not deal with a complaint until the firm has had an opportunity of dealing with the matter under its own internal procedures first. DISP 2.3.1R provides, however, that FOS may not deal with the complaint where there is less than eight weeks from the date when the firm received the complaint from the complainant, unless the firm has sent the complainant its final response (for an analysis of final response letter see **10.73–10.74** below).

Limitation period

10.35   **Step 5:** Is the complaint made within the required period of time?

Strict time limits are included in DISP 2.3.1R that essentially act as a limitation date for the FOS jurisdiction over complaints in both the Compulsory and Voluntary Jurisdiction. The limitation operates to restrict complaints in terms of the time between when they were finally responded to by a firm and when they were referred to FOS and also between the date when the event complained of occurred and the date when they were referred to FOS. DISP 2.3.1(b)R states that the FOS cannot consider a complaint if it is referred to it more than six months after the date when the firm sends the complainant the final response letter. DISP 2.3.1(c)R states that FOS cannot consider a complaint referred to it more than six years after the event complained of or if later more than three years from the date on which the complainant became aware or ought reasonably to have become aware that he had cause for a complaint.

10.36   Notwithstanding these limitations, FOS, however, has a general discretion under DISP 2.3.1(2)R to consider complaints outside of time where it considers that the complainant's failure to comply with the time limit was as a result of exceptional circumstances or where the firm consents to the complaint being dealt with[1]. The FSA provides in DISP 2.3.3G examples of the incapacity of a complainant or a firm's failure to properly notify a complainant of the time limits relating to their complaints as potential exceptional circumstances.

---

1 Ombudsman Transitional Order 2001, SI 2001/2326.

10.37 Special provisions do, however, apply to past business reviews approved under FSMA 2000, s 404 where the time limits above do not apply[1] and complaints relating to mortgage endowment complaints where the complaint must be referred to the FOS no later than three years from the date when the complainant receives a warning letter from the firm[2].

---

1 DISP 2.3.5R.
2 See **10.35** and **10.36**.

10.38 Where the Ombudsman considers that both the complaint and the complainant are eligible and that there is a reasonable prospect of resolving the complaint by mediation, he may attempt to negotiate a settlement between the parties[1]. The FOS approach to settlement enables it to come up with a solution that satisfies both sides, by taking a fresh look at the facts and identifying and agreeing the key issues as they see them.

---

1 DISP 3.2.9R.

Investigation and adjudication

10.39 If the FOS decides that it is necessary to investigate a complaint it will provide both parties an opportunity of making representations[1]. At this point the matter will be assigned to an FOS adjudicator. Commonly the adjudicator will write to both parties requesting information and providing them with an opportunity to answer any questions considered helpful to the investigation.

---

1 DISP 3.2.11R.

10.40 Following its investigation the FOS will send to the parties a provisional assessment, setting out his reasons and a time limit within which either party must respond and if either party indicates disagreement with the provisional assessment within the time limit prescribed the matter will proceed to determination by an Ombudsman[1].

---

1 DISP 3.2.11(3)R.

Request and analysis of evidence

10.41 DISP 1.6.1R requires firms to co-operate fully with the ombudsman in the handling of complaints against it. This requirement extends to the disclosure and production of all documents requested by the ombudsman within the time limits set out. Implicitly a firm in possession of evidence that has been requested, but which it does not disclose will be in breach of DISP 1.6.1 and be exposed to FSA enforcement action. Usually, during the initial assessment of a new compliant the ombudsman case adjudicator will make a specific request for any documents that he or she considers relevant to the adjudication of the complaint. DISP 3.5.1R entitles the ombudsman in relation to the evidence which may be required or admitted on a complaint, to give directions on the issues on which evidence is required, whether that evidence should be oral or in writing and the manner in which it should be presented. DISP 3.5.2R entitles the ombudsman to reach a decision on the basis of the evidence and documents that have been supplied as well as taking account any evidence that has not been supplied.

Reference to an ombudsman

10.42   The parties will be informed of their right to make representations before the Ombudsman makes a determination. If he considers that the complaint can be fairly determined without convening a hearing, he will so determine the complaint.

10.43   Oral hearings may take place where the Ombudsman considers that the complaint cannot be determined fairly without a hearing[1]. Either party to the complaint may request a hearing (they must do so in writing) setting out the issues they wish to raise and any reasons why they consider the hearing should be in private. The Ombudsman will then consider whether the issues are material and whether a hearing should take place and, if so, whether it should be held in public or private. In deciding if there should be a hearing and, if so, whether it should be in public or private, the Ombudsman will have regard to the provisions of the European Convention on Human Rights. If a hearing is to take place the parties will be invited to attend the hearing.

---

1 DISP 3.2.12R.

Case decisions, law and precedent

10.44   When determining complaints, under FSMA 2000, s 228(2) and DISP 3.8.1R the Ombudsman is required to determine a case by '… what is, in the opinion of the ombudsman, fair and reasonable in all the circumstances of the case.' When considering what is fair and reasonable DISP 3.8.1R states that the Ombudsman will take into account relevant law, codes of practice, and FSA rules and guidance. The manner in which the ombudsman must take into account relevant law and provide clear reasoning for a decision to depart from that law was considered in the case *R (on the application of IFG Financial Services Ltd) v Financial Ombudsman Services Ltd*[1]. In that case, IFG Financial

Services Ltd had advised a husband and wife client to invest monies into two investment funds which did not meet their stated attitude to investment risk. The funds advised by IFG were high risk investments and in the case of one of the investments (a fund called FCS) the fund manager improperly managed the monies. The clients complained to the Ombudsman and in relation to the FCS investment, IFG contended that the loss to the client arising from the fund manager's dishonesty was not a loss in respect of which compensation should be payable as in law such dishonesty was outside of their responsibility and liability. IFG relied on legal authority in the House of Lords case of *South Australia Asset Management Corporation v York Montague Ltd²*. The Ombudsman accepted that the law in that case relating to the irrecoverability of unforeseeable loss arising from the fraud of the fund manager was a correct conclusion of English law, but was entitled to depart from it when considering what was fair and reasonable in all the circumstances of the case. IFG contended that the Ombudsman was required to take that existing law into account and to clearly articulate reasons for departing from it. The case was found in favour of the Ombudsman Service and in his judgment Mr Justice Stanley Burnton stated,
'*... so far as the lack of a clear reason for coming to that conclusion, rather than the conclusion required by English Law is concerned, it does seem to me that it is sufficient for an ombudsman to make clear that which he considers to be fair and reasonable in the circumstances, at least in a case such as this. What is fair and reasonable will often be a matter of judgement and it may be difficult to articulate why one result is considered to be fair and another to be unfair or insufficiently fair. I am therefore not surprised that the ombudsman did no more than to say that a lack of recovery in the present case would have been neither fair nor reasonable ...*'

---

1 [2005] EWHC 1153 (Admin).
2 [1997] AC 191.

10.45   Where evidence is contradictory, the Ombudsman will make decisions on the basis of what he believes is most likely to have happened on the balance of probability. The FOS is not bound by legal precedent or their own previous decisions, but will aim to be consistent in approach when dealing with complaints of particular types.

Decisions, content and their affect

10.46   DISP 3.8.3R sets out the approach an Ombudsman must follow once an individual case has been determined. Initially the Ombudsman must send a signed written statements off to both the complainant and the firm setting out the reasons for the determination. This letter is a requirement in FSMA 2000, s 228(3).

10.47　As well as the reasons for the determination the written statement is required to specify a date by which the complainant must notify the Ombudsman in writing whether he accepts or rejects the determination. If the complainant accepts the determination within the time limit set, it is final and binding on both the complainant and the firm. If, however, the complainant either rejects the determination or does not notify the Ombudsman by the specified date that he accepts the determination, the complainant will be treated as having rejected the determination and the firm will not be bound by it.

The Ombudsman is required to notify the firm of the complainant's response (or lack of response).

Awards, redress and enforcement

10.48　FSMA 2000, s 229 sets out the FOS approach to making awards or redress in respect of complaints under the compulsory jurisdiction. Section 229(2) specifies that the FOS determination may include:

(a)　an award against the respondent [firm] of such amount as the Ombudsman considers fair compensation for loss or damage to compensate for financial loss or any other loss, or damage of a specified kind. This is referred to as a monetary award.

(b)　a direction that the respondent firm take steps in relation to the complainant as the Ombudsman considers appropriate (whether or not a court could order those steps to be taken).

10.49　In addition to or instead of awarding compensation for financial loss, the Ombudsman may award compensation for the following kinds of loss or damage, whether or not a court would award compensation[1]:

(a)　pain and suffering;

(b)　damage to reputation;

(c)　distress or inconvenience.

10.50　It is clear from the wording in s 229(2)(a) that in deciding on the appropriate amount of award the Ombudsman is not bound to follow the law when determining fair compensation. This was confirmed in the case of *R (IFRG Financial Services Ltd) v Financial Ombudsman Services Ltd*, Mr Justice Stanley Burton stated, ' ... *in my judgment ...the ombudsman is free to make an award which differs from that which a court applying the law would make, provided he concludes that the award he wishes to make is one which is fair and reasonable in all the circumstances of the case and provided he has taken into account the matters identified in rule 3.8.1 paragraph 2...*'

10.51 Under DISP 3.9.5R the maximum money award which the Ombudsman may make is £100,000, although he may recommend to the firm that it pays an amount more than the maximum where he considers that is fair compensation. However, the firm is not obliged to meet such recommendation[2].

1 DISP 3.9.2R.
2 DISP 3.9.6G.

10.52 The Ombudsman may specify in his award that reasonable interest must be paid on the award (at the rate and from the date he states). The FOS currently calculates interest at 8% simple per annum[1]. For the purposes of calculating the monetary limit in DISP 3.9.5R the amount of interest awarded by the Ombudsman does not form part of the award itself.

1 Ombudsman News, 33 November 2003.

10.53 The question of costs to be awarded following a determination in favour of the complainant often arises but in general it is unusual for costs to be awarded. FSMA 2000, s 230 and DISP 3.9.10R set out the FOS powers to make an award of costs, in addition to the basic monetary award or limit. No award may be made against the complainant in respect of the respondent firm's costs[1]. Given the rationale of the FOS being a free and independent complaints service to the consumer it seems unlikely that in the majority of cases that cost awards would be made and indeed guidance in DISP states, *'It is not anticipated that awards of costs will be common, since in most cases complainants should not need to have professional advisers to bring complaints to the Financial Ombudsman Service.'*

1 FSMA 2000, s 230(3).

10.54 The issue of costs was further clarified in the FOS newsletter in May 2002 when FOS presented a number of case studies illustrating when costs have been awarded and when they have been declined. FOS further stated, 'Very exceptionally, in certain successful complaints we may sometimes consider reimbursing part of the costs. But the circumstances would have to be unusual. We would also have to be convinced that:

●   it was entirely reasonable for the consumer to have sought the third party's assistance, in view of the complexity of the issues involved; and

●   the fees were reasonable.'

10.55 It is likely, however, that the majority of complaints will require conventional monetary compensation. Such compensation is most likely be calculated in accordance with general principles of damages. The FSMA 2000, s 229(8) states that a monetary award is enforceable by the complainant in accordance with Sch 17, Pt III. Schedule 17, para 16 provides that a monetary award, including any interest may, if a county court orders in England and Wales, be recovered by execution issued from the county court as if it were payable under an order of that court.

Appeals

10.56   There is no appeal available from the final decision of an Ombudsman. The Ombudsman independent assessor can consider complaints about the FOS service although does not have any jurisdiction to re-investigate complaints reviewed by an Ombudsman. The assessor, Michael Barnes CBE is appointed by the FOS Board and operates in accordance with a terms of reference. If a complainant is unhappy with the service provided by FOS he may refer the matter to the independent assessor who will consider the matter. If he thinks the service given by FOS is unsatisfactory, he will explain his reasons and will recommend the steps FOS should take to put the matter right. During the year ended 31 March 2005, the independent assessor dealt with 319 referrals and carried out investigations in 164 of these cases – an increase of 36% on the 121 investigations carried out in 2003/04. The assessor upheld the complaint about the Ombudsman Service (either wholly or in part) in 58 of the 164 cases and in all but seven of the 58 upheld complaints made a recommendation that compensation for distress or inconvenience should be paid – the amount of compensation ranging from £50 to £500. The ombudsman service accepted all the recommendations made[1].

---

1 Independent Assessor Annual Report, May 2005.

10.57   Complainants that do not accept the decision of an Ombudsman are not bound to accept their decision. They can, if they so choose, commence legal proceedings as a way of pursuing their complaint further. Firms, however, are bound to accept the Ombudsman's decision, although the FOS is subject to Judicial review. A number of firms have sought to review of Ombudsman's the final decisions. See *R (IRG) v Financial Ombudsman Service Ltd* above.

Consumers and the Ombudsman Service

10.58   The Ombudsman Service has identified its scheme as having the following objectives:

- provide consumers with a free one-stop service for dealing with disputes about financial services;
- resolve disputes quickly and with minimum formality;

343

- offer user-friendly information as well as adjudication and promote avoidance of disputes as well as their resolution;
- take decisions which are consistent, fair and reasonable;
- be cost-effective and efficient and be seen as being good value;
- be accessible to disadvantaged and vulnerable people;
- be forward-looking, adaptable and flexible, making effective use of new technology; and
- be trusted and respected by consumers, the industry and other interested parties.

10.59 For potential complainants the Ombudsman service has published seven points they recommend must be taken into account when making a complaint:

(1) It's usually best to complain to the firm in writing. But if you phone, ask for the name of the person you speak to. Keep a note of this information, with the date and time of your call – and what was said. You may need to refer to this later.

(2) Try to stay calm and polite, however angry or upset you are, that way you're more likely to explain your complaint clearly and effectively.

(3) If possible, start by contacting the person you originally dealt with. If they can't help, say you want to take matters further. Ask for details of the firm's complaints procedure.

(4) If you don't get the information you need, or you're not happy with the way your complaint is being dealt with, contact the most senior person in the firm. This will usually be the CEO.

(5) When you write a letter of complaint, set out the facts as clearly as possible. This will make it easier for the firm to start putting things right.

(6) Write down the facts in a logical order and stick to what is relevant. Remember to include important details like your customer number or your policy or account number. Put these details at the top of your letter.

(7) Keep a copy of your letter. You may need to refer to it later.

Relationship between FOS and the FSA

10.60 Given the Statutory relationship between the FSA and the Financial Ombudsman Service and because their functions are complimentary it has become vital that they both maintain a constructive relationships with each other. A Memorandum of Understanding (MOU) has been entered into between the FSA and FOS the terms being updated on 11 July 2002. The MOU contains terms setting out how both organisations should operate so as to support one anothers role in the regulatory system and provides in particular it provides for the following:

> 'Wherever appropriate the FSA and the Financial Ombudsman Service should achieve consistency of approach and avoid confusion or misunderstanding as to their respective roles'

> 'Authorised firms have a responsibility to identify issues (whether resulting in complaints or not) that may have regulatory implications and for drawing them to the attention of the FSA. The Financial Ombudsman Service also has a responsibility to inform the FSA where it sees indications of issues which may have regulatory implications. It is then the FSA's responsibility to evaluate those implications.[1]'

> 'The Financial Ombudsman Service will provide the FSA with:

> (a) *Briefing and, as required, detailed information on preliminary rulings and final decisions made by an Ombudsman (subject always to the appropriate privacy considerations).*

> (b) *Statistical and qualitative information about its complaints-handling activities on a monthly basis (to include the statistical return for the FSA complaints database).*

> (c) *Reports on the number of complaints made to the Independent Assessor, and their outcomes.'[2]*

> 'The FSA will provide the Financial Ombudsman Service with such information and briefing as is necessary and relevant to the performance of the Financial Ombudsman Service's statutory functions. This will include:

> (a) *Briefing and, as required, detailed information on regulatory action likely to affect the Financial Ombudsman Service in the exercise of its functions.*

> (b) *Briefing and, as required, detailed information on proposed changes to rules or guidance relating to complaints handling or the activities of the Financial Ombudsman Service general.'[3]*

> 'Subject to the appropriate privacy considerations, the Financial Ombudsman Service will provide the FSA with further detailed and specific information relating to a complaint (or complaints):[4]

> (a) Where the circumstances of the case appear to call into question

- a firm's fitness and propriety;

- or whether any person, who may be an approved person for the purposes of the Act, may not be a fit and proper person to carry on a relevant function;

- or if it appears that a criminal offence or a serious regulatory contravention has occurred.

(b) If it appears to the ombudsman that a complaint or a series of complaints may give rise or are giving rise to issues of regulatory relevance to the FSA (whether or not the firm has itself drawn the issues to the attention of FSA).

(c) If it appears that it would be desirable and appropriate for the FSA to consider using one or more of its regulatory tools including the exercise of its investigative and other enforcement powers, the making of rules or the giving of guidance to firms.

(d) In response to a request from the FSA where the FSA is or is contemplating using any of its regulatory tools in relation to a firm which is the subject matter of a complaint.

(e) Where it appears that a firm has failed to comply with an award made by an ombudsman.'

---

1 Memorandum of Understanding (MOU) between the Financial Services Authority and Financial Ombudsman Service, July 2002, para 8.
2 MOU paragraph 14. For further information in the Independent Assessor refer to para **10.56**.
3 MOU Paragraph 16.
4 MOU Paragraph 17 Specific Information sharing.

FSA rules on complaints procedures for firms

10.61 In this section we will consider the arrangements that firms are required to have in place for dealing with complaints they receive.

Pursuant to FSMA 2000, Sch 17, para 13(4) rules have been made requiring authorised firms to establish internal complaints rules to deal with complaints made against the firm. Schedule 17, para 13(4) requires that an authorised person who may become subject to the compulsory jurisdiction as a respondent, to establish such procedures as the FSA considers appropriate for the resolution of complaints which may be refered to the scheme. The basic premise for the combination of para 13(3) and (4) is to put in place an arrangement whereby firms are required to review compliants from their customers and if possible resolve them, and then only if the customer remains unsatisfied with the firm's response provide a mechanism through the FOS for the customer's complaint to be independently adjudicated upon.

10.62   The FSA's complaint rules for firms are set out in its Sourcebook DISP 'Dispute Resolution: Complaints'. DISP 1.2.1R sets out the basic requirement for a firm to operate and have written down internal complaint procedures.

It states:

> DISP 1.2.1 R A firm … must have in place and operate appropriate and effective internal complaint handling procedures (which must be written down) for:
>
> (1)   handling any expression of dissatisfaction, whether oral or written, and whether justified or not, from or on behalf of an eligible complainant about [the firms]… provision of, or failure to provide, a financial service; …

10.63   The rule introduces some basic requirements that must feature in both the firm's arrangements and the operation of a firm's complaint procedures. First the procedures must facilitate the investigation of complaints whether they are expressed in writing or presented orally. It is implicit from this requirement that it is not acceptable for a firm to argue that it will deal only with complaints that are made in writing. The arrangements must be appropriate and operate no matter whether the complaint is justified or not. Therefore even a complaint that has the appearance of being without merit will not allow a firm to argue that it has no obligation to deal with the complaint.

10.64   The FSA provide guidance at DISP 1.2.5G on those matters firms should take into account when designing internal arrangements. They should design their procedures in relation to the type of business they undertake, the size and organisational structure, the nature and complexity of the complaints they are likely to receive as well as the volume of complaints they are likely to receive. This guidance provides firms with a great deal of latitude to design a compliant handling process that works best for them, subject to meeting the required elements of the complaint rules. In addition the opportunity to establish procedures appropriate to the firm's business also demonstrates the importance the FSA attaches to a risk-based approach to regulation. When firms new to regulation are designing their complaints procedures they should undertake a review of their business and potential for complaints to ensure they are able to shape their proposed complaints process as well as justify the procedures they decide to establish. It is also seems sensible for all authorised firms to keep their complaints procedures under review in the context of changes to their business model and their complaints experience and where changes have occurred make necessary changes.

10.65   Further guidance is provided at DISP 1.2.4G in relation to matters that firms must provide for in their internal procedures. In particular, the guidance specifies that firms should make provisions for receiving complaints, responding to complaints and, where a complaint cannot be resolved forthwith, the appropriate investigation of complaints.

10.66 The Guidance relating to the receipt of complaints makes essential reading for all firms and effectively sets out concerns about the importance of ensuring that all individuals within a firms have the capacity to identify and act upon complaints received in their area of business. Complaints can be received in many parts of a large business, whether in the front office by a trader or broker, the back office, by an operations or administration department or even at more senior levels and often by the firm's chief executive officer. The internal procedure should therefore, ensure that all members of staff and departments are aware how they should deal with complaints when they are received and, also, how they can identify whether an item of correspondence or telephone call is in fact a complaint and once they are received what they should do with the complaint. It is not only a question of establishing internal rules to cover this point, but also to ensure that members of staff are adequately trained to be able to identify complaints when they are received. It should be noted that the FSA's own rules specify that complaints handling procedures are required when handling complaints about 'any expression of dissatisfaction'. A firm should, therefore, give proper consideration to ensuring that internal procedures not only deal with complaints alleging serious matters including financial loss, but also where customers are dissatisfied about the firm's service.

10.67 When designing its internal procedures a firm should consider the following:

- Should all complaints or expressions of dissatisfaction be referred imme- diately to a central complaint department?

- Is it feasible within the structure of the firm for complaints to be handled, in the first instance, by a customer services or operations department, and only if those complaints cannot be resolved, then escalated to a specialist complaints department?

Acknowledgements, responses and time limits

10.68 Firms are required (subject to certain exceptions) to acknowledge complaints in writing after receiving them and at various stages of their internal complaint investigation process as well as on notifying the complaintant of the outcome of the investigation provide information about the Financial Ombuds- man Service.

10.69 Upon receiving any complaint a firm is requird by DISP 1.4.1R to provide the complainant a written acknowledgement of the complaint within five business days. The acknowledgement must include the name or job title of the person within the firm with whom the complainant should have contact, together with details of the firm's internal complaints procedures.

10.70 If the complaint has been made orally it is good pratcice for the firm to also use the acknowledgement letter to confirm its understanding of the complaint and provide the complainant an opportunity to correct any misunderstanding. Some firms may choose also to have the customer sign, to acknowledge that the understanding of the complaint is correct. However, as the rules make it clear that complaints may be made in writing or orally, it does not seem acceptable for a firm to insist that such a written confirmation is a requirement before the complaint investigation can commence.

10.71 DISP 1.4.3G states that the firm should aim to resolve complaints at the earliest possible stage and in DISP 1.4.2G the FSA indicates that firms able to resolve a complaint within five business days may incorporate the acknowledgement of the complaint with the the final response letter (see **10.74** below). DISP 1.3.3R contains a useful exeption to the ackowledgement rule and indeed the rule for final letters. It provides that no acknowledgement is needed where the firm has taken reasonable attempts to determine that the complaint does not involve any allegation that the complainant has suffered, or may suffer financial loss, material distress, or material inconvenience or where the complaint can be resolved on the close of business on the business day following receipt of the complaint.

10.72 A firm is required by DISP 1.4.4R, to provide a complainant no later than four weeks from making a complaint, one of the following:

- a final response[1], which either accepts the complaint and, where appropriate, offers redress;

- an offer of redress, but without accepting the complaint; and

- a rejection of the complaint with reasons for doing so; or

- informs the complainant that the firm is not in a position to provide a final response, explains the reasons for the delay and gives an indication of when the complianant may receive a final response.

---

1 Final response is a defined term in the FSA Glossary.

10.73 The next communication requirement arises no later than eight weeks following receipt of the complaint and is set out in DISP 1.4.5R. These requirements also apply where the complainant receives a final responses if earlier than the eight week point. The requirements are:

- If the complaint remains outstanding at this point, the firm must provide the complainant with written reasons for the further delay, indicating when the firm will provide a written response; and

- The complainant must be informed that he may refer the complaint to the Financial Ombudsman Service if it remains dissatisfied.

10.74 If the communication with the client is a final response letter, that letter must as appropriate:

(a) accept the complaint, and, where appropriate, offer redress; or

(b) offer redress without accepting the complaint; or

(c) reject the complaint and gives reasons for doing so;

(d) and in all cases the final letter must inform the complainant that, if he remains dissatisfied with the firm's response, he may now refer his complaint to the Financial Ombudsman Service and he must do so within six months (see **10.35** and **10.36** above).

10.75 DISP 1.4.9R permits firms to operate a two-stage complaint process in essence building an additional layer of reference within the firm if the complainant remains dissatisfied when they receive the final response letter. The rule is designed to facilitate larger organisations that may have arrangements to investigate complaints at branch level and an opportunity for complainants to refer their complaint further to a more senior office or department within the firm if they remain dissatisfied. To satisfy the requirements in DISP 1.4.9R the firm's response must:

(1) offer redress (whether or not it accepts the complaint) or reject the complaint and give reasons for doing so;

(2) inform the complainant how to pursue his complaint with the firm if he remains dissatisfied;

(3) refer to the ultimate availability of the Financial Ombudsman Service if he remains dissatisfied with the firm's response; and

(4) indicate that it will regard the complaint as closed if it does not receive a reply within eight weeks.

10.76 If the complainant does not reply at all to the letter, the firm is not required to send a final response and furthermore is able to treat the complaint as closed for the purpose of the complaint reporting requirements see 10.21 below). If, however, the complainant does reply (within or after eight weeks), the firm must continue to comply with the complaints process and the time limits in DISP 1.4.5R resume subject to DISP 1.4.10R which allows the firm to exclude for the purposes of the time limits any time in excess of a week taken by the complainant to reply.

Disclosure of complaint arrangements

10.77 Firms are required to ensure that its customers, as well as any of its customers that complain, are given notice of the firm's arrangements for handling complaints as well as the fact that the firm is covered by the Financial Ombudsman Service. DISP 1.2.9R(1) deals with the requirement to refer all customers (that will be eligible complainants) in writing to the availability of its internal complaint handling procedures at, or immediately after, the point of sale of the investment or investment service they provide. This obligation does not require firms to provide customer with their actual written procedures only to draw their attention to the fact that they may obtain a copy upon request. Firms often choose to satisfy this requirement by drawing the customers' attention to their complaints procedures in their terms of business. DISP 1.2.14G requires that the firm's disclosure of its procedures is in clear and plain English.

10.78 DISP 1.2.10(2)R goes on to require a firm to publish it complaints procedures so that they may be provided to customers either on request or when a customer complains (save where the complaint is resolved by the next business day). Furthermore firms are required to display in each of its branches or sales offices to which eligible complainants have access a notice indicating that it is covered by the Financial Ombudsman Service. DISP 1.2.15G permits a firm to disclose that it is covered by the scheme by displaying a copy of the Financial Ombudsman logo in any literature or correspondence.

Complaint investigations, competence and indepedence

10.79 Firms' complaint procedures are required by DISP 1.2.16R to particularly make provison for the competence and objectivity of those persons given responsibility for investigating and responding to complaints. Firms must ensure that the person investigating the complaint has sufficient competence and skill relevant to the issues complained of, as well as not being a person directly involved in the subject matter of the complaint. The competence requirement will necessitate that the person investigating the complaint is not only familiar with the FSA compliant rules, but also technical issues including the nature of the investment to which the complaint relates, the firm's sales or advisory processes and the nature and calculation of any redress (we shall deal in more detail with competence and complaint handling skill later in this chapter). The issue of investigator independence is often a matter that can present practical problems for smaller firms, but is no less important for such firms to consider. DISP 1.2.5G allows firms to design their complaint procedures in the context of the size of the firms business. A firm's arrangements must therefore ensure that a complaint is never investigated by a person implicated, either directly or indirectly, in the matter complained of. Smaller firms that find that the person implicated in a complaint is the person that normally investigates complaints should necessarily identify another person to investigate the complaint in question. It is also important for firms to manage conflicts of interest, a requirement that will apply equally to a firm's complaint procedures as it applies to other areas of their business, and thus firms should ensure that their complaint arrangements do not allow a person to investigate complaints that might be bias in their appraoch to the complaint. By way of example this might necessitate avoinding the firm's sales management from any involvement in the complaints investigation and settlement process.

---

1 High level principle.

10.80 A firm is obliged by DISP 1.2.16(2)R to ensure that the person or persons with responsibility for investigating complaints has the authority to settle complaints (including the offering of redress where appropriate), or to have ready access to someone who has the necessary authority. Such requirement ensures that the complaint investigation remains independent and that the objectively reached outcome of the complaint will be followed through without any interference from persons at the firm otherwise motivated to take a defensive position about the matter complained of. Given the latitude allowed in DISP 1.2.5G for firms to design their complaints systems in the context of size and complexity as well as the requirement to have in place appropriate management control over their complaints systems under DISP 1.2.22R, it would be acceptable for larger firms to establish complaint investigation arrangements within a framework of tiered authority where certain decision making is reserved for more senior or experienced complaint investigators. It would also be acceptable in a small to medium sized firm, for an investigator to refer a complex or sizeable complaint to his department manager for final approval, or indeed, to the Chief Executive Officer, provided of course that the DISP 1.2.16R requirement for independence is met.

10.81 Where a firm's arrangements provide such a tiered level of authority, it will be important for such authority levels to be agreed or approved in advance and for them to be clearly articulated to ensure no unnecessary delay in the conclusion of the complaint investigation.

10.82 In conclusion, however, the rules are quite clear that no matter which individual within the firm is responsible for the investigation of a complaint, they must remain sufficiently objective and independent of the matter to ensure that the firm's response addresses adequately the subject matter of the complaint.

Offers of redress

10.83 Following the investigation of the complaint, if the investigator determines that it should be upheld in whole or part, he should turn is attention to the question of the appropriate remedy and the calculation of redress. DISP 1.2.16R requires that a firm's complaint procedures ensure that responses to complaints address adequately the subject matter of the complaint and, where a complaint is upheld, to offer appropriate redress.

10.84   DISP 1.2.17R makes it clear that a firm must, where it considers that redress is appropriate, provide a complainant with fair compensation. There is no specific guidance in the rules as to what constitutes redress although guidance at DISP 1.2.19G states that redress may not always be financial, and might in appropriate cases involve an apology. Importantly at DISP 1.2.18G firms when deciding whether or not to accept a complaint and determine the appropriate redress, may wish to consider any relevant guidance published by the FSA, the Financial Ombudsman Sevice, or any of the former schemes. The FOS do publish a monthly newsletter setting out its recent decisions relating to different complaint situations and these provide useful guidance on how to calculate redress for such cases. Moreover, the FSA from time to time publish guidance on appropriate redress in certain situations. By way of example Appendix 2 of DISP sets out the appropriate redress in mortgage endowment complaints. Any redress a firm provides is required by DISP 1.2.17R to be fair compensation for any acts or omissions for which the firm is responsible and the redress may include a reasonable rate of interest based on UK current rates.

10.85   As the rational behind the FSA's complaint rules is to ensure a speedy and informal mechanism for the resolution of complaints, logic would suggest that it is open for a firm, subject to compliance with any applicable FSA rules, to offer such redress as it and the customer considers appropriate. Remedies that may be acceptable to complainants may or may not be those which would be enforceable in the courts. This could include, for example, methods such as reinvesting customer's monies, the repurchasing of investments on dates or at rates that are favourable to the customer, offering ex gratia payments, gifts or tokens as a method of compensating a customer for inconvenience. Indeed it is clear from the rules (see DISP 3.9.1) that the Ombudsman Service can, if it finds in the complainant's favour, direct the firm to take such steps in relation to the complaint as considered appropriate, whether or not a court could order those steps to be taken.

10.86   Moreover FSMA 2000, s 229(2)(b) reflects the above approach to redress and states that, in determining the complaint, the ombudsman may make a direction that the respondent takes such steps in relation to the complainant as the ombudsman considers appropriate (whether or not a court could order those steps to be taken).

10.87   Firms must, however, respect that any unusual offer of redress, not acceptable to the customer, is unlikely to be recommended if the complaint were dealt with by the ombudsman. The Financial Ombudsman Service has developed a much more standard approach to settling complaints and thus where a customer seeks a standard approach to resolving their complaint there is little point in the firm attempting to press for settlement of the matter on unusual or informal terms.

Staff's awareness and understanding of complaints procedures

10.88 The FSA requires that all relevant staff within a firm, including appointed representatives are aware of the firm's internal complaint handling procedures. Firms should also endeavour to ensure that its employees and agents act in accordance with the procedures. Arguably, a firm that merely publishes its complaint procedures is not providing sufficient staff awareness and thus exposes its self to the risk of complaints not being dealt with in compliance with FSA rules. The firm should consider providing training to staff on how its complaint procedures operate, as well as details of which individuals in the firm have authority complaint investigation and resolution. This training requirement is particularly important for new members of staff within a firm. It is possible that any new member of staff on their first day at the firm could receive correspondence or a telephone call containing an expression of dissatisfaction. The member of staff must be able to know how to deal with that in accordance with the firm's internal procedures.

Identifying trends from complaints

10.89 DISP 1.2.22 R deals with the management control and manner in which complaints are to be handled internally. In particular, the rule is concerned with the fairness, consistency and promptness with which complaints are handled. It goes on to require that procedures are also required to identify and remedy any recurring or systemic problems, as well as any specific problems identified by the complainant. The latter point in DISP 1.2.22 goes to the very root of the concept of risk-based compliance and also features strongly in the FSA Treating Customers Fairly initiative. Given that complaints received in a firm can be a clear indicator to the firm of where its standards of compliance are falling down, it is imperative that complaint procedures do not deal with complaints in isolation from others that have been made. A firm should consider whether a complaint is indicative of a systemic problem within the firm or problems with an individual employee, department or even investment product, and thus arrangements should be established to collate trends and patterns about complaints and to escalate that information to the firm's senior management. However, a fair balance must be made between considering wider issues of the firm and dealing promptly with a complainant's individual concerns. The firm, therefore, should ensure that its procedures allow for the complainant's individual concern to be dealt with timely without its resolution being delayed as a result of any internal requirement to assess, report on or even attend to identified compliant trends.

A consistent approach to complaints handling

10.90   It is also essential for firms to ensure that their internal procedures allow for complaints relating to similar issues to be resolved in a consistent manner. Firm's are required to ensure that complaintant's interests are met and that appropriate remedies provided no matter the interest of the firm or member of staff that may be implicated by the complaint. It would therefore be inappropriate and potentially non-compliant for two similar complaints to be resolved differently. For example, it would not be appropriate for a complaint made against an area of a firm's business which is less productive, to be resloved differently from an identical complaint against an area of a firm which is highly successful. DISP 1.2.22(2) addresses specifically the procedures required to ensure consistency and compliments the provisions in DISP 1.2.16, which provides that the complaint should be handled or reviewed by members of staff who have sufficient experience, competence and authority as well as not being directly involved in the matter subject to the complaint. Those charged with the responsibility of complaint investigations within the firm should have sufficient authority to be able to make independent and objective decisions without fear of criticism from senior management. Although it would be acceptable for internal procedures to specify that complaints must be dealt with in accordance with basic concepts of law, it would be wholly inappropriate for a firm to place conditions on a complaints investigator's role by specifying that the primary objective is to defend the firm by attempting to find or develop a defence wherever possible.

Notifying professional indemnity insurers

10.91   Many firms are required to maintain professional indemnity insurance providing cover for liability caused by their acts or omissions. Where such indemnity insurance provides cover in relation to losses identified from customer complaints, it is likely to be a requirement of the insurance for the insurers to be notified of the potential claim before any admission of liability by the firm. The firm should consider approaching its professional indemnity insurer in advance of any complaint investigation with the view to agreeing with the insurer the firm's internal complaints process and the manner in which complaint investigations and correspondence should be managed. Certainly, where a larger volume of complaints is experienced, such prior agreement with insurers will ensure that individual complaints investigations can be concluded expeditiously. Where the firm maintains a good relationship with its professional indemnity insurer it may be the case that that insurer will allow the firm to conclude the investigation and accept liability without prior reference to the insurer. This should, of course, always be checked in advance with the professional indemnity insurance company.

10.92 Where fewer volumes of complaints are experienced, it will certainly be the case that the professional indemnity insurer will require notice of the potential claim in advance and will want to agree the outcome before there is any offer made to the complainant. If this is the case, then this should be considered to be an element of the compliance process and should be built into the firm's written complaints procedures.

Complaint management companies

10.93 Recent years have witnessed an increase in compliant management companies with many of them advertising their services to endowment policy complainants. DISP 2.4.1 R recognises that complainants may be represented by third party advisers. It states, 'A complaint may be brought on behalf of an eligible complainant, or a deceased person who would have been an eligible complainant, by a person authorised by the eligible complainant or authorised by law.'

10.94 The involvement of a complaint management firm in an individual complaint can cause challenges for authorised firms, the main issue usually being whether if offering redress a contribution should be made towards the complaint management cost should be covered. The FOS is unlikely to award a complainant the costs of being supported by a complaint management company although that may not stop such companies attempting to recover their costs when dealing directly with the firm. See section **10.53** and **10.56**. In August 2005 the FSA published a statement setting out its policy towards complaint management companies and the regulatory responsibilities for authorised firms. Although the statement did no more than affirm the current requirements in DISP it did provide a sense of the FSA concerns about the operation of such companies in the context of a free to the consumer independent ombudsman service. The FSA stated *inter alia*, '...*some consumers may choose to use the services of a third party such as a claims management company. We believe it is important that the consumer makes an informed choice in these circumstances – i.e. understands that there are likely to be costs involved in using a third party, and what those costs are ...*'

Management information and treating customers fairly

10.95 An analysis of a firm's complaints experience provides a valuable opportunity for the firm to analyse regulatory risks it is facing when transacting business. It is vital, therefore, that the firm, whether through its compliance or complaints departments, maintains a central record of all complaints received and analyses these regularly to identify complaint trends. That central record can be as simple or as complex as the firm considers necessary. However, it should at the very least contain the following vital information:

- The date the complaint was received. This will allow the firm to identify whether any compliance problems are date specific and may result from a particular action of the firm occurring at around that date.

- The name of the complainant.

- The product or investment held by the complainant: Once again, this will allow the firm to identify whether any particular compliance problem relates to specific investments or products that have been sold by the company.

- The person in the firm against whom the complaint is made: This will allow the firm to identify whether any particular compliance problems are being presented by an individual employee or broker or an appointed representative.

- A summary of the complaint allegations made: If the complaint analysis log is to be a useful tool, the firm should attempt to keep this summary as succinctly as possible. Once again, this will allow an analysis of various complaint types for the purpose of establishing whether a particular trend or pattern is emerging within the firm.

- Whether the complaint has been upheld in favour of the customer, defended, or whether the firm has decided to make an *ex gratia* offer to the customer without admitting liability.

10.96 The compliance department should determine the frequency at which complaint records are analysed. It may be appropriate if the firm is a large organisation and where complaints numbers may be quite high for the analysis to be frequent, to allow the firm to respond immediately to any patterns or trends that emerge. Smaller firms may determine that their complaints records can be analysed less frequently. No matter the frequency, the firm should always ensure that appropriate actions identified from complaint trends are taken. Those actions can relate to an individual employee concerned or company wide if complaints patterns suggest that a widespread failing is occurring. It should also be remembered that all records of complaints, whether they have been upheld in favour of the customer or not, can be a useful way to measure regulatory performance. Even a series of defended complaints relating to the same matter can identify a pattern of problems. For example, action might be taken if a number of customers have complained about the manner in which a particular product has been described when it has been sold, even where the firm has determined on investigation that it has no liability to the customer. Such a pattern of allegations may suggest that, in future, further care should be taken in a manner in which correct details are explained.

Complaints and staff education

10.97 The firm's senior management should also consider the method in which it communicates complaint trends to the organisation. It may be that details of complaints should be reported to the company's sales management or possibly directly to the training department. No matter what method the firm considers to be the most appropriate, it can be a useful compliance tool if details of these communications and the manner in which the firm agrees to act in relation to any compliance trends are recorded as evidence of the action the firm has taken.

10.98 At a more serious level, if the trends identified in the complaints record reveal that there is a widespread failing in relation to the sale of a particular product or conduct, the firm should, determine that a thorough review of that entire sales process be undertaken. This may result in individual customers being contacted for the purpose of identifying whether the firm has created a liability for them. Although such a method of approach may be contentious and certainly should be managed very carefully within the firm, it does provide an early opportunity for the firm to eliminate and manage any compliance breaches that have occurred early as opposed to allowing those breaches to go unattended and thus, over time, reduce any potential liability that the firm may have be exposed to.

10.99 The manner in which such broader reviews may be undertaken and the obligation firms may have to report such matters to the regulator is explored in more detail in Chapter 11.

Skills and competencies for complaints handling staff

10.100 Notwithstanding the regulatory requirements to comply with the FSA's complaint handling rules, it is important for a compliance officer and firms to consider the practical aspects of handling complaints received from customers. All expressions of dissatisfaction received by the firm can be used by the firm to assess the level and acceptability of the service that the firm is providing to its customers. A complaint may not only be an important indicator of compliance with regulatory issues but is also an excellent mechanism by which the firm can measure the failures in its service standards. It would, therefore, seem essential for a firm to attempt to keep not only for the purpose of compliance with its regulatory compliance but, for general assessment of service levels, statistics of all complaints received categorising those into complaint types.

10.101 In addition to using complaints as a method of measuring success, it is important that all customer complaints and expressions of dissatisfaction are handled promptly. It is often the case with customers that prevention is better that cure, and, if at all possible, it is better for the purpose of customer relations if a potential complaint is defused before the matter becomes out of hand. If a customer is of the opinion that they have a legitimate complaint, they are more likely to remain a loyal customer if they feel their complaint has been dealt with promptly, fairly and objectively than if they feel the matter has been subject to considerable delay and unnecessary defensiveness.

10.102 In the event that a complaint arises that does require investigation, then a series of actions will need to be undertaken, the effective application of which will help firms to more efficienly deal with its complaints and help ensure that all information necessary to assess the validity of the complaint is considered. A series of key pratcial steps can help the efficiency of complaint processing as well as help to defend those complaints that have no merit.

Scope of investigation

10.103 It is essential for the complaints investigator to understand exactly the nature of the complaint and what it is they are investigating. The length of time taken to investigate a complaint will be considerably extended if the investigator goes on a fishing expedition without any clear understanding, scope or limitation to their investigation.

10.104 It may be worthwhile at the stage of receiving a broadly worded complaint and particularly those expressed orally to agree with the complainant the precise matters that require investigation.

10.105 To assist case management, the investigator may consider the benefit of specifying the scope of the investigation, and identifying areas of the firm's practice which are to be reviewed, the individuals they wish to speak to, the documents they are going to examine and the regulatory rules and practices they may wish to analyse. The investigator should record the scope of the investigation, keeping that record on file and reviewing it periodically during the investigation to ensure they remain focused and on track.

10.106 Many complaint investigations require a significant assessment of evidential matters. The fundamentals of the complaint may either turn on what one person has said for example where what is alleged relates to the description of the features of an investment, or the complaint may require some analysis of documentation supplied to an investor. The investigator should, as early as possible, identify those documents that are critical to the investigation and those persons he or she wishes to interview.

Interviews

10.107   As part of the investigation into the complaint it may be necessary to speak to members of staff that have been involved in the subject matter of the complaint. Complaints of a technical nature may merely require an analysis of documents. However, typically, complaints made against the manner in which an investment has been sold, require an investigation that goes beyond a document analysis. Whilst a copy of the firm's 'Know Your Customer' or 'Factfind' record may demonstrate what the firm knew about the customer and record why the investment may have been suitable, it will often be of great assistance to the investigation if the broker or salesperson can explain the thinking behind the advice that was provided to the customer.

10.108   Often, a complaint may make allegations of matters where now record has been kept relating to that allegation or the client transaction. In such circumstances it becomes imperative that the sales advisor reports on the matter alleged before the complaint investigator decides what other lines of enquiry to follow.

10.109   The investigator should consider whether the interview should be conducted face to face or by telephone. Indeed, with simple interviews it may be possible to send to the interviewee a set of questions and have the interviewee respond in writing.

10.110   The investigator will find it beneficial to consider the scope of their interview in advance, planning the questions that need to be raised and answered. In this way, the interview can be much more focused and concentrate on the fundamental issues.

10.111   Consideration should also be given to the recording of the answers during the interview. This will ensure that a contemporaneous note of the interview is taken which can be referred to later, and provide the interviewee with an opportunity to check and confirm that the interviewer's understanding of the answers is correct. Lastly, it may be appropriate with some complaints, to put the interviewee's answers to the complainant for comment.

Document analysis

10.112   As part of the scope of the investigation, the investigator should identify those documents that need to be gathered and analysed. Many organisations arrange their record keeping in different ways to other firms. By way of example, a customer may make allegations regarding the manner in which a product is sold. Not only should the adviser be interviewed, but it may be appropriate to analyse the product's materials and brochures. It can not be safely assumed that all documents relating to the subject matter of the complaint will be present on the customer's file.

10.113 Almost as a matter of course for every investment-related complaint, the investigator should review the company's terms of business to establish whether the subject matter of the complaint is within the responsibility of the company. This should also include an analysis of any terms or conditions relating to the investment sold, key feature documents, illustrations and suitability letters for relevant packaged products.

10.114 It should also become standard practice for the investigator to consider the firm's compliance obligations provided by both the FSA rules and also the firm's own compliance manual. The investigator should seek to establish whether the firm has operated in a compliant manner in relation to the matter complained of. It should be remembered that under the FSMA 2000, s 150, a contravention of a rule by an authorised person is actionable by a private person who has suffered loss as a result of the contravention.

Obtaining expert opinion

10.115 In many cases, the person appointed to conduct the investigation will not be an expert in all matters material to the complaint. Provided the investigator appreciates this, it should in no way hinder the investigation. The investigator should be able to call upon impartial expertise to assist during the investigation. In this event, the investigator may wish to obtain a report or opinion from an expert. The expert may be found from within the organisation or, in appropriate cases secured from outside of the firm.

10.116 The investigator may also, during the investigation, consider it necessary to obtain external legal advice on aspects of the law affecting the subject matter of the complaint. It would be dangerous for the firm to assume that, simply because its practice is one which has been followed for a number of years, and has not been the subject of a previous complaint, that it is a practice which will be upheld by the courts.

Balancing the evidence obtained

10.117 Once the investigator has completed their enquiries and obtained all the necessary comments and documentation, it will be necessary to balance the evidence obtained. Where there is indisputable documented proof to support the company's point of view or, conversely, the complainant's point of view, then this task is a relatively simple one.

The process, however, becomes more complicated where the investigator is dealing with a situation of one person's word against another or where there is conflicting documentation.

10.118   The investigator should firstly consider some basic legal concepts:

- Who has the obligation to prove their case? In the majority of matters, the concept of 'he who asserts must prove' will operate. This means that the complainant must be able to prove their case if they are to be successful.

- In civil law matters, for a complainant to be successful, they must prove their case on a balance of probabilities. That is, the evidence must be able to show that it is more probable than not, that the alleged matters are accurate? This is a much lower standard of proof than the criminal one of 'beyond reasonable doubt'.

- Is it the firm's error, act, omission or breach that has caused the loss the customer is complaining about. It is not always the case that because someone has suffered a loss another person is to blame. It is important of the compliant investigator to identify a causal link between the loss being complained of and the firms behaviour.

A closing report

10.119   Once the complaint investigation has been completed and a decision reached, it is good practice for the investigator to write up a report on the matter, justifying their decision. This will be a useful document to remain on file, as it will justify the thought processes behind the decision together with the evidence relied upon to reach the decision. It will become a permanent record on a complaints file and can be used in the event of either regulatory scrutiny of the individual complaint investigation or if the matter is referred further on to the Financial Ombudsman Service.

Post-investigation matters

10.120   It is imperative that all actions to compensate or deal with individual complainants are dealt with timely. Any action taken within a firm either to adjust procedures or protect the firm's own position or deal with any rule breaches must not be conducted in a manner which does not prejudice the interest of the complaining customer.

FSA supervision and complaint reporting

10.121   The FSA relies on firms to notify them of the levels of complaints received and the extent to which the firm has been able to meet the timescales with in DISP. Firms are required to provide the FSA with a formal written report once per quarter setting out key information about the firms experience of complaints subject to DISP 1.4 to 1.6 The formal report is prescribed in DISP 1 Annex 1R.

10.122 Each report must contain the following information

(1) the total number of complaints received by the firm, broken down according to specified categories and in respect of each of specified product types

(2) the total number of complaints closed by the firm:

    (a) within four weeks or less of receipt;

    (b) within four to eight weeks of receipt; and

    (c) more than eight weeks after receipt;

(3) the total number of complaints

    (a) upheld by the firm in the reporting period;

    (b) that the firm knows have been referred to, and accepted by, the Financial Ombudsman Service in the reporting period;

    (c) outstanding at the beginning of the reporting period; and

    (d) outstanding at the end of the reporting period; and

(4) the total amount of redress paid in respect of complaints during the reported period.

10.123 Authorised firm's complaints experinces provide an essential opportunity for FSA to understand the extent of any problems being created by an individual firm's conduct of its business and by collecting complaint data from all firms the FSA is able to collect data that might reveal industry wide problems, possoibly allowing it to react early before the identified problems become widepread and create systemic issues impacting upon the FSA's Statutory Objectives. The manner in which the firm manages its investigation of individual complaints will also certainly reflect on its commitment to its customers as well as its compliance culure.

Chapter 11

Senior management systems and controls and managing a firm's relationship with the Financial Services Authority

11.1 Financial services regulators around the world are rightly concerned that senior management take responsibility for the effective organisation and control of the financial services firms for which they work. A study of recent financial service failures shows that in many cases the matters leading to the firms' failure were either a direct result of a breakdown in the firm's organisational systems or that the activities or practices of individuals were not properly managed and understood by senior management of the firm.

11.2 Following the failure of Barings Bank, the Bank of England in the Report of the Board of Banking supervision of inquiry into the collapse of Barings 18 July 1995 stated,

> 'The Chairman of Barings plc, Peter Baring, described the failure of controls with regard to BFS [Barings] as 'absolute'. We agree. It was this lack of effective controls which provided the opportunity for Leeson to undertake his unauthorised trading activities and reduced the likelihood of their detection. We consider that those with direct executive responsibility for establishing effective controls must bear much of the blame.

11.3 Participants in the financial marketplace range from sole traders to international businesses employing tens of thousands of staff. Despite the variations in business size, types and complexity they all will operate more efficiently and securely through the establishment and maintenance of appropriate arrangements to control the affective operation of their business.

11.4 In this chapter we will consider the basic FSA rules relating to organisational systems and controls together with mechanisms that firms should have in place to ensure that a business can operate compliantly and meet regulatory obligations. Where it is possible to illustrate FSA requirements by reference to past enforcement cases we have attempted to do so. The chapter will also consider the specific obligations placed on firms to report material information and compliance breaches to the FSA as well as the role senior management should have in managing their firm's relationship with the FSA.

11.5 It will be naïve of any firm to assume that because it operates in an environment where the FSA publishes rules and guidance, all members of its staff will as a matter of course work and operate compliantly. There can be a variety of reasons why compliance standards within a firm break down. It is not always the case that a firm's compliance breaches will be caused by the actions or omissions of a single member of staff. More often it is a breakdown in the firm's procedures, controls and systems that will lead to operating breakdowns. Moreover, where compliance breaches are caused by the actions of a single member or small group of staff , a breakdown in the firms controls will have often lead to the firm not dealing effectively with the errant individual or not mitigating the consequences of the failure. By way of example in the FSA's enforcement action against Citigroup Global Markets Limited (CGML)[1] announced on 28 June 2005, it was reported that the company developed and executed on 2 August 2004 a trading strategy on European government bond markets involving the building up and rapid sale over one hour of long positions in government bonds. The trade caused a temporary disruption to the volumes of bonds quoted and traded on a trading platform called MTS, together with a sharp drop in bond prices and a temporary withdrawal by some participants from quoting on the platform. This strategy, was actually developed by four traders on CGML's European Government bond desk following encouragement for their department to increase their profits through proprietary. Although the traders discussed their proposed strategy with their head of desk, who in turn sought and gained approval of the strategy from CGML's head of interest rate trading, it was reported by the FSA that there was no common or clear understanding between traders, head of desk or European head of interest rate trading as to the parameters of the size of the proposed trade and thus no effective communication of the arrangements CGML was to establish.

---

1 Citigroup Global Markets Limited, FSA Final Notice, 28 June 2005.

11.6 The FSA's action against CGML focused on breaches of High Level Principles 2 due skill, care and diligence; and Principle 3 organisation and control. FSA's Hector Sants when commenting on the case stated, '*... the lack of adequate systems and controls meant that the strategy was never fully considered, as would be expected, at an appropriate senior level within CGML ...*'

11.7 The FSA's Approved Persons regime (which is considered in more detail in Chapter 12) has a part to play in ensuring that individual officers and managers of a firm are held accountable, however, that regime on its own cannot sufficiently control how a firm manages and conducts its business. The stark reality is that despite its deterrent effect, FSA enforcement is only able to deal with the issues after a rule breach has occurred. The requirement for firms, to have in place arrangements to promote and maintain good standards of compliance, throughout their business operation is therefore paramount if problems are to be prevented.

11.8 For an effective compliance regime to exist within a firm, the concept of compliance must be embedded within its business. The entire firm's senior management must take responsibility for standards of compliance within their area of responsibility together with their influence over the entire organisation. That responsibility will extend to not only planning and operating effective systems and controls but also to how management deal with breaches and potential breaches as they occur.

11.9 This basic requirement is embodied in the FSA's Threshold conditions, a standard required for all firms seeking authorisation to conduct investment business in relation to the business permissions sought and a standard which they must continue to satisfy. Two particular Threshold Conditions can be said to apply directly to a firm's systems and controls. Condition 4[1] deals primarily with the firm's resources, but also talks in terms of the need for the FSA to be satisfied of the adequacy of resources having regard to the means by which it manages and, if it is a member of a group, which other members of the group manage the incidence of risk in connection with the firm's business. More specifically Condition 5[2] addresses the requirement for firms to satisfy the FSA of their suitability, fitness and properness including the need to ensure that the firm's affairs are conducted soundly and prudently.

---

1 FSMA 2000, Sch 6, para 4.
2 FSMA 2000, Sch 6, para 5.

11.10 The concept of systems and controls has been further refined beyond the fundamental Threshold conditions through a combination of the FSA High Level Principles for Business and Rules on Senior Management System[1] and Controls (SYSC). Both of these impose specific obligations for a firm's senior management to organise and control their business responsibly and effectively. FSA rules, in particular in SYSC, set out a series of requirements governing the arrangements that a firms' senior management are required to have in place. Such arrangements are wide in their nature and are designed to allow senior management to design and implement systems and controls that are appropriate to a firm's business as well as meeting specified regulatory obligations.

---

1 See para 11.12.

11.11   The FSA view of the role of senior management was emphasised by John Tiner FSA Chief Executive during a speech at the French Chamber of Commerce Lunch on 25 November 2005, when he said inter alia:

'... We believe it is managements' job to organise, manage and control their businesses in a way which meets a set of high level principles determined by the regulator necessary to safeguard the interest of customers and secure the safety and fairness of markets. Sometimes, it makes sense to underpin those principles with detailed rules or guidance, but it should not be the regulator's job to tell management how to run their business ...'

Senior management systems and controls

11.12   To properly appreciate the obligations placed on firms to have in place appropriate systems and controls, it is imperative to consider in some detail the systems and controls framework the FSA has created in its high level principles and SYSC. The combination of those high level principles that address senior management and their obligations to manage their business together with the key provisions of SYSC are intentionally drafted so as to allow firms to create control environments that are appropriate for their business, but at the same time impose strict obligations on firms to have in place effective arrangements.

11.13   Effective senior management oversight and internal systems and control are essential for effective regulation and minimise the need for detailed FSA rules. The FSA's Handbook provisions relating to SYSC although setting our basic principles of system and control, largely set out guidance that seeks to establish standards for firms. Although the FSA's high level principles and basic SYSC requirements relate to all authorised firms, a number of the FSA's provisions relating to systems and controls vary depending on the class of investment business conducted by the firm. It is important for all firms considering their compliance obligations to carefully consider the applicable provisions for their type of business and the standards that will be required of them.

11.14   New European legislation will have an impact on FSA rules relating to Systems and Controls. Both the Markets in Financial Instruments Directive (MiFID) and the Capital Requirements Directive (CRD) contain provisions relating to organisational controls. Most firms which conduct business which is subject to the CRD requirements (and that includes CAD firms) are also subject to MiFID requirements. In addition businesses falling outside of the directives such as insurance which is covered by existing standards, may only find their business impacted if they are part of a group subject to MiFID and the CRD. This development could potentially create a complex set of organisational obligations for multi-function firms and groups of firms. In light of this potential problem the FSA is proposing to establish a common systems and controls platform. Its proposals are set out in Consultation Paper 06/09 'Organisational Systems and Controls: Common Platform for Firms.'[1] The common platform provisions will be located in FSA's SYSC sourcebook in new topic-specific chapters covering matters such as Conflicts of Interest, Outsourcing and Risk Control. Although these changes will fundamentally alter the provisions of FSA's rules on organisational control, the FSA considers there will be minimal impact for firms that already have good practices and procedures supporting management oversight, effective risk management and other internal controls. Many of the system and controls matters we shall now consider may be impacted by the FSA proposed common platform. Where there is an insight into the FSA's proposals we have given an indication although at this stage it is not possible to predict in every occasion the likely practical impact of the proposed changes.

Let us first consider those High Level Principles that specifically address senior management obligations.

---

1 Consultation Paper 06/09, published 23 May 2006

High Level Principles

11.15 **Principle 2** deals with the standards of conduct and behaviour of regulated firms, it provides:

'A firm must conduct its business with due skill, care and diligence'

11.16 **Principle 3** is the main principle dealing with how senior management must organise and the control their firms business. It is of wide and general application and extends to both the financial affairs of the firm as well as the way the firm conducts its business. It deals with the general organisational expectations for a firm and introduces the requirement to include risk management systems, which is now a critical element to the effective design and maintenance of firms' internal arrangements. Principle 3 provides:

'A firm must take reasonable care to organise and control its affairs responsibly and effectively, with adequate risk management systems.'

11.17 **Principle 8** addresses the important area of effective management of conflicts of interest. The manner in which conflicts of interest are managed has come under increased regulatory scrutiny following a series of business failures that are seen as having been caused by a failure of senior management to manage effectively the conflicts that existed within the firm. The Principle acknowledges that conflicts of interest do and will exist between a firm and its customers as well as between different customers it is acting for, but for a firm to operate effectively all conflicts must be managed fairly. Principle 8 provides:

'A firm must manage conflicts of interest fairly, both between itself and its customers and between a customer and another client.'

11.18   **Principle 11** reflects the importance placed on openness and co-operation between the regulated community and the FSA. The relationship between the FSA and the firms it regulates is not meant to be an adversarial one. The system demands that firms take responsibility for their own standards of compliance with FSA rules and this extends to co-operating with the FSA during their supervisory activities as well as proactively drawing to the FSA's attention material failures within their business. Principle 11 is drafted generally and talks in terms of disclosures of anything that the FSA would reasonably expect notice. We consider in paras **11.61–11.90** below those matters that should be disclosed to the FSA. Principle 11 provides:

'A firm must deal with its regulators in an open and co-operative way, and must disclose to the FSA appropriately anything relating to the firm of which the FSA would reasonably expect notice.'

11.19   The FSA sets out in its Systems and Controls Sourcebook specific rules addressed at obligations for designing and maintaining systems and controls. Many of the rules in SYSC are supported by guidance providing firms an opportunity of understanding how the specific rules relate to their business as well as the FSA's expectations in relation to how the firms should translate into practice the generally drafted rules. Space limits the extent to which this book can address fully the requirements of SYSC and therefore we shall consider the basic systems and controls framework covering general systems and controls, operational risk and anti-money laundering.

11.20   The starting point as well as most fundamental requirements in SYSC is the requirement for the establishment and maintenance of appropriate systems and controls across all areas of the firm's business. SYSC 3.1.1R provides:

'A firm must take reasonable care to establish and maintain such systems and controls as are appropriate to its business.'

11.21   The manner of the drafting that this rule, although imposing a specific obligation on firms, allows a large degree of flexibility in how the firm's systems and controls are to be established and maintained and the extent of the systems and controls required. Firms are required to take reasonable care to establish and maintain their systems. The introduction of reasonableness in one part introduces an objective test when assessing individual firm's systems arrangements. Secondly it reconciles with the FSA's principles of good regulation which make clear at FSMA 2000, s 2(3)(c) that in discharging its general functions the FSA is required to have regard to the principle that a burden or restriction which is imposed on a person, or on the carrying on of an activity, should be proportionate to the benefits, considered in general terms, which are expected to result from the imposition of that burden or restriction. It infers that firms do not have to have in place or maintain systems and controls that deal with matters that could not be foreseen or are so remote that the cost of establishing them would be far in excess of the benefit that would be created by the control itself. The reasonableness test, however, does introduce an element of peer group comparison or benchmarking. To determine whether one firm's approach to systems and controls is reasonable, the FSA will view their arrangements and approach in comparison to other similar firms. Over time, having assessed many similar firms' arrangements the FSA may determine that one firm's approach is not reasonable when compared to the approaches adopted by the majority of other firms.

11.22 SYSC 3.1.1R also talks in terms of a firm's systems and controls being appropriate to its business. This provides firms with the scope to design and maintain their systems to suit their business. Once again, however, the question of appropriateness is based on an objective test and undoubtedly the FSA will compare one firm's arrangements with that of its peer group when determining the appropriateness of its arrangements. Indeed, arrangements that are appropriate for one firm may not necessarily be appropriate for another.

11.23 The FSA provide confirmation in SYSC 3.1.2 G of the variety of factors that might be taken into account and will affect the design and maintenance of a firm's internal controls which states:

(1) The nature and extent of the systems and controls which a firm will need to maintain under SYSC 3.1.1R will depend upon a variety of factors including:

   (a) the nature, scale and complexity of its business;

   (b) the diversity of its operations, including geographical diversity;

   (c) the volume and size of its transactions; and

   (d) the degree of risk associated with each area of its operation.

(2) To enable it to comply with its obligation to maintain appropriate systems and controls, a firm should carry out a regular review of them.

11.24 In the FSA's enforcement action against Citibank Global Markets Limited, the FSA observed that the company's systems and controls applicable to the trading desk in question were inadequate in a number of respects, in particular there was concern about the traders' knowledge of what they were required to escalate to senior management and that although eventually the strategy in question was escalated, overall there were inadequate systems and controls in place to ensure that the details of the strategy were escalated adequately and in advance to senior management as well as there being a failure to consult with applicable control functions resulting in the trading strategy not being considered by Compliance, Legal or independent Risk Management before it was executed[1].

---

1 FSA Final Notice, 28 June 2005.

11.25 What is clear is that compliance with SYSC3.1.R entails not only the maintenance of appropriate systems but having in place arrangements to regularly review those systems and controls. Regular reviews are an essential mechanism for ensuring that systems continue to be effective and appropriate, partly to assess whether the systems remain fit for the purpose for which they were designed and secondly to establish whether they are being operated in the intended manner. Firms do regularly experience process slippage finding after time that the systems and processes in operation have changed beyond those designed. This can occur as a result of staff members own application of the procedures and their interpretation of how processes should be applied in situations that were not originally anticipated. The consequence of such slippage can be that a firm's systems and controls become either too rigid and unnecessarily restrictive or less effective than intended.

11.26 SYSC 3.1.2G goes on to set out that although detailed requirements regarding systems and controls relevant to particular business areas or particular types of firm are specifically covered in the FSA Handbook, there are areas that the FSA would typically expect to see covered by the systems and controls referred to in SYSC 3.1.1R. These matters are set out in SYSC 3.2. We will now consider some of the arrangements of application to most firms.

For an overview of arrangements that may be used to construct a risk assessment refer to Chapter 4.

Apportionment of responsibilities

11.27 In order to ensure that a firm's system and control arrangements work in the organisation, the firm needs to ensure that responsibilities are clearly divided up among the senior management team, so that everyone knows who is responsible for what. In SYSC 2.1.1R the requirement is that a firm's apportionment arrangements must be such that it is clear who has which of those responsibilities and the business and affairs of the firm can be adequately monitored and controlled by the directors, relevant senior managers and governing body of the firm. The FSA require that a person be appointed to act as the apportionment and oversight officer. It anticipates that in most firms the person with this responsibility is the Chief Executive Officer.

Compliance arrangements

11.28 SYSC 3.2.6R sets out the general requirement applying to all firms. It states:

'A firm must take reasonable care to establish and maintain effective systems and controls for compliance with applicable requirements and standards under the regulatory system and for countering the risk that the firm might be used to further financial crime.'

11.29 This rule clearly provide firms with the latitude to design compliance systems and controls that are appropriate to their business model and unique business risks rather than providing a one size fits all approach. Further guidance is provided in SYSC 3.2.7G (1) which makes it clear that an individual firm's approach to its compliance arrangements will be dependent on the nature, scale and complexity of its business. The FSA will expect to see that the compliance function is staffed by an appropriate number of competent staff and that the compliance staff are both sufficiently independent to perform their duties objectively as well as havie unrestricted access to the firm's records and ultimate recourse to its governing body. For further information on independence see **11.43** below.

11.30 It is essential for firms to consider whether they need to have a separate compliance function. Once again this decision will be driven by the size, nature and complexity of the firm's business. The interrelationship between the need to devote adequate resource to compliance and the decision to have a separate compliance function need not be confused. Scenarios are possible where a firm determines that its regulatory obligations can be met with dedicated resource within business units with oversight being undertaken by a small team of specialist compliance resource. The important test is whether the arrangements established by the firm are appropriate for its business. There are circumstances, however, when the oversight of compliance must be allocated to a senior manager or director of the firm. SYSC 3.2.8R provides that:

(1) A firm which carries on designated investment business with or for customers must allocate to a director or senior manager the function of:

    (a) having responsibility for oversight of the firm's compliance; and

    (b) reporting to the governing body in respect of that responsibility.

11.31 Ultimately, the compliance arrangements established by a firm must be thoroughly documented, moreover SYSC 3.2.7G provides that the organisation and responsibilities of a compliance function should be documented, however in order to demonstrate that the arrangements are appropriate it also seems imperative that the firm's reasoning and methodology in establishing the arrangements are documented.

11.32   Matters relating to compliance systems and the involvement of senior management relevant to SYSC 3.2.6R were addressed in the FSA's enforcement action against Carr Sheppards Crosthwaite Ltd (CSC)[1]. That case related to inadequate and inappropriate systems and controls to monitor and demonstrate compliance. In particular the FSA was concerned that CSC did not have in place systems and controls appropriate to its business in relation to the performance of its compliance function. It was reported that the FSA found CSC's compliance policies and procedures to be inadequate and incomplete. A major problem for firms can occur when it is found that there are serious defects in their compliance manual or where it is not complete or inadequate. Indeed such defect appears to have been the catalyst for the FSA's action against CSC.It was reported that CSC's Compliance manual failed to adequately address matters such as financial promotions, outside business interests, out of hours trading, an authorised signature list containing names of former members of staff and in fact was out of date including copies of documents from the Securities and Futures Authority rules which had been superseded by the FSA rules.

---

1 FSA final notice, 19 May 2004.

11.33   The FSA's Final Notice reported that CSC had experienced a material failing in its maintenance of senior management arrangements, which the FSA regarded as a key safeguard to ensuring the proper application of FSA rules and principles. This included criticism of the informal arrangements for reporting of compliance matters to CSC management. There was a lack of detailed written reporting such that CSC could not provide evidence that its management had been fully aware of key compliance issues or that management had sufficient tools with which it could measure future progress and monitor compliance issues. CSC had not established and implemented a detailed monitoring programme covering FSA rules and its business.

11.34   Although most firms think of SYSC 3.2.6R in terms of general compliance arrangements, the rule does also require firms to have systems and controls for countering the risk that the firm might be used to further financial crime. Once again, it is the nature and complexity of the firm's business that will determine the arrangements the firm will need to have in place. To determine the nature of a firm's response it is essential for it to carry out a financial crime risk assessment, establish controls and procedures to reduce its risk to criminal activity and establish regular monitoring of the effectiveness of its arrangements. Although, firms will think in terms of its risk exposed from customers and third parties intent on exploiting the firm, many firms face the risk of criminal conduct from their own employees.

11.35   The FSA took enforcement action for the very first time in respect of a firm's poor anti-fraud controls against Capita Financial Administrators Ltd (CFA) in March 2006[1].

---

1 Final Notice published 16 March 2006.

11.36   The FSA's criticism of CFA was that it did not use appropriate skill, care and diligence when considering the risk of fraud in its business. The FSA further criticised CFA for not undertaking sufficient analysis of the fraud risk that the firm was running and was too focused on the risk of external fraud. CFA was fined £300,000 for breaches of Principle 2 in failing to conduct its business with due skill, care and diligence in considering the risks posed by financial crime; Principle 3 for failing to take reasonable care to organise and control its affairs responsibly and effectively, with adequate risk management systems; and SYSC 3.2.6R by failing to take reasonable care to establish and maintain effective systems and controls to counter the risk that CFA might be used to further financial crime. The case is valuable in that it highlights a number of potential financial crime risks and provides an insight into the FSA's view on steps firms should take to deal with such risks.

11.37   The FSA's Final notice in the matter sets out the following information in particular: CFA was a third party administrator for collective investment schemes responsible for maintaining clients' records and carrying out client instructions for the purchase and repurchase of investments. Between August 2004 and December 2004, CFA following enquiries from clients discovered that a number of actual and attempted frauds appeared to have been carried out by a small number of CFA staff. In August 2004, CFA discovered that a client's name and address had been changed without instructions from the client and the sale of units was being processed without any instruction from the client. CFA subsequently found that the data held for five other clients had been subject to unauthorised changes and fraudulent requests for payments had been made. Although these payments were stopped by CFA before they were made, the value of the requested payments was £1,134,938.

11.38   The arrangements CFA had in place to deal with customers' requests illustrate the risk the firm faced and the FSA's subsequent concern. By way of example the Final Notice highlighted that where a client requested a change of address they would be required to put their request in writing. On receipt of the letter CFA's internal processes required staff to enter the change onto the IT system. There was no check that the signature on the letter corresponded to the signature held on file by CFA. Once changes to a client's address had been processed, CFA would take the details from the letter and write to the new and old address giving the client the opportunity to act if the change was not genuine. In respect of placing a telephone deal, callers were identified by reference to their account number, name, address and date of birth. This information (apart from the date of birth) was written on the annual statement that is sent to the client in the post. Rather than using passwords or other client specific information to verify client identity, CFA used publicly available information that could be found in electoral roles, from the internet, through theft of annual statements or other correspondence sent to clients by CFA. Importantly all of this information could easily be accessed by staff working in the areas processing changes to client data and sale and purchase instructions.

11.39   The FSA points out in its Final Notice that the effect of CFA's systems was that a fraudster could have changed a client's address and then instructed CFA to sell units. The fraudster would then have been able to return the confirmation for the sale instruction, request payment to an account controlled by him and the transaction would have been processed.

Money laundering

11.40   An integral part of a firm's compliance arrangements will be the systems it establishes to combat anti-money laundering. Since 2002 the FSA has taken enforcement actions against a number of major UK banking groups for failing to establish effective anti-money laundering arrangements. In the matter of Abbey National plc[1] which resulted in a £2,000,000 financial penalty, the FSA stated in its final notice:

'... Abbey National has demonstrated extremely serious control failings in respect of its AML procedures which occurred within the context of weak compliance controls across the Group. In particular the failure to report SARs on a timely basis undermines a crucial aspect of the UK's AML regime ... The serious nature of the AML breaches and the risk they posed to the FSA's statutory objective to reduce financial crime demand that a very substantial financial penalty be imposed in this case ...'

---

1 Final Notice, 9 December 2003.

11.41   Although SYSC 3.2.1R which applies to all authorised firms talks in terms of compliance arrangements to combat financial crime, with effect from 31 March 2006[1] certain firms have specific anti-money laundering SYSC obligations following the removal of the FSA money laundering sourcebook[2]. The FSA place great importance on the standard of a firm's anti-money laundering arrangements, and any failure at firm level can have a direct impact on the FSA statutory objective to reduce financial crime. The basic obligation addressed in the new SYSC 3.2.6AR requires firms to have in place arrangements to enable the identification, assessment, monitoring and management of money laundering risk; which is defined in SYSC 3.2.6B (G) as the risk that a firm may be used to further money laundering. Once more, as in SYSC3.2.4, a firm's anti-money laundering arrangements are to be designed so that they are comprehensive and proportionate to the nature, scale and complexity of its activities. The specific AML SYSC requirements, go on, however, to require at SYSC 3.2.6C R that a firm must carry out regular assessments of the adequacy of these systems and controls to ensure that it continues to comply with SYSC 3.2.6AR.

---

1 PS06/01 sets out a transitional period allowing existing authorised firms from 31 March 2006 until 31 August 2006 to comply with the new SYSC provisions.
2 This change has come about as part of FSA rule book simplification project.

11.42 The new requirements set out an obligation for firms to have in place two senior management positions with responsibility for a firms day-to-day anti money laundering systems. The first as a senior manager or director with responsibility for the establishment and maintenance of effective anti-money laundering systems and controls[1], the second as Money Laundering Reporting Officer (MLRO) with responsibility for oversight of its compliance with the FSA's rules on systems and controls against money laundering[2]. The firms must ensure that its MLRO has a level of authority and independence within the firm and access to resources and information sufficient to enable him to carry out his responsibility. The MLRO position is a controlled function, however, the senior manager responsible for systems establishment and maintenance is not designated as a controlled function in its own right, although firms should consider whether the person exerts a significant influence and as a result requirines approved person status.

Finally it is important to note that there remains an overlap between the FSA's Anti Money Laundering requirements in SYSC and the best practice framework in the JMLSG guidance notes. For further information see Chapter 7 money laundering and financial crime.

---

1 SYSC 3.2.6H R.
2 SYSC 3.2.6I R.

Audit committee

11.43 Once more depending on the nature, scale and complexity of a firm's business, at SYSC 3.2.15 G the FSA consider that it may be appropriate for a firm to establish an audit committee comprising an appropriate number of non-executive directors and with a formal terms of reference for the purpose of examining management's process for ensuring the appropriateness and effectiveness of systems and controls, examining the arrangements made by management to ensure compliance with requirements and standards under the regulatory system, overseeing the functioning of the internal audit function (if applicable) and providing an interface between management and the external auditors. Financial service companies that have also listed their shares for public sale also have to take into account the provisions of the Combined Code on Corporate Governance which sets out requirements for an audit committee. The guidance in that code is also a useful reference for all companies whishing to establish an audit committee. A firms arrangements for governance might be more effective if the Compliance and risk departments have a reporting line into the audit committee with responsibility to that committee for reporting on progress against their compliance plan for the year, areas of regulatory development, the firm's relationship with the FSA and its progress in meeting its FSA risk mitigation programme, together with any areas of regulatory risk and material regulatory breaches. By reporting to an Audit Committee the firm can help ensure that the compliance function within the firm is appropriately independent from the business areas it has responsibility for overseeing.

Management information

11.44 To allow senior management to operate their business effectively it is vital that they have access to reliable data and measurements about the performance of the overall business as well as their own discrete area of responsibility. Appropriate management information will ensure that management are able to identify positive areas of performance as well as receive prompt warning of risks or failures. As part of the guidance to SYSC 3.2.1R the FSA recognise at SYSC 3.2.11G the value of management information and once again the nature of the detail and extent of information required will depend on the nature, scale and complexity of the firm's business. In the guidance the FSA set out an expectation that a firm's arrangements should be such as to furnish in a timely manner its governing body with relevant and reliable information needed to identify, measure, manage and control risks of regulatory concern. The FSA go on to describe risks of regulatory concern as those risks which relate to:

* the fair treatment of the firm's customers,
* the protection of consumers,
* confidence in the financial system, and
* the use of that system in connection with financial crime.

Business strategy

11.45 Not only will the complexity, size and type of a firm's business determine the arrangements it needs to put in place but also the business strategy it plans to undertake may require controls and safeguards as well as planned responses from senior management including special compliance focus. Firms will often and necessarily embark on new business strategy which will impact on the existing senior management arrangements and require a revised approach either for the entire organisation or specialist focus for the new business that is being created. Senior management must never underestimate the impact that a new business strategy will have on their existing business arrangements. The new strategy might divert away valuable resource from other departments or even introduce product or processes that are beyond the competence of existing staff. Firms must also take into account that any new business strategy that involves a material change to the firm's business may necessitate the firm applying for revision to their FSA business permissions, see Chapter 12 or require the firm to notify the FSA of the detail of such change under Principle 11 and SUP 15.3.8G (see para **11.70** below).

11.46   Thorough and appropriate planning for any new strategy should be undertaken with sufficient time and resource devoted to an assessment of the impact of the change, a risk assessment and planning on the new systems and controls that will be required. The firm should concern itself with the impact the changes will have on their compliance planning for the year ahead and how they will manage any additional risks presented by the new business strategy. FSA consider that a firm should plan its business appropriately so that it is able to identify, measure, manage and control risks of regulatory concern as part of its business strategy planning and in the guidance in SYSC 3.2.17G the FSA stress the importance of documenting the business strategy decisions, it provides,

> 'In some firms, depending on the nature, scale and complexity of their business, it may be appropriate to have business plans or strategy plans documented and updated on a regular basis to take account of changes in the business environment.'

Business continuity

11.47   The need to build into every firm's systems and controls planning for the continued functioning of the business following an interruption to the business or a catastrophic event has existed as responsible business planning for some time. The need for effective business continuity planning was highlighted by the interruption to business that occurred after the Terrorist events in New York on 11 September 2001 and the suicide bombings in London on 7 July 2005. The guidance in SYSC 3.2.19G makes clear an FSA expectation that a firm should have in place appropriate arrangements to ensure that it can continue to function and meet its regulatory obligations in the event of an unforeseen interruption. Once more the question of what is appropriate will be determined having regard to the nature, scale and complexity of the firm's business as well as third party provider systems and arrangements that are readily available in the market and those the FSA see utilised by other members of the firm's peer group. The guidance also makes clear that an integral part of a firm's business continuity arrangements will be a programme to regularly update and test the continuity arrangements to ensure their effectiveness.

Operational risk

11.48   As part of the FSA's plan to introduce a single integrated prudential sourcebook, in Consultation Paper 142, it set out proposals for revised guidance to firms on the establishment and maintenance of appropriate systems and controls. The guidance applies to almost all regulated firms. Operational risk covers matters such as the risk from employees, managing inadequacies in a firm's processes, outsourcing and business continuity management. The basic guidance is provided at SYSC 3A7.1G which states:

'A firm should establish and maintain appropriate systems and controls for managing operational risks that can arise from inadequacies or failures in its processes and systems (and, as appropriate, the systems and processes of third party suppliers, agents and others).'

11.49   In managing its operational risk a firm[1] should take into account both the importance and complexity of the processes and systems it uses during the overall operating cycle for its business activities as well as the products it offers its customers. The FSA have set an expectation in SYSC 3A.7.1(3) G that it will when considering the adequacy of a firm's systems take into account whether the design and use of its processes and systems allow it to comply adequately with regulatory and other requirements. The FSA also highlight in SYSC 3A7.2G the role that internal documentation has in enhancing an understanding of and aiding continuity of operations. It points out in particular that a firm should ensure the adequacy of its internal documentation of processes and systems (including how documentation is developed, maintained and distributed) in managing operational risk.

---

1 SYSC 3A 7.1G.

11.50   It is important, however, that the firm establishes a control framework that will help it to prevent system and process failures as well as identify any such failures so as to allow for prompt resolution. FSA set out in SYSC3A.7.1(4) and (5) that firms need to include:

• arrangements for the continuity of operations in the event that a significant process or system becomes unavailable or is destroyed; and

● the importance of monitoring indicators of process or system risk (including reconciliation exceptions, compensation payments for client losses and documentation errors) and experience of operational losses and exposures.

11.51 The reliance most firms now place on Information Technology solutions raises a particular risk for senior management, both in terms of senior management's technical ability to appreciate the IT solutions that have been implemented and the technology's fitness for providing the intended solution as well as the importance of providing appropriate security within the system to misuse or even prevent financial crime. The FSA will expect firms to have in place appropriate systems and controls for Information Technology risk. See SYSC3A.7.5G.The extent of a firm's structure and its reliance on IT solutions will have an effect on the arrangements the FSA would expect to see in place. Of particular importance, however, are arrangements needed for the management of IT system acquisition, development and maintenance as well as the interaction and allocation of responsibilities between IT development and operational areas, together with the embedding of security requirements into systems. For further information about financial crime risk see the FSA's action against Capita Financial Management Ltd above at para **11.35**.

Outsourcing

11.52 Use of and reliance on outsourced arrangements by the financial service industry has shown marked increase over recent years. Firms now routinely consider outsourcing business arrangements and systems ranging from core business requirements such as client administration, and sales process, through to support services such as training and development of staff. Outsourcing arrangements have the potential to transfer risk, management and compliance of the business to third parties, who may not be regulated and who may operate offshore. Many companies' decision to outsource is based on reasons of efficiency and for others the decision is based on economic grounds. Notwithstanding the varied reasons, all outsourcing arrangements challenge a firm's ability to remain in control of their business risks and to comply with regulatory responsibilities. Despite a decision to outsource, the firms regulatory responsibilities for the function cannot be transferred and as a result firms with outsourcing arrangements must have in place systems and controls to both assess the viability of the outsourced function, the risk associated with the outsourced arrangement and then to manage the arrangement whilst it is being maintained.

11.53 The question of the outsourcing of functions material to a firm's business has become a matter of concern to international regulators as well as the FSA. In January 2005, the Joint Forum and IOSCO issued guiding principles and, at European level, in April 2006 the Committee for European Banking Supervisors published draft principles for consultation. Moreover both the Markets in Financial Instruments Directive and Capital Requirements Directive deal with the risks associated with outsourcing.

11.54 The FSA rules currently in SUP 15.3.8 G (1)(e)require that a firm should notify the FSA when it intends to enter into a material outsourcing arrangement. The FSA define material outsourcing as[1]:

'an outsourcing services of such importance that weakness, or failure, of the services would cast serious doubt upon the firm's continuing satisfaction of the threshold conditions or compliance with the Principles'.

---

1 Defined in FSA Handbook Glossary.

11.55 SYSC sets out guidance on the arrangements firms should put in place to manage outsourcing arrangements. SYSC 3A.9.4G sets out five key matters that senior management should address before entering into, or significantly changing, an outsourcing arrangement. It states that a firm should:

(1)   analyse how the arrangement will fit with its organisation and reporting structure; business strategy; overall risk profile; and ability to meet its regulatory obligations;

(2)   consider whether the agreements establishing the arrangement will allow it to monitor and control its operational risk exposure relating to the outsourcing;

(3)   conduct appropriate due diligence of the service provider's financial stability and expertise;

(4)   consider how it will ensure a smooth transition of its operations from its current arrangements to a new or changed outsourcing arrangement (including what will happen on the termination of the contract); and

(5)   consider any concentration risk implications such as the business continuity implications that may arise if a single service provider is used by several firms.

11.56 In its Consultation Paper 'Organisational Systems and Controls: Common Platform for Firms[1] the FSA proposes a unified set of arrangements for system and controls for outsourcing. The FSA plans on introducing rules that will introduce requirements to ensure:

●   the investment firm, its auditors and relevant competent authorities have effective access to data related to the outsourced activities, as well as to the business premises of the service provider;

- the service provider must protect confidential information belonging to the investment firm or its clients;

- the investment firm and the service provider must have a contingency plan that provides for disaster recovery and the outsourcing agreement must be in writing;

- a firm takes appropriate action where it appears the service provider is not carrying out the functions effectively or in compliance with applicable laws and regulatory requirements.

1 Consultation Paper 06/09.

11.57 The rules proposed in the consultation paper will require firms subject to the common platform to take reasonable steps to avoid undue operational risk impairing the quality of its internal control or the activities of its supervisor where the firm relies on a third party for the performance of operational functions, critical or important for the provision of continuous and satisfactory service. The FSA proposals specify that in taking reasonable steps a firm should be satisfied that:

- the service provider has the ability, capacity and necessary authorisation to perform the outsourced activities reliably and professionally;

- the firm can assess the standard of performance;

- it can supervise the third party appropriately and manage risks associated with the outsourcing.

Training and competence

11.58 Although a study of the FSA's training and competence rules are beyond the scope of this Chapter, it is important to reflect on the role that appropriate training has in contributing to robust systems and controls. For many reasons, in addition to meeting regulatory requirements, having appropriately trained staff enables them to operate effectively within the firms framework of systems and controls. Firms may develop system, processes and procedures to support the functioning of their business but unless their management and staff are made aware of the existence of those procedures and trained on how to apply them, then those systems will inevitably fail.

11.59 The FSA place significant emphasis on the role that training plays in helping to ensure that a firm meets its regulatory obligations. In the FSA's enforcement case against Berkely Independent advisers Ltd[1] the FSA expressed concerns about sales training delivered to support that company's new sales strategy. It was particularly concerned that the company did not assess whether attendees had sufficient expertise following the training to implement the new sales strategy. It can be observed from the final notice that this weakness in training in part contributed to the company's systems and controls failure.

---

1 Final Notice, 1 December 2005.

11.60 Furthermore, in the FSA's enforcement case against Citigroup Global Markets Limited[1], the FSA expressed concerns about the quality of training received by the trading desk that had established the failed trading strategy. The FSA observed that the Desk was inadequately trained in respect of observing proper standards of market conduct. In particular, there had been inadequate compliance training on what matters needed to be escalated to management, inadequate market abuse training was only provided on the introduction of the market abuse regime on 1 December 2001 and not thereafter, but despite this weakness in training, the traders in question did not attend at all the market abuse training provided; and although the desk did receive some compliance training in respect of observing proper standards of market conduct, the language used by the traders in their communication of their proposed strategy to their senior management suggested that they had inadequate knowledge of market conduct issues and thus by implication the general training they had received was inadequate.

---

1 FSA Final Notice, 28 June 2005, para 6.1.5. See para **11.24**.

FSA relationship building and notifiable events

11.61 Senior management must not lose sight of the importance and benefits of regular interaction and communication with the FSA. These may come about as a result of either regular reporting requirements such as the new RMAR, complaints reporting, special notifications that may be necessary where errors have happened, as well as where there is direct communication with FSA staff during Arrow and thematic review visits. Firms may even consider the benefits of general dialogue with its FSA supervisory staff as part of a wider relationship building exercise.

11.62 How a firm chooses to manage its relationship with the FSA and in particular its FSA supervision team can have a significant impact on the FSA's perception of the strengths of the firm and ultimately how it chooses to manage its dealings with the firm. A strong and positive relationship can lead to a trusting and co-operative relationship whereas a negative and aggressive relationship can give rise to a relationship of caution or even lack of trust. Senior management must consider methods that may be utilised to manage and promote a firm's relationship with the FSA. In this section we will consider the positives of a strong FSA relationship programme, how firms can develop methods to improve their working relationship with the FSA as well as efficiently manage rule breach reporting rule. We will then go on to consider the more contentions issue of how senior management might manage a response to an FSA enforcement actions against a firm, the affect that such actions may have on a firm and whether these affects can be mitigated through a predetermined enforcement risk management plan.

Relationship building

11.63 In Chapter 4 we considered the FSA's risk-based approach to the supervision of firms. As part of the FSA's individual firm risk assessment it might be the case that a firm's management might only be exposed to direct contact with it supervision team once every 2–3 years. For high risk firms, however, the contact between the FSA and the firm's senior management might be significantly more frequent.

11.64 No matter how frequently the FSA might schedule direct contact with a firm's senior management, there is a great deal of merit for firms, their compliance departments and senior management, to proactively develop and maintain a good working relationship with the FSA. Indeed there is argument that a programme of relationship building will support a firm's compliance with Principle for Business 11 and significantly contribute to a firm dealing with the FSA in an open and co-operative manner. FSA Principle for Business 11 states:

> 'a firm must deal with its regulators in an open and co-operative way and must disclose to the FSA appropriately anything relating to the firm of which the FSA would reasonably expect notice.'

11.65 Any firm whether authorised or regulated by the FSA should consider establishing a programme of regular contact with its supervision staff. The contact should be conducted with a view to ensuring that the firm's business model and approach to regulatory obligations are explained and understood by the FSA. It should be acknowledged that such a programme of events can only provide comfort to the regulator and cannot be used as a method of allowing the regulator to test the firm's approach to compliance. Nonetheless, a well thought out and conducted programme of contact can significantly contribute to the development of the FSA's confidence in the firm.

11.66 Senior management should consider introducing the FSA to the following aspects of their firm

- its business model;
- the types of business it conducts;
- its general approach to the conduct of business;

- the organisational structure within the firm;
- the role of the compliance department;
- activities performed by the compliance department;
- a brief overview of how compliance activities are conducted;
- the experience of senior compliance staff;
- methods used by the compliance department to communicate compliance procedures and policy;
- an open and honest approach to areas of risk within the firm and how the compliance department and senior management of the firm deal with those matters.

11.67   The firm should consider the frequency with which it might most appropriately have direct contact with the FSA's staff. For more complex firms, a contact frequency of once a quarter may be sufficient. With less complex firms, an attempt to make contact once every six months may be appropriate. At the beginning of a firm's FSA relationship, whether that follows from the initial granting of authorisation, or a change in business permission, or even the transfer of a firm from one regulator supervision team to another, steps should be taken to explain the fundamentals of the firm's business, its regulatory history and its organisational arrangements. Thereafter, the firm should attempt to keep the FSA's staff up to date with any business issues arising at the firm. Matters such as changes to senior staff or management, launch of new products or investment offerings, or changes in business direction could all be explained.

11.68   The key objective in maintaining a programme of dialogue and communication is to ensure that the FSA has a firm understanding of the firm's business and is confident that the firm is able to deal with any regulatory issues or breaches that occur. Methods of managing potential enforcement actions brought against the firm are explored at para **11.101**. However, it is fair to say that the FSA might be more inclined to avoid serious enforcement action where it is confident that an authorised firm is able to deal with any rule breaches in a sound, organised and controlled manner. Whereas if the FSA holds the view that rule breaches have been caused by the firm's lack of controls and that such identified rule breaches will not be managed adequately then enforcement action is more likely.

11.69   The key message for all firms is that regulator staff do not like surprises. Where the FSA identifies problematical issues or even rule breaches for which they have not had prior notification, then the regulatory tools they may use are likely to be more intrusive and wide ranging. Whereas, if the firm has proactively reported details of any its business developments, problems, concerns and rule breaches in a logical and controlled manner within an environment of trust and co-operation between the FSA and the firm, formal intervention is less likely. In discharging any communication programme with the FSA a firm's senior management must ensure that information presented to the FSA, whether written or oral is accurate and not likely to mislead. Indeed it is a criminal offence under, s 398(1) of the FSMA 2000 (the Act) for a person who, in purported compliance with any requirement imposed by or under the Act, to knowingly or recklessly give the FSA information which is false or misleading in a material particular.

Required notifications to the FSA

11.70 For most firms the most testing time for senior management's relationship with the FSA is when the firm finds that it has breached one of its regulatory obligations and is faced with the requirement of drawing this breach to the attention of the FSA. Firms are obliged by Principle for Business 11 to notify the FSA of '...*anything relating to the firm of which the FSA would reasonably expect notice.*[1]' The FSA provide guidance in SUP 15.3.8G of the types of matters that should be disclosed to ensure compliance with Principle 11. These will include matters such as:

- any proposed restructuring, reorganisation or business expansion which could have a significant impact on the firm's risk profile or resources, such as setting up a new undertaking within a firm's group, or a new branch (whether in the United Kingdom or overseas, commencing the provision of a new type of product or service, entering into, or significantly changing, a material outsourcing arrangement;

- any significant failure in the firm's systems or controls, including those reported to the firm by the firm's auditor;

- any action which a firm proposes to take which would result in a material change in its capital adequacy or solvency.

---

1 High Level Principle for Business 11.

11.71 Moreover, general and specific notification obligations are set out in the FSA's Supervision sourcebook. A series of general notification requirements is provided in relation to:

- Matters that might have a serious regulatory impact.

- Breaches of FSA rules and the Act.

- Civil, criminal and regulatory proceedings.

- Fraud and irregularities.

- Insolvency, bankruptcy and winding up.

11.72 Each of these matters may be classified as issues that might if left unattended increase the risk the firm presents to the FSA's Statutory Objectives that thus require careful regulator scrutiny and possibly intervention.

11.73 The FSA requires notification under SUP 15.3.1R of matters that will have a serious regulatory impact in particular relating to the firm's authorisation, its reputation in the market, its ability to service is customers or have financial impact of the financial system or other firms. Each of the specific requirements, although potentially overlapping, must be notified to the FSA immediately the firm becomes aware, or has information which reasonably suggests, that the matters have occurred or may occur in the foreseeable future. The matters are:

(1) the firm failing to satisfy one or more of the threshold conditions; or

(2) any matter which could have a significant adverse impact on the firm's reputation; or

(3) any matter which could affect the firm's ability to continue to provide adequate services to its customers and which could result in serious detriment to a customer of the firm; or

(4) any matter in respect of the firm which could result in serious financial consequences to the financial system or to other firms.

11.74 Notifications are also required under SYSC 15.3.11R when the firm has identified breaches of FSA rules or provisions of the Act by or against the firm, its directors or employees, approved persons or appointed representatives. The firm is required to make notification under SYSC 15.3.11R immediately it becomes aware, or has information which reasonably suggests, that any of the following matters have occurred, may have occurred or may occur in the foreseeable future. These matters are:

(a) a significant breach of a rule (which includes a Principle) or Statement of Principle; or

(b) a breach of any requirement imposed by the Act or by regulations or an order made under the Act by the Treasury (except if the breach is an offence, in which case (c) applies); or

(c) the bringing of a prosecution for, or a conviction of, any offence under the Act, by (or as regards (c) against) the firm or any of its directors, officers, employees, approved persons, or appointed representatives.

11.75 SYSC 15.3.11R talks in terms of significant rule breaches. This suggests that there is a category of breaches that could be classified as not significant that would not require notification. In determining significance the FSA expect firms to have regard to potential financial losses to customers or the firm, the frequency of the breach, the implications for the firm's systems and controls and if there were delays in identifying rectifying the breach[1].

---

1 See SUP 15.3.12G.

11.76   Civil or regulatory proceedings against the firm can give rise to an obligation to report those matters to the FSA under SUP15.3.15R. Such matters can give rise to financial liabilities that would threaten the viability of the authorised firm or in the case of actions by other regulatory organisations indicate that the firm may no longer be able to meet the threshold conditions.

11.77   The requirement in SUP 15.3.1R states:

A firm must notify the FSA immediately if:

(1)   civil proceedings are brought against the firm and the amount of the claim is significant in relation to the firm's financial resources or its reputation; or

(2)   any action is brought against the firm under section 71 of the Act (Actions for damages) or section 150 (Actions for damages); or

(3)   disciplinary measures or sanctions have been imposed on the firm by any statutory or regulatory authority, professional organisation or trade body (other than the FSA) or the firm becomes aware that one of those bodies has started an investigation into its affairs; or

(4)   the firm is prosecuted for, or convicted of, any offence involving fraud or dishonesty, or any penalties are imposed on it for tax evasion; or

(5)   it is an OPS firm, which is a trustee, and is removed as trustee by a court order.

11.78   Further the FSA is concerned to receive notification of matters relating to fraud, matters impacting upon honesty and integrity and accounting or record irregularities. SUP 15.3.17 R provides:

A firm must notify the FSA immediately if one of the following events arises and the event is significant:

(1)   it becomes aware that an employee may have committed a fraud against one of its customers; or

(2)   it becomes aware that a person, whether or not employed by it, may have committed a fraud against it; or

(3)   it considers that any person, whether or not employed by it, is acting with intent to commit a fraud against it; or

(4) it identifies irregularities in its accounting or other records, whether or not there is evidence of fraud; or

(5) it suspects that one of it employees may be guilty of serious misconduct concerning his honesty or integrity and which is connected with the firm's regulated activities or ancillary activities.

11.79 Once again SUP 15.3.17R expresses the obligation in terms of events that are significant. In relation to that requirement the FSA provide guidance and expect firms when determining whether a matter is significant to have regard to both size of any monetary loss or potential monetary loss to itself or its customers and the risk of reputational loss to the firm. The FSA is also concerned as to whether the incident or a pattern of incidents reflects weaknesses in the firm's internal controls.

11.80 Where the firm experiences major financial difficulties, that lead to insolvency or bankruptcy or where a decision is taken to wind up the business, notification is required by 15.3.21R, which requires:

A firm must notify the FSA immediately of any of the following events:

(1) the calling of a meeting to consider a resolution for winding up the firm; or

(2) an application to dissolve the firm or to strike it off the Register of Companies; or

(3) the presentation of a petition for the winding up of the firm; or

(4) the making of, or any proposals for the making of, a composition or arrangement with any one or more of its creditors; or

(5) an application for the appointment of an administrator or trustee in bankruptcy to the firm; or

(6) the appointment of a receiver to the firm (whether an administrative receiver or a receiver appointed over particular property); or

(7) an application for an interim order against the firm under section 252 of the Insolvency Act 1986 (or, in Northern Ireland, section 227 of the Insolvency (Northern Ireland) Order 1989); or

(8) if the firm is a sole trader:

(a) an application for a sequestration order on the firm; or

(b) the presentation of a petition for bankruptcy; or

(9) anything equivalent to (1) to (8) above occurring in respect of the firm in a jurisdiction outside the United Kingdom

11.81 Once any compliance breach has been identified the firm should give serious considerations to whether the breach should be notified to the FSA. In Chapter 4 various risk assessment tools were considered, including the use of breach and near miss logs. These records can be used by senior management to plot not only risk tends within a firm but also the basis of senior management's internal management intelligence of the rule breaches that occur and the extent of the breaches across the firm's business. This data can then be used by senior management to determine whether a matter is serious enough to require notification. Senior management should then as a matter of practice, record their rationale for and decisions to report the matter. The question of whether or not to report regulatory issues or rule breaches to the FSA can be a difficult one for a firm. It is certainly the case that not all rule breaches should be reported, but a firm must be able to demonstrate that any identified rule breaches have been managed internally in an appropriate manner, whether or not they have been reported. It may be difficult for senior management of the firm to predict whether an isolated incident or more widespread rule breach should be reported. In determining whether a report is necessary the following questions may be asked:

- Is the matter sufficiently material that the regulator will want to be notified of the matter? Materiality can be defined as something of great importance or consequence.

- Is the issue widespread within the organisation? For example, if during the firm's compliance monitoring programme it is identified that the firm has failed to meet its regulatory obligation either universally or for a statistically significant number of customers, then the firm should consider reporting this matter. However, if the incident is related to no more than one or a few customers then it may be sufficient not to report.

- Where there is a clear obligation to the regulator to make a report, such as in the requirement under the approved persons regime to make a statement in relation to the reasons for the dismissal by the firm of an approved person.

11.82 The question of whether or not to report a matter to a regulator presents many firms and compliance departments with a dilemma. Save those matters provided in the specific guidance Principle 11 and SUP 15.3.1R and 15.3.11R are not specific about either the type of issues to be notified or the timing of notifications and thus senior management are often faced with the dilemma of whether to report a matter and if so how quickly to report and how to phrase the report made. Management has to balance between its obligation to notify the FSA quickly and provide an accurate and thorough response demonstrating that the firm has both identified the full extent of the issues and is in control of remedying the problem. The firm's obligations to report and its desire to keep control of the management of the problems become pronounced when the matter is so serious that it might reasonably lead to enforcement. When potential enforcement issues are identified within a firm it is not merely a question of addressing the matter internally. Consideration must then be given to how notification should be provided to the FSA and the consequences of providing that notification. It must also be remembered that any action that the FSA may take arising from the reported breaches, whether against the firm or any individuals within the firm, will be viewed in the context of the firms notification and the manner in which the firm has dealt with the rule breach in question. This should be balanced against the likelihood that, if the rule breach in question is serious, and is identified by the FSA during a risk assessment or themed supervision visit, any enforcement action taken will be more severe if they conclude that the matter should have been reported but was not.

11.83   The first concern for senior management, however, is often whether the notification will lead to FSA intervention or potentially an enforcement action. Whilst it is not the notification itself but the rule breach in question that might lead to FSA action against the firm or any individual within the firm, it is the case that the firm's prior relationship with the FSA, its track record of strong and compliant management and the manner in which it proposes to deal with the rule breach will have either positive or negative on the manner in which the FSA determines to deal with the matter notified.

11.84   A report of rule breaches presented to the FSA should be clear and in writing, containing as much support material as necessary to justify the methodology applied in identifying the breach, the investigation the firm is conducting to identify the extent of the breaches and any corrective work either undertaken or proposed to eliminate the risk of further recurrence. The report should also contain, where necessary, a clear timescale over which corrective action will be completed. It may be that there needs to be milestone dates at which certain actions are to be taken and this may well include further contact with the regulatory authority. In the case of systemic breaches within the firm, the compliance department or senior management may also wish to retain a firm of external advisers or reporting accountants to review periodically the corrective work it will undertake to ensure that it is carried out to the standard deemed acceptable by the regulatory authority. Moreover, the firm may wish to offer external adviser reports to the regulatory authority as a way of providing further comfort.

11.85   When reporting a notifiable to the FSA, it is essential to ensure that the report is clearly composed and includes an explanation of the following:

- the extent of the problem or issue;

- the background to the problem or issue;

- the extent of any rule breach;

- any actions taken by the firm to identify the extent of the breach;

- the actions taken to ensure that the breach does not recur;

- actions taken to identify any liability that has been caused for customers;

- the calculated compensation due; and

- any procedural changes that have become necessary within the organisation.

11.86 It is an important element of reporting to convey a clear impression of the control the firm has over the reported matter and corrective action it proposes to put in place to deal with the rule breaches. If the FSA concludes that there is little merit in it becoming involved in the matter it will leave the resolution of the problem to the firm. However, if the FSA feels uncomfortable with the firm's methodology in identifying the extent of the problem and steps taken to eliminate any potential recurrence of the problem then it is possible that it might choose to intervene on either a formal or informal footing.

11.87 Preparation of rule breach reports should be carefully considered. Particular care should be given to the planning of any corrective work that is proposed and the timescales over which corrective work should be completed. Whilst it is important to ensure that the response of the firm to any identified rule breaches will be acceptable to the FSA, it is also vital to ensure the firm does not fall into the trap of over committing itself to corrective work. Such over commitment can occur as a result of the extent of the work proposed and the timescales over which the work is to be completed. It is vital for a firm not to try and impress the FSA with its commitment to dealing with the matter by an over elaborate and unrealistic programme of remedial work. Whereas it undoubtedly will be the case that the FSA will be more impressed with a realistic approach to corrective work. It will no doubt be distressed by any failure by the firm to complete any corrective work which with hindsight is proven to have been over commited by the firm.

11.88 Finally, dependent upon the nature of any rules breaches identified and reported upon, it may be necessary for the firm to negotiate and agree with the FSA the extent of any corrective work. Whether this suggested approach is correct is very much based on the judgement of the firm's senior management and any advice received from external advisers. It would certainly be prudent for the firm to suggest the type of corrective work it considers appropriate, followed by an invitation to the FSA to discuss whether the proposals are suitable.

11.89 In conclusion, whenever a firm is placed in a position where it must make a formal report on rule breaches, it is important that the firm's response and written report clearly conveys its commitment to resolving the problem in a controlled and structured manner. Such an approach should not only contribute to a lessoning of regulatory risk, but can also allow the firm to retain control of its proposed redial action.

11.90 Needless to say, for some firms the extent or nature of rule breaches reported will be sufficiently serious for the FSA to exercise greater scrutiny over the matter and perhaps deal with the rule breaches through the enforcement process. The FSA policy towards using its regulatory tools including enforcement actions is considered in Chapter 5 and the methods of approach that can be taken by firms towards enforcement proceedings are explored in detail at para **11.101** below.

Management's involvement with FSA supervision visits

11.91 All authorised and regulated firms are potentially subject to detailed and thorough FSA supervision visits. For higher risk firms, these visits may take the form of risk assessment reviews designed to consider all the areas of the firm's business. All, firms, however are subject to selection for thematic reviews which will focus on specific areas of the firm's business and concentrate on the regulatory issues impacting upon the FSA's priorities for the year. It may be considered appropriate during a visit or a formal investigation to focus on a specific area of the firm's business activities for the purpose of identifying whether or not rule breaches have occurred. All firms need to be aware of the benefits of full and timely preparation for such visits and ensuring that its senior management engage with the FSA supervision staff in a constructive, open and structured manner. A firm that professionally handles an FSA visit will help convey a strong impression that the firm is in control of its regulatory responsibilities and will help to portray the firm in a good light. Firms must, however, be concerned that any attempt to over manage and control the visit will be viewed cynically by supervision staff and needless to say any attempt to disguise materials or misrepresent information requested during a visit will certainly contravene Principle 11 and potentially be an offence under FSMA 2000, s 398(1) which provides that

> 'A person who, in purported compliance with any requirement imposed by or under this Act, knowingly or recklessly gives the Authority information which is false or misleading in a material particular is guilty of an offence.'

11.92 An imperative for any firm is always to be prepared. It may be that the FSA has requested information from the firm in advance of the visit to assist the FSA's supervision staff to conduct the visit more productively. Where material has been requested in advance, the firm should always ensure that it is compiled diligently and made available to the FSA's staff on time, whether that is in advance of the visit or at a time requested during the visit. It is, of course, good practice for the firm to ensure that it understands the information that it is presents to the FSA and, if the information reveals any particular risks or potential rule breaches, that it is in a position to respond to any questions providing further information to demonstrate, where it is the case, the actions it has already taken to deal with the matter in question.

11.93 It may also be appropriate, depending upon the type of visit being conducted, for the firm to agree a visit schedule with the FSA. Such schedules may identify particular staff that need to be made available for interview, the areas of the firm's business that the interview will relate to as well as the extent of the interviews. The schedule may also identify the areas of the firm's business to be reviewed and the manner in which the review will take place. Once again, this will allow the firm to ensure that all relevant and appropriate materials are made available to the regulatory authority promptly and in a manner which is meaningful to the visit being conducted.

11.94 It is certainly the case that any staff potentially exposed to FSA interviews should appreciate the responsibility they have when being interviewed and the skills that they should apply during the interview. It may be the case that members of staff exposed to FSA interviews for the very first time will be unnerved by the prospect and senior managers might, therefore consider providing briefing staff in advance of any FSA visits as means of clarify any areas of business likely to be reviewed and the types of questions that may be raised. During a visit, compliance staff should also be prepared to accompany regulators' staff. This can serve a number of purposes:

- to ensure that any interviews or visits remain focused;

- to provide comfort to the member of staff being interviewed;

- to allow the compliance staff to explain any misunderstood items that may be addressed during an interview; and

- to ensure that other compliance staff and management of the firm are kept up to date with the progress of the visit.

Feedback meetings

11.95 Once the FSA's visit is concluded, a short feedback meeting may take place during which an explanation might be provided of any findings from the visit. Any informal or verbal feedback meetings must always be accepted in the informal context in which they are given, and senior management must appreciate the potential for the any formal feedback to vary from the informal, once the final report has been through its internal FSA moderation[1].

---

[1] See Chapter 4 for discussion of the FSA Risk Mitigation programme process relating to reports.

11.96 Feedback meetings can, however, be a valuable opportunity to discuss any immediate findings from the FSA visit and can provide the firm with indications of the likely items that will be reported by the FSA.

11.97 Ultimately, following a visit, it is likely the FSA will formally report its findings in writing and will expect written responses to any corrective or risk mitigation actions required. Some corrective actions may be specific whereas others may require a response from the firm setting out actions it is prepared to take to deal with a particular item that has been identified. Chapter 4 provides fuller detail on the FSA Risk Assessment programme and its approach to individual firms' risk mitigation.

11.98 Any written reports required from the firm should be carefully considered and, once again, it is important for the firm not to over commit itself when promising remedial work or its completion timescale. It is certainly the case that the FSA will not object to a further discussion about the proposed corrective action or if senior management considers that an alternative approach or timescale may be more appropriate to that proposed by the FSA. In this instance, it is always sensible for dialogue to take place and an agreement reached between the firm and the FSA supervision team manager.

11.99 When responding to visit reports, the firm should ensure that the response it provides is articulated in a clear and unambiguous manner and, of course, that any corrective work required is in fact conducted.

11.100 It is a useful discipline for a firm, when completing more complex corrective work, to have that work independently verfified whether by the firms internal audit department or an external professional services firm. This can be a useful mechanism to ensure that corrective work will be completed to the satisfaction of the FSA prior to any attempt by the Authority to verfify the completion of the corrective work. It should always be remembered that any corrective work might be subject to further review by the FSA. It will undoubtedly be the case that, if the FSA considers that corrective work has not been completed adequately or in accordance with specifications set, it may very well treat this failure as a regulatory breach and escalate as an enforcement issue.

Management's interaction with FSA enforcement proceedings

11.101 Where a firm runs into major regulatory difficulties, the FSA may determine that in its opinion the only course of action is to take enforcement action against the firm. In Chapter 5 we consider the FSA's use of enforcement proceedings as a regulatory tool. It is important, however, for a firm's senior management to consider how they might react in situations when enforcement proceedings are either possible or threatened. Few firms are ever prepared for the many difficulties that will inevitably confront them. Valuable time and energy is often wasted in deciding how to manage the firm's response to the enforcement action and identifying how the FSA's enforcementg process operates. Moreover, it is often the case during an enforcement action that the working relationship between the firm's senior management can become very strained, as individual managers come to terms with the fact that the firm is being accused of significant rule breaches that are considered deserving of enforcement. Many firms, having been disciplined, often observe that they had no idea of the pitfalls they would encounter at the start of the process.

An enforcement risk management plan

11.102 Developing an enforcement risk management plan enables a firm to make provision for a structured management response to any future enforcement action. It can create policy mechanisms with a view to safeguarding its future business conduct and ensuring that the regulator receives a response to allegations that are in the interest of effective regulation and not to the complete disadvantage of the firm or its customers. The latter can certainly happen in a company's hasty attempt to demonstrate that it is keen to co-operate with the FSA.

11.103 Whilst some may consider that prior planning for a potential but unknown enforcement action is a cynical manoeuvre, it can make good operational sense. It should be viewed no differently from other areas of risk management or disaster recovery. Who would ever suggest that a company's back-up systems for dealing with computer system failure, lapse of health and safety standards or the involvement of the company in high profile litigation, have a cynical motive behind them? A contingency plan may very well help the firms save time, energy and unnecessary expense should the worst happen.

11.104 Fundamentally, an enforcement risk management plan can be designed to plan for procedural responses to the issues and risk that are likely to arise during enforcement proceedings and allocate responsibilities to specified staff for dealing with the identified actions. At a fundamental level, certain issues can be specified in a disciplinary risk management plan. These could include:

- establishing a management steering committee to oversee the firm's regulatory, public and internal response to the allegations;

- ensuring management separation of the handling or defence of the enforcement proceedings, FSA corrective work and ongoing compliance responsibility, so as to avoid regulatory overload;

- eliminating from the management steering committee and day-to-day enforcement case management any personnel who may have a conflict of interest in the firm's defence or response;

- ensuring that the firm responds to the allegations swiftly, intelligently and openly so as to avoid or limit the possibility of FSA intervention;

- the objective analysis of the FSA's allegations and whether the action should be defended or settled;
- the immediate need to start communicating with the FSA; and
- how best to protect the firm's business reputation.

The separation of enforcement action management from continuing compliance

11.105 Experience suggests that compliance departments and senior compliance personnel often bear the brunt of dealing with and responding to any enforcement proceedings. Their task will often include:

- co-ordinating corrective work with the FSA;
- developing methods of revised compliance;
- briefing and co-ordinating any external advisors instructed to act for the firm during the enforcement proceedings;
- dealing with any internal corporate changes that come about as a result of the matter;
- trying to develop a better relationship with the FSA; and
- preparing the firm for any follow-up or verification visit from the FSA which will be checking to see whether the corrective work has been completed.

11.106 Compliance staff faced with these many tasks often experience regulatory overload. They are expected to deal with many competing areas of the firm's business. Each of these areas often requires detailed and urgent attention and, inevitably, the compliance officer or compliance department will cease to function effectively. It can be self-defeating for a firm to operate in this manner and therefore makes sound sense for the management of any enforcement proceedings and resulting corrective work to be managed by a person or department separate from the person or department that has day-to-day compliance responsibility.

Avoiding conflicts of interest

11.107 When allocating responsibility for the management of enforcement proceedings to any person, a firm should take into account and manage in so far as it is possible, any conflicts of interest. It is often the case that an allegation of regulatory misconduct invariably involves some direct or indirect criticism of a firm's staff and senior management. It is absolutely essential that managers or other persons who are subject to any such direct or indirect criticism are not involved in the management of the firm's response to the enforcement action. Firms often make this mistake and soon discover that these people then embark on a campaign to protect their own reputation, pursue self-serving avenues of enquiry or to defend the indefensible as a way of defending their own position or involvement in the alleged breaches.

Limiting enforcement action and intervention

11.108 Depending on the circumstances which have given rise to the enforcement action, firms may find it possible to mitigate or eliminate some of the more exacting enforcement remedies available to the FSA if they act quickly. If, despite its misconduct, the firm is able to act effectively and responsibly in correcting the compliance failures in question, its responsible behaviour may persuade the FSA not to exercise powers of intervention. In turn such response may even assist the firm in mitigating the outcome of the enforcement action, although it is unlikely that it will act to prevent or withdraw the enforcement action completely.

11.109 The firm's responses will of course have to be commensurate with the misconduct in question and may, in severe circumstances, restrict its ability to take on new business for a time. It is, however, far better if the company is seen to be in control of its rule breach rectification than if the FSA is 'setting the pace'.

11.110 Firms can only respond promptly if the circumstances giving rise to the proceedings come to its attention quickly. If the firm has identified the problem itself but is obliged to tell the FSA, it ought to accompany the notification with a full statement of how it proposes to respond. If, however, the firm only becomes aware of misconduct when it receives formal notification about the conduct from the FSA, that notification may take the form of an intervention order. In that case, the company ought to provide the FSA with a speedy description of how it can respond to the misconduct and manage any corrective work that may be necessary.

Identifying the FSA's objectives

11.111 Those responsible for the management of a firm's response to enforcement proceedings should always aim to identify the FSA's overall objective in commencing the enforcement proceedings. An understanding of the objective of the case will allow them to understand:

- how receptive the FSA will be to the firm's own proposals for corrective work;

- whether there is scope for a negotiated settlement; and

- how to plan a public relations exercise to protect the firm's reputation.

11.112 In understanding these, firms should consider any statement the FSA has published about its approach to enforcement which can be used to calculate how seriously it may treat disciplinary cases. In Chapter 5 the FSA's current approach to enforcement proceedings is considered in more detail.

Admit or defend?

11.113 The FSA's enforcement process is in part designed to facilitate actions to be brought to a speedy end through a process of admission and negotiated settlement. The extent to which a regulated firm is prepared to accept a disciplinary settlement is undoubtedly dependent on the penalty the FSA is seeking to impose. Those regulated firms facing expulsion or exceptionally large financial penalties may be more inclined to contest the allegations, but there are many advantages to a firm which settles disciplinary proceedings as promptly as possible.

11.114 When faced with the prospect of enforcement actions, few firms are prepared for the many difficulties that will inevitably confront them. Valuable time and energy is often wasted in deciding how to manage the company's response to the enforcement action and identifying how the FSA enforcement process operates. In addition, it is often the case during enforcement proceedings, that the working relationship between the firm's managers can become very strained, as individual managers come to terms with the fact that the firm is being accused of significant rule breaches that are considered deserving of discipline. Many firms, having been disciplined, often complain that they had no idea of the pitfalls they would encounter at the start of the process.

11.115 For most regulated firms involved in enforcement proceedings, it is soon apparent whether the FSA has a strong case. If it has, little is to be gained from contesting the allegations. Those acting for the regulated firm should decide how strong the allegations are and should quickly begin a dialogue with the regulator's enforcement staff, seeking to identify the disciplinary sanctions the regulator is seeking. This approach is best in the majority of disciplinary actions. Negotiations at least allow the firm some involvement in the outcome of its own case. They also ensure that the firm has some control over the content of any resulting press release. Many regulated firms find that the conclusion of enforcement proceedings is something of a release; it relieves tension that can often build up within the firm, it ends speculation amongst the media and competitors and it allows management effort to be re-channelled into managing improvements to compliance procedures and repairing the damage to the firm's reputation.

Protecting the firm's reputation

11.116 Publicity and comment about the outcome of enforcement action will obviously cause some damage to the reputation of the company. The extent of the damage is determined by the scale of the regulatory misconduct, the penalty involved, the notoriety of the firm and the immediate political atmosphere. Other matters may also play their part. Issues such as the time of year, other items of news at the time and the actions of other regulated firms which are involved in enforcement actions will all contribute to the attention the media give to an individual firm's case. News of the enforcement action may come to the attention of the media – often through 'leaks' – months before formal conclusion of the action is expected. The most logical solution to this is for regulated firm to brief and enlist the services of a specialist public relations company.

Chapter 12

Authorisation, business permissions, and approved persons

'... under the FSA there will in future be just one authorisation available – authorisation by the FSA to carry out financial business in the UK. That authorisation will be rather like a driving licence. In other words you will have a licence, but with a list of permissions on it – all those things which the regulator allows you to do ...'

Howard Davies, Chairman, Financial Services Authority, 19 June 2000[1].

1 From a speech by Howard Davies at the BBA banking supervision conference 19 June 2000.

Introduction

12.1   One basic concept is consistent throughout the financial services regulatory systems in developed countries, is that of regulatory control over entry and participation in the financial services market through a system of authorisation. Such system of control ensures only persons considered by the regulatory laws of the county to be suitable to conduct financial services business are allowed to participate in the market. In addition, a process to approve key personnel involved in the management and operation of authorised firms goes some way to ensure that companies will be managed in accordance with regulatory standards.

In this chapter we will consider the requirement for authorisation and permission to conduct investment business together with the impact of the approved persons regime on both firms and the individual occupying a controlled function.

The requirement for authorisation

12.2   The FSMA 2000 controls entry and participation in the market through the general provision in s 19. Section 19(1) states that no person may carry on a regulated activity in the UK or be thought to be doing so unless he is:

- an authorised person; or

- an exempt person.

An integral part of the of the requirement for authorisation is the FSMA 2000 treatment of those investments treated as regulated investments and in s 22 and Sch 2 those activities treated as regulated activities. These are explored in more detail in Chapters 1 and 9.

The test to determine whether a person needs to be authorised to carry on a particular activity requires an analysis of three issues:

- Does the person's activity relate to a specified type of investment?

- Is the person's activity specified under the Act?

- and whether that activity is carried on by way of business.

Section 31 of the FSMA 2000 specifies the manner in which a person may be authorised and includes provision for the granting of authorisation to certain firms already authorised to conduct investment business in EU or EEA member states, known as qualifying firms. Section 31(1) specifies the categories of authorised persons for the purpose of the Act as:

- a person who has a Pt IV permission to carry on one or more regulated activities;

- an EEA firm qualifying for authorisation under Sch 3 to the Act;

- a Treaty firm qualifying for authorisation under Sch 4 to the Act;

- a person who is otherwise authorised by a provision of, or made under, this Act.

Under Pt IV of the FSMA 2000, provision is made for the application for obtaining permission from the FSA. We consider in para **12.16** below the FSA process for applying for permission to carry on regulated activities. Under s 40(1) of the FSMA 2000, permission may be granted to an individual, a body corporate, a partnership or an unincorporated association. Section 41(2) specifies that, in order to obtain permission, the FSA must ensure that the person will satisfy and continue to satisfy certain threshold conditions[1]. Section 41(3) goes on to provide that the duty imposed on the FSA under subsection (2) does not prevent the FSA, having due regard to that duty, from taking such steps as it considers are necessary, in relation to a particular authorised person, in order to secure its regulatory objective of the protection of consumers. In essence the provision in s 41(3) ensures that applications for Pt IV permission will be considered in the light of the risk to consumers of the applicant's business. Reference should be made to s 5(2) of the FSMA 2000 in relation to the protection of consumers which provides:

'In considering what degree of protection may be appropriate, the Authority must have regard to:

(a) the differing degrees of risk involved in different kinds of investment or other transaction;

(b) the differing degrees of experience and expertise that different consumers may have in relation to different kinds of regulated activity;

(c) the needs that consumers may have for advice and accurate information; and

(d) the general principle that consumers should take responsibility for their decisions.'

In its annual report for 2004/05 the FSA reported that of the 79 enforcement cases that it concluded by the use of powers, 45 related to fitness and propriety[2].

---

1 Refer to FSMA 2000, Sch 6.
2 FSA Annual Report 2004/2005, page 12 enforcement as a regulatory tool.

The by way of business test

12.3 Section 19 of the FSMA 2000 was intended to consolidate the different test for authorisation set out in the regulatory regimes brought together in the FSMA 2000. It is generally considered that s 19 and the ancillary test in s 22 which states that activity is a regulated activity if it is carried on by way of a business has broadened the scope of authorisation from the requirement in the Financial Services Act 1986. The FSMA test requires authorisation for specified activities that are incidental to another business. Conversely, the s 19 test is considered to be narrower than the business test in the Banking Act 1987 which required authorisation where a person held himself out as accepting deposits on a day-to-day basis or accepted deposits on more than specified occasions. During the report stage of the Financial Services and Markets Bill in Parliament, the Government stated that its approach was to catch, along with any mainstream activity, any activity that falls short of constituting a business in its own right but which should be regulated. It is clear from the wording of s 19 that even business with incidental investment activities requires authorisation. In order to ensure that the legislation does not inadvertently include or exclude activities that reasonably should or should not require authorisation as the case may be. The Treasury has exercised its powers under s 419 of the FSMA 2000 to define the meaning of 'carrying on a regulated activity by way of business' for the purpose of any Business Order it may make under s 22[1].

The Orders made by HM Treasury are supported by the provision of FSA guidance in PERG 2.3 guidance on the application of the by way of business test in respect of certain types of business.

The Orders made by HM Treasury under s 22 has resulted in a variation of identifying features in the 'by way of business' test between regulated activities, in part reflecting differences in the nature of the activities that might be unique to one each individual activity. The result is best illustrated by two examples. In relation to the activity of accepting deposits, the determining factor is frequency of the activity as Deposit Taking is no regarded as carried on by way of business by a person if he does not hold himself out as accepting deposits on a day-to-day basis and if the deposits he accepts are accepted only on particular occasions. To determine whether deposits are accepted only on particular occasions, the frequency of the occasions and any distinguishing characteristics must be taken into account. Alternatively in relation to a person who carries on an insurance mediation activity the key factor is whether the activity is undertaken for remuneration. In PERG 2.3.3G FSA state that the question of whether or not an activity is carried on by way of business is ultimately a question of judgment and that it is necessary to take into account of several factors including the degree of continuity, the existence of a commercial element, the scale of the activity and the proportion which the activity bears to other activities carried on by the same person but which are not regulated. The guidance does, furthermore make clear that the analysis of the proposed regulated activities and the impact of the by way of business test is one of fact and each of the described factors above are not necessarily conclusive.

---

1 This includes the Financial Services and Markets Act 2000 (Carrying on Regulated Activities by Way of Business) Order 2001, SI 2001/1177, the Financial Services and Markets Act 2000 (Regulated Activities) (Amendment) (No 2) Order 2003, SI 2003/1476 and the Financial Services and Markets Act 2000 (Carrying on Regulated Activities by Way of Business) (Amendment) Order 2005, SI 2005/922. Refer to FSMA 2000, Sch 6.

Threshold conditions

12.4   FSMA 2000, s 41 of the refers to the need for firms to satisfy certain Threshold Conditions in order to be granted authorisation and for such conditions to continue to be met for a firm to remain authorised. Schedule 6 provides further detail regarding these conditions providing definition to their application. In addition FSA has made rules contained it is handbook at COND, regarding the Threshold Conditions and how they are to be applied to firms applying for authorisation as well as the continuing obligation for all firms to meet those conditions. The Threshold Conditions are currently divided between five areas of requirement as follows with additional conditions added in relation to office locations in respect of the type or origin of certain types of insurance business:

- Condition 1: Legal status.
- Condition 2: Location of offices.
- Condition 3: Close links.

- Condition 4: Adequate resources.
- Condition 5: Suitability[1].

---

1 Special conditions under FSMA 2000, Sch 6, Pt III, para 8.

Threshold Condition 1: Legal status

12.5   This condition sets out specific legal status requirements for those seeking permission to carry on investment business. The person either must be a body corporate, registered friendly society or a member of Lloyd's. Moreover, a person seeking permission to carry on business of deposit taking must be either a body corporate or a partnership. The Financial Services and Markets Act 2000 (Variation of Threshold Conditions) Order 2001[1] imposes certain additional conditions on non-EEA insurers, under FSMA 2000, Sch 6, para 8. It requires furthermore if the person is not a Swiss General Insurance Company it must be must be a body corporate formed under the law of the country where its head office is situated.

---

1 SI 2001/2507.

Threshold Condition 2: Location of offices

12.6   It is a requirement that a body corporate constituted under any part of the UK must have its head office and registered office in the UK. Furthermore, where a person has a head office in the UK but is not a body corporate, he must carry on business in the UK. The Financial Services and Markets Act 2000 (Variation of Threshold Conditions) Order 2001 imposes certain additional conditions on non- EEA insurers, under FSMA 2000, Sch 6, para 8. It requires that that a non-EEA insurer (including a Swiss General Insurance company must appoint an authorised UK representative.

---

1 SI 2001/2507.

Threshold Condition 2A: Appointment of Claims Representatives

This condition inserted by the Financial Services and Markets Act 2000 (variation of Threshold Conditions) Order 2001[1] provides that if it a person is seeking to carry on, or carrying on, motor vehicle liability insurance business, that person must have a claims representative in each EEA State other than the

United Kingdom. Condition 2A (3) defines a claims representative as a person with responsibility for handling and settling claims arising from accidents of the kind mentioned in Article 1(2) of the fourth motor insurance directive.

1. SI 2001/2507.

Threshold Condition 3: Close links

12.7   Close links are specified in the FSMA 2000, Sch 6, Pt I, para 3(2). These will include, for example, where another person is a parent or subsidiary undertaking of the person seeking permission, where the third party owns or controls 20% or more of the voting rights, or capital of the person seeking permission. Or where the person seeking permission owns or controls 20% or more of the voting rights or capital of the third party. In the event that a close link exists, the FSA has to be satisfied that the links are not likely to prevent effective supervision of the person seeking permission[1].

1. FSMA 2000, Sch 6, Pt I, para 3.

Threshold Condition 4: Adequate resources

12.8   The person seeking permission must have resources which, in the opinion of the FSA are adequate in relation to the regulated activities they seek to carry on. In reaching the opinion, the FSA may take into account the person's membership of any group[1].

The FSA is required to ensure that a firm has adequate resources in relation to the specific regulated activity or regulated activities which it seeks to carry on, or carries on. The FSA interprets the term 'adequate' as meaning sufficient in terms of quantity, quality and availability, and "resources" to include all financial resources, non-financial resources and means of managing its resources, for example capital, provisions against liabilities, holdings of or access to cash and other liquid assets, human resources and effective means by which to manage risks[2]. The Financial Services and Markets Act 2000 (Variation of Threshold Conditions) Order 2001[3] imposes certain additional conditions on non-EEA insurers, under FSMA 2000, Sch 6, para 8. It requires that that a non-EEA insurer (including a Swiss General Insurance company must appoint an authorised UK representative and must have assets in the United Kingdom to a value specified in the FSA rules and where the applicant wants to carry on insurance business in other EEA States, the applicant must have assets in those other as are agreed between the FSA and the other States supervisory authorities

In its assessment of adequate resources, the FSA may have regard to any person appearing to it to be, or likely to be, in a relevant relationship with the firm, in accordance with s 49 of the FSMA 2000, for example, a firm's controllers, directors or partners, other persons with close links to the firm and other persons that exert influence on the firm which might pose a risk to the firm's satisfaction of the threshold conditions.

---

1 FSMA 2000, Sch 6, Pt I para 4.
2 COND 2.4.2 (2)G.
3 SI 2001/2507.

12.9   In *NDI Insurance Brokers v Financial Services Authority Ltd*[1] the Financial Services and Markets Tribunal was required to consider the question of adequate resources as it applied to the fitness and propriety of one of the directors of the applicant firm NDI (a Mr Greengrass who was also another applicant in the reference). The FSA's position in relation to Condition 4 was that a director by reason of his prior dealings was not fit and proper and that if the application for approval of him to perform the controlled function of director was refused, NDI would not have the requisite resources[2]. In the case the Tribunal found that Mr Greengrass was not fit and proper but considered there was no other reason to refuse the application. It considered that if Mr Greengrass were to resign as director and dispose of his shares that would be sufficient to distance himself from company and that the company would then be able to satisfy Threshold Condition 4. The Tribunal stated,

> '… As we have indicated, we came to the conclusion that while the reference so far as it related to Mr Greengrass must fail, there was no reason why it should fail in relation to NDI and Mr Britton if that outcome could be avoided without offending FSMA. The principal difficulty was NDI's connection with Mr Greengrass; as long as he remained a director and the holder of more than ten per cent of the shares (see FSMA section 179) he would not merely be connected with NDI but, for the purposes of the Act, controlling it …'

---

1 See Financial Services and Markets Tribunal reference FIN 2004/0027.
2 The FSA also contended that in relation to Condition 5 Suitability that if Mr Greengrass remained a director and the controlling shareholder of NDI, NDI's connection with him means that it too was not fit and proper. Given the Tribunal's decision in relation to Condition 4 this contention seems to be rejected.

12.10   In *Vrajlal Laxmidas Sodha v Financial Services Authority*[1], the Tribunal was required to consider the extent of resources necessary in a sole trader's business given the history of the sole trader's business activities. The applicant Mr Sodha had applied under s 40 of the FSMA 2000 for Pt IV permission as a sole trader to carry on the regulated activities of advising on and/or arranging mortgages and general insurance products (the Application). The FSA refused the application, as it was not of the view that Mr Sodha satisfied, nor would continue to satisfy, Threshold Conditions 4 and 5. In respect of Condition 4 (adequate resources) the FSA contended that having regard to all the circumstances, including that Mr Sodha proposed to carry on business by himself, he could not satisfy Condition 4 as there were not appropriate human resources which would effectively oversee the relevant systems and controls at all times. In particular the FSA was concerned by the level of complaints made against the applicant during the course of his career and the proportion of those complaints upheld by SJP and Barclays, 2 companies that Mr Sodha had been previously engaged by.. Whilst at Barclays Mr Sodha received 22 complaints over a 10-year period, all of which were upheld and 7 of which resulted in compensation being paid. During his 12-year period (ending in June 2004) with SJP Mr Sodha was the subject of 55 complaints of which 17 were upheld.

Mr Sodha sought to demonstrate to the Tribunal that although a sole trader he was prepared to retain the services of a compliance consultant to provide monitoring services of his new client mortgage business. The Tribunal was not satisfied that Mr Sodha met Condition 4. In its judgment it is clear that the Tribunal was concerned about Mr Sodha's own ability to operate his business compliantly, it considered that as a sole trader Mr Sodha would be the person responsible for managing his business; he would choose the level of compliance support and training which he requires; he would be responsible for dealing with clients' concerns including how to fulfil their requirements and deal with their complaints. There is no obligation on Mr Sodha to continue a contract with the compliance consultant he proposed using. The Tribunal placed particular emphasis on Mr Sodha's past experience and clearly considered that the resource he proposed would not be adequate. The Tribunal referred to his past experience and stated:

> '... We note that even after Mr Sodha was placed under constant supervision at SJP the level of complaints remained high due to the use of flawed procedures and advice. Weekly monitoring is less supervision than constant supervision.
>
> Monitoring is inherently something which occurs after the event and dependent upon adequate records being maintained ...'

1 Financial Services and Markets Tribunal reference FIN 2005/0031.

12.11 The FSA's Handbook on Threshold Conditions sets out, at COND 2.4.4(2)G, useful guidance on those matters the FSA will have regard to when considering resources. Relevant matters may include, but are not limited to:

(a)   whether there are any indications that the firm may have difficulties if the application is granted, at the time of the grant or in the future, in complying with any of the FSA's prudential rules;

(b) whether there are any indications that the firm will not be able to meet its debts as they fall due;

(c) whether there are any implications for the adequacy of the firm's resources arising from the history of the firm, for example whether the firm has:

— been adjudged bankrupt, or

— entered into liquidation, or

— been the subject of a receiving or administration order, or

— had a bankruptcy or winding-up petition served on it, or

— had its estate sequestrated, or

— entered into a deed of arrangement or an individual voluntary agreement (or in Scotland, a trust deed) or other composition in favour of its creditors, or is doing so, or

— within the last ten years, failed to satisfy a judgment debt under a court order, whether in the United Kingdom or elsewhere,

(d) whether the firm has taken reasonable steps to identify and measure any risks of regulatory concern that it may encounter in conducting its business (see COND 2.4.6G) and has installed appropriate systems and controls and appointed appropriate human resources to measure them prudently at all times: see SYSC 3.1 (systems and controls) and SYSC 3.2 (areas covered by systems and controls); and

(e) whether the firm has conducted enquiries into the financial services sector in which it intends to conduct business (see COND 2.4.6G) that are sufficient to satisfy itself that:

— it has access to adequate capital, by reference to the FSA's prudential requirements, to support the business including any losses which may be expected during its start-up period, and

— client money, deposits, custody assets and policyholders' rights will not be placed at risk if the business fails.

The FSA will expect firms to plan business appropriately so that the likely risks of regulatory concern can be identified, measured and managed. The FSA observes that any newly-formed firm can be susceptible to early difficulties. Such difficulties could arise from a lack of relevant expertise and judgment, or from ill-constructed and insufficiently tested business strategies. It is also recognised that a firm may be susceptible to difficulties where it substantially changes its business activities. As a result, the FSA would expect a firm which is applying for a Part IV permission, or a substantial variation of that permission, to take adequate steps to satisfy itself and, if relevant, the FSA that:

(a)   it has a well-constructed business or strategy plan for its product or
service which demonstrates that it is ready, willing and organised to
comply with the relevant requirements in IPRU and SYSC that apply to
the regulated activity it is seeking to carry on;

(b)   its business or strategy plan has been sufficiently tested; and

(c)   the financial and other resources of the firm are commensurate with the
likely risks it will face.

Threshold Condition 5: Suitability

12.12   When determining whether the firm will satisfy and continue to satisfy
threshold condition 5, the FSA will have regard to all relevant matters, whether
arising in the UK or elsewhere. Relevant matters set out in COND 2.5.4G
include, but are not limited to, whether a firm:

(a)   conducts, or will conduct, its business with integrity and in compliance
with proper standards;

(b)   has, or will have, a competent and prudent management; and

(c)   can demonstrate that it conducts, or will conduct, its affairs with the
exercise of due skill, care and diligence.

The authority has to be satisfied that the person seeking permission is a fit and
proper person, which will include an analysis of any connection the person may
have with any other individual, the nature of the regulated activity to be carried
on, and the need to ensure that the person's affairs are conducted soundly.

As to suitability, the firm is required to satisfy the FSA that it is 'fit and proper'
to have a Part IV permission having regard to all the circumstances, including its
connections with other persons, the range and nature of its proposed (or current)
regulated activities and the overall need to be satisfied that its affairs are and will
be conducted soundly and prudently (see also PRIN and SYSC)[1].

The FSA will also take into consideration anything that could influence a firm's
continuing ability to satisfy this threshold condition. Examples include the
firm's position within a UK or international group, information provided by
overseas regulators about the firm, and the firm's plans to seek to vary its Part IV
permission to carry on additional regulated activities once it has been granted
that permission by the FSA.

The FSA make it clear, at COND 2.5.3G, that the emphasis of the threshold
condition of suitability is on the suitability of the firm itself. It states that,
generally, the suitability of each person who performs a controlled function will
be assessed by the FSA under the approved persons regime. It further states that,

410

in certain circumstances, however, the FSA may consider that the firm is not suitable because of doubts over the individual or collective suitability of persons connected with the firm.

---

1 COND 2.5.2G.

A Conducting business with integrity and in compliance with proper standards

12.13 At COND2.5 the FSA also consider the question of a person's ability to conduct its business with integrity and in compliance with proper standards. In determining whether a firm will satisfy, and continue to satisfy, threshold condition 5 in respect of its conduct of business the following issues will be considered as set out in COND 2.5.6G:

- whether the firm has been open and co-operative in all its dealings with the FSA and any other regulatory body and is ready, willing and organised to comply with the requirements and standards under the regulatory system and other legal, regulatory and professional obligations; the relevant requirements and standards will depend on the circumstances of each case, including the regulated activities which the firm has permission, or is seeking permission, to carry on;

- whether the firm has been convicted, or is connected with a person who has been convicted, of any unspent offence involving fraud, corruption, perjury, theft, false accounting or other dishonesty, money laundering, market abuse or insider dealing, offences under legislation relating to insurance, banking or other financial services, companies, insolvency, consumer credit or consumer protection or any significant tax offence; where relevant, any spent convictions excepted for this purpose under the Rehabilitation of Offenders Act 1974 will be taken into consideration;

- whether the firm has been the subject of, or connected to the subject of, any existing or previous investigation or enforcement proceedings by the FSA, the Society of Lloyd's or by other regulatory authorities (including the FSA's predecessors), clearing houses or exchanges, professional bodies or government bodies or agencies; the FSA will, however, take both the nature of the firm's involvement in, and the outcome of, any investigation or enforcement proceedings into account in determining whether it is a relevant matter;

- whether the firm has contravened, or is connected with a person who has contravened, any provisions of the FSMA 2000 or any preceding financial services legislation, the regulatory system or the rules, regulations, statements of principles or codes of practice (for example, the Society of

Lloyd's Codes) of other regulatory authorities (including the FSA's predecessors), clearing houses or exchanges, professional bodies, or government bodies or agencies or relevant industry standards (such as the Non-Investment Products Code); the FSA will, however, take into account both the status of codes of practice or relevant industry standards and the nature of the contravention (for example, whether a firm has flouted or ignored a particular code);

• whether the firm, or a person connected with the firm, has been refused registration, authorisation, membership or licence to carry out a trade, business or profession or has had such registration, authorisation, membership or licence revoked, withdrawn or terminated, or has been expelled by a regulatory or government body; whether the FSA considers such a refusal relevant will depend on the circumstances;

• whether the firm has taken reasonable care to establish and maintain effective systems and controls for compliance with applicable requirements and standards under the regulatory system that apply to the firm and the regulated activities for which it has, or will have, permission;

• whether the firm has put in place procedures which are reasonably designed to:

(a) ensure that it has made its employees aware of, and compliant with, those requirements and standards under the regulatory system that apply to the firm and the regulated activities for which it has, or will have permission,

(b) ensure that its approved persons (whether or not employed by the firm) are aware of those requirements and standards under the regulatory system applicable to them,

(c) determine that its employees are acting in a way compatible with the firm adhering to those requirements and standards, and

(d) determine that its approved persons are adhering to those requirements and standards;

• whether the firm or a person connected with the firm has been dismissed from employment or a position of trust, fiduciary relationship or similar or has ever been asked to resign from employment in such a position; whether the FSA considers a resignation to be relevant will depend on the circumstances, for example if a person is asked to resign in circumstances that cast doubt over his honesty or integrity; and

• whether the firm or a person connected with the firm has ever been disqualified from acting as a director.

The quality and accuracy of a person's application for FSA permission can have a bearing on the FSA's decision to grant permission. Where information material to the application is intentionally or recklessly omitted the FSA may very well conclude that the person in question is not fit and proper. In *Vrajlal Laxmidas Sodha v the Financial Services Authority 2006[1]*, the applicant omitted to disclose that he had previously received a written warning from a previous employer regarding his activities as an investment advisor. That failure, together with a history of high levels of complaints, led the Tribunal to conclude, '... His failure to disclose the SJP warning was consistent with a failure to appreciate the importance of the purpose of regulation set up under FSMA. Accordingly we are not satisfied that he has adequate non-financial resources or is a fit and proper person to be authorised in the light of the matters before the Tribunal ...'

---

1 Financial Services and Markets Tribunal reference FIN 2005/0031.

B Competent and prudent management and exercise of due skill, care and diligence

12.14   COND 2.5.7G also addresses the question of the whether the applicant will exercise competent and prudent management and due skill, care and diligence and suggests that that in relation to competent and prudent management FSA will consider [1]

- the governing body of the firm is made up of individuals with an appropriate range of skills and experience to understand, operate and manage the firm's regulated activities;

- if appropriate, the governing body of the firm includes non-executive representation, at a level which is appropriate for the control of the regulated activities proposed, for example, as members of an audit committee (see SYSC 3.2.15G (audit committee));

- the governing body of the firm is organised in a way that enables it to address and control the regulated activities of the firm, including those carried on by managers to whom particular functions have been delegated (see SYSC 2.1 (apportionment of responsibilities) and SYSC 3.2 (areas covered by systems and controls));

- those persons who perform controlled functions under certain arrangements entered into by the firm or its contractors (including appointed representatives) act with due skill, care and diligence in carrying out their controlled function (see APER 4.2 (Statement of Principle 2)) or managing the business for which they are responsible (see APER 4.7 (Statement of Principle 7));

- the firm has made arrangements to put in place an adequate system of internal control to comply with the requirements and standards under the regulatory system (see SYSC 3.1 (systems and controls));

- the firm has approached the control of financial and other risk in a prudent manner (for example, by not assuming risks without taking due account of the possible consequences) and has taken reasonable care to ensure that robust information and reporting systems have been developed, tested and properly installed (see SYSC 3.2.10 (risk assessment));

- the firm, or a person connected with the firm, has been a director, partner or otherwise concerned in the management of a company, partnership or other organisation or business that has gone into insolvency, liquidation or administration while having been connected with that organisation or within one year of such a connection;

- the firm has developed human resources policies and procedures that are reasonably designed to ensure that it employs only individuals who are honest and committed to high standards of integrity in the conduct of their activities (see, for example, SYSC 3.2.13G (employees and agents));

- the firm has conducted enquiries (for example, through market research or the previous activities of the firm) that are sufficient to give it reasonable assurance that it will not be posing unacceptable risks to consumers or the financial system;

- the firm has in place the appropriate money laundering prevention systems and training, including identification, record-keeping and internal reporting procedures (see SYSC); and

- where appropriate, the firm has appointed auditors and actuaries, who have sufficient experience in the areas of business to be conducted (see SUP 3.4 (auditors' qualifications)).

---

1 COND 2.5.7G.

The granting of permission

12.15   Section 42(6) of the Act gives the FSA power to describe the regulated activities for which it gives permissions in such manner as the FSA consider appropriate. The Permissions that a firm may apply for are set out in PERG 2 Annex 2G and relate to regulated activities and the specified investments associated with those activities. Moreover PERG 2 Annex 1 contains a flow-chart setting out a useful process for helping a person establish whether authorisation may be required.

If the FSA grants permission to the applicant to carry on the regulated activity or activities, the authority may incorporate in the description of the regulated activities either:

- such limitation as it considers appropriate, specific to an activity or investment. Limitations may be applied for by the applicant for permission or be incorporated by the FSA. and they are generally necessary as method of limiting a firms activities within the broadly drafted permission it is being granted. FSA provide further information regarding 'Limitations' at AUTH 3.6;

- a narrower or wider description of the regulated activities than that applied for; and

- permission for carrying on of regulated activities which are not included within the application[1].

Furthermore, under FSMA 2000, s 43, the FSA may impose requirements on the condition, which could include the requirement that the person seeking permission takes specified action or refrains from taking specified action. This could include an action by reference to the person's relationship with other members of a same group of companies, or activities which are not themselves regulated activities. Requirements differ to limitations in that they will either be unrelated to the performance of regulated activities affecting a firm's operational matters or will relate to all, or a number of, the firm's regulated activities. FSA provide further information regarding 'Requirements' at AUTH 3.7.

---

1 FSMA 2000, s 42(6) and (7).

Procedure for making an application

12.16 The FSA's authorisation manual sets out guidance and procedures to be followed by the authority when dealing with an application for authorisation and permission. At AUTH1.6.9 the FSA also sets out useful general guidance for persons considering applying for authorisation. It states:

'Among other things, the applicant will need to:

(1) determine the precise scope of the permission it wishes to apply for; this should include the regulated activities (the specified activities and the specified investments in respect of which the activities are carried on: see PERG 2 Annex 2G) and any limitations and requirements the applicant wishes to apply for to refine the scope of the regulated activities; an example includes a limitation on the types of client it wishes to carry on business with or a requirement not to hold or control client money;

(2) determine whether it needs to apply to the Society of Lloyd's for admission to the register of underwriting agents or to any other bodies; the timing of these applications should be included in the applicant's plans;

(3)   determine which prudential category (and, if relevant, sub-category) will apply, and therefore its minimum regulatory financial requirements;

(4)   determine the rules in the Handbook which will apply to the activities it proposes to carry on, and take all reasonable steps to ensure that it is ready, willing and organised to comply with those rules;

(5)   determine the systems and controls necessary both to support its activities and to comply with the relevant rules, and have plans to implement and test these systems before the FSA determines its application;

(6)   prepare a business plan setting out the planned activities (and related risks), budget and resources (human, systems and capital);

(7)   determine which persons will fall under the FSA's approved persons regime and apply for the necessary approval; and

(8)   obtain any auditors' or reporting accountants' reports that are required to support its application or have been requested by the FSA; the auditors or other professionals should be involved early in the process to ensure that the planned work on the application will be sufficient to enable them to provide any opinions required.'

A person, when making an application for permission, must complete an application which should include the following[1]:

'(a)   A business plan which describes the regulated activities and any unregulated activities which the applicant proposes to carry on, the management and organisational structure of the applicant and details of any proposed outsourcing arrangements. The level of detail required in the business plan will be appropriate to the risks to consumers arising from the proposed regulated and unregulated activities. For an applicant seeking to carry on insurance business, the business plan should include a scheme of operations in accordance with SUP App 2 (Insurer and friendly societies: schemes of operation).

(b)   Appropriately analysed financial budget and projections which demonstrate that the applicant expects to comply with the relevant financial resources requirements appropriate to the applicant's prudential category (and in some cases sub-category).

(c)   Details of systems to be used (which do not have to be in place at the time of initial application), compliance procedures and documentation.

(d)   Details of the individuals to be involved in running the proposed business (such as directors, partners and members of the governing body, all of whom will be performing controlled functions) and any connected persons.'

The FSA would expect the level of detail in a firm's business plan or strategy plan to be appropriate to the complexity of the firm's proposed regulated activities and unregulated activities and the risks of regulatory concern it is likely to face (see SYSC 3.2.11G (management information)). General guidance on the contents of a business plan is given in the business plan section of the application pack for a Part IV permission.

The application pack should be accompanied by such other information as the applicant reasonably considers the FSA should be aware of for the purposes of determining the application. Any relevant supporting documentation should also be enclosed. The guidance notes to the application pack give further details about information to be provided by applicants, to enable them to answer the questions.

Applicants should be aware that there may be a delay in processing applications if the information given to the FSA is inaccurate or incomplete; for example, if the business plan for an applicant does not describe in adequate detail the regulated activities for which the applicant seeks Part IV permission. Applicants should discuss any problems with the corporate authorisation department before submitting the application or, if necessary, consider seeking appropriate professional advice.

At any time after receiving an application and before determining it, the FSA may give notice to the applicant to require it to provide additional information or documents. The circumstances of each application will determine what additional information or procedures are appropriate.

While applicants will often wish to discuss applications with the corporate authorisation department during the application process, similarly, the FSA will often need to discuss and clarify information that has been submitted within the application pack. The exchange of information during the application process is viewed as important by the FSA, since the final decision about an application needs to be based on as complete a picture of the application as possible.

In addition, in considering the application, the FSA make clear at AUTH 3.9.15G that it may:

*   carry out any enquiries which it considers appropriate, for example, discussions with other regulators or exchanges;
*   ask the applicant, or any specified representative of the applicant, to attend meetings at the FSA to give further information and explain any matter the FSA considers relevant to the application;

- require any information given by the applicant to be verified in such a way as the FSA may specify (for example, see AUTH 3.9.16G);

- take into account any information which it considers appropriate in relation to the application, for example any unregulated activities which the applicant carries on or proposes to carry on; and

- visit the premises which the applicant intends to use as its place of business.

Under FSMA 2000, s 51(6), the FSA may require the applicant to verify information provided in such a way as the FSA directs. Thus, as part of the application for authorisation, the FSA may require the applicant to provide, at its own expense, a report by an auditor, reporting accountant, actuary or other qualified person approved by the FSA. The report may be on such aspects of the information provided, or to be provided, by the applicant as the FSA may specify.

Under the FSMA 2000, s 49 the FSA will, when considering an application for permission, have regard to any person who appears to be, or is likely to be in a relationship with the applicant which is considered relevant.

When granting an application for permission, the FSA will confirm the permission in a written notice. The notice will state the date from which permission has effect[2].

---

1 FSA Authorisation Manual at 3.9.9(G).
2 FSMA 2000, s 52.

Application refusal or granting of permissions with limitations and requirements

12.17   Generally, pursuant to FSMA 2000, s 52(1) an application for permission has to be determined by the FSA within a six month period from the date that it first receives the completed application. Where the FSA determines to grant permission but impose limitations or requirements, or to refuse an application then it will provide the applicant with a warning notice under FSMA 2000, s 52(6) or (7). Furthermore, where the FSA is minded to refuse an application for permission, once again a warning notice will be provided. Any person who is aggrieved by the manner in which an application for permission is determined may refer the matter to the Financial Services and Market Tribunal.

Exempt persons

12.18   Sections 38 and 39 of the FSMA 2000 set out certain exemptions from the requirement to obtain authorisation. In particular, an appointed representative is an exempted person. An appointed representative is defined as "a party to a contract with an authorised person, which permits or requires them to carry on investment business ... and whose activities in carrying on that business are the accepted responsibility of the authorised person."

Contravention of the requirement to be authorised

12.19   The general prohibition in the FSMA 2000, preventing a person from conducting regulated activities without being authorised, is enforced by criminal sanction. (the general prohibition is explored in further detail in Chapter 1) Section 23 specifies that a person conducting regulated activity without authorisation is guilty of an offence and liable either (a) on summary conviction to a term of imprisonment not exceeding six months, or a fine not exceeding the statutory maximum or both or (b) on conviction on indictment to imprisonment for a term not exceeding two years or a fine or both.

Authorised person acting without permission

12.20   Whilst it is not an offence for an authorised person to conduct a regulated activity for which they have not gained a permission under Pt IV of the FSMA 2000, the authorised person will be considered to have acted in contravention of a requirement imposed on him by the FSA under the Act. This will subject the authorised person to enforcement proceedings by the FSA[1]. Section 20(2) makes it clear that such a contravention does not give rise to a criminal offence or to void or unenforceable transactions (for further information about acting without appropriate permission see Chapter 1).

---

1 FSMA 2000, s 20.

Enforceability of agreements

12.21   A further consequence of conducting a regulated activity without authorisation is that the agreement entered into by the person is unenforceable against any other party[1]. Persons are entitled to recover from unauthorised persons any money or property they have paid or transferred, and obtain compensation for loss sustained as a result of having parted with it. Section 28 of the FSMA 2000 specifies the amount of compensation that may be recoverable to such amount as agreed to by the parties or on an application to court, the amount determined by the court.

A further provision in s 27 of the FSMA 2000 effectively imposes an obligation on authorised persons to ensure that they only accept business in consequence of something said or done by another person, where that person is themselves an authorised person. This would relate, for example, where a financial adviser has recommended that a consumer purchase a package product with a life assurance company. Where that person is himself not an authorised person, then the investment contract is unenforceable against the provider. This will entitle the investor to recover any money or properties paid and obtain compensation for losses sustained. Providers should, therefore, always ensure that business introduced to them is introduced by an authorised person.

---

1 FSMA 2000, s 26.

Approved persons

12.22 As part of a firm's application for authorisation it must take reasonable care to ensure that no person performs a controlled function in relation to its carrying on of regulated activity, unless the FSA has approved that person to perform in a controlled function. All controlled functions are listed in the table to SUP 10.4.5R.

This issue has been recognised by regulators for many years, and most regulators have introduced methods of gaining accountability from senior employees of an organisation where their acts or omissions may give rise to a breach of regulatory requirements. Under the FSMA 2000, an approved persons regime has been created. This regime, which will be explored in further detail at para 12.23–12.33 ensures that all members of staff within an organisation that fulfil a controlled function must obtain approval to fulfil that role before it can be commenced. Approval is gained from the FSA, and will only be granted where the authority considers that the applicant for approval is a fit and proper person. Consequently, it is open for the authority to remove approval or impose disciplinary measures where the regulatory breach or misconduct is identified.

As part of the FSA's programme of rule book simplification it began consultation in July 2005 on proposals to simplify in certain respects its Approved Person regime and to consolidate certain controlled functions. A further round of consultation began in August 2006 with CP06/15 'Reforming the Approved Persons regime' which in particular considers the removal of specific Controlled Functions as well as the consolidation of others. It is proposed that the new rules arising from this consultation will come into force from November 2007.

Significant influence functions

12.23 Those functions performed within an organisation that have been designated as controlled functions have been set out in the table to SUP 10.4.5.

In determining the current controlled functions, the FSA has sought to establish and mark the boundaries of the Approved Persons regime. They specify those functions, which it sees as key to the performance of regulated activities. Not all of the Controlled Functions are required or apply to every type of investment business and it is important for firms to identify their own category of business to determine from SUP 10.1 the Controlled Functions that either they are required to have in place or those that will apply to their business. Each of the functions is then ordered by the type of functions to be performed. These are listed in paras **12.24–12.31**, but include governing functions, required functions, systems and controlled functions, significant management functions and customer functions. Furthermore, the FSA has identified that the governing functions, required functions, systems and controlled functions and significant functions are ones which are likely to result in the person responsible for the performance exercising a significant influence on the conduct of its regulated activities.

Whilst an analysis of each of the controlled functions is beyond the scope of this work, authorised firms and those seeking authorisation should consider the manner in which they identify whether a control function exists within their authorisation and the process that they should follow in ensuring a person who performs that function obtains approval from the FSA.

Governing body functions

12.24   These consist of being:

- a director of either a company or a holding company;

- a non-executive director of a company;

- a chief executive officer. This is widely interpreted and covers joint chief executives operating under the immediate control of the board where there is more than one. In the case of a UK branch of a non-EEA insurer, the role includes the principal UK executive;

- partners and limited partners (where appropriate) are all regarded as carrying on controlled functions where the firm is primarily carrying on regulated investment business. Limited partners whose role is that of an investor are excluded. If a partnership's primary business does not relate to specified investments but a separate part of the business does then, provided a distinct partner or set of partners deal with that aspect of the business, only they need be approved;

- directors of unincorporated associations;

- those directing or regulating the specified activities of a small friendly society; and

- sole traders.

Required functions

12.25   There are seven of these:

- the director or other senior member responsible for apportionment and oversight;
- EEA Investment business oversight function
- Compliance oversight function, that is the director or senior manager responsible for investment business compliance;
- the money laundering reporting officer;
- in the case of insurance companies, the appointed actuary;
- With Profits actuarial function; and
- Lloyds actuarial function.

Management functions

12.26   These consist of the members of senior management reporting to the governing body in relation to the following activities:

- the financial affairs of the firm;
- setting and controlling risk exposure; and
- internal audit.

Significant management functions in relation to business and control

12.27   The functions set out below are added to cover those situations where the firm concerned has senior managers whose functions are equivalent to that of a member of the firm's governing body. They do not apply if the activity is a specified activity as this would automatically be an approved persons' role. They fall into five categories of senior management:

- those operating in relation to investment services, such as the head of equities. This will often be a controlled function in any event;

- those operating in relation to other areas of the firm's business than specified investment activity, e g head of personal lending or corporate lending, head of credit card issues etc;
- those responsible for carrying out insurance underwriting other than in relation to contractually-based investments, e g head of aviation underwriting;
- those responsible for making decisions concerning the firm's own finances, e g chief corporate treasurer; and
- senior management settlement function.

Temporary and emergency circumstances

12.28   Should the function of undertaking such a role continue for more than eight weeks in a 12-month period, then the person primarily responsible will need to be an approved person.

Dealing with customer functions

12.29   There are seven main functions within this category:

- Investment adviser function;
- Investment adviser trainee function;
- Corporate finance adviser function;
- Pension transfer specialist;
- Adviser on syndicate participation of Lloyds function;
- Customer trading function; and
- Investment management function.

Appointed representatives

12.30   The FSMA 2000, s 19 states:

'No person may carry on a regulated activity in the United Kingdom, or purport to do so, unless he is–

(a)   an authorised person; or

(b)   an exempt person.'

There is a continuation of the exception that existed under the previous regime whereby the FSMA 2000, s 39 exempts appointed representatives. An 'appointed representative' is defined by the section as being: someone who is:

> '(a) a party to a contract with an unauthorised person (his principal) which–
>
> > (i) permits or requires him to carry on business of a prescribed description, and
> >
> > (ii) complies with such requirements as may be prescribed, and
>
> (b) is someone for whose activities in carrying on the whole or part of that business his principal has accepted responsibility in writing.'

Anyone satisfying this description is exempt from the general prohibition in relation to any regulated activity when they are acting within the remit of the area of business for which their principal has accepted responsibility. Thus, the principal will be responsible for the appointed representative's acts[1] and will therefore need to be an authorised person. There is some protection for the principal, though, as the FSMA 2000, s 39(6) states that 'nothing … is to cause the knowledge or intentions of an appointed representative to be attributed to his principal for the purpose of determining whether the principal has committed an offence, unless in all the circumstances it is reasonable for them to be attributed to him'.

The process that is to be undertaken in making an application for approval to perform a controlled function is specified in the FSMA 2000, s 60 and will be considered in further detail below[2].

---

1 FSMA 2000, s 39(4).
2 FSMA 2000, s 59.

Undertaking a review of business structure

12.31 It is important to note that a number of the controlled functions are required to exist within relevant organisations. Where appropriate, persons should perform the functions of: (a) apportionment and oversight; (b) EEA investment business oversight function; (c) compliance oversight function; (d) money laundering reporting function and (e) appointed actuary function.

Firms should assess whether controlled functions are required to be occupied and also whether any individuals are performing certain activities that are subject to the Approved Persons regime. To aid such an understanding firms should compile an organisational chart reflecting the manner in which it s business functions are organised, the reporting lines that exist within the organisation and the functional senior management positions that exist. When completing such an organisational chart for the first time, it would also be essential to ensure that all appropriate required functions are included.

Responsibility statements or job descriptions should also be compiled for each of the controlled functions that exist in an organisation. This will not only satisfy regulatory requirements but also ensure that each person performing a controlled function understands and appreciates the extent of their responsibilities within the organisation. This will also help them to appreciate the extent of the responsibility under the approved persons regime.

Fitness to be an approved person

12.33   A person authorised to conduct regulated activities should take reasonable care not to allow persons to exercise controlled functions without the approval of the FSA[1]. The restriction is imposed in relation to both natural and corporate persons and where the person to perform the controlled function is employed or engaged under an arrangement entered into by a contract of the authorised person.

Authorised firms have a general obligation not to appoint any member of staff without ensuring the appointee is a fit and proper person. This obligation for firms exists also in respect of those persons to be appointed to a controlled function. The FSA's rules relating to the fitness and propriety of approved person are set out in its sourcebook 'Fit and Proper test for Approved Persons' referred to as FIT. FIT relates Approved Persons' fitness and properness to honesty and integrity (in FIT 2.1); Competence and capability (in FIT 2.2); and Financial Soundness in (FIT 2.3). A number of refused applications for approved person status have been referred to the Financial Services and Markets Tribunal and many of these provide a useful insight into the matters that will influence the FSA decision as to whether an applicant is a fit and proper person and often show the impact that approved person refusal have on a firm's application for authorisation.

In *Rajiv Kungar and Kungar Homeloans Ltd v Financial Services Authority Ltd*[1]. The FSA had issued a decision notice that it was not satisfied that Mr Kungar was a fit and proper person to perform the controlled functions of Director and Responsibility for Apportionment and Oversight. The application for those control functions formed part of Kungar Homeloan's application for authorisation to carry on certain categories of mortgage and insurance business. It was reported in the Tribunal's decision that the FSA was concerned that Mr Khungar had not been straightforward in his dealings with it and that Mr Khungar had failed to disclose a number of criminal convictions, a previous bankruptcy and an investigation and warning by the FSA in 1999 and that in turn indicated that he is not a fit and proper person. The facts leading to the FSA's Decision Notice where summarised by the Tribunal as follows: Mr Khungar had in 1992 been convicted on his own plea of guilty of nine counts of procuring the execution of a valuable security by deception and was sentenced to two years imprisonment. In all cases the valuable security had been a cheque issued by a mortgage lender and the form of deception in each case had been to falsely represent to the lender that the borrower had been employed for a certain period at a certain salary. The FSA view was that these offences related to the work now proposed to be done by Khungar and KHLL. They went on to question of Mr Khungar's integrity. Moreover, the Authority say, Mr Khungar took no steps to make good the losses (some £1,000,000) that the lenders had suffered as a result of his criminal conduct. In addition Mr Khungar had petitioned and been declared bankrupt on 31October 1991 with the bankruptcy being discharged three years later. The performance by Mr Khungar of his business activities since 1992 had also been taken into account by the Authority. In 1999 an inquiry had been conducted by the Financial Services Authority into Mr Khungar's involvement with an Isle of Man based institution. It was reported by the Tribunal that Mr Khungar, through Khungar Associates, had been providing advice to UK residents about investment products. This led to the Financial Services Authority issuing him with a warning letter dated 25 January 2000.

It was reported that Mr Khungar had explained to the Tribunal that he had been in business arranging mortgages since 1993 and had received no complaints. Regarding the convictions and sentence in 1992, Mr Khungar contended that he had paid the penalty for these and had lost everything and it would have been impossible to make reparations to the mortgage lenders. He also argued that it was wrong and unduly harsh of the FSA to have sought to bring the past into the present and that the right approach was for the FSA to concentrate on the present situation. In relation to the alleged failure to disclose and wrongly answered questions in the application for approval to the FSA Mr Kunghar said that he had either not read them or where he had he had misinterpreted them or had forgotten facts to which the questions related.

In reaching its decision the Tribunal considered that the earlier events, such as the convictions and the bankruptcy, had sufficiently close similarity between the nature of Mr Khungar's business activities in the1980's and the business activities of KHLL today, to make those earlier events relevant to the FSA's role in granting authorisation and approved person status. The Tribunal particularly addressed the applicant's disclosures to the FSA in the context of integrity and made it clear that it was for the FSA to decide what is relevant in determining a person's fitness and propriety to carry on a particular business. It considered that the questions in the form were clear and unambiguous. The Tribunal stated:

'... Mr Khungar's answers in the form were misleading and we do
not accept that they were given as the result of advice that he had

received. We think that the answers he gave to the Authority's
enquiries and the explanations that he produced when giving evidence show that he was not at any stage prepared to be frank with the
Authority, as regulator, or indeed, with the tribunal. That feature
itself demonstrates a lack of integrity on Mr Khungar's part ...'

1 (2005) FIN2004/0028.

12.34 Firms should establish an internal process by which they screen the
applicant's background for certain matters prior to offering that person employment. In addition, they must ensure that prior to the person taking up employment an application under the approved persons regime is also submitted to the
FSA. It should be noted that it is a requirement under the approved persons
regime that no one may perform a controlled function without receiving prior
approval from the FSA to do so.

A firm's own process in screening an applicant to ensure they are a fit and proper
person can be time consuming. Firms must take into account the time required
to properly screen when considering the appropriate time to make an offer of
employment and the candidate's desired start date. Firms may consider that the
following should be screened or verified before an offer of employment is
made:

- **Past employment history:** Firms should consider the importance of
  verifying the past employment record of an applicant. The dates between
  which a person has been employed by an organisation and the actual
  employment should be verified. In addition, any gaps in between employers may also be verified to ensure that the applicant has not attempted to
  avoid reference to a period of their employment which has caused
  problems.

- **Written references:** In addition to verification of employment, it will, in
  many cases, also be appropriate to obtain from past employers written
  comment about the applicant's standard of employment. In many cases
  now most employers will not be prepared to supply verbal references. It is
  therefore necessary to obtain written references containing comments
  about the conduct of a person's work, their general performance, the
  reason for them leaving and inviting any other general comments can be a
  useful insight into determining whether a person is fit and proper.

In both verification and written referencing firms should determine the
period of time over which they wish to screen the applicant. The FSA
provides no specification for the period of time over which background
screening should be conducted. It is merely a question of firms
determining what is reasonable in all the circumstances. Some firms
may choose to verify and reference the employment for the past ten

years of an applicant's employment background, whereas others choose to go back no further than three or four years.

- **Credit checking:** It is now almost standard practice for firms to undertake, with a credit checking agency, a credit reference on applicants. Such practice should continue to be applied to all persons to be employed in a controlled function. Firms should ensure that they utilise a reliable credit checking agency and respond to all the information that is reported to them. It may be that the agency is not able to identify the applicant from their address and, therefore, return a negative report. In this instance, the applicant should always be asked to provide more reliable information to confirm their address and any prior addresses should also be used to screen the applicant. Where credit referencing identifies particular credit problems, these should be followed through by the firm and a reasonable decision should always be taken as to whether a firm considers it appropriate to appoint a person into a controlled function where they have an adverse credit history.

- **Academic and professional qualifications:** There are numerous instances of firms identifying, some time after employment, that an employee has overstated their professional or academic qualifications. Certain controlled functions have minimum educational requirements. The firm has a general obligation to ensure that all staff are competent to perform the role they are employed for. Where a firm is relying on the applicant's qualifications, they should ensure they obtain independent verification that the examinations have been passed and are held. Where professional qualifications are held, firms should obtain a reference from the applicant's professional body to identify whether there are any existing or outstanding disciplinary actions against the applicant.

- **Criminal background:** Firms should consider whether it is appropriate to screen an applicant's background for any past or outstanding criminal convictions. The firm may consider that some criminal convictions are not relevant to an individual's employment and may wish to consider screening an employee applicant through the Criminal Records Bureau. These may very well include minor road traffic offences. However, offences involving fraud, dishonesty or even violence will often be considered unacceptable for somebody wishing to be employed in the financial services industry.

---

1 FSMA 2000, s 29(1).
2 Supervision Manual, Chapter 10.

Matters of concern to the FSA

12.35 As part of an employee's screening consideration should also be given to those matters which are considered by the FSA as impacting upon a person's fitness and properness. When making an application for approval a standard FSA application form is completed. This sets out a series of questions relating to the proposed controlled functions' employee's background, including the involvement they have had with previous financial service companies that may have run into difficulties. It is sensible practice for an employing firm to address each of these matters with an applicant in advance of an offer of employment. It would cause difficulties for an employer to have made an offer of employment only to find that the FSA either declines an application or imposes requirements based on answers to the questions in the approved person application form.

Applications for approval by the FSA

12.36   All persons wishing to perform a controlled function and seeking approval to do so from the FSA must submit a standard application. Application forms are available from the FSA and are set out at Annex 4 of the FSA Handbook at reference SUP 10.

The FSA will only grant an application for approval if it is satisfied that the applicant is a fit and proper person. The FSA has a period of three months from the date it receives the application to determine whether to grant the application or provide to the applicant a warning notice that it proposes to refuse the application. All applications, which are granted, are confirmed to the applicant on written notice. A copy of that notice is also provided to all interested parties.

Where the authority is minded to refuse an application, it must provide a warning of its proposal to refuse. The applicant and each interested party may then refer the matter to the Financial Services and Markets Tribunal[1].

---

1 FSMA 2000, s 62(4).

Training and competence

12.37   The competence of a firm's employees and in particular those occupying client advisory, supervision and senior management controlled functions has a significant bearing on the FSA decision to grant a firm authorisation, as well as the firm's continuing ability to meet the requirements of Threshold Condition 4 relating to resources, and Condition 5 relating to suitability. In particular the impact of the requirement for competence in the context of a firm's overall suitability can be read into Threshold Condition 5 which includes provision as to whether the firm:

(a)   conducts, or will conduct, its business with integrity and in compliance with proper standards;

(b) has, or will have, a competent and prudent management; and

(c) can demonstrate that it conducts, or will conduct, its affairs with the exercise of due, skill, care and diligence.

The FSA is clear that the competence of those working in the financial industry is a key factor influencing its ability to deliver its regulatory objectives. At the FSA's training and competence conference in December 20004, it was made clear by Andrew Proctor, formerly head of enforcement at FSA, that when considering enforcement action, the two factors that will have the most significant affect are a firm's systems and controls and its training and competence arrangements. The FSA will and does in appropriate cases take enforcement action firms where there has been a breakdown in a firms training arrangements. By way of example in its enforcement case against Bank of Ireland case published in a final notice dated 31 August 2004, FSA fined the bank £375,000 for breaches of anti money laundering requirements, In relation to the bank's failings the FSA raised concerns regarding training and competence and stated in its Final Notice:

'...[*The Bank*} did not take appropriate steps to ensure that it had in place a system to check that staff had understood the money laundering training that was delivered to them, specifically that they had sufficient understanding to recognise and report suspicious transactions ...'

Nonetheless the FSA's approach to its Training and Competence rules appears markedly different from the detailed prescription of Training and Competence requirements operated by a number of the FSA's legacy regulators (such as Lautro and IMRO) that operated under the regime within the Financial Services Act 1986. Such an approach can be traced back to 1989 when the Securities and Investment Board commissioned Dr Oonagh McDonald to report the training requirements for the industry. The McDonald report was published in May 1990 making the following main recommendations:

● Firms should have thorough and well recorded recruitment procedures;

● Training should include the ethos of a firm, knowledge of the regulatory system, knowledge of personal finance matters including social security and tax affairs as well as product knowledge;

● There should be regular knowledge updating and assessment.

● Firms should have in place arrangements for supervision to ensure that individuals act with competence and integrity

At that time the industry regulators response to the report and the resulting SIB requirements was mixed with for example Lautro and subsequently the PIA putting in place Training and Competence arrangements focusing on knowledge and skill testing together with obligations for ongoing competence supervision. Conversely other regulators viewed competence in the context of technical knowledge and thus measured competence through the qualifications that an individual held.

Compliance with the FSA's Training and Competence commitments, which are provided in its sourcebook 'TC' set out a series of competence principles for all staff as well as specific requirements for Approved Persons, certain client facing and operational staff. It is a requirement that a firm ensures its entire staff is fit and proper to perform their responsibilities. From a practical standpoint there is little difference between the competence requirement for Approved Person and those staff that do not occupy a Controlled Function. Each has to be shown to have the capability to meet their responsibilities. Whilst the passing of appropriate examinations continues to be a measure of an individual's knowledge competence, a requirement to ensure that staff have and continue to display the appropriate level of skill and practical application remains an inherent part of TC, and firms should not overlook that the maintenance of competence requires refresher and sometimes remedial training, as well as developmental activity covered by the continual professional development programmes of professional bodies. Moreover, Training and Competence as a regulatory concept is closely aligned with FSA's systems and controls requirements and with the FSA's development of its risk-based approach to compliance, a more risk orientated approach has emerged towards the operation of the FSA's Training and Competence rules. Nonetheless firms are required to have in place a their own arrangements to secure the delivery of their approach to Training and Competence, and thus it is essential that those charged with managing a firm's regulatory risk have a good understanding of their Training and Competence obligations, as well as the tools to judge if their firms arrangements meet regulatory requirements.

With the FSA's less invasive approach to the assessment of compliance with its Training and Competence it is no longer the case that FSA will routinely carry out detailed assessments of firms' Training and Competence arrangements, they do nonetheless consider that the competence of those working in the financial market contributes fundamentally to market confidence and consumer protection. Speaking at SII annual awards ceremony on 6 February 2006, Hector Sants FSA Managing Director Wholesale and Institutional Markets said,

> '… You may also have noticed that ensuring satisfactory levels of competence is a prerequisite for achieving the FSA's statutory objectives – consumer protection, market confidence, public awareness and the reduction of financial crime. It is important to have competent people providing financial services to consumers to help build confidence in the financial markets and ultimately protect consumers from unsuitable conduct …'

It is not surprising therefore, that when fundamental failings are identified within firms training arrangements are identified that FSA will take action even though such enforcement action might be expressed in terms of system and controls failings rather than discrete breaches of the FSA Training and Competence rules. For example issues arising from training and competence failings were raised by the FSA's in its enforcement case against *Carr Shepherds Crosthwaite* (CSC) an action that comes close to being about compliance in training and competence. CSC's failings resulted in the firm being fined £500,000 and at a fundamental level arose because the firm failed to keep fully up-to-date with the regulatory developments that had taken place since the establishment of the FSA. The enforcement action and final notice highlighted the fact that CSC's compliance policies, procedures and their monitoring were inadequate and incomplete, and that they had not kept pace with regulatory developments. The final notice dated 19 May 2004 refers to breaches of FSA high level principles 2 and 3 as well as breaches of senior management systems and controls at SYSC 3.1.1 and 3.2.6, together with specific breaches of the COB rules.

Following the enforcement action the FSA stated in its press release about the action:

> 'If a compliance department is to be fully effective, it needs to keep up to date with the regulatory requirements and market developments. The creation of the FSA has led to important changes in that landscape, of which CSC has failed to stay fully appraised.'

The CSC enforcement action highlights the FSA's concerns about the importance of compliance, culture and up-to-date training that might expose a firm's clients to the risk of loss even where there is no evidence that individual customers had experienced an actual loss. It illustrates that lack of proper training affects not just those staff engaged in the sale of or advice on investment products to consumers, but extends to the organisation as a whole and its ability to organise and control its senior management systems and controls. The thrust of the case is an illustration, if one was needed, of the importance of an organisation's compliance culture in meeting FSA rules and that affective training and competence is not a regulatory obligation that can be addressed only by the passing of examinations.

Chapter 13

The role of the Financial Services and Markets Tribunal

Introduction

13.1   In this chapter we will consider the Financial Services and Markets Tribunals (the Tribunal) contribution to the accountability of the FSA's decision-making and enforcement powers. We shall assess the legal provisions from which the Tribunal gains its powers and the arrangements that exist for the governance of the Tribunal. We shall then consider the Tribunal's rules of procedure, scope for appeals from Tribunal decisions and the legal assistance scheme.

The FSA uses a number of the regulatory tools, some of which have been considered in Chapter 5 , to regulate entry and participation in the financial services market. The FSA often uses its enforcement process as a last resort to facilitate the the punishment of firms and individuals that have caused rule breaches or engaged in transactions that abuse the market and as a deterrent against others that might otherwise engage in breaches of regulatory requirements. FSA enforcement and supervisory powers also act as a means of protecting the investing public and in the most serious of cases, enforcement proceedings will be used to withdraw a firm's authorisation to conduct investment business, thus prohibiting firms and individuals from operating in the financial market. The effect of formal disciplinary proceedings on an authorised person's business activities can be enormous. Indirect costs, such as the disruption of working practices, the diversion of management time, damage to a business's reputation, together with the direct costs of rectifying non-compliant procedures and compensating the victims of non-compliance, can vastly exceed any financial penalty arising from the actual enforcement proceedings. The FSA's internal decision-making process is designed to allow the FSA to take informed yet prompt action against regulated firms, approved persons and market participants that breach regulatory requirements. The impact of the FSA's enforcement proceedings, however, can in serious cases have lasting affects on a business or individual reputation and result in considerable expense. By way of example it has been reported that Paul Davidson spent three years and in excess of £1m successfully fighting an FSA decision to bring a market abuse case against him. It is vital that market participants have confidence in the fairness of the FSA's decision-making and enforcement process and although an informal and speedy system provides many benefits, a facility to allow an independent review of FSA's decisions is an imperative. The Tribunal provides a vital tool in ensuring the FSA is accountable for its enforcement decision making and aspects of its decision making.

In a landmark reference brought by Legal and General Assurance Society in 2003, the enforcement process of the Financial Services Authority was scrutinised by the Financial Services and Market Tribunal (the Tribunal). The substantive hearing lasted from 13 September to 21 October 2004, and necessitated the close examination of 40,000 pages of documents. The Tribunal reported that the FSA's closing argument alone amounted to 171 pages with 2 appendices. Both sides to the dispute initially claimed victory and although Legal and General did not find that its processes were vindicated by the Tribunal, the FSA found the independence of its enforcement process seriously criticised by the Tribunal. That criticism was the catalyst for a full-scale internal FSA review of its enforcement process resulting in a series of changes being made, particularly in relation to the independence of its regulatory decisions committee and reliance on external skilled person reports during FSA investigations into firms. The Legal and General case serves to illustrate the role the Tribunal plays in contributing to the accountability of the FSA's decision making. Ultimately the Tribunal in the case did not make formal recommendations to the FSA, however, that only appears to have been the case because of the prompt response of the FSA board to set up a review of its enforcement processes. In the written reasons of the Legal and General case the Tribunal stated:

> '... We do not however accept FSA's claims about the extent of mis-sales. FSA have proved 8 mis-sales to the required standard from the 13 cases about which we heard evidence. It would not be just for us to find any mis-sales in the other 47 cases for the reasons set out elsewhere. Although a sales review such as that relied on by FSA is a valid and acceptable tool in the vital work of identifying and proving regulatory breaches, the exercise in this case was flawed. We do not accept FSA's case that the conclusions of the sales review and our findings on individual cases can be taken to reflect the pattern of mis-sales generally ...In our view the RDC was in error in its approach to the mis-selling case and reached conclusions not justified by the material before it ...'

Although the impact of the Tribunal's criticism of the FSA in the Legal and General case was the catalyst for a wide reaching review of the FSA enforcement process, historically the extent to which references are made to the Tribunal appear limited to small businesses objecting to FSA decisions that would otherwise deprive them of their business or individuals who face the prospect of reputational damage arising from FSA decisions, and up until

1 November 2006 only 41 Tribunal references have been published.(this includes a number of decisions on preliminary issues and costs applications). In the context of the FSA's priority activities, it has experienced particular difficulties in defending its decision making before the Tribunal in high- profile market abuse cases suggesting a mismatch between the way the FSA Regulatory Decisions committee and the Tribunal evaluate evidential material. Although at the time of writing the FSA's reaction to these cases is not known, it is almost certain that the FSA will react with a view to ensure that lessons learned from these cases are factored into its future market abuse enforcement work.

The legal basis for the Tribunal

13.2   The Tribunal is an independent tribunal created under Part IX of the FSMA 2000. The Tribunal provides a forum for the review of certain decisions of the Financial Services Authority. It is not an appellate body as its role is to conduct fresh hearings of the matters referred to it from all the evidence available[1]. Following its determination of an individual case it is able to direct the FSA to take appropriate actions in relation to an individual case[2], as well as make recommendations to the FSA considered appropriate from the issues considered during a particular reference[3].

---

1 FSMA 2000, s 133.
2 FSMA 2000, s 133(4) and (5).
3 FSMA 2000, s 133(8).

Tribunal governance and constitution

13.3   To ensure the Tribunal's independence the Act sets out arrangements for the Tribunal's governance. These arrangements in essence ensure that the Tribunal is not put into a position where it might be influenced or controlled by the FSA or persons subject to FSA regulation. Schedule 13 to the FSMA 2000 sets out requirements for the Tribunal's governance, panel membership, decision making and the rules of procedure.

Panel members

13.4   The Tribunal comprises two panels, members of which are appointed by the Lord Chancellor. The first, a panel of chairmen, is appointed from legally qualified persons with the following minimum requirements as required by para 3(2) of Sch 13 to the FSMA 2000 and provided that at least one member of the panel is an advocate or solicitor in Scotland of the kind mentioned in (b) below. They are required to:

(a)   have a seven-year general qualification within the meaning of s 71 of the Courts and Legal Services Act 1990; or

(b)   be an advocate or solicitor in Scotland of at least seven years' standing; or

(c)   be a member of the Bar of Northern Ireland of at least seven years' standing or a solicitor of the Supreme Court of Northern Ireland of at least seven years' standing.

The second panel comprises lay members who are qualified by experience or otherwise to deal with matters of the kind that may be referred to the Tribunal[1]. Lay members are selected to assist with the determination of questions of fact and industry practice that arise during references.

The Lord Chancellor must appoint one of the members of the panel of chairmen to preside over the discharge of the Tribunal's functions (the current President is His Honour Stephen Oliver QC) and one of the members of that panel as Deputy President, to have such functions in relation to the Tribunal as the President may assign to him and to discharge the functions of the President where he is absent or is otherwise unable to act. In circumstances, however, where there is no Deputy President or he too is absent or otherwise unable to act, the Lord Chancellor is able to appoint a person from the panel of chairmen to discharge the functions of the President[2].

Both the President and Deputy President must be a person that:

(a)   has a ten-year general qualification within the meaning of s 71 of the Courts and Legal Services Act 1990;

(b)   is an advocate or solicitor in Scotland of at least ten years' standing; or

(c)   is:

    (i)   a member of the Bar of Northern Ireland of at least ten years' standing; or

    (ii)   a solicitor of the Supreme Court of Northern Ireland of at least ten years' standing.

Paragraph 4 specifies the terms of office for each chairperson and lay panel member. Each is required to hold and vacate office in accordance with the terms of his appointment. Each panel member is entitled to resign office by notice in writing to the Lord Chancellor. The Lord Chancellor is, however, entitled to remove panel members from their office on the ground of incapacity or misbehaviour[3].

To insure independence of the Tribunal, members' remuneration and expenses in respect of their service as panel members are paid by the Lord Chancellor at such rates as he may determine.

436

1 FSMA 2000, Sch 13, para 3(4).
2 FSMA 2000, Sch 13, para 2(7).
3 FSMA 2000, Sch 13, para 4(2).

Government oversight

Tribunal service

13.5   The government has established a framework of oversight of the functions and performance of certain Judicial Tribunals. The Tribunals Service launched on 1 April 2006 is a government agency providing common administrative support to the main central government tribunals. The Tribunals Service is an executive agency of the Department for Constitutional Affairs (DCA) and its launch followed a government review started in May 2000 of the Tribunal system by Sir Andrew Leggatt. Sir Andrew's report, 'Tribunals for Users: One System, One Service' published in August 2001 was critical of the arrangements for supporting tribunals. The report observed the need to achieve independence and coherence in the Tribunal system and recommended that all tribunals should be supported by a common administrative service, independent of those bodies whose decisions the tribunals were reviewing.

The government's response to Sir Andrew's report was published in March 2003 and subsequently in a White Paper entitled 'Transforming Public Services: Complaints, Redress and Tribunals', published in July 2004 the government set out its proposals in the wider context of reform of the administrative justice system and dispute resolution to create within the DCA an independent Tribunals Service.

The Financial Services and Markets Tribunal, for administrative purposes now forms part of the Finance and Tax Tribunals service. Details of this service, rules of procedure covering the Tribunal sit serves together with published decisions is available on its website www.financeandtaxtribunals.gov.uk

Council on Tribunals

13.6   The Council on Tribunals was established by the Tribunals and Inquiries Act 1958 and now operates under the Tribunals and Inquiries Act 1992. Its role is to oversee large tribunals such as Employment Tribunals and smaller tribunals including the Financial Services and Markets Tribunal. The Council does not involve itself with particular cases which a tribunal or inquiry is hearing, or deal with complaints about a particular case or a tribunal decision. Of special importance is the requirement for the Council to be consulted before procedural rules are made for any tribunal specified in Sch 1 to the 1992 Act.

The principal functions of the Council on Tribunals provided in the 1992 Act are:

(a) to keep under review the constitution and working of the tribunals specified in Sch 1 to the 1992 Act, and, from time to time, to report on their constitution and working;

(b) to consider and report on matters referred to the Council under the 1992 Act with respect to tribunals whether or not specified in Sch 1 to the Act; and

(c) to consider and report on matters referred to the Council, or matters the Council may consider to be of special importance, with respect to administrative procedures which involve or may involve the holding of a statutory inquiry by or on behalf of a Minister.

The Council consists of not more than 15 or less than 10 members appointed by the Lord Chancellor and the Scottish Ministers. During the appointment process regard must also be had to the need for representation of the interests of persons in Wales. In addition, the Parliamentary Commissioner for Administration (the Parliamentary Ombudsman) by virtue of his office is a member of the Council.

The Council takes the view that proceedings in a tribunal should:

- make the tribunal easily accessible to members of the public who would like the tribunal to deal with their case;
- be cheap, quick and as informal as possible;
- provide the right to an oral hearing;
- be held in public;
- conclude with the tribunal giving adequate reasons for its decisions;
- have time limits where necessary to prevent delay (although these limits should not be too short); and
- be seen to be independent, impartial and fair to all.

The Council is required to produce an annual report covering the period from 1 August to 31 July and present it to Parliament and the Scottish Parliament, usually in December. The annual report must set out:

- matters which concern the Council; and
- important business during the period of the report. This includes the main consultations in which the Council gave advice.

Functions and role of the Financial Services and Markets Tribunal

13.7   The Tribunal has the functions conferred on it by the Act. The following table shows the occasions which give rise to the right to make a reference to the Tribunal:

Provision in FSMA 2000	Reference
	In relation to authorised and regulated firms
Section 55	A reference may be made in relation to the determination of matters relating to business permissions granted under Part IV of the Act. This would include: • applications for permissions; • where the FSA seeks to impose requirements; • variations and cancellations of permissions; • variations to permissions at the FSA's own initiative; • variations to permissions following acquisition of control of a business; • variations or cancellations at the request of an overseas regulator; and • prohibitions and restrictions.
Section 57	Prohibition orders against individuals performing specified functions or activities falling within a specified description.
Section 58	Applications relating to variations or revocations of prohibition orders.
Section 186	Decisions relating to applications for control of authorised persons.
Section 187	Decision relating to a person's existing control over an authorised person.
Section 189	Decisions regarding the improper acquisition of controlling shares in an authorised person.
Section 197	FSA imposition of requirements on incoming firms (an EEA or EU Treaty firms as defined in s 193(1)).
Section 200	FSA's own decision to vary or revoke its intervention over incoming firms.
Section 208	Decision notices in relation to public censures under s 205 and financial penalties under s 206.
Section 386	Decisions regarding the FSA's powers to require restitution of profits of authorised persons.
	In relation to approved persons, auditors and actuaries
Section 62	Refusals of applications for approval to perform a controlled function.
Section 63	Determining matters relating to the withdrawal of approval to perform a controlled function.
Section 67	Determination of a proposal to impose disciplinary measures against an approved person.
Section 345	Disqualification from being an auditor or actuary of an authorised person.

	In relation to FSA's role as UK Listing Authority[1]
Section 76	Relating to decisions to refuse an application for listing.
Sections 77 and 78	Decisions on the discontinuance or suspension of listing.
Section 87D	Decision to refuse to approve a prospectus.
Section 87N	Public censure of the issuer of a transferable security.
Section 87O	Decision relating to suspension or prohibition of admission to trading on a regulated market.
Section 88	Decisions relating to refusal of approval or cancellation of approval to act as a sponsor.
Section 89	Public censure of a sponsor.
Section 92	Decisions relating to contravention of Pt 6 official listing rules.
Section 96C	Decisions relating to suspension of trading in financial instruments.
	In relation to market abuse
Section 127	In respect of the market abuse regime, determining decisions to impose penalties in cases of market abuse under s 123.
	In relation to collective investment schemes
Section 245	Refusals of applications for unit trust scheme authorisation.
Section 252	Refusal of approval of a proposal to replace trustee or manager of an authorised unit trust scheme.
Section 255	Decisions relating to the revocation of authorisation of a unit trust scheme.
Section 256	Decisions relating to a request for an authorisation revocation order.
Section 259	Direction to require a manager to cease unit trust issue or wind up a scheme.
Section 260	Decision relating to an FSA proposal to vary a direction or refusal to varay or revoke a direction of a schemes authorisation.
Section 262	Power granted to tribunal under this section relating to open-ended investment companies. See in particular the Open Ended Investment Companies Regulations 2001, SI 2001/1228.
Section 265	Notice to the FSA relating to recognised overseas schemes.

---

1 Certain amendments made by Prospectus Regulations 2005, SI 2005/1433, Sch1 and came into force on 1 July 2005.

Making a reference and Tribunal procedures

Rules of procedure

13.8   Section 132 of the FSMA 2000 sets out the requirement for making rules of procedures for the conduct of proceedings before the Tribunal. The

Lord Chancellor may by rules make such provision as appears to him to be necessary or expedient in respect of the conduct of proceedings before the Tribunal. The Tribunal's current rules are set out in the Financial Services and Markets Tribunal Rules 2001[1].

---

1 SI 2001/2476.

Beginning the reference

The process and time limits

13.9   The applicant's notice is required to be filed (sent to the Tribunal) no later than 28 days from the date of the FSA's notice, that is the decision notice, supervisory notice or other notice relating to the referred action that was given to the applicant by the FSA. Under rule 4(3) the applicant's notice is required to state the following:

(a)   the name and address of the applicant;

(b)   the name and address of the applicant's representative (if any);

(c)   if no representative is named under sub-paragraph (b), the applicant's address for service in the United Kingdom (if different from the address notified under sub-paragraph (a));

(d)   that the notice is a reference notice; and

(e)   the issues concerning the FSA's notice that the applicant wishes the Tribunal to consider. This will set out the basis of the applicant's case against the FSA's decision in the relevant notice.

Rule 4(1) requires that any notice must be made by way of written notice signed by or on behalf of the applicant and sent to the Tribunal. The Tribunal offers a standard form for individuals or corporations who wish to file a reference. A copy of the form is reproduced at Table 1 below. The Tribunal also provides an explanatory leaflet giving information on the Tribunal's procedures. This is available on the Tribunal's website www.financeandtaxtribunals.co.uk under forms and leaflets. The applicant is also required to file with the reference notice a copy of the FSA notice to which the reference relates[1].

At the same time as filing the reference notice, the applicant is required to send a copy of that notice and of any application for directions (see **13.14** below) to the FSA.

Subject to any directions given by the Tribunal, upon receiving a reference notice the Secretary to the Tribunal enters particulars of the reference in the Tribunal register and informs the parties in writing of the matters below as well as specifying the date on which the information is being sent[2]:

(i)   the fact that the reference has been received;

(ii)   the date when the Tribunal received the notice; and

(iii)   the Tribunal's decision on any application made for directions (and include a copy of any direction given).

Following issue of a reference the FSA is prohibited under s 133(6) of the FSMA 2000 from taking the action specified in the referred decision notice until the reference, and any appeal against the Tribunal's determination, has been finally disposed of.

---

1 Financial Services and Markets Tribunal Rules 2001, SI 2001/2476, r 4(5).
2 Financial Services and Markets Tribunal Rules 2001, r 4(9).

The FSA's statement of case and document disclosure

13.10   Once the applicant's reference has been sent to the Tribunal, the FSA is required to file a written statement of its case within 28 days[1] from the date it received the information from the Tribunal described in **13.9** above. The FSA's written statement of case is required by r 5(2) to:

(a)   specify the statutory provisions providing for the referred action;

(b)   specify the reasons for the referred action;

(c)   set out all the matters and facts upon which it relies to support the referred action; and

(d)   specify the date on which the statement of case is filed.

Rule 5(3) obliges the FSA to undertake full disclosure of documents that both support and might undermine the FSA case.

The FSA is required to submit with the statement of its case a list of:

(a)   the documents on which it relies in support of the referred action; and

(b)   the further material which in the opinion of the FSA might undermine the decision to take that action.

A definition of the term 'documents' is provided in the tribunal rules and means: information recorded in any form and, in relation to information recorded otherwise than in legible form, references to its production include references to producing a copy of the information in legible form. Further material is defined as including materials that were considered by the FSA in reaching or maintaining the decision to give an FSA notice or materials that were obtained by the FSA in connection with the matter to which that notice relates (whether they were obtained before or after giving the notice) but which were not considered by it in reaching or maintaining that decision.

Under r 5(4), at the same time as the FSA files its statement of case it is required to send to the applicant a copy together with the list of documents and further material.

Having received the FSA's statement of case the applicant under r 6(1) is then required within 28 days to file with the Tribunal a reply which shall:

(a)   state the grounds on which the applicant relies in the reference;

(b)   identify all matters contained in the statement of case which are disputed by the applicant;

(c)   state the applicant's reasons for disputing them; and

(d)   specify the date on which it is filed.

The applicant's reply must be accompanied by a list of the documents on which the applicant intends to rely in support of its case. We consider the requirements for document disclosure further below in **13.15**.

---

1 Financial Services and Markets Tribunal Rules 2001, SI 2001/2476, r 5(1).

Third party references

13.11   The rights set out in s 393 of the FSMA 2000 ensure that third parties should not be identified and adversely criticised in a warning notice issued by the FSA without having had an opportunity to make representations in response and if they are identified and criticised in a decision notice, they should have the right to challenge such criticisms in the Tribunal.

To enable us to consider the Tribunal's role in any reference under s 393 we need to consider the rights under that section.

Section 393(1) of the FSMA 2000 deals with third parties that are identified in FSA warning notices, it provides:

'If any of the reasons contained in a warning notice to which this section applies relates to a matter which-

(a)   identifies a person ('the third party') other than the person to whom the notice is given, and

(b)   in the opinion of the Authority, is prejudicial to the third party

a copy of the notice must be given to the third party.'

Section 393(3) of the FSMA 2000 provides the right for a third party that has received a copy of a warning notice to make representations to the FSA within 28 days of the warning notice.

Section 393(4) of the FSMA 2000 deals with third parties that are identified in FSA decision notices, it provides:

'If any of the reasons contained in a decision notice to which this section applies relates to a matter which

(a) identifies a person ('the third party') other than the person to whom the decision notice is given, and

(b) in the opinion of the Authority, is prejudicial to the third party

a copy of the notice must be given to the third party.'

Because the warning and decision notice procedure created by the Act might prejudice parties other than the direct recipients of the notices the third party rights in s 393 of the FSMA 2000 allow for the third party to make representations to the FSA as well as make a reference to the Tribunal where either they are not satisfied with the FSA response or the FSA has not provided them with a copy of the relevant notice. The purpose of s 393 was described by Lord Bach (the Minister who introduced the amendments to the Financial Services and Markets Bill which became s 393), in the following terms[1]:

'The new clause on third party rights ... rationalises the existing provisions dealing with the rights of third parties identified in warning or decision notices in a way that is prejudicial to them. These provisions were designed to deal with cases where there is some wrongdoing alleged on the part of a third party who is not himself the subject of action by the FSA. For instance, in disciplinary cases under Part XIV, it was felt that action might be taken against a firm for reasons which implied that there has been some failing by one of its directors or employees; or in market abuse cases, where other parties might well be involved in the transactions giving rise to the allegation that market abuse has been engaged in. The provisions give third parties, who are identified in prejudicial terms in the reasons for a warning or decision notice, the right to receive a copy of the notice, and to make representations or refer the matter to the tribunal in the same way as the person who is the subject of the FSA's proposed action. We took the view that although these rights create an administrative burden for the FSA, they are necessary to give the third party the right to defend himself against any implied blame arising from the reasons given for the action.'

In respect of the right to make a reference to the Tribunal, s 393(9) makes provision for references in respect of both the FSA decision based on any opinion expressed by the FSA in relation the third party. It states:

'A person to whom a copy of the notice is given under this section may refer to the Tribunal-

(a)   the decision in question, so far as it is based on a reason of the kind mentioned in subsection (4)[2]; or

(b)   any opinion expressed by the Authority in relation to him'

There may be occasions where the FSA considers that it has no obligation to provide a person with a copy of a relevant notice, but the third party disagrees. In such circumstances the third party may make a reference to the Tribunal under s 393(11) which provides:

'A person who alleges that a copy of the notice should have been given to him, but was not, may refer to the Tribunal the alleged failure and-

(a)   the decision in question, so far as it is based on a reason of the kind mentioned in subsection (4); or

(b)   any opinion expressed by the Authority in relation to him'

---

1 Hansard HL Col 1026, March 30 2000.
2 FSMA 2000, s 393(4).

13.12   The Tribunal in an application on a preliminary issue in the case of *Sir Philip Watts v Financial Services Authority* was required to consider the meaning of identification under s 393. The application turned on the provision in s 393(4) and in essence, whether Sir Philip was identified in the notice by virtue of the external publicity about him following the events that led to the FSA's enforcement activities against Royal Dutch Shell Corporation. The applicant's reference arose out of the problems with the Royal Dutch Shell Group's calculation of its oil and gas reserves. Sir Philip Watts had been the Chairman of Royal and Dutch Shell. On 9 January 2004, Shell announced a re-categorisation representing 3.9 billion 'barrels of oil equivalent' of its proved hydrocarbon reserves. This was 20% of its proved reserves at that date. Following the announcement, Shell's share price fell 7.5%. In mid-April, after further adjustments, Shell announced that the total re-categorisation was about 4.3 billion 'barrels of oil equivalent'.

Shell's stock is traded in New York as well as London and the calculation of its reserves prompted action by the regulatory authorities in the UK and USA. On 23 April 2004, the FSA began investigating alleged misstatements of Shell's proved hydrocarbon and at the same time as the FSA investigation, the Securities and Exchange Commission in the USA also began its own investigation. On 29 July 2004, Shell announced that it had reached agreement in principle with the regulators, without admitting or denying their findings or conclusions. Shell agreed to the FSA issuing findings that Shell had breached the market abuse provisions of FSMA, as well as the Listing Rules. It agreed to pay a penalty of £17 million. Similar findings were made by the SEC and in the US Shell agreed to pay a $120 million civil penalty, and an additional $5 million to developing a comprehensive internal compliance program.

The FSA's penalty was levied by way of the notice procedure laid down in the relevant provisions of the FSMA. These involve a warning notice, followed by a decision notice, culminating in a final notice, which in this case was issued on 24 August 2004. Because of the agreed settlement Shell did not contest these notices. The applicant was given written notice of the FSA's investigation on 27 May 2004 as an additional subject of the investigation for the purposes of s 170(2) of the FSMA 2000.

It was reported that the applicant had been subject to extensive adverse comment in the media and he was concerned to protect his reputation against what he considered to be wholly unjust criticism. In the tribunal reference the applicant asserted his rights as a third party under s 393 of the FSMA 2000. He said that even if he was not explicitly identified in the relevant notice, he was entitled to the statutory rights of a third party if he was identifiable by reference to publicly available sources as the individual responsible for the matters complained of.

The Tribunal concluded that the proper construction of s 393(4) affords third party rights to a person who is identified in the decision notice itself, and not as the applicant had argued, to a person identified in the 'matter' as ascertained by looking at external sources. In reaching this conclusion the Tribunal determined that the term 'matter' as used in s 393 relates to the matter of the decision taken by the FSA as defined in the relevant notice and not to a wider context in which the individual may be identified or criticised. The Tribunal considered that this construction is consistent with other instances where the term 'matter' is used in FSMA 2000. It provided a series of examples to illustrate this point, in particular s 127(4) of the FSMA 2000 which states 'if the Authority decides to take action against a person [for market abuse], that person may refer the matter to the Tribunal.' It considered therefore, that there was no reason to give the term 'matter' a wider meaning in s 393(3). In the context of s 393(4), the Tribunal considered that the use of the term 'matter' serves to make it clear that identification can be found from the entire notice, and not from the reasons alone, or one of them. Other provisions of s 393 strongly suggest that the section envisages that identification will be in the decision notice. By way of example, subsection (6) provides that a copy need not be given to the third party under subsection (4) if the FSA issues him with a separate decision notice at the same time as it issues 'the decision notice which identifies him'.

In its decision judgment the Tribunal stated,

> 'We have to say that we regard the contrary interpretation as a very artificial one. A company is (as the Applicant reminds us) an

abstraction, but it is one which is basic to the law. There is no reason in our view why a market abuse allegation directed at a company must necessarily be taken to impute criticism to particular individuals. We doubt whether undertaking the threefold steps which are said to be required, and looking at "publicly available sources" to see whether any and if so which individuals were identified, would be a workable process.'

Withdrawal of reference

13.13 Tribunal rule 14 sets out the procedure for withdrawal of a reference. Should the applicant want to withdraw the reference at any time before the substantive hearing he may do so with without permission of the Tribunal by filing a notice to that effect. Where the decision is taken by the applicant to withdraw the reference during the hearing itself the Tribunal's permission to do so is required under r 14(1)(b). Neither the Tribunal rules nor the FSMA state when a hearing of the reference begins and the question of what is meant by the 'before the hearing' under r 14(1)(a) was considered by the Tribunal in the case of *Eurolife v Financial Services Authority*. In that case the hearing was listed to start on 2 September 2002, but before the hearing started the parties asked for further time to see if they could agree to certain matters. The Tribunal agreed to this but by 4.00pm on 3 September the parties had still not reached an agreed position and asked in open court for further time. The Tribunal consented to this further application on the basis that the FSA would open its case at 10.30am on 4 September. At 10.30am on 4 September in open court but before the FSA had commenced its opening, the applicant's representative handed the Tribunal a letter from the applicant dated 4 September withdrawing its reference. The Tribunal concluded that until the FSA opens its case the determination process will not have begun and the expression 'the hearing of the reference' is directed at the time from which the hearing has effectively begun. The Tribunal considered that it is not required to give its permission for the withdrawal of a reference when as in the instant case all that has happened is that an application for further time has been successfully made. The Tribunal has a statutory obligation under s 133(4) of the FSMA 2000 to determine the appropriate action (if any) for the Authority to take in relation to the matter, including where the reference has been withdrawn. Such determination might be necessary to ensure that the terms of the FSA's supervisory notice (which may have been suspended by direction under r 10) or the FSA decision notice is given effect.

Similarly under r 14(2)(a) the FSA may state that it does not oppose the reference or that it is withdrawing its opposition to it before the substantive hearing by filing a notice to that affect. By way of example see *Greenfield Financial Management Ltd v FSA*[1]. Where the FSA wishes to withdraw its opposition or no longer oppose a reference at the hearing of the reference it must obtain the Tribunal's permission to do so. In this event it will be necessary for the Tribunal to determine the reference, either to direct that the terms of the FSA's supervisory or decision notice are not to take effect or even potentially to dismiss the reference, although where it is minded to do so it is required under r 14(3) to notify the applicant that it is minded to do so and give him an opportunity to make representations.

---

1 FIN 2005/0022.

Directions

13.14 - The applicant may include with the reference notice an application for directions on the case. Appropriate directions from the Tribunal are a necessary and essential element of proper preparation of the parties' case. They will serve to guide the parties on the steps they should take, setting time limits, assist the Tribunal to determine the issues and generally to ensure the just, prompt and economical determination of the reference. Certain directions may be given as a way of dealing with matters to ensure that the case is ready for a hearing. Directions may be applied for by either party or given by the Tribunal on its own initiative. Rule 10 sets out certain directions that may be given by the Tribunal; these deal with matters such as fixing the time and place for the hearing, extending time limits for making a reference, the disclosure of certain documents and in appropriate cases directing to suspend the FSA's action being subject to the application, pending the determination of the case. Such an application was considered by the Tribunal in *Theophilus Folagbade Sonaike trading as Ft Financial Services v Financial Services Authority*[1]. The reference in that case arose out of the FSA on 19 May 2005 issuing two notices directed to the applicant. Mr Sonaike had been a sole trader carrying on business in the name of 'FT Insurance Services', he had had permission, in accordance with Part IV of the FSMA 2000 to carry on various regulated activities, in advising on and arranging investments and mortgages. The first notice, a supervisory notice given in accordance with s 45 of the FSMA 2000, removed all of the regulated activities from Mr Sonaike's permission, with immediate effect. The second, a warning notice, also given under s 45, indicated an intention to cancel Mr Sonaike's permission altogether. The FSA's supervisory notice arose out of Mr Sonaike's conviction at Manchester Crown Court on 26 January 2004, of five counts of furnishing false information, (false accounting) contrary to s 17(1)(*b*) of the Theft Act 1968. Although he had pleaded not guilty to each count, he had been convicted by the jury and sentenced to a community punishment order for 150 hours, concurrent on each count and ordered to pay compensation of £11,871. Mr Sonaike referred the notices to the Tribunal, and asked the Tribunal to consider whether the effect of the supervisory notice should be suspended pending the final determination of the reference. In considering the application the Tribunal stated:

'Our task at this stage in the reference is not to evaluate the evidence with a view to determining the merits of the opposing cases, but to undertake a balancing exercise. We must weigh the protection of the public – the primary focus of the Act – against the burden to the Applicant of his being deprived of his livelihood pending the final determination of the reference, bearing in mind the risk that the temporary closure of a sole trader's business may lead to its demise even if the reference is ultimately decided in his favour. But in carrying out the balancing exercise we must keep very much in mind the fact that the power to suspend a person's authorisation immediately was given to the Authority by the Act for good reason, namely that a delay in withdrawal may itself be prejudicial to the public.'

The Tribunal considered that in principle a recent conviction for an offence of dishonesty necessarily gives rise to serious doubts about the fitness of the person concerned to be authorised for the purposes of the Act. It was of the view that in this case the balancing of the need to protect the public against depriving the applicant of his livelihood led to the conclusion that the supervisory notice should not be suspended pending determination of the reference. It stated 'There must, we think, be some compelling reason in a case of this kind before the tribunal might come to the opposite conclusion.'

In all cases where an application for directions is made the Secretary of the Tribunal will refer the application for directions to the Tribunal for determination and no further action in relation to the reference notice is taken by the Tribunal until the application for directions has been determined. The process for applying for directions is set out in r 9. An application for directions must be filed with the Tribunal and under r 9(3) include the reasons for making that application. It is possible that both parties will consent to the directions being applied for, in which case the application should be accompanied by the written consent of all the parties[2]. The party making the application shall at the same time send a copy to the other party. In situations where the opposing party objects to the directions applied for, then under r 9(5) the Tribunal shall consider the objection and, if it considers it necessary, it will give the parties an opportunity to make representations.

The Tribunal's response to an application for directions (or directions it gives on its own initiative) may under r 9(6) either present orally or in writing, and notice of the written direction (or refusal to give a direction) shall be given to the parties, although the Tribunal may decide not to give notice in any particular case. In giving directions containing a requirement the Tribunal may under r 9(7) specify a time limit for complying with the requirement including a statement of the possible consequences of a party's failure to comply with the requirement. Such consequences might range from preventing the party taking the procedural step addressed in the direction to in extreme situations the withdrawal of the applicant's reference or the FSA's response.

The Tribunal rules permit a person to whom a direction is given to subsequently apply to the Tribunal showing good cause why the direction should be varied or set aside. Where such an application is made and it relates to a direction applied for by the other party the Tribunal will notify that other person and give them an opportunity to make representations.

---

1 FIN 2005/0021.
2 Financial Services and Markets Tribunal Rules 2001, SI 2001/2476, r 9(4).

Documents and disclosure

13.15   The process for the exchange of lists of documents disclosed by the FSA under r 5(3) and the applicants under r 6(3) appears to be designed to ensure that all documents supporting both the FSA's decision and the applicant's reference are revealed to the parties early in the Tribunal process. There is particular emphasis on the disclosure of documents that might reasonably assist the applicant's case. Under r 7(1), following the filing of the applicant's reply, the FSA is required to file a further list of documents that might reasonably be expected to assist the applicant's case that are not already disclosed in the FSA list accompanying the statement of its case. Such list must be filed so that it is received by the Tribunal no later than 14 days after which the FSA received the applicant's reply. A party who has filed a list under r 5(3), 6(3) or 7(1) is required under r 8(7) and upon the request of the other party, to provide that other party with a copy of any document specified in the list or make any such document available to that party for inspection or copying.

During the compilation of both parties' lists the question as to whether certain documents must be disclosed often arises. Certain documents may be particularly sensitive or be subject to privilege. Disciplinary cases in particular may rely on evidence in material relating to third parties and consumers the disclosure of which may reveal sensitive and personal financial data about those third parties. Rule 8 contains three specific exclusions to document disclosure as well as the power for the Tribunal to make directions relating to disclosure of documents.

Under r 8(1) the FSA need not disclose in its lists any documents relating to a case involving a person other than the applicant which was taken into account by the FSA in the applicant's case only for the purposes of comparison with other cases. Rule 8(2) provides that neither the applicant's list nor the FSA's list of documents need contain any documents that are material and the disclosure of which for the purpose of or in connection with any legal proceedings is an intercepted communication as prohibited by s 17 of the Regulation of Investigatory Powers Act 2000. Finally the parties may apply to the Tribunal under r 8(4) for directions on whether documents are required to be disclosed on grounds that the disclosure of the document would:

(a)   not be in the public interest,

(b)   not be fair, having regard to:

    (i)   the likely significance of the document to the applicant in relation to the matter referred to the Tribunal; and

    (ii)   the potential prejudice to the commercial interests of a person other than the applicant which would be caused by disclosure of the document.

In considering an application under r 8(4) the Tribunal may require that the document in question be produced to the Tribunal together with a statement of the reasons why its inclusion in the list would (as the case may be) not be in the public interest; or not be fair; and the Tribunal may invite the other party to make representations. Once the application has been determined and if the Tribunal determines that the document in question should be disclosed it will provide a direction under r 8(6) to revise the list so as to include the document and file a copy of that list as revised and send a copy to the other party.

Cases before the Tribunal

Pre-hearing review

13.16   In most cases to ensure the appropriate case preparation as well as ensuring necessary arrangements are made for the hearing, the Chairman of the Tribunal will direct that it is necessary to hold a pre-hearing review. Where such direction is given the parties will under r 9(10) be given 14 days' notice of the time and place for the review. The Chairman has discretion to give such directions that appear in the circumstances of the actual case to be necessary to ensure an expeditious and economical conduct of the reference. This may include fixing the time and place for the hearing and, providing for the manner in which any evidence may be given. In addition it is often the case that certain matters or facts relating to the reference will not be in dispute and to save such matters from having to be formally put to the Tribunal during the hearing, during the pre-hearing review the Chairman will endeavour to secure that the parties make all admissions and agreements as they ought reasonably to have made in relation to the proceedings.

Witnesses and evidence

13.17   Section 133 of the FSMA 2000 provides that the Tribunal may consider any evidence relating to the subject-matter of the reference, whether or not it was available to the Authority at the material time. References before the Tribunal are determined in accordance with the civil law. The FSA has to prove the breaches of the rules or issues that it alleges and to do so on the balance of probabilities. In *Hoodless and Blackwell v FSA* the Tribunal endorsed the judgment in *Re Dellow's Will Trusts, Lloyd's Bank Ltd v Institute of Cancer Research*[1] which very simply explains that the more serious the matter alleged the greater the evidence required to prove the allegation. Ungoed-Thomas J set out the extent of evidence required in civil cases, he stated:

> 'The more serious the allegation, the more cogent is the evidence required to overcome the unlikelihood of what is alleged and thus proven.'

Rule 12(1) authorises the Tribunal to require by summons any person to attend, at such time and place as is specified in the summons, to give evidence as a witness as well as file, within the time specified in the summons, any document in his custody or under his control which the Tribunal considers necessary to examine. Any such witness summons must be sent so as to be received by the summonsed witness not less than seven days before the time specified in the summons[2].

Witnesses summonsed to give evidence are entitled to receive expenses in advance where they are required to travel more than 16 kilometres from their place of residence. When the summons is issued at the request of a party, those expenses shall be paid by that party[3].

Failure to comply with a Tribunal witness summons is a criminal offence. Paragraph 11(3) of Sch 13 to the FSMA 2000 prescribes that persons who without reasonable excuse refuse or fail to attend following the issues of a witness summons or to give evidence are liable on summary conviction to a fine not exceeding the statutory maximum. Those persons that alter, suppress, conceal or destroy, or refuse to produce a document which they may be required to produce for the purposes of proceedings before the Tribunal are guilty of an offence which is punishable on summary conviction, to a fine not exceeding the statutory maximum or on conviction on indictment, to imprisonment for a term not exceeding two years or a fine or both.

The Tribunal may under r 12(6), following an application of the person to whom the witness summons is addressed, direct that the witness summons be set aside or varied and moreover no person is required under r 12(2) to file a document if the Tribunal is satisfied that such document is a protected item under s 413 of the FSMA 2000 or exempted under r 8(1) and (2) or should not be disclosed under r 8(4). See **13.15** above.

During any hearing the Tribunal may under para 11(2) of Sch 13 to the FSMA 2000 take evidence on oath or instead of administering an oath the Tribunal may require the witness to declare the truth of the matters of which he is examined.

1 [1964] 1 All ER 771.
2 Financial Services and Markets Tribunal Rules 2001, SI 2001/2476, r 12(3).
3 Financial Services and Markets Tribunal Rules 2001, SI 2001/2476, r 12(5).

Legal representation

13.18 There is no restriction over representation or assistance at any hearing before the Tribunal and parties may in accordance with r 18(1) appear in person, be assisted by any person and may if they choose be represented by any person, whether or not that person is legally qualified. The Tribunal may, however, where it is satisfied that there are good and sufficient reasons for doing so, refuse to permit a person to assist or represent a party at the hearing[1]. The question of whether to rely on legal representation will usually be one of cost. In qualifying cases, the applicant may be able to rely on funding under the legal assistance scheme to provide representation.

1 Financial Services and Markets Tribunal Rules 2001, SI 2001/2476, r 18(2).

Preliminary hearings

13.19 The Tribunal may direct under r 13(1) that any question of fact or law which appears to be in issue in relation to the reference be determined at a preliminary hearing. Such a direction may help ensure that material issues, that have a bearing on the reference, can be determined both early and without the need for a full hearing. Indeed it is possible that the outcome of a preliminary hearing will dispose of the reference. Under r 13(2) if, in the opinion of the Tribunal, the determination at the preliminary hearing substantially disposes of the reference, the Tribunal may treat the preliminary hearing as the hearing of the reference and may make such order disposing of the reference as it thinks fit.

Hearings

13.20 Subject to the FSMA 2000 and the rules of procedure in the Financial Services and Markets Tribunal regulations the Tribunal may conduct hearings in such manner as it considers most suitable to the clarification of the issues in the matter and for the just, expeditious and economical determination of the proceedings. Evidence may be admitted by the Tribunal whether or not it would be admissible in a court of law and whether or not it was available to the FSA when taking the referred action. At the hearing and subject to any directions by the Tribunal, the parties shall be entitled under r 19(2):

(a)   to give evidence (and, with the consent of the Tribunal, to bring expert evidence);

(b)   to call witnesses;

(c)   to question any witnesses; and

(d)   to address the Tribunal on the evidence, and generally on the subject matter of the reference.

If a party fails to attend or be represented at any hearing of which it has been duly notified, the Tribunal pursuant to r 19(4) may if it is satisfied that there is no good and sufficient reason for the absence:

(a)   in the case of the hearing of the reference, hear and determine the reference in the party's absence; and

(b)   in the case of any other hearing, give any direction, determine any issue or adjourn the hearing.

In general, hearings before the Tribunal are conducted orally and are held in public. The Tribunal may determine a matter without an oral hearing under r 16(1) where either the parties agree in writing, or the issues concern an application for directions hearing. Furthermore where the FSA decides not to oppose a reference or does not file a statement of case or where the applicant does not file a reply, then the Tribunal may deal with the matter without an oral hearing, but under r 14(3) it shall not dismiss a reference without notifying the applicant that it is minded to do so and giving him an opportunity to make representations.

When considering whether to dispense with the need for an oral hearing the Tribunal is required under r 16(2) to consider whether there are circumstances making it undesirable to make a public pronouncement of the whole or part of its decision. The Tribunal will invite the parties to make representations as to whether it should anonymise the decision, edit the text of the decision or not publish the whole or part of the decision. Any such decision of the Tribunal must be made with a view to ensuring there is the minimum of restriction over the publication of the decision and which is consistent with the need for the restriction[1].

---

1 Financial Services and Markets Tribunal Rules 2001, SI 2001/2476, r 16(2).

Whether hearings should be in public or private

13.21   Rule 17 provides that all hearings of the Tribunal shall be held in public, save where on the application of all of the parties to the reference the Tribunal is satisfied that a hearing in private would not prejudice the interests of justice, or on the application of any of the parties the Tribunal is satisfied that a hearing in private would not prejudice the interests of justice and is necessary having regard to[1]:

(i)   the interests of morals, public order, national security or the protection of the private lives of the parties; or

(ii) any unfairness to the applicant or prejudice to the interests of consumers that might result from a hearing in public.

Upon hearing an application under r 17 (if the application is made by one of the parties the other party is entitled to make representations[2]) the Tribunal will consider not only the requirements of r 17(3) but will also give due consideration to whether the entire hearing should be held in private or only part of the hearing. Under r 17(3) if the Tribunal is satisfied that the requirements of r 17 have been met it may direct that all or part of a hearing shall be in private. The word 'may' indicates that the Tribunal, even when so satisfied, is not bound to order a private hearing, but has a discretion as to whether the hearing should be held in public or private.

The question of whether a private hearing would result in unfairness came before the Tribunal in *Eurolife v Financial Services Authority*[3]. Although the circumstances giving rise to this case arose prior to the implementation of the FSMA 2000, following representations from Eurolife the FSA agreed to proceed with the matter under the provisions of the supervisory regime in the Act and issued a supervisory notice under s 53(4) of the FSMA 2000 withdrawing Eurolife's authorisation to conduct new insurance business from 1 December 2001. It also required assets sufficient to meet Eurolife's liabilities within the European Community to be held by an approved trustee. On 21 December 2001, Eurolife referred that action to this Tribunal in accordance with s 55 of the FSMA 2000 and subsequently applied, pursuant to r 17(3) of the Rules, for the hearing of that reference to be in private. Its application was made on two grounds, first, a public hearing would cause irreparable damage to Eurolife's reputation, whatever the outcome and second, the consequential damage to Eurolife's business would be so disproportionate as to be unfair. In support of its application Eurolife claimed that the reaction to a public hearing would be an immediate lack of confidence in all the companies comprised in the Eurolife Group. It also predicted that independent financial advisers would no longer be able to recommend Eurolife products and new business would dry up with the consequence that Eurolife Group would cease to be viable. Because the Eurolife Group was at that time relatively small, damage to any part of the group would, it believed, impact unfairly on other parts of the group.

Eurolife's application was made under r 17(3)(b), relying on sub-paragraph (ii). To justify an order that the hearing be in private under this provision the Tribunal must be satisfied that: (1) a hearing in private is necessary, having regard to any unfairness to the applicant or prejudice to the interests of consumers that might result from a hearing in public, and (2) a hearing in private would not prejudice the interests of justice. The Tribunal rejected Eurolife's application. In reaching its decision it addressed the requirements that had to be satisfied in r 17 applications as well as the fundamental requirement for court hearings to be held in public.

---

1 Financial Services and Markets Tribunal Rules 2001, SI 2001/2476, r 17(3)(b).
2 Financial Services and Markets Tribunal Rules 2001, r 17(4).
3 (26 July 2002, unreferenced).

Unfairness to the applicant

13.22   In the Eurolife refernce the Tribunal was asked to make a judgment under the terms of r 17 as to whether reputational risk arising out of a public hearing gave rise to unfairness or not. It concluded that it is necessary to consider the circumstances of each particular case. In the circumstances of the Eurolife case it did not consider that the reputational risk was such to give rise to unfairness, but it did not go as far as saying that reputational risk can in certain situations give rise to unfairness to the applicant. In its judgment it gave an example of the reputational damage occurring during the progress of the hearing such as to destroy the applicant's business. The suffering of disproportionate damage would be unfair.

The Tribunal pointed out that the prospect of unfairness or prejudice does not arise simply through knowledge of the action or decision taken by the FSA as in many cases the existence of the proceedings will already be a matter of public knowledge, prior to the hearing taking place. In addition after the hearing the Tribunal's decision will normally be made public. An application under r 17(3) is confined specifically to the unfairness or prejudice that might result from the holding of the hearing in public and the concern is likely to be with the effect of publication of allegations or evidence during the hearing itself and in the period up to the publication of the Tribunal's decision. The Tribunal gave examples of when such concerns might arise: 'such concerns may arise because press reporting may not always succeed in being accurate, or because during the hearing the allegations are more prominently reported than the applicant's answers to them, or because a decision by the Tribunal in the applicant's favour after the conclusion of the hearing may not in practice be sufficient to undo the damage done by the publicising of the allegations. There may also be concerns over other matters, such as unnecessary public disclosure of commercially sensitive or other confidential information.'

The Tribunal found that it must be satisfied that the risk of unfairness or prejudice resulting from holding the hearing in public makes it 'necessary' to hold the hearing in private. To reach this decision it stated that it must weigh both the likelihood and the seriousness of the possible unfairness or prejudice and consider whether, in the circumstances, a private hearing is really needed.

Interest of justice

13.23   If the Tribunal is satisfied that a hearing in private is necessary having regard to any unfairness to the applicant or prejudice to the interests of consumers that might result from a hearing in public, the Tribunal may still only direct that all or part of the hearing shall be in private if the Tribunal is satisfied that a hearing in private would not prejudice the interests of justice.

The Tribunal was guided by the judgment in the European Court of Human Rights case of *Diennet v France*[1] in which it was said:

> 'The Court reiterates that the holding of court hearings in public constitutes a fundamental principle enshrined in Article 6. This public character protects litigants against the administration of justice in secret with no public scrutiny; it is also one of the means whereby confidence in the courts can be maintained. By rendering the administration of justice transparent, publicity contributes to the achievement of the aim of Article 6(1), namely a fair trial, the guarantee of which is one of the fundamental principles of any democratic society, within the meaning of the Convention.'

Article 6 of the European Convention on Human Rights does, however, sanction the exclusion of the public where (among other things) publicity would prejudice the interests of justice. Lord Diplock said in *Attorney-General v Leveller Magazine Ltd*[2]:

> '... since the purpose of the general rule is to serve the ends of justice it may be necessary to depart from it where the nature or circumstances of the particular proceeding are such that the application of the general rule in its entirety would frustrate or render impracticable the administration of justice or would damage some other public interest for whose protection Parliament has made some statutory derogation from the rule.'

The Tribunal considered that, if the unfairness or prejudice condition is fulfilled, the interests of justice in the particular case are likely to be better served by the holding of the hearing in private. However it was concerned to stress that it must keep in mind the important public interest in open justice, and before making a r 17 direction the Tribunal must in every case be satisfied also that the interests of justice in this more general sense will not be prejudiced.

---

1   (1995) 21 EHRR 554 at para 33.
2   [1979] AC 440 at 843–844.

Decision making and reason for decisions

13.24   A decision of the Tribunal may under para 12(1) of Sch 13 to the FSMA 2000 be taken by a majority and the Tribunal is required under para 12(3) of Sch 13 to the FSMA 2000 to inform each party to the reference of its decision and as soon as reasonably practicable, send to each party and, if different, to any authorised person concerned, a copy of the document in which the decision is set out. A copy of the Tribunal's decision must also be sent to HM Treasury[1]. Copies of all Tribunal decisions that have been published are available on the Tax and Financial Tribunal website.

Under para 12(2) of Sch 13 to the FSMA 2000 the Tribunal's decision must contain a statement of the reasons for the decision, state whether it was reached unanimously or by a majority and be signed and dated by the person acting for the Tribunal. The Tribunal is required under r 20(1) to make arrangements for the public pronouncement of its decisions. It may make such pronouncements orally in open court or by publishing its decisions in writing, although under r 20(2) where the whole or any part of any hearing was in private the Tribunal having regard to the reason for the hearing or any part of it being in private and the outcome of the hearing, will invite representations from the parties on the matter[2] and will consider whether it would be undesirable to make a public pronouncement of the whole or part of its decision and if so the steps it should take to pronounce the decision. It may take the following steps[3]:

(a) anonymise the decision;

(b) edit the text of the decision;

(c) decline to publish the whole or part of the decision.

---

1 FSMA 2000, Sch 13, para 12(4).
2 Financial Services and Markets Tribunal Rules 2001, SI 2001/2476, r 20(4).
3 Financial Services and Markets Tribunal Rules 2001, r 20(3).

The effect of Tribunal decisions

13.25 The Tribunal's powers in determining references are unusual in order to enable it to effectively deal with decisions that will have already been taken by the FSA. Section 133(5) of the FSMA 2000 makes clear the Tribunal's power in giving effect to its determination of a reference is to remit the matter to the FSA with such directions (if any) as the Tribunal considers appropriate. Where the Tribunal finds in favour of the FSA to direct that the relevant notice is to have effect or where it finds in favour of the applicant a direction that the FSA do not take the action in the relevant notice. Section 133(6) and (7) of the FSMA 2000 limits the extent of the directions that the Tribunal is able to prevent it from directing that the FSA take any action in a decision notice that it would not have had power to take when giving the decision notice and in respect of a supervisory notice, which would have otherwise required the giving of a decision notice. Under s 133(10) of the FSMA 2000, the FSA is obliged to act in accordance with the Tribunal's determination and any directions.

Tribunal recommendations

13.26   The Tribunal may, pursuant to s 133(8) of the FSMA 2000 on deter-mining a reference, in addition to any direction it gives to the FSA make recommendations as to the FSA's regulating provisions or its procedures, although there is no provision in the Act obliging the FSA to act in accordance with Tribunal recommendations.

The question of making recommendations to the FSA came close in the matter of *Legal and General v FSA*, where the Tribunal stated that:

> 'We also have the power to make recommendations as to FSA's regulating provisions or procedures under Section 133(8) of the Act. This is not a power which we will exercise unless at least one party urges us to do so and both parties then make submissions about what if any those recommendations should be.'

Although in the refernce formal recommendations were not made the criticism of the FSA in the Tribunal's determination nonetheless led to a full FSA review of its enforcement process and ultimately changes to the way in which the FSA manages investigations and enforcement actions by its regulatory decisions committee[1].

---

1 Financial Services Authority Enforcement Process Review consultation paper CP05/11 and revised enforce-ment process rules PS05/11.

Costs and awards

13.27   Unlike court proceedings where, as a general rule, the successful party can make an application for its costs to be paid by its opponent, the Tribunal only has discretion to make awards of costs and expenses where one of the parties has acted vexatiously, frivolously or unreasonably. Paragraph 13(1) of Sch 13 to the FSMA 2000 provides that if the Tribunal considers that a party to any proceedings on a reference has acted vexatiously, frivolously or unreason-ably it may order that party to pay to another party to the proceedings the whole or part of the costs or expenses incurred by the other party in connection with the proceedings. In addition under para 13(2) the Tribunal may also only award costs and expenses against the FSA where it considers that a decision of the FSA which is subject of a reference was unreasonable. The reason why the question of costs is dealt with by two sub-paragraphs of para 13 is not totally apparent although para 13(2) addresses only the question of the FSA acting unreasonably in reaching a decision and para 13(1) appears to be limited to conduct during the Tribunal proceedings.. In *Baldwin and WRT Investments v Financial Services Authority Ltd*[1], the Tribunal concluded that it is entitled to take into account conduct which took place before the reference was made and the proceedings commenced. Although it determined that the conduct must have some bearing on the proceedings. That is the Tribunal's discretion can only be exercised on the basis of facts connected with or leading up to the proceedings, as contrasted with conduct wholly unconnected with the proceedings.

The Tribunal has no general power to award costs to the exonerated applicant. Such an approach to cost awards can have the effect of ensuring that persons aggrieved by a decision of the FSA are not put off from making a reference to the Tribunal through fear of the cost consequences for them should their reference be unsuccessful. As we will see, however, the Tribunal's discretion is limited to certain types of behaviour and persons making successful references may feel that although the Tribunal's decision has vindicated them, they have incurred unnecessary and unrecoverable costs in dealing with a decision that the FSA could not sustain.

The question of whether a decision of the FSA was an unreasonable one was considered by the Tribunal in *Baldwin and WRT Investments Ltd v Financial Services Authority*[2]. The case was an application for costs following a successful reference of the FSA's decision to impose on the applicants a financial penalty for market abuse. The application was made under both para 13(1) relying on allegations concerning the FSA's investigation of the case and para 13(2) regarding the nature of the FSA's decision. The FSA's original decision turned on there having been a phone call during which price sensitive information was disclosed. The Tribunal determined that there was no evidence that such telephone call had been made and found in favour of the applicants that they were not guilty of market abuse and that no penalty should be imposed. The applicants argued that the FSA investigation into the alleged market abuse and its decision to impose a financial penalty were unreasonable. In the case the Tribunal observed that '[it] has no general power to award costs to exonerated parties. The hardship suffered by [the applicant] might impel us towards exercising our discretion in his favour, but the discretion only arises if we first find that there was unreasonableness in the relevant sense.'

The Tribunal considered the appropriate test for unreasonableness. It considered the test in *Associated Provincial Picture Houses Ltd v Wednesbury Corpn*[3]. The Wednesbury test was formulated for the purpose of determining whether a public authority had acted outside its statutory powers. Lord Greene MR stated that a decision is 'Wednesbury unreasonable' if it is '... so unreasonable that no reasonable authority could ever have come to it ...'

In *Council of Civil Service Unions v Minister for the Civil Service*[4], Lord Diplock stated that Wednesbury unreasonableness '... applies to a decision which is so outrageous in its defiance of logic or of accepted moral standards that no sensible person who had applied his mind to the question to be decided could have arrived at it ...'

In *Baldwin and WRT Investments Ltd v Financial Services Authority*, the Tribunal determined, however, that the Wednesbury test was not appropriate for the discretion to award costs it is granted under Sch 13, para 13. It stated that '... The Tribunal, unlike the court in the Wednesbury case, is expressly directed by paragraph 13 to make its own judgment of what is reasonable ...'

In its judgment the Tribunal also followed the decision in *Secretary of State for Education and Science v Tameside Metropolitan Borough Council*[5] and gave the reminder that judging whether something is reasonable or unreasonable is wholly distinct from judging whether it is right or wrong: a decision may be wrong without being in the slightest degree unreasonable.

The Tribunal found that the FSA had not acted unreasonably and rejected the application for costs. The judgment made clear that the right approach is to ask whether it considered that the Authority's decision was unreasonable, given the facts and circumstances which were known or ought to have been known to the FSA at the time when the decision was made. In the *Baldwin* case the Tribunal followed the decision in *Legal and General v Financial Services Authority* where the Tribunal determined that the FSA should not be expected or compelled to follow procedures, or to express its conclusions, as required of a court. In *Baldwin* the Tribunal stated 'In taking this approach, we remind ourselves that the process leading to the FSA's decision was not a full judicial hearing of the kind conducted by the Tribunal ...'

With regard to the application under para 13(1) the Tribunal considered it important to keep in mind the broader picture and not to over-emphasize the significance of any individual feature of the FSA's investigation. It considered that even though the investigation may have made mistakes in balancing the evidence available to it that would not necessarily make the investigation unreasonable. It also pointed to the fact that while the investigation was part of what led to the proceedings, the regulatory decision committee's decision was critical in the FSA's decision to issue a decision notice and the Tribunal having found that the FSA's decision was not unreasonable under the application under para 13(2) it did not consider it right on the facts to award costs against the FSA on the basis of the criticisms of its investigation.

---

1 FIN 2005/0011.
2 N 1.
3 [1948] 1 KB 223, CA.
4 [1985] AC 374 at 410.
5 [1977] AC 1014, HL.

13.28 The question of the unreasonable conduct of the FSA came before the Tribunal following two separate costs applications in *Paul Davidson and Ashley Tatham v Financial Services Authority*. The first application related to the costs incurred by the Applicant and thrown away as a result of the withdrawal of the original Tribunal members on 28 June 2004. One of the questions before the Tribunal was whether the actions of the Chairman of the FSA's regulatory decisions committee were the actions of the FSA when determining whether the FSA's actions were unreasonable.

Paul Davidson, the applicant, had referred to the Tribunal a decision of the FSA to impose a penalty of £750,000 for market abuse in respect of the placement of spread bets on the price of shares in the company Cyprotex. The hearing of the applicant's reference commenced on 14 June 2004 before a Tribunal chaired by the President with one other member selected from the panel of chairmen and two other members selected from the lay panel.

On 16 June 2004 the respondent became aware of a conversation which had taken place on the evening of 15 June 2004 between the chairman of the respondent's Regulatory Decisions Committee and the member of the Tribunal selected from the panel of chairmen hearing the reference of the applicant. On 17 June 2004 the respondent informed the Tribunal that it believed such a conversation had taken place. The hearing of the reference was then adjourned and it was suggested that the applicant might wish to take legal advice which he did.

On 18 June 2004 the chairman of the respondent's Regulatory Decisions Committee tendered his resignation with immediate effect. On 24 June 2004 the member of the Tribunal selected from the panel of chairmen hearing the reference of the applicant withdrew himself from the reference. Following an application of Mr Davidson, on 28 June the remaining three members of the Tribunal withdrew themselves on the basis that the fair minded and informed observer would not be able to exclude the real possibility of unconscious bias. Thereafter a newly constituted Tribunal was selected.

On the facts mentioned the Tribunal concluded that it was clear that the chairman of the respondent's Regulatory Decisions Committee did act unreasonably. His actions had been described by the FSA as inappropriate and they led to his resignation with immediate effect. On the application for costs the Tribunal stated 'At the time the chairman of the Respondent's Regulatory Decisions Committee was an employee of the Respondent and his actions were, therefore, those of the Respondent. However, I would like to emphasise that in all other respects the Respondent behaved correctly, especially in drawing the conversation to the attention of the Tribunal.'

The second cost application followed Davidson and Tatham's successful substantive reference, and related to the FSA's conduct in issuing a market abuse decision notice. The Tribunal ordered the FSA to pay the costs or expenses incurred by Mr Davidson and Mr Tatham in connection with the proceedings, including the costs hearing. In reaching this decision the Tribunal had found that the FSA's approach to the evidence before the RDC had been unreasonable, its approach to the law relating to the reasonable user of the market was unreasonable and that the level of penalties imposed by the FSA was also unreasonable. The Tribunal did, however stress that it is considered in unlikely that these failures would reoccur as they had predated the FSA's review of its enforcement process following the Legal and General decision[1].

Before the Tribunal may make a costs order it is required under r 21(2) of the Financial Services and Markets Tribunal Rules 2001 to first give the paying party an opportunity to make representations against the making of the costs order.

Where the Tribunal makes a cost order it may order under r 21(3):

(a)   that an amount fixed by the Tribunal shall be paid to the receiving party by way of costs or (as the case may be) expenses; or

(b)   that the costs shall be assessed or (as the case may be) expenses shall be taxed on such basis as it shall specify:

    (i)   in England and Wales, by a costs official[2];

    (ii)   in Scotland, by the Auditor of the Court of Session;

    (iii)   in Northern Ireland, by the Taxing Master of the Supreme Court of Northern Ireland.

---

1 *Davidson and Tathum v Financial Services Authority (2nd cost application)* 11 October 2006 FIN 2003/016 and 2003/021.

2 In *Paul Davidson v Financial Services Authority* the Tribunal ordered that the FSA pay to the applicant one-half of the costs thrown away by the applicant in connection with the previous hearing; the costs shall be assessed on the standard basis by a costs official under r 21(3)(b)(i).

Review and appeals

13.29   The Tribunal rules of procedure provide for the Tribunal to review its own decision determining a reference where either it was wrongly made as a result of an error on the part of the Tribunal staff or new evidence has become available since the conclusion of the hearing, the existence of which could not have been reasonably known of or foreseen. Under r 22(2) an application for review may be made by either party immediately following the hearing of the decision or no later than 14 days after the day on which notification of the decision of the hearing was sent to the parties. Moreover, the Tribunal may on its own initiative decide to review its own decision and if so is required to notify the parties of that proposal not later than 14 days after the date on which the decision was sent to the parties[1].

The parties shall have an opportunity to make representations on any application or proposal for a review of a Tribunal decision. Rule 22(4) provides that review may be determined either by the same members of the Tribunal who decided the case or by a differently constituted Tribunal appointed by the President. Having reviewed its own decision the Tribunal may set aside the original decision and either impose an alternative decision or remit the case for a re-hearing. Where the original decision is to be set aside the Chairman of the Tribunal is required by r 22(1) to sign a certificate to that effect and the Tribunal will make immediately such correction as may be necessary in the register and shall send a copy of the entry so corrected to each party[2].

Where an original decision in favour of the FSA is set aside on review the parties as well as the Tribunal will have to give consideration to whether the FSA's notice should continue to have effect. The Tribunal may direct under r 10(1)(e) to suspend the effect of the FSA's notice until the reference has been finally disposed of[3].

Section 137 of the FSMA 2000 sets out the legal basis on which appeals may be made from decisions of the Tribunal. Appeals may be made by either party from a decision of the Tribunal may be made to the Court of Appeal or in Scotland to the Court of Session. Appeals may only be made on a point of law and require the permission of the Tribunal, Court of Appeal or Court of Session. Rule 23 of the Tribunal rules of procedure sets out the process of applying to the Tribunal for permission to appeal. Applications to the Tribunal may be made orally at the hearing after the decision is announced by the Tribunal or by written application filed not later than 14 days after the decision is sent to the party making the application[4]. Written applications must state the name and address of the appellant and any representative of the appellant; identify the decision of the Tribunal to which the application relates; and state the grounds on which the appellant intends to rely in the appeal[5]. At this point it would be important where the appellant is the applicant of the reference for him to apply for a direction under r 10(1)(e) to suspend the FSA's action.

If on an appeal the Court of Appeal or Court of Session considers that the decision of the Tribunal was wrong in law then it may either remit the matter to the Tribunal for re-hearing or itself make a determination of the case. Appeals from decisions of the Court of Appeal or Court of Session can be made to the House of Lords but only with leave of either the Court of Appeal or Court of Session (as appropriate) or the House of Lords.

1 Financial Services and Markets Tribunal Rules 2001, SI 2001/2476, r 22(3).

2 Financial Services and Markets Tribunal Rules 2001, r 22(6).

3 See for an example of the FSA's decision making on whether to suspend the effect of the FSA's supervisory notice *Theophilus Folagbade Sonaike trading as Ft Financial Services v Financial Services Authority* (although this case did not arise from a review of the Tribunal's own decision).

4 Financial Services and Markets Tribunal Rules 2001, r 23(2).

5 Financial Services and Markets Tribunal Rules 2001, r 23(4).

Legal assistance scheme

13.30   The legal assistance scheme established under s 134 of the FSMA 2000 to support applicants of limited means in relation to certain FSA's decisions relating to market abuse allows for the funding of legal services in market abuse cases brought before the Tribunal. During the Financial Services and Markets Bill's passage through Parliament, there was much concern expressed about whether the Bill would be compliant with the European Convention on Human Rights. Legal advice given to the government was that the market abuse regime bore the hallmarks of criminal law with the convention. In particular there was concern that the regime's extension to cover all users of the financial markets and not just authorised persons required that additional protections would be necessary to ensure the market abuse provisions would be compliant. In response the government decided to import the ECHR criminal protections into market abuse penalty proceeding. In evidence before the Joint Committee on the Bill, Patricia Hewitt Economic Secretary to Treasury stated:

'... The Convention requires legal assistance to be made available where that is necessary in the interests of justice. I think what that suggests is clearly one has to look at the means of the person, the individual or the company, against whom market abuse fining proceedings are being brought. One also has to look at the complexity of the case and whether or not it is actually reasonable to expect the individual concerned to put his own case or whether legal representation is going to be required in order for that person to have a fair hearing. ... If you have proceedings against somebody who is extremely wealthy, then the same thing probably applies, but if you do have proceedings against someone who, although those proceedings have not been concluded, has nonetheless been dismissed from his firm and does not have substantial accumulated wealth, then I think you probably need to take a different view, and that is what we are looking at in order that we can come forward with an appropriate scheme for subsidised legal assistance ...'[1]

The assistance scheme is a free standing scheme and not part of the legal aid system. Its funding is provided for under s 136 of the FSMA 2000 by contributions made by both Parliament and the FSA to the Lord Chancellor (special provision is made in s 136 for the repayment to the FSA of any sums received by the Lord Chancellor in excess of the monies expended on the legal assistance scheme in a determined period). Regulations made under s 134(1) of the FSMA 2000 set out the operation of the scheme.

The Financial Services and Markets Tribunal (Legal Assistance Scheme – Costs) Regulations 2001, SI 2001/3633 provide for the method of calculation of assistance, expenses, interim payments, staged payments, final payments.

The Financial Services and Markets Tribunal (Legal Assistance) Regulations 2001, SI 2001/3632 set out arrangements for applying for legal assistance, eligibility, assessment and contributions. Applications for legal assistance are made to the Tribunal under reg 4. The Tribunal is required under reg 8 to grant legal assistance to an individual if it is satisfied that it is in the interests of justice to do so and the individual's financial resources are such that he requires assistance in meeting the legal costs he would be likely to incur in relation to the proceedings before the Tribunal. A series of tests are set out in the regulations allowing the Tribunal to take into account not only the applicant's financial position but the position of persons supporting the applicant[2].

When deciding whether it is in the interests of justice for legal assistance to be granted, reg 9 provides assistance and requires the Tribunal to take all relevant factors into account, including:

(a)   whether the individual would, if any matter arising in the proceedings before the Tribunal is decided against him, be likely to lose his livelihood or suffer serious damage to his reputation;

(b)   whether the determination of any matter arising in the proceedings may involve consideration of a substantial question of law;

(c)   whether the individual may be unable to understand the proceedings or to state his own case;

(d)   whether the proceedings may involve the tracing, interviewing or expert cross-examination of witnesses on behalf of the individual; and

(e)   whether it is in the interests of another person that the individual be represented.

The Tribunal, may order legal assistance for all or part of the anticipated legal costs of the applicant and in deciding what legal assistance to grant it is required to take all relevant factors into account, including those required by reg 37(2), that is:

(a)   whether the case appears to involve substantial, novel or complex issues of law or fact;

(b)   whether the case is exceptional compared with the generality of such cases; and,

(c)   the number and level of advocates instructed on behalf of the Authority.

---

1 Evidence taken before the joint committee on financial services and markets, 19 May 1999.

2 In particular see the Financial Services and Markets Tribunal (Legal Assistance) Regulations 2001, SI 2001/3632, regs 10–35.

Table 1 Form of Reference to Financial Services and Markets Tribunal

13.31

	Reference Number:
(For Tribunal use only)	

FINANCIAL SERVICES AND MARKETS TRIBUNAL REFERENCE NOTICE

Department for Constitutional Affairs

First read the accompanying notes (Write clearly in black ink)

Part A REFERENCE

1. Name of Applicant:

(*Please read Note 1*)

Address:

Telephone No:

Fax No:

2. Address for service in the UK: (if different from 1)

(*Please read Note 2*)

3. Name of Representative: (if any)

Address:

(*Please read Note 3*)

Telephone No:

Fax No:

Status: (e.g. Solicitor, Barrister)

4. Date of disputed Authority Notice:

(*Please read Note 4*)

A copy of the Authority Notice is attached ☐ (tick box)

(*You must send a copy of the Authority Notice*)

---

5. I wish the Tribunal to consider the following issues concerning the Authority Notice:–

(Please read Note 5)

(Here set out your reasons for making the reference to the Tribunal)

(Continue on separate sheet if necessary)

6. TIME LIMITS (Tick one box only)

(Please read Note 6)

☐ This Reference is in time (i.e. within 28 days of receipt of Authority Notice).

☐ I apply for an extension of time to file my Reference Notice on the following grounds:

7. OTHER APPLICATIONS (Tick boxes as required)

(Please read Note 7)

☐ I apply for a direction suspending the effect of the Authority Notice on the following grounds:

☐ I apply for a direction that the Register contain no particulars of the Reference on the following grounds:

☐ The Authority Notice is in respect of a penalty for market abuse and I apply for legal assistance regarding this Reference.

8. SIGNATURE

(Please read Note 8)

Signed:

Status:

Date:

Send this completed Reference Notice and a copy of the Authority Notice to:

The Financial Services and Markets Tribunal

15–19 Bedford Avenue

London

WC1B 3AS

Tel. No. 0207 612 9700 Fax No. 020 7436 4151(alt 4150)

You must also send a copy of this Reference Notice to the Authority.

Appendix

Websites for Financial Services Authority Regulation and Risk-based Compliance

FSA

http://www.fsa.gov.uk

Financial Ombudsman Service

www.fos.org.uk

Office of the Complaints Commissioner

www.fscc.org.uk

Consumer Panel

www.fs-cp.org.uk

Practitioner Panel

www.fs-pp.org.uk

Bank of England

www.bankofengalnd.co.uk

HM Treasury

www.hm-treasury.gov.uk

Department of Constitutional Affairs

www.dca.gov.uk

Tribunal Service

www.tribunals.gov.uk

Finance and Tax Tribunals

www.financeandtaxtribunals.gov.uk

Office of Public Sector information

www.opsi.gov.uk

The Cabinet Office

www.cabinetoffice.gov.uk

UK Parliament

www.parliament.uk

Council on Tribunals:

www.council-on-tribunals.gov.uk

Better Regulation Task Force

www.brtf.gov.uk

OFT

www.oft.gov.uk

The Home Office

www.homeoffice.gov.uk

European Court of Human Rights

www.echr.coe.int

Assets recovery Agency

www.assetsrecovery.gov.uk/

Joint Money Laundering Steering Group

www.jmlsg.org.uk/

Serious Organised Crime Agency

www.soca.gov.uk

Metropolitan Police Fraud Alert

www.met.police.uk/fraudalert

Financial Action Task Force

www.fatf-gafi.org

The Fraud Advisory Panel

www.fraudadvisorypanel.org

Institute of Business Ethics

www.ibe.org.uk

Institute of Risk Management

www.theirm.org

Committee of European Securities Regulators

www.cesr-eu.org

International Organisation of Securities commissioners

www.iosco.org

International Association of Insurance Supervisors

www.iaisweb.org

Committee of European banking supervisors

www.c-bs.org

Financial Stability Forum

www.fsforum.org

Financial Services Skills Council

www.fssc.org.uk

European Commission financial services

http://ec.europa.eu/internal_market/top_layer/index_24_en.htm

Serious Fraud Office

www.sfo.gov.uk

Association of British Insurers

www.abi.org.uk

British Bankers Association

www.bba.org.uk

Futures and Options Association

www.foa.co.uk

Investment Management Association

www.investmentuk.org

Association of Private Client Investment Managers and Stockbrokers

www.apcims.co.uk

European Corporate Governance Institute

www.ecgi.org

International Monetary Fund

www.Imf.org

Bank for International Settlements

www.bis.org

European Central Bank

www.ecb.int

Index

[*all references are to paragraph number*]